Political Campaigning and Communication

Series Editor
Darren Lilleker
Bournemouth University
Bournemouth, Dorset, United Kingdom

The series explores themes relating to how political organisations promote themselves and how citizens interpret and respond to their tactics. Politics is here defined broadly as any activities designed to have impact on public policy. Therefore the scope of the series covers campaigns conducted by parties and candidates for election to legislatures, pressure group campaigns, lobbying, and campaigns instigated by social and citizen movements. Campaigning is an important interface between organisations and citizens, they present opportunities to study the latest strategies and tactics of political marketing as well as their impact in engaging, involving and mobilising citizens.

More information about this series at
http://www.springer.com/series/14546

Robert E. Denton, Jr.
Editor

The 2016 US Presidential Campaign

Political Communication and Practice

Editor
Robert E. Denton, Jr.
Department of Communication
Virginia Tech
Blacksburg, Virginia, USA

Political Campaigning and Communication
ISBN 978-3-319-52598-3   ISBN 978-3-319-52599-0 (eBook)
DOI 10.1007/978-3-319-52599-0

Library of Congress Control Number: 2017943375

Cover illustration: REUTERS / Alamy Stock Photo

This Palgrave Macmillan imprint is published by Springer Nature
The registered company is Springer International Publishing AG
The registered company address is: Gewerbestrasse 11, 6330 Cham, Switzerland

This book is dedicated to Ellie Reeser, my mother-in-law. While we are not of the same ideological or political persuasion, she has always been tolerant of my views, opinions, and ranting. Only at family reunions and gatherings are my first amendment rights suppressed. Actually, Ellie has always been most supportive personally and professionally. She provides an endless source of encouragement, optimism, and support. With my utmost gratitude and love.

PREFACE

Nearly forty years ago, as a graduate student, I was struck by a quote by noted political science scholar James David Barber. As I was beginning my journey into what is now the disciplinary area of political communication and campaigns, the quote struck a chord from communication and campaign perspective. "Every four years a gong goes off and a new Presidential campaign surges into the national consciousness; new candidates, new issues, a new season of surprises. But underlying the syncopations of change is a steady, recurrent rhythm from election to election, a pulse of politics that brings up the same basic themes in order, over and over again."[1] Every modern presidential campaign is different, yet the same.

Since 1992, I have edited a volume on the presidential election. In all the previous volumes, I have noted that every presidential election is historic from policy, issues, and cultural perspectives. To characterize the 2016 presidential election as historic is an understatement indeed. Donald Trump pulled off one of the greatest political feats in modern history. There were a couple of "firsts" related to gender in this election. Of course, Hillary Clinton was the first female presidential nominee of a major party. In addition, Kellyanne Conway, Republican strategist, was the first woman to manage a presidential campaign.

Donald Trump put together the winning coalition of non-college educated, working class, and non-urban voters. Those turned out in record numbers for him. In those critical Midwest battleground states, the disaffected wanted change. After the election there was the meme of Trump's victory based on hate, racism, xenophobic, misogynistic, and homophobic attitudes of his supporters. Others claim it was not an election based on issues. On the latter claim I would offer some caution. Just before the election, Rasmusen poll found that 62 percent of voters indicated that the candidates' specific policy proposals are more important than their character.[2] Examining the Exit Polls would suggest issues indeed played a role in the election:

- 56 percent of voters who saw the Supreme Court nominations as "the most important factor" supported Trump.
- 64 percent of voters who thought immigration was the "most important issue" voted for Trump, as did 86 percent of those who want a wall built on the U.S.-Mexico border.
- 83 percent of voters who felt Obamacare "went too far" supported Trump.
- 57 percent of those who viewed terrorism as the top issue backed Trump, as did
- 85 percent of those who thought the fight against ISIS was going "very badly."
- 73 percent of voters who felt the "government [is] doing too much" went for Trump.

At the very least these reflect issues of national security, rule of law, and the nature and scope of government. In addition the vast majority of voters expected Clinton to continue the policies of President Obama. Thus, for some, the election did represent a rejection of the Obama administration. Others argued that for the Trump true believers, he was "refreshing," "non-professional politician," "an outsider, "authentic," and "told it like it is." Some even make the argument that Trump's use of social media made a difference.

After the election there were numerous explanations being offered for Clinton's defeat. They include Clinton as a poor candidate, the campaign ignoring the Rust Belt battleground states, FBI Director James Comey's surprise announcement of reopening the private server investigation, and the thousands of leaked emails from the campaign, to name only a few. Others cite tactical errors of the Clinton campaign and a sense of "change" versus "continuity" of the Obama policies and administration. On Election Day, the Clinton campaign underperformed among young people, minorities, and white working class. She also underperformed in the 13 swing states where Obama enjoyed a 3.6 percent margin of victory, whereas Trump won those states by 1.8 percent.[3] In addition, what is now clear, voters deciding within the last week of the election broke for Trump.

Yes, Hillary Clinton won the popular vote. Of the 58 presidential elections in the United States, the popular vote and the Electoral College vote have matched in 54 of them (the exceptions in 1824, 1876, 1888, and 2000). Interestingly, just 77,759 votes combined in the states of Wisconsin, Pennsylvania, and Michigan determined the Presidency for Donald Trump.[4]

The 2016 presidential election was one of the most polarized elections in contemporary history along the lines of ideology, party, income, gender, and age. Polls revealed that the public was frustrated with the direction of the nation and with the institutions of government. Americans in general were angry, especially the middle class, blue collar workers, and minorities. There was a broad anti-government and anti-establishment mood across America. Not since the 1990s have we witnessed such general anger and political fragmentation. The general frustration largely explains the candidacies of Donald Trump and Berney Sanders.

There was also a noticeable shift in media coverage during the campaign in tone and aggressiveness. Many within the journalism academic community note how Trump's relationship with media has changed political journalism.[5] Because of Trump's confrontational style and often sweeping generalizations or falsehoods, journalists were more aggressive, challenging, contextualizing, fact checking, and even editorializing than in the past. However, for many Americans, it made the "main stream media" appearing bias, overtly hostile, liberal, and cheerleading for Clinton. According to Dartmouth political scientist, Brendan Nyhan, this was "the most consequential election for political journalism in my lifetime."[6] For Nyhan, the election drove "a stake through the heart of he said, she said journalism."[7] If "truth" is the standard, then more aggressive approach is warranted. Those on the right have a different interpretation. We are witnessing where news organizations are more open and comfortable with their biases. Rich Lowry, editor of *National Review* believes "going forward news organizations may become less apologetic about those biases. It could be a step to a British-style journalism that's a little more partisan and wears its biases on its sleeve."[8]

I think there is little evidence to suggest that journalists will treat Trump any differently as president. Thus, perhaps American political journalism has changed for the long term. As Ron Schiller, former NPR chief, said, "There's a newfound toughness, a pugilist form that reporters have been embracing."[9] Certainly Trump was the catalyst for it, the question is whether or not it is here to stay.

For communication scholars, the essence of politics is "talk" or human interaction. The interaction may be formal or informal, verbal or non-verbal, public or private, but always persuasive, forcing us as individuals to interpret, to evaluate, and to act.

I have argued for years that presidential campaigns are our national conversations. They are highly complex and sophisticated communication events: communication of issues, images, social reality, and personas. They are essentially exercises in the creation, recreation, and transmission of "significant symbols" through human communication. As we attempt to make sense of our environment, "political bits" of communication comprise our voting choices, worldviews, and legislative desires.

The purpose of this volume, as were the others, is to review the 2016 presidential campaign from a communication perspective. The chapters are clustered within three sections. The first section contains chapters that focus on major areas of political campaign communication in the 2016 election to include the nominations, the conventions, the debates, political advertising, and new media. The second section provides more detailed studies of specific topics and issues of the campaign, such as the role of Trump's persona in treatment of opponents, gender in general and in the debates, hate speech, and Benghazi. The final section summaries the campaign finance and its impact in the election and explains the vote in 2016. The analyses presented here go beyond the quantitative facts, electoral counts, and poll results of the election. Thus, each chapter focuses on a specific area of political campaign communication. All the contributors are accomplished scholars. Most have participated in past volumes.

In Chapter 1, Craig Allen Smith explores how our four-year national conversation rhetorically reconstituted the electoral landscape and shaped the subsequent nomination campaigns. In describing the surfacing phase of the 2016 campaign, Smith identifies three kinds of surfacing. It was a national conversation that concerned not only aspiring candidates, but evolving structures such as laws, rules, and calendars as well as evolving issue priorities and their publics. Smith argues that the 2016 presidential campaign occurred in a rhetorical political landscape quite different from that of 2012 that greatly influence the nomination campaigns of both parties. It is equally unlikely that the 2016 landscape will frame the 2020 campaign.

In Chapter 2, Rachel L. Holloway analyzes the political conventions of 2016. Both Trump and Clinton faced significant rhetorical challenges in the conventions. Both were widely unpopular among Americans and both faced divisions within their party. The conventions provided an opportunity for the candidates to unify party supporters and broaden appeals to general voters. Holloway analyzes the themes, strategies, speakers, and messages of both conventions. The conventions were very much in contrast. The Democrats effectively managed and enhanced the communication potential of a nominating convention through strategic and well-orchestrated presentations. The Republican convention was less successful largely void of party leadership participation and painted a dark and angry perception of America. The parties offered opposing explanations and responses to the nation's challenges.

Ben Voth in Chapter 3 examines the 2016 presidential debates. He begins by noting the rhetorical significance of the 2016 debates and identifies four essential ingredients of a debate. In reviewing the presidential primary debates, Voth explains why 2016 was a blockbuster year with so many initial candidates among the Republicans and a surprisingly tough contest for the Democrats between Clinton and Sanders. Voth addresses the unprecedented role and impact of the media on the debates. Trump received overwhelmingly more negative press than Clinton and the moderators became active participants during the debates. Voth concludes with considerations of why Trump's vulgarity and offensive arguments worked and five lessons from the debates that will influence the 2020 presidential debates.

In Chapter 4, Scott Dunn and John C. Tedesco reviews the strategies that dominated the candidate's televised advertising messages and discuss some of the opportunities seized or missed by the campaigns. Unlike the past several presidential elections, televised advertising spending *did not* exceed the prior election spending. In addition, the narratives of the campaigns *were not* driven by the rhetoric of the ads. Both candidates relied heavily upon negative advertising. The ads reinforced perceptions that neither candidate was fit for office. The authors suggest perhaps if either candidate had run a few more positive ads to give voters an affirmative reason to vote for them rather than trying to convince voters they were the lesser evil, they could have pulled away and won the election convincingly.

John Allen Hendricks and Dan Shill review the use of new media in the 2016 presidential campaign in Chapter 5. Social media radically upended the traditional campaign norms and practices in the presidential contest. Its use was unprecedented in volume, scope, and tactics. The Trump campaign was transformative in relying on social media as the primary communication channel. This chapter reviews how both campaigns utilized social media to include Quora, Tumblr, Pinterest, Vox, Buzzfeed, Upworthy, Facebook, Instagram, Longform, Twitter, Reddit, Snapchat,

YouTube, and LinkedIn. Hendricks and Shill caution that although social media and digital communication were critical in the 2016 contest, it would be an overstatement to claim that social media elected Donald Trump. However, the campaign changed the way social media will be used the future.

In Chapter 6, Deronda Baughman and Dennis D. Cali explore the candidate persona of Donald Trump. It specifically describes how Trump's campaign persona inoculated him from attacks from opponents. The analysis demonstrates how Trump used persuasive inoculation to imprint his version of the other Republican candidates' personae on the public and to enfeeble the influence from the candidates themselves. During the presidential campaign of 2016, while Trump's rivals carefully scripted their own personae, Trump effortlessly and offhandedly destroyed each in turn. Trump's persona assignment against his rivals operated best at the emotional level, vitiating his opponents with his swamp-draining caricatures of them and raising the capital of his own celebrity billionaire belligerence in the process.

In Chapter 7, I provide an overview of how issues of gender played out across the primaries, general election and post-election phases. From the beginning of the political season, there was no question that gender was going to be a major consideration in the presidential campaign. Challenges women face in political campaigns are well documented. Most of the gender characterizations and portrayals noted in the 2008 race also appeared in the 2016 contest, to the detriment of Clinton. The two unexpected aspects were the negative reactions of Third Wave feminists and younger women to the candidacy of Clinton and the statements, attitudes and behavior Trump displayed toward women throughout the campaign, not to mention much of his life. In the end, Trump enjoyed strong support among Republican women, married white women and evangelical white women.

The election of 2016 stands out for its volume of hate-filled messages. The election changed the climate for discourse throughout society. In Chapter 8, Rita Kirk and Stephanie Ann Martin identify the hate stratagems used by both the Trump and Clinton campaigns as well as how they functioned in the course of the election. Kirk and Martin argue that the use of hate stratagems prevented discussion of policy issues during the general election campaign. They conclude by evaluating the impact of hate speech on civil discourse, the media, and self-governance.

In Chapter 9, David R. Dewberry argues that the Benghazi and e-mail scandals were no exception to the American political scandal narrative in

American political culture. Dewberry describes the American political scandal narrative and recount of the Benghazi attack. He focuses on how scandals related to Benghazi followed the scandal narrative in both the 2012 and 2016 presidential elections. Both attempts at scandal unfolded in a similar manner as other historical political scandals. Although both attempts failed to reveal a cover-up, Dewberry addresses the nature of the narrative as reflecting the use of scandals as a discursive political weapon.

Cayce Myers in the Chapter 10 explores the campaign finance issues in the 2016 presidential election. Because understanding campaign finance requires a grasp of federal election laws, this chapter provides a brief and understandable overview of campaign finance laws. Next, Myers discusses the campaign expenditures and impact the hotly contested presidential primaries meant for the general election campaign. He concludes with a detailed analysis of the campaign fundraising and expenditures of the Clinton and Trump campaigns as well as joint fundraising committees and super-PACs, and finally provides some analysis of why Donald Trump lost the money contest, but won the presidential election in 2016.

The study of political campaign communication focuses on the elements of the political environment, messengers, messages, channels of communication (print, radio, television, social media, etc.), audience, and effects. In Chapter 11, Henry C. Kenski and Kate M. Kenski explain the presidential vote in 2016, and it draws upon the key factors in political campaign communication to explain it. Henry Kenski and Kate Kenski focus on: (1) the overall political environment, (2) the rules of the game and the electoral college, (3) the salience of party identification, (4) the messengers, (5) the messages and campaign strategies, (6) the channels of communication, and (7) the audience or the region/state and demographic bases of the presidential vote, with special attention to the roles of gender and race ethnicity in recent elections and the 2016 campaign.

There is no question that this election campaign will generate a great deal of analysis and scholarship. I would offer a word of caution and hope that our collective scholarly endeavors will not and would not reflect the polarization, blindness, and bias of much that was written by the popular press and as reflected by the opinions and attitudes among the general public. I attended a national professional conference within days of the election and was saddened by the "commentaries" and "observations" that were presented as scholarship. We must strive to understand the dynamics of the election of 2016 without overt bias and share our understanding with our students and the public. And yes, we *should* also engage in thesis-driven and argumentative works as well.

Presidential campaigns communicate and influence, reinforce and convert, motivate as well as educate. Former mentor and early scholar of political communication Bruce Gronbeck argues that campaigns "get leaders elected, yes, but ultimately, they also tell us who we as a people are, where we have been and where we are going; in their size and duration they separate our culture from all others, teach us about political life, set our individual and collective priorities, entertain us, and provide bases for social interaction"[10] (496).

As I have argued in the past in nearly every volume dealing with political communication, I believe strongly that political communication scholars should remember that *more* communication does not mean *better* communication. More technology does not mean more *effective* communication. For well over 200 years, America has incrementally moved toward a more "inclusive" democracy: greater participation of women, minorities, and the young. We have also witnessed unparalleled advances in communication technologies beyond belief just a decade ago. Yet, for well more than a quarter of a century during a time of increased opportunity for participation and information, sadly citizen political awareness, knowledge, and understanding have declined. A Democracy cannot stand without an informed and engaged citizenry.

The central task is how to cultivate an active, democratic citizenry. Civic responsibility and initiative should once again become a keystone of social life. It is my hope that perhaps by better understanding the role and process of communication in presidential campaigns, we may somehow improve the quality of our "national conversations."

NOTES

1. James David Barber, *The Pulse of Politics* (New York: W.W. Norton, 1980), p. 3.
2. Fran Coombs, "Issues Matter After All," Rasmussen Reports, November 9, 2016, http://www.rasmussenreports.com/public_content/politics/com mentary_by_fran_coombs/issues_matter_after_all, retrieved November 9, 2016.

3. "56 Interesting Facts About the 2016 Election," The Cook Political Report, December 16, 2012, http://cookpolitical.com/story/10201, retrieved December 20, 2016.
4. Ibid.
5. Dylan Byers, "How Donald Trump changed political journalism," Money. CNN.Com, November 2, 2016, http://money.cnn.com/2016/11/01/media/political-journalism-2016/index.html?iid=Lead, retrieved November 15, 2016.
6. Ibid.
7. Ibid.
8. Ibid.
9. Ibid.
10. Bruce Gronbeck, "Functions of Presidential Campaign," in *Political Persuasion in Presidential Campaigns,* ed. Lawrence Devlin (New Brunswick, NJ: Transaction Books, 1987), 496.

ACKNOWLEDGMENTS

I have had the privilege to edit well over a dozen volumes over the years. There are always challenges working with very smart, busy, and diverse group of scholars. However, I have actually come to enjoy the process. This project was no exception. This project brought together colleagues and friends, "new" and "old." I am most fortunate to work with such an outstanding group of scholars. Once again, the contributors have made this a most rewarding and enjoyable endeavor. I genuinely appreciate their participation in this volume. I also value their friendship.

I want to thank my colleagues in the Department of Communication at Virginia Polytechnic Institute and State University (Virginia Tech). As now a continuing and long-term administrator of various sorts over the years, I am grateful to my colleagues for their continued collegiality and encouragement, as well as for their recognizing the importance of maintaining an active research agenda. Thanks also to Robert Sumirchrast, Dean of the Pamplin College of Business, whose support allows my continued association with the Department of Marketing and the college. I am also most grateful to Elizabeth Spiller, Dean of the College of Liberal Arts and Human Sciences, who understands the importance of the "right mix" that makes the job of department head a privilege and pleasure. They both are outstanding mentors and administrators. I also want to personally thank Laura Purcell, a wonderful graduate student in the department, who heroically and under deadline assisted me with editing footnotes and preparing the Selected Bibliography. She certainly allowed me to be more efficient and on time.

Finally, as always, countless thanks to my wonderful wife, Rachel, a true blessing, friend, colleague, and partner in my life. And also to my now grown sons, Bobby and Chris, who now have their own wonderful spouses Christen and Sarah. The boys and Rachel have always been tolerant of the countless hours in the study, perhaps too tolerant and too many hours. Together the five, plus our precious dogs Daisy and Abby enrich and fulfill every moment of my life.

CONTENTS

LIST OF FIGURES

LIST OF TABLES

Political Campaign Communication in the 2016 Presidential Campaign

CHAPTER 1

Setting the Stage: Three Dimensions of Surfacing for 2016

Craig Allen Smith

Americans agreed on little in 2016 except that the presidential election was surprising. Although establishment Republicans tried to avoid nominating Donald Trump, Democrats attacked him, and 54% of voters cast their votes for someone else, he won 304 electoral votes to become President of the United States. How? Many surprising results are difficult to explain if we focus solely on the ending. This is not to say that the ending yields no explanations. But such explanations discourage thoughtful inquiry into the evolving dynamics that made the "winning shot" possible.

The purpose of this chapter is to explore how our four-year national conversation rhetorically reconstituted the electoral landscape and shaped the subsequent campaign. Imagine the four years between elections as a 24-hour day beginning with President Obama's 2012 victory at 12:00 AM and ending with Donald Trump's victory in 2016. In that context Americans voted at 11:58 PM, the conventions began at 11 PM, and the primaries began at 7:15 PM. This chapter considers the conversations that occurred between midnight and 7:15 PM to understand the dynamics that would shape the "prime time" campaign.

C.A. Smith (✉)
North Carolina State University, Raleigh, NC, USA
e-mail: casmith.nc@gmail.com

© The Author(s) 2017
R.E. Denton, Jr. (ed.), *The 2016 US Presidential Campaign*,
Political Campaigning and Communication,
DOI 10.1007/978-3-319-52599-0_1

The Surfacing Trialogue

Presidential Campaign Communication, second edition, provided the theoretical framework that we here apply to 2016.[1] Underlying the theory is a functional view of communication: people communicate to fulfill their own purposes. Some people say similar things for different reasons, while some people respond differently to the same words. What people say (or do not say) and do (or do not do) reshapes or "rhetorically reconstitutes" the menu of available rhetorical and political choices.

The Theoretical Essentials

Six principles form the foundation of the theory. They are:

1. *An American presidential campaign is a complex network of "rhetorical transactions."* To conceive of communication as a rhetorical transaction is to highlight its mutuality and reciprocity. Candidates say things to get coverage, money, and votes from reporters, donors, and citizens who, in turn, grant their support to the candidates who say what they long to hear.
2. *The rhetorical transactions are negotiated in a "trialogue" among three sets of role-defined communicators—citizens, campaigners, and reporters.* "Citizens" engage in the conversation to decide whom to prefer and whether to vote. "Campaigners" are all those who work strategically to win resources from the others in order to elect their candidate. "Reporters" are the assorted scholars, entertainers, pollsters, pundits, bloggers, and journalists who observe and assess the campaign in explanatory narratives that cultivate an audience that makes their work sustainable and sometimes profitable.
3. *Political circumstances create rhetorical opportunities for communication that redefines the political circumstances and rhetorical opportunities.* Everything is fluid, and campaigners, reporters, and citizens continually define and redefine issues and priorities, thereby constituting and reconstituting clusters of interests.
4. *The trialogue unfolds in four functional stages—surfacing, nominating, consolidating, and electing.* During each stage the participants trade words and symbolic actions for attention, campaign resources, and votes. They must navigate the surfacing stage to reach the nominating stage, win the nominating stage to control the party

consolidating stage, and consolidate their support to compete effectively in the electing stage. Success in each stage unlocks the next stage, much as winning sports teams advance to the playoffs.

5. *All three kinds of communicators pursue their agendas by interpreting their environment, saying some things (but not others) to some audiences (but not others) with the intention of improving their environment.* All of this talk creates a trail of words that can be studied and effects changes that yield data points.

6. *Contemporary communication technologies provide us with boundless information and data that can be used to study the dynamic, evolving campaign.* We now know that some of it is "fake news," some of it is only partially correct, and some of it is wishful thinking; but some of it is systematically gathered, objective, and potentially useful. Our theory provides a framework for interpreting such data points.

The surfacing stage crystallizes the elements of the campaign to come. The surfacing stage began when President Obama was reelected and people started pondering the next election; it culminated in the February 1, 2016, Iowa precinct caucuses. Iowa provides the first opportunity for citizens to vote (or not vote) in a statewide contest, but Iowans decided only who would represent them at their county party conventions the following month. The nominating stage—the quest for national convention delegates—began the next day as attention and the viable candidates turned to New Hampshire.

Three Kinds of Surfacing

Our theory conceives of surfacing more broadly than have other research projects. Specifically, we shall explore three kinds of surfacing: "structural surfacing," "issue surfacing," and "candidate surfacing." In structural surfacing, the national conversation reconstitutes the rules and processes for campaigning. Rules and laws are verbal texts by which decision-makers prescribe some choices and proscribe others. In fact, it is those rules and laws that distinguish election campaigns from social protests: they determine when elections will be held, who is allowed to vote, how they vote, how their votes are tabulated, and how votes determine the result. Electoral disputes are adjudicated by authorized panels including courts. But before the election campaign begins the interested parties tinker with the rules to "improve" the process.

In issue surfacing, the national conversation reconstitutes the "issues" (recognized by students of argumentation as our points of disagreement), their relative importance or priority, and the number of people who consider each issue important. Every month Gallup asks respondents to name the most important problem facing the country. The Gallup reports identify the general issue frames such as the "general economy," "national security," and "race relations" and calculate the percentage of respondents regarding each issue as "most important." Those percentages represent the "issue publics"—the cluster of people most worried about each issue frame. These clusters vary in size and compete for the attention of candidates and reporters. Put differently, the issue publics provide the potential followers for the candidates who can appeal to them. Changes in these issue publics during the three years of surfacing can reveal how the surfacing trialogue reshaped the electorate.

In candidate surfacing, the aspiring presidents develop organizations, resources, and strategies for competing in the nominating stage. Functionally, they need an organization sufficient to do the necessary work, endorsements from people respected by potential voters, sufficient money to underwrite the cost of their campaigns, news coverage to keep them in the public eye, name recognition sufficient to score well in national polls, and the potential to finish among the top four in their party's Iowa precinct caucuses.

Most of the surfacing literature has studied candidate surfacing, for a candidate who fails to surface effectively has little opportunity to thrive in the primaries. But to focus exclusively on candidate surfacing is to ignore the dynamics of structural and issue public surfacing that both invite and constrain those candidates' rhetorical choices.

STRUCTURAL SURFACING FOR 2016

As we consider structural surfacing, we will discuss the structure of the electoral process and the structure of the media environment in which we learned about it.

Restructuring the Electoral Process

The conversation about structural aspects of the 2016 presidential campaign began with President Obama's reelection, but the most important structural question was largely ignored. In 2000, George W. Bush won the

Electoral College but lost the national popular vote to Al Gore. There followed a period of controversy in which several calls for reform emerged. Some called for direct popular election of the president while an intriguing compromise called for electors to cast their votes for the winner of the national popular vote. Not surprisingly, most of those calls for reform came from disappointed Democrats, and two subsequent victories by Barack Obama drained support for electoral college reform...until late 2016 when Hillary Clinton won the national popular vote and lost in the electoral college. Sometimes the conversations we defer prove to be important.

Other surfacing conversations established the rules and procedures by which the nominating, consolidating, and electing stages would be conducted. Those included the primary, caucus, and convention schedules, the parties' delegate allocation rules, the rules and schedules for televised debates, and state laws enacted to prevent "voter fraud."

The national party organizations and state governments devote a great deal of time and attention to the schedule of primaries and caucuses. New Hampshire's constitution requires their primary to be "first in the nation" but what of the others? Many states hope to vote early, thinking that they can decisively impact the campaign. Others prefer to position themselves later so they can vote on the survivors and decide the nomination. By setting their calendar for primaries and caucuses, the Republican National Committee (RNC) and Democratic National Committee (DNC) structure the nominating stage.

The parties also set their rules for allocating their national convention delegates to the states. Democrats adopted a simple formula—the average of each state's percentage of the total popular and electoral votes for past three presidential elections.[2] Republicans adopted a more complex formula for allocating delegates to the states. Each state received ten at-large state delegates (five per senate seat), three delegates for each congressional district, and bonus delegates for having elected Republican senators and/or governors, for providing a 2012 majority for Romney, for the state's three Republican party officials, and for Republican control of their congressional delegation and/or state legislative chambers.[3]

The contrast between the parties' allocation formulas is stark. The RNC rewarded with delegate strength all state parties that had won elections—for state legislatures, congress, senate, governor, and president—while the DNC ignored everything but presidential votes. Put differently, the Republican Party restructured itself as an organization of victorious state parties, whereas the Democratic Party restructured itself as an organization of presidential voters. DNC rules advantaged California and New York where huge populations provided large popular and electoral margins for Kerry and Obama and disadvantaged smaller, competitive states. RNC rules advantaged states with strong party organizations that won elections.

The parties also established the rules for awarding those state delegates on the basis of primary and caucus votes. Since 1972 Democrats have allocated state delegates proportionately to candidates winning 15% or more of a primary or caucus vote. That winnows from the field candidates winning less than 15%, which is important when the Democratic field is crowded. Five Democrats tried to surface for 2016 but Jim Webb and Lincoln Chaffee abandoned their campaigns early when they could not escape single digit polling. Had Democratic rules provided delegates proportionately to *all* candidates receiving votes, Martin O'Malley might have fought on after Iowa (although his failure to muster other resources suggests not). With the Democratic field reduced to two candidates, both were poised to exceed the 15% needed for delegates and neither was likely to win the 86% needed to win them all. Thus, the rules defined a landscape in which two candidates would split convention delegates from every state and prolong the nominating campaign.

Much would later be made of the Democrats' "Super Delegates"—their elected office holders and members of the Democratic National Committee. Yet those Super Delegates—who worked with and knew the candidates—accounted for just 15% of Democratic convention delegates, with the other 85% distributed on the basis of primaries and caucuses. It was also likely that those Democratic party officials would prefer a lifelong Democrat over a lifelong independent socialist who caucused with Democratic senators. Thus the DNC's decision to offer both sorts of delegates created a rhetorical wedge between "the choice of the insiders" and "the choice of the people" even as Clinton won the majority of both groups.

More importantly, it would develop, was a Republican requirement that delegates allocated through primaries and caucuses were pledged to their candidate *through the convention*. Any state breaking that pledge would be penalized 50% of its delegates.[4] The establishment Republicans' effort to "Dump Trump" ran headlong into this rule.

The RNC also laid out a more complicated calendar than the Democrats. Until recently Republicans had expedited nomination with winner-take-all primaries, several of them clustered on "Super Tuesday" in early March. But after those rules brought them John McCain, Mitt Romney, and two defeats, the RNC decided to prolong the process by allowing no winner-take-all contests until after March 15. Thus, Republican February and March contests would award state delegates in proportion to the 17 aspiring nominees' votes, week after week; should they all tie, then each would get 5.88% of the state's convention delegates. Unlike the Democrats, every Republican with votes won some delegates, so unlike the Democrats the RNC gave lesser candidates an incentive to keep running, and unlike the Democrats the RNC made it difficult for a Republican to pull ahead early but easy to pull away in mid-March when winner-take-all primaries began.

In short, Republican rules encouraged a large early field and bound splinter delegations to their candidate throughout the convention. Primaries would slowly winnow the field until the finalists reached the winner-take-all contests. If that reminds you of sports playoffs or reality television, then you have a sense of how those rules advantaged an inexperienced candidate unfamiliar with party rules who was, however, a reality television host familiar with professional wrestling. These rules—early proportional delegations pledged through the convention—would severely hamper the establishment Republicans' effort to "stop Trump."

The laws governing voter eligibility also changed during surfacing. In 2012, 4 states required a photo ID to vote but, by 2016, 32 states had enacted such laws.[5] These laws were controversial. Proponents considered them necessary to stop the fraudulent voting that they had some difficulty documenting. Opponents charged that the photo ID laws were a veiled attempt to disenfranchise minorities who were less likely to have the requisite photo ID. North Carolina's photo ID law was judged unconstitutional when it was discovered that legislators researched the kinds of identification least common among minorities before deciding which to require. The point here is that the surfacing stage altered the rules for voter eligibility and thus reconstituted the electorate.

In summary, the surfacing stage established the parties' primary and caucus schedule and their delegation allocation rules and revised 28 states' voter eligibility laws. Moreover, the conversation strayed from reforming the Electoral College.

Restructuring the Media Environment

During surfacing, citizens decide where to find the campaign information they want. We reconstitute our networks by revising our viewing and reading habits, even as the information providers revise their services to better serve their target audiences. The rhetorical transaction is a combination of "I will rely on you for my political information if you provide the information I want" and "We will provide the political information our audience wants." The Pew Research Center reported that 91% of their respondents had learned about the presidential campaign by the end of surfacing, with half of their respondents using five or more sources.[6]

Cable news networks were considered the most helpful single source by 24% of respondents—the same percentage Pew had found in October 2012.[7] Social media were judged most helpful by 14% by the end of surfacing in 2016 (up 8% from 2012). Oddly, although only 1% had found local television news helpful in 2012 and only Iowa and New Hampshire had any significant local campaign news by the time of this February survey, local television news was judged most helpful by 14%, tying for second with social media. News apps were considered most helpful by 13% in 2016 (up from 3%), while radio dropped in perceived helpfulness from 16% to 11% in 2016. Still fewer respondents found traditional television networks helpful (10%). Local and national print newspapers, issue-based emails and websites, and candidate mailings and websites were all considered most helpful by less than 5% of respondents in both years.

The Pew findings suggest a pattern—citizens found "most helpful" the sources of news that they themselves selected. We select our preferred cable news network, our social media friends, our news apps, and our locale. Respondents found less helpful those news sources that aim their news at a broad audience: national newspapers and nightly network news. That is consistent with Stroud's finding that citizens rely on partisan selective exposure and perception to select their news sources.[8]

The media environment saw several important personnel changes. In 2012, the #1 network news anchor was NBC's Brian Williams, who by 2016 had been moved to MSNBC. His arrival there coincided with MSNBC's dismissal of Melissa Harris-Perry, an African-American political science professor whose program had provided a unique perspective on current events.

In 2012, 12% of Pew respondents reported getting political news from late night comedy programs including "the Daily Show with Jon Stewart," "The Colbert Report," "David Letterman," "The Tonight Show with Jay Leno," and "Saturday Night Live"; yet only 1% found comedy "most helpful." During the surfacing stage, Jon Stewart, David Letterman, and Jay Leno all left the air and Colbert replaced Letterman. Those and other changes in the entertainment sphere deflected the political conversation.

But surprisingly, by February 2016 substantially more Pew respondents counted late night comedy among their five or more sources of political news (25%, up from 12%) and 12% found comedy shows "most helpful" (up from 1%). Did the new generation of late night comedy hosts take a more political approach or did citizens find the other sources of political news less helpful? The Pew data are inconclusive on that question, but it is apparent that respondents found nonserious news increasingly helpful by early 2016.

ISSUE SURFACING FOR 2016

To understand issue public surfacing we can track the percentages of people who name an issue frame as the "most important problem" in Gallup's monthly surveys. Let us begin with a snapshot of public concerns from the period just before President Obama won reelection.

In October 2012, five problems accounted for 91% of Americans' perceived "most important problems":[9]

37%—General economy
26%—Unemployment/jobs
12%—Federal deficit
9%—Dissatisfaction with government
7%—Health care

Eight other issues polling at 5% or less concerned other Americans: a lack of money (5%), education, foreign aid, and ethical/moral decline all tied at 4%, the wars in Iraq and Afghanistan (3%), and immigration/aliens, national security, and aid for the elderly/Medicare all tied at 2%.

By the end of surfacing in February 2016, the issue publics' issue concerns had fragmented. The top eight problems accounted for 69% of respondents (as compared to 91% for five issues in late 2012).[10]

17%—General economy (down 20% but still #1).
13%—Dissatisfaction with government (up 4% from #4).
10%—Immigrants and aliens (up 8%) to tie unemployment/jobs (down 16% and one rank).
7%—National security (up 5%) to tie terrorism (absent from prior poll).
6%—Health care (down 1% and two ranks) and the federal deficit/debt (down 6% and four ranks).

In short, the 2012 issue publics had been transformed.

Although 75% had named the general economy, unemployment/jobs, or the federal deficit as the nation's most important problems in late 2012, only 39% did so in early 2016—a shift of 36%. But those respondents apparently gave no credit for that perceived economic improvement to government, for dissatisfaction with government increased from 9% to 13% and second place. Americans' concern about immigrants/aliens, national security, and terrorism increased by a combined 17% to move into the top five concerns.

This section has explained how Americans' sense of the most important problems changed during the surfacing stage. Between October 2012 and February 2016, the trialogue of citizens, reporters, and campaigners had reconstituted the issue publics that would decide the presidential nominations.

But presidential nominations are decided by the two major parties, not in at-large contests. Moreover, the distribution of citizens across political parties is not random. Thus, Gallup also reported the "most important problems" of February 2016 by party preference.

In February 2016, Republican respondents' priorities were dissatisfaction with government, the general economy, and immigration, whereas Democratic respondents' priorities were the general economy, unemployment, and dissatisfaction with government. But notice the gaps dividing the parties' issues[11]:

- 10% Difference: National Security—13% of Republicans vs. 3% of Democrats
- 7% Differences:
  - Dissatisfaction with Government—17% of Republicans vs. 10% of Democrats
  - Immigration/aliens—15% of Republicans vs. 8% of Democrats
  - Federal Deficit—10% of Republicans vs. 3% of Democrats
- 6% Difference: Race relations—2% of Republicans vs. 8% of Democrats
- 5% Differences:
  - Education—3% of Republicans vs. 8% of Democrats
  - Unemployment/jobs—7% of Republicans vs. 2% of Democrats
- 2% Difference:
  - Terrorism 8% of Republicans vs. 6% of Democrats.

With their partisan target audiences worried about different problems, it should not be surprising that candidates for the two parties' nominations articulated different rhetoric agendas.

Newsweek and *The New York Times* both tracked the topics debated during the surfacing stage and posted visualizations that suggested the parties' divergent issue spheres.[12] Democratic candidates argued about income inequality, Wall Street's influence, education, criminal justice, race, women's right, energy, and the environment. Republican candidates argued about excessive government, the Constitution, the legacy of Ronald Reagan, religious liberty, gay marriage, immigration, military power, Israel, North Korea, and China. Additionally, the Republican candidates exchanged (frequently undignified) personal attacks, whereas the Democrats contested policies.

Both reports suggest that the parties' candidates developed distinct rhetorical agendas consistent with their partisans' sense of the most important problems. Reporters and debate questioners—presumably trying to assist partisans considering candidates within their parties—rarely raised the same issues for the two parties' candidates. Thus, reporters helped to advance the separate agendas and exacerbated the polarization between the partisan communities.

The foregoing discussion suggests a deceptively simple question: Did the campaigners influence their partisans' concerns or did the partisans' concerns drive the campaigners' rhetoric? Because these are rhetorical transactions, the answer is "both." Campaigners strategically chose to discuss their partisans' "most important issues" AND their comments attracted news coverage and still more citizen reflection. Moreover, citizens surely adjusted their preferred news sources so as to receive news about their concerns. The result was that the trialogue cultivated a spiral effect that drove the two partisan communities further apart as they headed into the nominating stage.

It is important for us to recognize that neither party perceived a need to address independents or nonpartisans during the surfacing and nominating stages. Participation in most primaries and caucuses is restricted to registered partisans, and precious few of them actually participate. Instead, campaigners work to crystallize their partisan spheres and to emerge as the candidate best able to represent those audiences in the nominating stage. To see how they do so, we turn now to candidate surfacing.

CANDIDATE SURFACING

Some 22 aspiring candidates—17 Republicans and 5 Democrats—surfaced well enough by 2015 to appear in televised primary debates. But they faced an arduous journey before they could compete in the nominating stage. Our theory suggests tracking candidates' surfacing progress on five indices: fundraising, endorsements, media coverage, national polls, and success in Iowa's caucuses.[13] Let us apply those indices to candidate surfacing for 2016.

Fundraising

Campaigners trade words for dollars to finance their campaigns. People who want to contribute more than their votes browse the aspiring candidates for good investments; candidates who need funding browse the issue publics and articulate the positions favored by those willing to write checks. The worries common among wealthy people (including deregulation and tax cuts) have been blue chip investments—elusive, highly competitive, but lucrative. Populist ideas (including tax increases on the rich and free tuition) are penny stocks that individually yield little but offer a vast number of investors. As the campaigns develop their rhetorical portfolios they reconstitute their team of stockholders; their choice of stockholders, in turn, reconstitutes and constrains their subsequent rhetorical choices, their finances, and issue surfacing.

The Federal Election Commission requires quarterly fundraising reports from all campaigns, and reports them online. California, New York, New Jersey, Texas, Florida, and Washington, DC accounted for the most contributions during surfacing, providing a different early influence than those states with early contests (Iowa, New Hampshire, South Carolina, and Nevada). Several mega-donors who had invested heavily in Mitt Romney's unsuccessful 2012 campaign (including the Koch brothers) decided early on to withhold their hundreds of millions of dollars until the Republican nominee was decided; a choice that surely complicated their anti-Trump campaign.

The most effective fundraisers for 2016 were Democrats Hillary Clinton ($76 million) and Bernie Sanders ($41 million), and Republicans Ben Carson ($31 million), Ted Cruz ($26 million), and Jeb Bush ($24 million).[14]

Donald Trump defied the odds by self-financing most of his surfacing campaign and raising only five million dollars. Pundits and adversaries mocked his choice, but it freed him from binding commitments to donors.

More importantly, with few significant stockholders to hold him accountable, his rhetorical portfolio of stated positions could "evolve" without betraying donors. But a low-budget operation complicates staffing and advertising buys, a rhetorical challenge that Trump surmounted by using personal tweets to attract free media coverage.

Endorsements

The political parties nominate presidential candidates, so many elected party officials endorse aspiring candidates. The importance of endorsements was a particular emphasis of *The Party Decides*[15] which became one of the most influential political science studies to shape reporters' perspective on the 2016 surfacing. Endorsements are rhetorical transactions. Some elected officials are eager to see a candidate in the Oval Office, some are anxious about opposing the next president, and others play hard to get. Candidates trade words for endorsements and elected officials browse the field for a promising ally. And once again, candidates compile portfolios of issue promises and establishment support.

Nate Silver's FiveThirtyEight.com was sufficiently influenced by *The Party Decides* to develop an "Endorsement Primary," updated daily.[16] It awarded one point for each congressional endorsement, five points for senatorial endorsements, and ten points for each state governor's endorsement. This endorsement primary provides a useful metric for tracking the role of endorsements in 2016 as well as a sense of the candidates' commitment to establishment politics.

Hillary Clinton finished the surfacing stage with 463 endorsement points; Jeb Bush led Republicans with 51 and Marco Rubio had 43. Bernie Sanders, Donald Trump, Ben Carson, and Ted Cruz were essentially shut out in the endorsement primary.[17] Clearly, the Democratic establishment was rallying around Clinton while the Republican establishment—like their mega-donors—mostly held back.

Obviously, the notion of the endorsement primary presumed that endorsements by elected officials would be helpful. After all, the endorsers had won their elections and knew personally both the political skills required to perform their official duties and most of the aspiring candidates. But citizens' displeasure was so deep and widespread in 2015–2016 that these political endorsements were essentially toxic. While Clinton racked up Democratic endorsements the three other candidacies that would last the longest—Sanders, Trump, and Cruz—received essentially no endorsements during surfacing. This proved to be one of the biggest surprises of 2016 as the candidate with the fewest endorsements defeated the candidate with the overwhelming majority of endorsements. Here again, the Republican establishment that would later try to "Dump Trump" failed to invest their endorsements in candidates with the potential to do so.

Media Coverage

Candidates need media coverage to reach citizens, to enhance their name recognition, and to position themselves in the national conversation. Although challenged by social media, television remains the leading source of political information.[18] Google created a Television News Tracker they called "Gdelt" as a searchable database. Gdelt allows us to see how widely televisions news covered each candidate, and which networks did so.

The Gdelt database shows that Donald Trump led all candidates with 213,000 mentions (43% of Republican coverage). Surprisingly, most of Trump's surfacing coverage came from MSNBC (34%) and CNN (27%), while Fox News provided much less (only 17%).[19] Put differently, Trump received more television coverage on center-left cable networks than from the conservative Fox. Hillary Clinton's 143,000 mentions provided 74% of Democrats' coverage. Jeb Bush ranked third (80,000) and Bernie Sanders fourth (42,000).[20]

Trump attracted a great deal of coverage by saying outlandish, provocative things. Rather than spending money on television ads, Trump gave speeches and sent tweets. Journalists, pundits, and bloggers found his tweets irresistible. MSNBC and CNN took his bait more readily than the others and thus expanded his early media exposure. Although their coverage of Trump's tweets was rarely positive, their coverage made his campaign the centerpiece of the national conversation.

Bernie Sanders was understandably displeased about receiving only 24% of the Democrats' television coverage. But Clinton's coverage was largely unfavorable and investigative. Indeed, Sanders fared better than 15 Republican candidates who struggled in vain to reach citizens.

National Polls

National opinion polls abound during election years. But what do they tell us? Each asks a theoretically representative sample of the country's likely voters whom they prefer for president. That might be a productive exercise if the election were a national popular vote, but American presidents have always been elected in a set of state elections with differential electoral vote weighting. National polls might be important if we held one national popular primary election to decide the nominations, or if we held all state primaries on the same day. But because the United States does none of those things, national polls are basically a major industry with no meaningful purpose—except one.

National polls provide a crude measure of positive name recognition across the country, and name recognition is important when one reads a ballot. As campaign conversations produce years of rhetorical transactions, some names become familiar. We ordinarily think of surfacing as a time for lesser known aspiring candidates to become widely known, but some names are already familiar. In 2016, the Clinton name was more familiar than Sanders or O'Malley, and Bush was more familiar than Cruz or Rubio. Barack Hussein Obama frequently joked about his "funny name" and its unfortunate similarity to those of Saddam Hussein and Osama bin Laden (not all of his critics ignored those similarities). Although familiar names, we might expect a Fred Hitler or a Ben Arnold to have trouble cultivating positive name recognition. Thus, polls provide but a crude estimate of positive branding.

Since no single national poll is of much value and because we are blessed with so many, we can improve our understanding by softening our focus and averaging a set of polls taken about the same time to get a very general sense of the candidates' desirability among Americans. Daily during 2015–2016, *realclearpolitics.com* reported the averages of the three most recent candidate polls.

A Quinnipiac University poll from July 8, 2014, provides an early baseline for comparison. Hillary Clinton dominated the Democratic field (58%), followed by Senator Elizabeth Warren (11%), Vice-president Joe Biden (9%), New York Governor Andrew Cuomo (4%), and others below 1%[21] (Quinnipiac 2014). But there was little separation among the Republicans:

- Rand Paul 11%
- Chris Christie, Mike Huckabee, and Jeb Bush 10%
- Scott Walker, Ted Cruz, and Paul Ryan 8%
- Marco Rubio 6%

No pollsters asked about Donald Trump.

On November 1, 2015—roughly 16 months later and still a year before the election, after several primary debates, and with 3 months of surfacing still to go—RCP showed 4 of the 21 candidates exceeding 20%:

- Hillary Clinton 48% (down 10%)
- Donald Trump and Bernie Sanders 27% (absent from the previous poll)
- Ben Carson 22% (absent from the previous poll)[22]

For a variety of reasons, Elizabeth Warren, Joe Biden, Scott Walker, and Paul Ryan had left the field (although the Warren and Ryan names would periodically return). Trump, Sanders, and Carson had climbed the polls, while many others failed to achieve traction. Indeed, eight candidates were polling between 1% and 10 %, and six others could not even muster an average of 1% in polls that typically had a ±3% statistical margin for error.

By surfacing's end on February 1, 2016, the RCP average of likely voter polls showed:

- Hillary Clinton 52% (up 4% but 6% below 2014)
- Bernie Sanders 37% (up 10% since 2015 and 37% since 2014)
- Donald Trump 35% (up 35% since 2014 and 2015)
- Ted Cruz 20% (up 12% since 2014) and Marco Rubio 20% (up 14% since 2014 and 10% since 2015).[23]

Most observers were surprised by Trump's polling success, but we need not have been. Positive name recognition is important, but it does not only come from politically relevant exposure. The Trump brand had become familiar through his businesses, and he had been a celebrity for years, even hosting a popular television series. Long before Donald himself became known to us, card players knew "trump" as the suit that beats everything else. By announcing his availability, Trump transferred his name recognition into a political account.

Iowa Precinct Caucuses

Surfacing culminated in the February 1 Iowa precinct caucuses. Nomination depends on party convention delegates of whom Iowa provides only 1%. Moreover, by rule Iowa decides their national convention delegate assignments in state party conventions that take place after all other primaries and caucuses have finished. But candidates' success in Iowa does reflect each campaign's ability to strategically mobilize resources to attract actual voters. If the Iowa precinct caucuses are mainly symbolic, symbolic events have the potential to shape news narratives.

Journalists and pundits have long emphasized the importance of "winning Iowa" in the precinct caucuses, but that narrative is misleading. Since Iowa began using their caucuses for presidential purposes in 1972 roughly half of all eventual presidential nominees have failed to win them. Instead, the record shows that no candidate has been nominated by either party after faring worse than fourth in the precinct caucuses. So, the candidates' strategic objective should be to finish among their party's top four in Iowa's precinct caucuses. Nominations cannot be won in Iowa, but candidates' future prospects can be severely damaged by poor performances in Iowa.[24]

Iowa Republicans attend their local caucuses and participate in a straw poll. Attendees write the name of their preferred candidate on a slip of paper; precinct chairs tabulate and report them to the state Republican Party. Iowa Republicans who attended their local caucuses voted for a top four of Ted Cruz (27.6%), Donald Trump (24.2%), Marco Rubio (23.1%), and Ben Carson (9.3%).[25]

Democrats attend their caucuses and cluster themselves into candidate preference groups of 15% or more of those in attendance (regrouping themselves as necessary). Those candidate preference groups then elect their precinct delegates to the county conventions. Clinton won those county delegates 667–663 for Sanders.[26]

The traditional approach to influencing Iowans has seen candidates spending many days there. The logic is that candidates can drum up support there through personal appearances, score well in the precinct caucuses, and then parlay news reports of their Iowa success into national prominence. In 1984, Gary Hart did so and became an overnight challenge to Democratic Vice-president Walter Mondale's nomination. In 2012, Rick Santorum appeared to win by speaking at hundreds of events while Mitt Romney relied on national coverage.

The *Des Moines Register's* website reports all candidate events in Iowa. We can therefore calculate the number of local Iowa events by each candidate per percentage of their caucus votes. Doing so suggests that campaigning in Iowa worked well in 2016 only for Bernie Sanders (3.1 events per 1%) and Ted Cruz (5.5 per 1%). Rick Santorum again relied on Iowa events, but parlayed 293 visits into just 1% of the caucus votes; Mike Huckabee, Martin O'Malley, Carly Fiorina, and Bobby Jindal fared even worse.[27]

Meanwhile, Hillary Clinton, Donald Trump, and Marco Rubio fared well in Iowa without seeming to move there. All three campaigned efficiently by balancing their time in Iowa with attention to the other aspects of surfacing.

The Candidate Surfacing Sweepstakes

For campaigners, surfacing is a scramble toward the top. We can perhaps best assess it by aggregating their rankings on the five surfacing indices such that the lowest total ranking points suggest the best overall success.

Among Democrats, Hillary Clinton ran the Surfacing table, trailed by Sanders and O'Malley on all five indices. The Surfacing contest that had already discouraged Jim Webb and Lincoln Chaffee claimed Martin O'Malley on caucus night, leaving only Clinton and Sanders to advance to the nominating Stage.

Republican surfacing was more complicated. Surfacing difficulties ended the campaigns of George Pataki, Bobby Jindal, Lindsay Graham, and Scott Walker before Iowa. Shortly after Iowa they were joined by Rick Santorum, Mike Huckabee, and Carly Fiorina.

Across the five indices Marco Rubio and Ted Cruz tied for first. Rubio ranked well on all five measures whereas Cruz received fewer endorsements and less television coverage. Jeb Bush performed well except, problematically, for national polls and Iowa voters. Trump led in coverage, national polls, and Iowans but received no endorsements and few dollars from others, whereas Ben Carson surfaced well except for endorsements. John Kasich finished only eighth in Surfacing but nevertheless chose to persist into the nominating stage (where he won only his home state of Ohio).

DISCUSSION

While Americans were looking elsewhere during 2013–2015, the ongoing trialogue among citizens, campaigners, and reporters rhetorically reconstituted our political landscape. Democrats stopped worrying about the Electoral College after Obama's second victory while Republicans were satisfied to enact photo identification voting laws. Democrats were content to have primaries and caucuses decide 85% of their convention delegates, while Republicans delayed winner-take-all primaries until mid-March and pledged their delegates through the convention.

Although we continued to worry about general economics, jobs, unemployment, and the federal deficit, we largely forgot about reforming the electoral process and respecting one another, fewer of us worried about race relations and more of us worried about immigration and aliens. Citizens inclined toward each party began to worry about different issues, and the campaigners' courting them began articulating different issue agendas.

We continued to rely on selective sources for political information—cable news channels and social media—while relying less on print newspapers, radio, and candidate or issue-based websites. Our appetites for political information consistent with our beliefs seemed to increase accordingly.

After the 2012 Romney defeat, several of the Republicans' megadonors delayed their contributions and most Republican officials deferred their endorsements. Perhaps early generous contributions and endorsements could have helped an establishment Republican defeat Trump. But because the Republican rules awarded proportional delegates to so many candidates for so long, the not-Trump field provided the mega-donors with no promising alternative.

Hillary Clinton remained the most popular candidate for a majority of survey respondents, as she was eventually preferred by a majority of voters. But national polls predict no outcome of consequence and she was widely endorsed by elected Democrats who were themselves objects of the public's dissatisfaction with government. Although she received 74% of Democrats' television news coverage, her values and policy proposals received less of that attention than did her email server and trustworthiness. One would expect a candidate so well funded, endorsed, and covered to gain ground during surfacing; instead, she actually declined in the national polls.

Bernie Sanders, Donald Trump, Marco Rubio, and Ben Carson surfaced from nowhere, and Ted Cruz more than doubled his initial support. Jeb Bush—perhaps buoyed initially by the family name—disappointed potential voters; Rand Paul's approval declined, perhaps as Republicans learned the full range of his libertarian foreign policy positions. Many other aspiring candidates in both parties failed utterly.

Once considered a requirement for surfacing success, public dissatisfaction with government rendered political endorsements largely toxic. Both parties saw challenges to their established leadership—the Democrats from independent socialist Bernie Sanders, the Republicans from political novices Donald Trump and Ben Carson.

CONCLUSIONS

The Surfacing stage of the 2016 American presidential campaign—from November 2012 through February 1, 2016—rhetorically reconstituted the American political landscape on which the rest of the campaign would take place. Inevitably, the challenges of Surfacing eliminated many candidates and winnowed the field of competitors for the primary elections of the nominating stage. Atypically, endorsements by Republican officials proved toxic and fundraising paled. Social media became more helpful to citizens and generated news coverage at low cost.

This chapter has described the Surfacing stage of the 2016 campaign. It was a national conversation that concerned not only aspiring candidates, but evolving structures such as laws, rules, and calendars as well as evolving issue priorities and their publics. The 2016 election did not begin with the primaries or the conventions—it began when Mitt Romney conceded to Barack Obama in 2012.

Thus, the 2020 Surfacing stage began with Donald Trump's victory speech and Hillary Clinton's concession. The new trialogue has begun. Many Democratic voices, and some Republicans, are now seeking to obstruct President Trump, much as Republicans blocked many of Obama's initiatives, but that may well be a mistake. President Trump will surely succeed in some areas and come up short in others; whatever happens will create new perceptions of the "most important problem" we face as a country, new aspiring presidents, and new rules and procedures for electing that president.

This chapter has shown that the 2016 presidential campaign occurred in a rhetorical political landscape quite different from that of 2012. It is equally unlikely that the 2016 landscape will frame the 2020 campaign. The 2020 election may well entail new rules and laws, different issues and publics, and at least one different candidate (it is not inconceivable that establishment Republicans will challenge President Trump's renomination). Whether that happens, and how that happens, will depend on the national trialogue among citizens, reporters, and campaigners that has already begun.

NOTES

1. Craig Allen Smith, *Presidential campaign communication*, 2nd ed. (Cambridge: Polity, 2015).
2. Green Papers, "Democratic Detailed Delegate Allocation". greenpapers. com. Accessed December 12, 2016, http://www.thegreenpapers.com/ P16/D-Alloc.phtml.
3. Green Papers. "Republican Detailed Delegate Allocation—2016". green papers.com, February 3, 2013. Accessed April 15, 2016 http://www.the greenpapers.com/P16/R-Alloc.phtml.
4. Green Papers. "Republican Detailed Delegate Allocation—2016". green papers.com, February 3, 2013. Accessed April 15, 2016 http://www.the greenpapers.com/P16/R-Alloc.phtml.
5. Jasmine C. Lee, "How States Moved Toward Stricter Voter ID Laws," New York Times, November 3, 2016. Accessed November 4, 2016 http://www. nytimes.com/interactive/2016/11/03/us/elections/how-states-moved-toward-stricter-voter-id-laws.html.
6. Jeffrey Gottfried, Michael Barthel, Elisa Shearer, and Amy Mitchell, "The 2016 Presidential Campaign: A News Event that's Hard to Miss," *Pew Research Center: Journalism & Media*, February 4, 2016. Accessed March 3, 2016 http://www.journalism.org/2016/02/04/the-2016-presiden tial-campaign-a-news-event-thats-hard-to-miss.
7. Pew Research Center. (2012. October 25). "Internet Gains Most as Campaign News Source but Cable TV Still Leads," *Pew Research Center: Journalism & Media*, October 25, 2012. Accessed December 8, 2016 http://www.journalism.org/2012/10/25/social-media-doubles-remains-limited.
8. *Natalie Jomini Stroud, Niche News: The Politics of News Choice.* (New York: Oxford University Press, 2011).
9. Lydia Saad, "Economy is Dominant Issue for Americans as Election Nears," gallup.com, October 22, 2012. Accessed December 22, 2016 http://www. gallup.com/poll/158267/economy-dominant-issue-americans-election-nears.aspx.
10. Rebecca Riffkin, "Economy Tops Americans' Minds as Most Important Problem," gallup.com, February 11, 2016. Accessed December 22, 2016 http://www.gallup.com/poll/189158/economy-tops-americans-minds-important-problem.aspx.
11. Riffkin, 2016.
12. Polly Mosendz, "Chart: How Republican Presidential Debate Topics Compare with the Democratic Debate," newsweek.com, January 14, 2016. Accessed January 26, 2016 http://www.newsweek.com/chart-republican-debate-gop-democrate-debate-compare-416025 and Josh Keller and Karen

Yourish, "Party Debates, or Ignores," *New York Times*, March 10, 2016. Accessed March 12, 2016 http://www.nytimes.com/interactive/2016/03/11/us/elections/what-parties-debate-or-ignore.html?_r=1.

13. Smith, 2015.
14. Federal Election Commission. "2016 Presidential Campaign Finance", Accessed February 6, 2016 http://www.fec.gov/disclosurep/pnational.do.
15. Marty Cohen, David Karol, Hans Noell and John Zaller, *The Party Decides: Presidential Nominations Before and After Reform*. (Chicago: University of Chicago Press, 2008.
16. Aaron Bycoffe, A. "The Endorsement Primary," fivethirtyeight.com, February 1, 2016. Accessed February 1, 2016 http://projects.fivethirtyeight.com/2016-endorsement-primary.
17. Bycoffe, 2016.
18. Gottfried et al., 2016.
19. Gdelt, "Presidential Campaign 2016: Television News Tracker". gdeltproject.org. Accessed February 10, 2016 http://television.gdeltproject.org/cgi-bin/iatv_campaign2016/iatv_campaign2016.
20. Gdelt, 2016.
21. Quinnipiac University Poll. "Clinton Owns Dem 2016 Nod; Tops Top Republicans, Quinnipiac University National Poll Finds," *Quinnipiac University Poll*, July 8, 2014. Accessed December 17, 2016 https://poll.qu.edu/national/release-detail?ReleaseID=2058.
22. Real Clear Politics. "Polls", realclearpolitics.com, November 1, 2015. Accessed November 1, 2016 http://www.realclearpolitics.com/epolls/2016/president/us/2016_republican_presidential_nomination-3823.html.
23. Real Clear Politics, "Polls," realclearpolitics.com, February 1, 2016. Accessed February 1, 2016 http://www.realclearpolitics.com/epolls/2016/president/us/2016_republican_presidential_nomination-3823.html.
24. Smith, 2015.
25. *Des Moines Register*, "Take a Deeper Look at Iowa Caucus Results," desmoinesregister.com, February 2, 2016. Accessed February 2, 2016 http://www.desmoinesregister.com/story/news/elections/presidential/caucus/2016/02/05/take-deeper-look-iowa-caucus-results/79839784.
26. *Des Moines Register*, "Take a Deeper Look".
27. *Des Moines Register*, "Iowa Caucuses 2016: Candidate Tracker," desmoinesregister.com, February 2, 2016. Accessed February 2, 2016 http://data.desmoinesregister.com/iowa-caucus/candidate-tracker/index.php.

Craig Allen Smith is professor emeritus, North Carolina State University. He is the author of *Presidential Campaign Communication, 2nd ed.* (2015) and *Persuasion and Social Movements, 6th ed.* with Charles J. Stewart and Robert E. Denton, Jr. as well as chapters and articles about American political rhetoric.

CHAPTER 2

Midnight in America: The Political Conventions in 2016

Rachel L. Holloway

Presidential nominating conventions mark the transition from the primary campaign to the general election and serve multiple communication functions for the presidential campaign. If effective, the conventions reaffirm and celebrate the democratic selection of candidates, thereby legitimizing both the process and the nominees. The conventions also create a communicative moment through which the political parties set aside the divisions evident in the primary campaign and establish party unity, commitment, and excitement for the general election. Finally, the conventions afford the candidate a platform to introduce and elaborate campaign issues and messages in a highly controlled, choreographed, and scripted production.[1]

The convention (and campaign) messages, at the highest level, construct competing conceptions of national identity.[2] The candidates and their parties compose a narrative of the nation constructed around core principles and values with an attendant vision for the future, all in the hope of building a winning coalition for the general election. Candidates draw on an American story composed of two competing myths, according to Walter Fisher.[3] One is a materialistic myth guided by values of

R.L. Holloway (✉)
Virginia Tech's Department of Communication, Blacksburg, VA, USA
e-mail: rhollowa@vt.edu

© The Author(s) 2017
R.E. Denton, Jr. (ed.), *The 2016 US Presidential Campaign*,
Political Campaigning and Communication,
DOI 10.1007/978-3-319-52599-0_2

self-reliance, achievement, and success historically aligned with the Republican Party. The alternative conception of the American story is moralistic, focused on the values of equality, tolerance, and cooperation to create a public good. This focus on communal effort to move toward "a more perfect union" is associated historically with the Democrats.[4] Rowland and Jones argued that President Barack Obama achieved "narrative victory" through a careful balancing of individual and communal values into what Obama called the "American Promise": "That's the promise of America, the idea that we are responsible for ourselves but that we also rise and fall as one nation, the fundamental belief that I am my brother's keeper. I am my sister's keeper."[5] In 2012, Obama shifted the balance of values more strongly toward communal principles to sustain his vision for America, asking citizens to persevere in the "long journey" of American progress.[6]

Yet, as Obama's administration neared its end, the American people were deeply anxious about the direction of the country. Obama's promised change had failed to meet the expectations of many in the electorate. Gallup reported the American public's satisfaction with the "way things are going in the U.S." dropped 12% in July 2016 among all respondents, the largest drop since Gallup began the monthly tracking in 2001. Republicans accounted for little of the change having expressed dissatisfaction throughout the Obama presidency, registering only 6% satisfaction in July 2016. The drop in satisfaction was primarily among Democrats and Independents with Democrats' satisfaction dropping from 55% to 29% from June to July. Independents dropped from 24% to 16%.[7] The issues topping the "most important" list also changed in order during the early summer, with racism/race relations moving to the top of the list. Dissatisfaction with government, the economy in general, and unemployment followed. The number of people identifying "crime and violence" and "guns and gun control" as important increased over previous months.[8]

In addition to a highly dissatisfied public, both Republicans and Democrats faced internal challenges as they prepared to transition to the general election. The Republican primary battle fractured the party. Seventeen candidates participated in the primary election process. Their attempts to differentiate their candidacy often devolved into an exchange of insults, frequently initiated by Donald Trump's name calling. As Trump's campaign gained support, the attacks on his candidacy became increasingly pointed and negative, including statements from candidates and others in Republican leadership calling Trump unfit to serve as president. Over the spring, candidates dropped out of the race one by one, with Florida Senator Marco Rubio suspending his campaign in March and Ohio Governor John Kasich in May, leaving Ted Cruz as Trump's primary rival. The media speculated throughout the late spring about the possibility of a "contested" or "brokered" convention.[9] However, after a loss in Indiana, Ted Cruz too suspended his campaign. Trump remained standing as the party's presumptive nominee.[10] While Trump accurately claimed the most primary votes of any Republican candidate in history, he also held the record for the most votes *against* a Republican primary candidate, eclipsing John McCain's previous record.[11] Trump had overcome what he called a "rigged, disgusting dirty system that's designed so that the bosses can pick whoever they want."[12]

The Democratic primary was equally divisive. Vermont Senator Bernie Sanders launched a "revolution" among citizens who responded to his Progressive agenda, surprising both the Clinton campaign and political pundits. He too complained of a "rigged system" designed to favor an establishment candidate. Sanders scored an upset in Michigan in March and won key victories in the Midwest and west through May. Even after Clinton was named the presumptive Democratic nominee in June, Sanders continued his campaign.[13] Finally, barely two weeks before the convention, Sanders pledged his support for Clinton, although many Sanders supporters refused to give up the fight, preparing to bring their energy and voice to the Democratic National Convention. Thus, both political parties had significant internal discord and dissent to overcome within the conventions.

Both candidates also entered the conventions with little public support. A Gallup poll completed one month before the conventions reported 25% of respondents held an unfavorable view of both candidates. Only 35% held a favorable view of Clinton and 28% claimed a favorable view of Trump.[14] In July, when Gallup asked individuals to describe the candidates, the negative characterizations outranked positive descriptors for both candidates. Clinton was described as "untrustworthy" or "dishonest," while Trump was described as an "idiot," a "joke," a "racist," and as "dangerous or reckless."[15] A Fox News Poll conducted in June reported similar dissatisfaction with the candidates. While both Clinton and Trump were perceived as "intelligent" and "patriotic" by a majority of respondents, only 45% said Clinton "cares about people like me" and Trump received an even lower 35% positive rating on the same item. While Clinton scored a 77% on "experienced" to Trump's 34%, both candidates scored below 35% on the descriptor "honest and trustworthy."[16]

Thus, both candidates faced significant rhetorical challenges as they prepared for the nominating conventions. The candidates themselves were generally unpopular with the American people and a significant portion of the electorate was uncommitted to either party. Both candidates needed to overcome deep divisions within their parties to launch their campaigns into the general election. Above all, both candidates needed to convince an anxious and dissatisfied electorate that they would lead toward a more prosperous and peaceful future. Over the course of eight days in July, the candidates made their case to their own parties and to the American people. The Republican National Convention convened first. The Democratic National Convention began four days later in Philadelphia. The conventions together presaged a campaign during which both candidates would promise to fight for the American people, to "have their back," and to restore the American Dream for all Americans as each also declared their opponent unfit to hold the office of president. The remainder of this chapter describes their convention strategies and messages.

THE REPUBLICAN NATIONAL CONVENTION

The Republican National Convention convened in Cleveland's Quicken Loans arena from July 18 to 24, 2016.[17] The convention organizers announced a strategy focused on Trump's primary campaign theme, "Make American Great Again" that would be elaborated through a subtheme each night. On Monday, "Make America Safe Again" would focus attention on national security and military readiness. Tuesday's theme, "Make America Work Again," would emphasize Trump's accomplishments as a successful businessman and demonstrate his ability to move the country forward economically. "Make America First Again" on Wednesday would highlight how "under a Trump administration, America will once again be a beacon of progress and opportunity." On the final night of the convention, Republicans would explain how a Trump administration would "Make America One Again" by moving "beyond divisive identity politics that have been holding us back by restoring leadership, building trust, and focusing on our shared love of country and our common goal of making America great again."[18]

The Republican National Convention was not nearly as organized or clear in its communication as its press release proposed. The order of speakers and their messages were disjointed. Long musical interludes filled time between speakers. The number and caliber of speakers failed to elevate Trump's candidacy. Most importantly, errors in preparation and planning raised questions about the Trump campaign's ability to undertake an effective general election campaign.

Political nominating conventions traditionally feature elected leaders from the party and other party leaders in key speaking roles to demonstrate unity, endorse the candidate's legitimate leadership of the party, and to generate excitement for the party's nominee. Trump's convention faced an unofficial boycott. While all primaries are contentious, Trump's personal attacks on his rivals, his brash and often offensive statements, and controversial policy positions had alienated many in the Republican Party. Neither President George H.W. Bush nor President George W. Bush attended. 2008 Republican nominee John McCain and 2012 nominee Mitt Romney as well as party leaders such as South Carolina Senator Lindsey Graham and New Hampshire Senator Kelly Ayotte, among others, bypassed the convention. Republican primary candidate John Kasich refused to participate, even though he served as Governor of the host state. Politico reported having contacted more than 50 prominent governors, senators, and congressional representatives to gauge their interest in speaking at the convention and found only a few open to an invitation.[19] Even Trump's affiliation with the entertainment industry produced few stars to boost excitement and interest in the convention.

Trump's primary campaign also failed to generate support from many traditional conservatives, including Evangelical Christians. "Average" Republicans, especially those who voted for another candidate in the primary, did not believe that the party would unify behind Trump.[20] Trump named Indiana Senator Mike Pence as his vice presidential running mate to reassure the conservative core of the party. Speaker of the House Paul Ryan described Pence as "from the heart of the conservative movement—and the heart of America."[21] Yet Pence's selection was not enough to assuage members of the "Never Trump" movement within the party, a group of delegates who worked to change convention rules to free delegates to vote "according to their conscience" rather than as bound by the primary election outcomes.[22] Their opposition to Trump created a dramatic opening to the convention.

Having failed to secure the desired rules changes in behind-the-scenes negotiations and action in the convention rules committee, the Never Trump constituency launched a floor fight. The nominating convention's first order of business is approval of the convention rules, an action usually accomplished through a simple voice vote. The "Never Trump" leadership brought a motion to the floor calling for a roll call vote. They hoped to delay the opening of the convention and to gather sufficient support to allow "unbound delegates" to vote independently from their state delegations. As the convention moved toward the vote on the rules change, delegates chanting "Roll Call Vote" were countered by shouts of "We Want Trump" and "U.S.A!" The chair called for a voice vote on the motion and ruled the motion was defeated. Shouting escalated as delegates screamed for their right for a roll call vote. The chair left the podium as Republican National Convention leadership and Trump campaign staff moved to the convention floor, lobbying key delegations to withdraw from the petition for a roll call. Ultimately, party leadership quashed the roll call and the rules change. The Colorado delegation and others walked out of the convention in protest. While the Trump campaign effectively ended the challenge to Trump's nomination, the division within the party remained and would resurface later in the convention.[23]

As the convention moved forward, speakers articulated the primary message of the convention. They painted a stark picture of a dangerous world, both domestically and internationally, and attributed responsibility for the nation's insecurity to the Obama administration and specifically to Hillary Clinton. The only way to make American safe again in their narrative was to defeat Clinton and elect Trump.

One of the dominant stories of the first evening was a recounting of the attack on the American Embassy in Benghazi, Libya, in 2012. Pat Smith, mother of Sean Smith, one of the victims of the Benghazi attack, recounted her last conversation with her son and then said, "For all of this loss, for all of this grief, for all of the cynicism, the tragedy in Benghazi has brought upon America—I blame Hillary Clinton."[24] A video narrated by retired military and intelligence officers followed and created a timeline of action in the Benghazi attack and response. Two members of the Benghazi Annex Security team shared their story, including a decision to move to defend the consulate despite an order to "stand down." They held Hillary Clinton responsible for a failure to "protect her people on the ground." The Benghazi story was raised throughout the convention as evidence that Clinton was not fit to serve as commander-in-chief.

Others speakers turned attention to "law and order" at home. Three parents of children killed by undocumented immigrants shared their grief over the loss of a child and their support for Trump's strong stance on illegal immigration. David Clarke, Sheriff of Milwaukee County, Wisconsin spoke of a sense of anxiety across the nation: "many Americans increasingly have an uneasiness about the ability of their family to live safely in these troubling times. This transcends race, religion, ethnicity, gender, age, and lifestyle."[25] Citing a Gallup poll, he reported, "More than half of all Americans now worry a great deal about crime and violence, consistently up from a few years ago. And for African Americans, that number is 70%." His answer to address the problem was "the rule of law" and a Trump administration. Similar themes emerged in the remarks of Rep. Senate candidate Darryl Glenn, an African-American who described himself as a "unapologetic Christian constitutionalist conservative," who called for support of law enforcement and for the military, asking the audience to recognize that "evil exists" and that "the battle can be won."[26]

In the critical primetime hour, former New York Mayor Rudy Giuliani delivered a scathing denunciation of the Obama Administration and Hillary Clinton's record as Secretary of State.[27] He accused the Obama administration of being afraid "to define our enemy" leading the U.S. to be perceived as "weak and vulnerable." The response, he argued, must be to name the enemy, "radical Islamic terrorism," and to "commit ourselves to unconditional victory against them." Giuliani charged Clinton with advocating for the overthrow of Gaddafi in Libya that resulted in "chaos." He called the Benghazi attack a "dereliction of duty" and a "gross failure as Secretary of State," the Iran nuclear agreement "one of the worst deals American ever made" and decried Clinton's plans to allow Syrian refugees, who might "actually be terrorists," to enter the country and "come here and kill us." He returned to the Benghazi attack and Clinton's Congressional testimony afterwards. He accused her of "arrogant disregard" and said, "Anyone who can say that it makes no difference how or why people serving America are killed, should not be entrusted with the awesome responsibility to protect them and us and should not be allowed to be our Commander-in-Chief." Giuliani elevated the sense of crisis: "there's no next election. This is it. There's no more time for us left to revive our great country. No more time to repeat our mistakes of the Clinton/Obama years. Washington needs a complete turnaround, and Donald Trump is the agent of change and he will be the leader of the change we need."

Giuliani's speech encapsulated the Trump message. The nation was in crisis due to Obama's leadership and policies. Hillary Clinton, a key leader in the administration, would continue the same failed policies. She was a flawed leader who failed to recognize the threats facing the nation. Restoration of the U.S. to strength and safety, to make American safe again, required dramatic and immediate change. A Trump presidency was the answer.

Giuliani's intense and highly negative presentation energized the delegates. They cheered and jeered throughout the speech. As they continued to shout after the end of his speech, the lights on the stage suddenly dimmed and a bright white light and fog filled the stage. The song, "We are the Champions," played and Donald Trump's distinctive silhouette appeared. The crowd roared.

Trump walked to the podium, repeating "thank you" and "we love you" and "we're going to win so big" while the delegates continued to cheer. Finally, Trump gave what was perhaps the shortest speech of his campaign, "Ladies and gentlemen, it is my great honor to present the next first lady of the United States, my wife, an amazing mother, an incredible woman, Melania Trump."[28]

Melania entered the stage, embraced her husband, and walked to the podium. She spoke of growing up in Slovenia and learning the values of hard work, integrity, and showing respect to others. She talked of achievement as limited only by the strength of dreams and hard work. Her work in fashion led her to Milan, then Paris, and finally to New York where she became a U.S. citizen in 2006. She described becoming a U.S. citizen as "the greatest privilege on planet earth." Melania Trump's story stood in stark contrast to the stories of illegal immigrants preying on communities featured earlier in the evening.[29]

Melania Trump devoted much of her speech to describing Donald Trump's positive personal attributes. She called him "kind and fair and caring," "intensely loyal," and respectful to his family. The caring and mentoring of his children made them an "amazing testament to who he is as a man and a father." She described her husband as someone who thinks big and gets things done. In response to the many characterizations of Donald Trump as a racist and bigot, Melania described her husband as an inclusive leader:

> Donald intends to represent all the people, not just some of the people. That includes Christians and Jews and Muslims. It includes Hispanics and African-Americans and Asians and the middle class. Throughout his career,

Donald has successfully worked with people of many faiths and with many nations. Like no one else, I have seen the talent, the energy, the tenacity, the resourceful mind and the simple goodness of the heart that God gave to Donald Trump.

Turning away from Giuliani's strident rhetoric, Melania Trump articulated an alternative set of values to unite the party:

As the citizens of this great nation, it is kindness, love, and compassion for each other that will bring us together and keep us together. These are the values Donald and I will bring to the White House. My husband is ready to lead this great nation. He's ready to fight every day to give our children the better future they deserve. Ladies and gentlemen, Donald J. Trump is ready to serve and lead this country as the next president of the United States.

Melania's personal story grounded in the American Dream, her testament to Donald Trump's good character, his heart, and his commitment to serve all people created a positive contrast to the dark depiction of the nation's state throughout the evening.

Unfortunately, Melania Trump's speech was quickly embroiled in controversy. Comparisons of Melania Trump's speech to First Lady Michelle Obama's speech at the 2008 Democratic National Convention prompted allegations of plagiarism. News outlets created side-by-side media clips demonstrating duplicated phrases and even a striking similarity in the timing of the speech's delivery.[30] The story dominated the next morning's media coverage of the convention. The Trump campaign denied plagiarism, discounting the similarities as a simple expression of common values. The controversy presented a second distraction from the core message of the convention and raised questions about the caliber of the Trump campaign.

The convention's second night was to focus on "Make America Work Again," presenting Trump's acumen as a businessman as critical experience related to restoring and building the nation's economic future. Speakers across the evening celebrated Trump's successful business career. Donald Trump, Jr. described his father's "unrelenting determination," his respect for common sense, and for those who worked in his businesses.[31] His father's leadership style was hands on and engaged:

He didn't hide out behind some desk in an executive suite, he spent his career with regular Americans. He hung out with the guys on construction sites pouring concrete and hanging sheetrock. He listened to them and he valued their opinions as much and often more than the guys from Harvard and Wharton locked away in offices away from the real work.

Donald Trump was not an elitist, according to his son. He focused on an individual's performance and character rather than external validation gained through credentials:

> He's recognized the talent and the drive that all Americans have. He's promoted people based on their character, their street smarts and their work ethic, not simply paper or credentials. To this day, many of the top executives in our company are individuals that started out in positions that were blue collar, but he saw something in them and he pushed them to succeed.

Through his son's characterization, Donald Trump became the champion of the blue-collar worker, a person who valued people based on their performance. West Virginia Senator Shelley Moore Capito contrasted Trump's leadership with lack of understanding and respect for workers within the Obama administration: "People across the country feel the Obama administration has kicked them to the curb with a callousness that's damaged their ability to trust and respect government."[32]

Kimberlin Brown, former actress and business owner, spoke to the needs of small business owners and called for "A president who will bring common sense regulations and eliminate unnecessary ones, who will fix our tax system, who will start us on the path to rebuild our infrastructures. We need someone who knows how to build things, who knows how to create jobs, and who knows how to negotiate, who's going to tackle problems head-on, ladies and gentlemen, so we can have true progress."[33] Kerry Woolard, General Manager of Trump Winery, talked about Trump's engaged leadership and support for the people who work for him. Video presentations reinforced the in-person presentations, featuring a number of women who worked in the Trump organization.

For all the positive support for Trump's business acumen, the keynote speakers returned to direct attacks on Hillary Clinton and the threat of a Hillary Clinton presidency. Governor Chris Christie launched the most scathing attack, inviting the audience to participate as a "jury of Clinton's peers" as he presented his case against Hillary Clinton.[34] Even before Christie began the litany of "charges," the crowd began to chant, "Lock her up." He presented his summary of Clinton's actions related to Libya and then asked the audience, "guilty or not guilty?" The audience shouted, "Guilty." He produced the same refrain for Iran, Russia, Cuba, and her explanations related to her use of an unsecure personal email server. Christie's summary: "Here it is everybody. We didn't disqualify Hillary Clinton to be President of the United States, the facts of her life and career disqualify her."

When Ben Carson took the stage, he too raised the dangerous specter of a Hillary Clinton presidency, speaking very directly to Christian Evangelicals.[35] He denounced the "secular progressive agenda" and the "politically elite and the media." The effects of a Hillary Clinton administration would last for generations, he said, and "America would never recover from that." In a surprising move, Carson referenced Hillary Clinton's senior college thesis about Saul Alinsky, author of "Rules for Radicals," describing Alinksy as one of Clinton's heroes and mentors. He noted that Alinsky's book dedication acknowledged Lucifer.

> Now, think about that, this is a nation where our founding document, the Declaration of Independence talked about certain inalienable rights that come from our creator. This is a nation where our Pledge of Allegiance says we are one nation under God. This is a nation where every coin in our pocket, and every bill in our wallet says, "In God We Trust." So, are we willing to elect someone as president who has as their role model somebody who acknowledges Lucifer? Think about that.

Carson's conclusion was far from secular. He said: "The secular progressive agenda is antithetical to the principals of the founding of this nation, and if we continue to allow them to take God out of our lives, God will remove himself from us, we will not be blessed, and our nation will go down the tubes. And, we will be responsible for that. We don't want that to happen."

The convention's second day reiterated the argument for change based in the country's dire circumstances. Speakers elevated Trump's credentials as a leader while they undermined Hillary Clinton's leadership and character.

As the convention moved into its third day, the controversies of previous days continued to distract from the convention's primary message. A Trump speechwriter finally answered for the plagiarism in Melania Trump's speech and offered her resignation.[36] And, the appearance of Texas Senator Ted Cruz once again demonstrated the divisions within the Republican Party.

Trump had worked to move beyond the divisiveness of the primaries through inclusion of his primary rivals as speakers at the convention. Only Ted Cruz accepted an invitation to speak without also promising an endorsement of Trump. Cruz arrived early on Wednesday and scheduled an outdoor "thank you rally" for his supporters. Cruz said, "In an amazing campaign field of 17 talented dynamic candidates, we beat 15 of those candidates. We just didn't beat 16. Our party now has a nominee." Just as Cruz said the word "nominee," members of the crowd pointed overhead as Trump's massive jet, emblazoned with his name, flew directly over the venue.[37] Although Cruz laughed off the timing of the jet's appearance, it clearly angered his supporters.

Anticipating Cruz's appearance later in the evening, speakers called for party unity. Conservative political commentator Laura Ingraham called out those who had yet to endorse Trump: "I want to say this very plainly, we should all—even all you boys with wounded feelings and bruised egos, and we love you, we love you, but you must honor your pledge to support Donald Trump now. Tonight. Tonight."[38] The crowd cheered in support. Governor Scott Walker said, "last August right here in Cleveland, I stood on this stage and I said that any of the Republicans running for office would be better than Hillary Clinton. I meant it then, and I mean it now. So let me be clear, a vote for anyone other than Donald Trump in November is a vote for Hillary Clinton."[39] Florida Senator and Republican primary candidate Marco Rubio appeared on the screens behind the stage, offered direct comparisons between Clinton's record and Trump's agenda, and said, "After a long and spirited primary, the time for fighting each other is over. It's time to come together and fight for a new direction for America. It's time to win in November."[40]

Throughout the evening, other speakers carried forward the evening's primary goal—an inclusive Republican vision for the nation. A series of speakers representing diverse constituencies supported Trump. Attorney General Pam Bondi represented the key state of Florida and spoke directly to those most focused on "law and order." Michelle Van Etten represented small business owners and Millenial entrepreneurs. Ralph Alvarado, a Kentucky state senator, called Hispanic citizens to vote Republican. Darrell Scott, an African-American pastor, said, "Donald Trump will rebuild the broken trust that now exists between our citizens and our government which over the last eight years has brought the rhetoric of hope but the reality of higher minority unemployment, crime, drug use, with more civil unrest and national distress. This election is one of the most crucial elections in American history." Harold Hamm, CEO of Continental Resources, not only spoke of the need for American energy independence but also told his story as the son of a sharecropper. Trump and Pence, he said, would "restore the American dream for the next would-be visionary from small town America." Lydia Patton, Vice President of the Eric Trump Foundation, narrated a video celebrating the philanthropic spirit of the Trump family. When she came to the stage, Patton spoke frankly as an African-American woman:

> There's not one person in this room who can deny that, historically, black lives have mattered less. My life mattered less. And whether we like it or not, there are people out there who still believe this to be true. But tonight, as a minority myself, I personally pledge to you that Donald Trump knows that your life matters. He knows that my life matters, He knows that LGBTQ lives matter. He knows that veterans' lives matter. And he knows that blue lives matter.

Across the evening, speakers answered Trump's critics and promised that a Trump presidency would unify Republicans in support of all Americans.

Finally, Cruz took the stage and clearly had a different agenda. He congratulated Donald Trump and said, "Like each of you, I want to see the principles that our party believes prevail in November." Cruz asked the audience, "What if this right now is our last time? Our last moment to do something for our families, and our country? Did we live up to the values we say we believe? Did we do all we really could?" Just as Cruz asked the questions, the camera showed Donald Trump entering the arena. For viewers at home, depending on the media outlet, Cruz appeared to be providing a voice- over for Trump's entrance. As the camera cut back to Cruz, he said, "That's really what elections should be about. That's why you and millions like you devoted so much time and sacrifice to this campaign. We're fighting not for one particular candidate, or one campaign, but because each of us wants to be able to tell our kids and grandkids ... that we did our best for their future and our country."

Cruz articulated a conservative agenda guided by the value, "freedom." Toward the end of his speech, Cruz called for action but failed to endorse Trump's campaign. Cruz said: "If you love our country, and love our children as much as you do, stand, and speak, and vote your conscience, vote for candidates up and down the ticket who you trust to defend our freedom, and to be faithful to the constitution." Cruz's admonition to "vote your conscience" called on the Never Trump movement to support his cause. Boos and shouts erupted. Delegates began chanting, "We want Trump." Cruz acknowledged the "enthusiasm" of the New York delegation. As Cruz reached the final lines of his speech, Donald Trump entered the main hall, the camera moved away from Cruz at the podium to show Trump's reaction as Cruz said, "We will unite the party; we will unite the country by standing together for shared values by standing for liberty. " Boos drowned out Cruz and escorted him from the stage.

The producers in the hall immediately launched a video featuring Trump's three adult children. And, at the top of the 10 o'clock hour, Eric Trump came to the stage and returned to the primary populist message of the evening. He told unemployed workers, teachers, veterans, laborers, oil and gas industry workers, single mothers, families of special needs children, and middle-class families without medical benefits, "my father is running for you." He implored voters to "Vote for the candidate who can't be bought, sold, purchased, bribed, coerced, intimidated, or steered from the path that is right and just and true."[41]

When former Speaker of the House Newt Gingrich came to the podium following Eric Trump, he quickly took on the most immediate challenge of the night: "I'm also proud to be here as a Republican activist to see the extra effort Donald Trump has invested in bringing the Republican Party together. With no requirement for endorsement, he encourages competitors to speak once again. Governor Rick Perry, Governor Scott Walker, Dr. Ben Carson, Senator Marco Rubio, and Senator Ted Cruz have all responded to Donald Trump's generosity."[42] The mention of Cruz's name prompted another loud protest from the audience. Gingrich continued:

> Now I think you misunderstood one paragraph that Ted Cruz, who is a superb orator, said, and I just want to point it out to you, Ted Cruz said you can vote your conscience for anyone who will uphold the Constitution. In this election, there is only one candidate who will uphold the Constitution. [Cheers] So to paraphrase Ted Cruz, if you want to protect the Constitution of United States, the only possible candidate this fall is the Trump-Pence Republican ticket.

Gingrich then turned to his primary theme: a reprise of the challenges to the nation's safety and security. He began with a litany of recent terrorist attacks and then endorsed Trump's position: "Let's be clear, Donald Trump is right. We are at war with radical Islamists. We are losing the war. And we must change course to win the war." Gingrich outlined his analysis of the threat to the U.S., saying, "it is about our safety and survival as a country." He then articulated the Trump-Pence responses—rebuild the military, secure the borders, take care of our veterans, rebuild infrastructure and reenergize the economy, restore law and order. Gingrich called for a change of course and restated the four major themes of the convention:

> So tonight, the challenge for everyone in this hall and everyone Republican, Democrat, or independent who is watching at home, and knows we cannot continue on our current course, is to rise above our factions, and rise above the politics we have inherited, to ignore the lies of the news media and the old order, to reject the suicidal dishonesty of Hillary Clinton and her establishment allies, and to stand with Donald Trump and Mike Pence for what we know is true. We can make America safe again. We can make America work again. We can make America first again. And together, we can make America great again for all Americans.

Gingrich had brought the convention back to its primary message. The night's final speaker, Vice Presidential nominee Mike Pence, provided a balance to the ticket and represented the core of the Republican Party. He contributed a record of government service and strong conservative credentials, having served in the U.S. House of Representatives and as Governor of Indiana. Paul Ryan introduced him to the audience as a "Reagan conservative through and through. Pro-growth, pro-life, pro-strong defense."[43]

Pence used his speech to lift up his running mate to the audience and to reach out to a broad constituency of voters.[44] Pence reported his observations of Trump: "Now, I'll grant you he can be a little rough with politicians on the stage, and I'll bet we see that again. But I've seen this good man up close, his utter lack of pretense, his respect for the people who work for him and his devotion to his family." He described Trump as "the outsider who turned a long-shot campaign into a movement," "an uncalculating truth-teller," and "a doer in a game usually reserved for talkers." Pence said, "You know, the choice couldn't be more clear. Americans can elect someone who literally personifies the failed establishment in Washington, D.C. or we can choose a leader who will fight every day to make America great again. It's change versus status quo."

Pence reach out to citizens "who feel like Democrat politicians have taken them for granted." He named union members, African-Americans, Hispanic Americans and said, "During these difficult days, it will be our party and our agenda that opens the doors for every American to succeed and prosper in this land." Pence extended the theme of unity beyond the convention hall:

> There seems to be so many things that divide us and so few great purposes that unite us as they once did. And it's at moments like this, moments when politics fail, that I believe we'd do well to remember that what unites us far exceeds anything that sets us apart in America. That we are, as we have always been, one nation under God, indivisible, with liberty and justice for all.

The endorsements from representatives of diverse interests, Trump's willingness to include his rivals, and ability to "stand up" to Cruz's challenge demonstrated the potential for party unity.

African-American Pastor Mark Burns, founder of NOW television network, articulated the theme of the final day of the convention, "Make American One Again." His rousing speech accused the Democrats of "race-baiting" saying; "Those Democrats will do whatever it takes to keep us Americans focusing on the colors that divide us and not the colors that unite us." He built to a crescendo as he declared: "Under a Donald Trump administration, all lives matter! [CHEERING] All lives! [CHEERING] All lives! [CHEERING] And that means Black lives, White Lives Hispanic lives, Asian Lives, Muslim lives! All lives!" He challenged Republicans to "listen to the cries of the disenfranchised, the low income, the African-American community" and to "solve the problems together."[45] Women including Tennessee Representative Marcia Blackburn, Oklahoma Governor Mary Fallin, and Dr. Lisa Shin, representing the National Diversity Coalition for Trump, called for a Trump presidency to renew the American Dream. Peter Thiel, co-founder of PayPal and a Venture capitalist, painted a bleak picture of the nation describing the economy and the government as "broken." But significantly, he also represented the LGBTQ community. Theil took on the cultural divide between the Republicans and Democrats:

> When I was a kid, the great debate was about how to defeat the Soviet Union and we won. Now we are told that the great debate is about who gets to use which bathroom. This is a distraction from our real problems.

Who cares? Of course, every American has a unique identity. I am proud to be gay. I am proud to be a Republican. But most of all, I am proud to be an American! I don't pretend to agree with every plank in our party's platform, but fake culture wars only distract us from our economic decline. And nobody in this race is being honest about it except Donald Trump.[46]

Thiel claimed Trump's convention themes as forward-looking: "When Donald Trump asks us to make America great again; he's not suggesting a return to the past. He's running to lead us back to that bright future. Tonight, I urge all of my fellow Americans to stand up and vote for Donald Trump."

A biographical video narrated by Donald Trump, Jr. recounted Donald Trump's career as a New York real estate developer. Tom Barrack, close friend of Donald Trump and founder of the Rebuild America Now Super Pac, came to the stage with a handheld microphone and said, "But what I'm going to do is something different. And you're going to hate me for it, because you're not going to hear one negative thing out of my mouth. I have nothing negative to say about Hillary. I have only amazing things to tell you about Donald."[47] He said, "What I want to do is spend a little time talking to you about the message, the man. Without his armor, without his weaponry, walking down the tunnel into the arena. Who is he? What is he made out of?" Barrack told a series of anecdotes through which he portrayed Trump as a person who reaches his goals through "relentless and beautiful habits. He shows up on time. He believes that punctuality is the courtesy of kings. He doesn't confuse efforts with results. He befriends the bewildered. He pushes everybody around him, including you, through comfort barriers that they never thought that they could ever, ever shatter." Barrack described the campaign as an adventure, one like a Michener tale. And he said to the audience, "It's up to you, all of you tonight to unite in one pen, one hand and make once upon a time, once upon this time."

Signs throughout the hall called out constituencies—Hispanics for Trump; Women for Trump; Families for Trump—as Ivanka Trump introduced her father.[48] She called him an "outsider," a "fighter," a person who "spent his entire life doing what others said could not be done." She characterized him as a man of empathy and generosity. She said, "It is just his way of being in your corner when you're down. My father not only has the strength and ability necessary to be our next President, but also the kindness and compassion that will enable him to be the leader that this country needs." Ivanka Trump said her father was "color blind and gender neutral. He hires the best person for the job, period." Ivanka then called her father the best person for *this* job.

> This is the fighter, the doer that you have chosen as your nominee, in ways no one expected, this moment in the life of our country has defined a mission and given it to an extraordinary man. He is ready to see it all the way through, to speak to every man and every woman, of every background, in every part of this great country. To earn your trust and to earn your vote.

Finally, for the fourth and final time of the convention, Donald Trump entered the stage. His nomination acceptance lasted for more than an hour.[49] Trump described a nation in "crisis." He recounted attacks on police, increasing violent crime rates, increasing illegal immigration, high unemployment among African-American youth, Latino and African-American families in poverty, dropping household incomes, an increasing trade deficit, and a national debt at $19 trillion and growing. The infrastructure he described as "falling apart" and said, "43 million Americans are on food stamps."

His description of foreign affairs was equally stark. He said the nation was "humiliated" in the Iran nuclear deal, the Obama administration's approach to Syria, and in the destruction and deaths at the consulate in Benghazi. He said, "After 15 years of wars in the Middle East, after trillions of dollars spent and thousands of lives lost, the situation is worse than it has ever been before. This is the legacy of Hillary Clinton: death, destruction, terrorism and weakness." Over the course of the speech, he called Clinton's policies "failed," "radical and dangerous," "job-killing," "massive," "disastrous," and the "worst." Trump described Clinton as participating in a "rigged system." He said, "Big business, elite media and major donors are lining up behind the campaign of my opponent because they know she will keep our rigged system in place. They are throwing money at her because they have total control over every single thing she does. She is their puppet and they pull the strings." He previewed the message the Democrats would offer in just a few days. He said, "So if you want to hear the corporate spin, the carefully-crafted lies, and the media myths, the Democrats are holding their convention next week." Trump positioned himself as the truth-teller.

The answer to the nation's many challenges, according to Trump, was simple: "A change in leadership is required to produce a change in outcome." He challenged his audience to "break free from the petty politics of the past. America is a nation of believers, dreamers and strivers that is being led by a group of censors, critics, and cynics." Trump said his plan of action would "put America first." He promised safety in neighborhoods and a secure border and a thriving economy that would add millions of new jobs. He promised a better life for those who have been "ignored, neglected and abandoned." He took on the role of champion of the disenfranchised: "I have joined the political arena so that the powerful can no longer beat up on people who cannot defend themselves. Nobody knows the system better than me. (Laughter) which is why I alone can fix it." He promised "law and order," especially in the inner cities, to ensure that "all of our kids are treated equally and protected equally." He said he would think of "young Americans in Baltimore, in Chicago, in Detroit, in Ferguson, who have . . . the same right to live out their dreams as any other child in America, any other child." As he turned his attention to terrorism and listed recent attacks in the U.S. from the Boston Marathon to the attack on a nightclub in Orlando, FL, Trump said, "As your president, I will do everything in my power to protect our LGBTQ citizens from the violence and oppression of a hateful foreign ideology." Applause and cheers followed, and Trump added, "And I have to say, as a Republican, it is so nice to hear you cheering for what I just said. Thank you."

On foreign policy, Trump indicated that he would focus on three things: intelligence gathering, a strong alliance with Israel and a demand for NATO to engage in anti-terrorism activity, and a suspension of immigration from "any nation that has been compromised by terrorism." He said, "Anyone who endorses violence, hatred or oppression is not welcome in our country and never, ever will be!" He argued that record immigration resulted in "lower wages and higher unemployment for our citizens, especially for African American and Latino workers." He reminded the audience of the presentations on Monday of families whose children were killed by illegal immigrants. He said, "These wounded American families have been alone, but they are not alone any longer." He renewed his pledge to build a great border wall and to build a "lawful" immigration system, saying, "we are going to be considerate and compassionate to everyone, but my greatest compassion will be for our own struggling citizens."

On the economy, Trump promised a "new fair trade policy that protects our jobs and stands up to countries that cheat." He said, "I am going to bring back our jobs to Ohio and Pennsylvania and New York and Michigan and all of America. And I am not going to let companies move to other countries, firing their employees along the way without consequence. Not going to happen anymore." He promised relief from high taxes and regulation, especially restrictions on the production of energy. His policies would include school choice, repeal of "Obamacare," reform of the Transportation Safety Administration, and strategies to address student debt. He announced his commitment to rebuild the military, to care for veterans, and to eliminate wasteful spending projects. And he said, "we are going to appoint justices of the United States Supreme Court who will uphold our laws and our Constitution.... This will be one of the most important issues decided by this election." He spoke directly to the evangelical and religious community, thanked them for their support, noting, "I'm not sure I totally deserve it," and said he would work to repeal language in the tax code that limited political speech of religious organizations.

He promised all this and "so much more." At the end of his speech, Trump declared:

> I am your voice. So to every parent who dreams for their child, and every child who dreams for their future, I say these words to you tonight: I am with you, and I will fight for you, and I will win for you! (APPLAUSE) To all Americans tonight, in all our cities and towns, I make this promise: We will make America strong again! We will make America proud again! We will make America safe again! And we will make America great again!

As the celebration began, Donald Trump's family joined him on stage followed by Mike Pence and his family. Fireworks lit the video screens, confetti and balloons fell from the ceiling, and the delegates celebrated. And, the 2016 Republican Nominating Convention was over. Over the course of four days, the Republicans portrayed a nation in distress, a country drifting away from the American dream. Parents were struggling to imagine a nation in which their children's lives would be better than their own. They pointed to violence at home and danger abroad, an increasingly divided nation, with large segments of the population believing their leaders and their government had forgotten then and left them behind. The Republicans blamed the nation's challenges on the failed leadership of the Democrats and offered a change—Donald Trump.

THE DEMOCRATIC NATIONAL CONVENTION

Just as the Democrats prepared to make their case to the American people, a controversy rocked the Democratic National Committee and its convention. Despite Sanders' pledge to support Clinton, many of his supporters were not ready to concede based on their resistance to what they called a "rigged system." One group, Occupy DNC, announced its goal as "to bring all Bernie Sanders supporters together at the DNC Convention to fight for the will of the people—a Bernie Sanders's nomination, NOT a fraudulent Hillary nomination."[50] Then, just days before the convention, Wikileaks posted nearly 20,000 Democratic National Committee (DNC) emails, including email showing clear favoritism for the Clinton campaign, giving credence to complaints from the Sanders campaign throughout the primaries. As a result, DNC chairwoman Debbie Wasserman Shultz resigned on July 24 and eventually was excluded from gaveling in the convention. Donna Brazile, a long-time Democratic operative and leader in the party, stepped in as interim chairwoman and issued an apology to Bernie Sanders and his supporters. The apology attempted to set a positive tone for the convention: "We are embarking on a convention today that— thanks to the great efforts of Secretary Clinton, her team, Senator Sanders, his team, and the entire Democratic Party—will show a forward-thinking and optimistic vision for America, as compared to the dark and pessimistic vision that the GOP presented last week in Cleveland."[51]

An apology failed to mollify Sanders supporters. They took to the streets, protesting the primary system. CNN video showed Sanders supporters chanting, "Hell, no, DNC, we won't vote for Hillary."[52] Supporters inside the hall disrupted proceedings and similar to the Never Trump movement at the Republican convention tried to change convention rules in favor of their candidate. The Sanders campaign had challenged the use of superdelegates within the Democratic Party nominating process. Superdelegates, elected officials and other key party leaders, were not bound to the outcome of primary or caucus results in their states. By June, Clinton had secured the support of 547 superdelegates with Sanders only able to count on 46.[53] The pledged superdelegates clearly gave Clinton a significant base of support to achieve the nomination. After contentious meetings and protests both outside and within the Rules Committee meeting room, the Clinton and Sanders campaigns worked out a concession, forming a "unity commission" that would, in part, require approximately two-thirds of superdelegates to follow the results of their states' primary results. It made no difference in the 2016 outcome but potentially would change the Democratic Party process in subsequent elections.[54]

The initial controversy did not disrupt the convention. To the contrary, unlike the Republican convention, the Democrats ran a highly scripted and choreographed convention. Each hour featured multiple segments to articulate key messages. Each segment featured Democratic Party elected leaders from across the country and citizens who represented Clinton's past achievements and future promises. Video segments designed to communicate Clinton's experience and achievements and frame the speakers introduced most segments. Short video attacks on Trump's character and policies were interspersed throughout each night's presentation.

Clinton's overarching theme, Stronger Together, was articulated as the convention opened by the Rev. Leah Daughtry:

> When Democrats say 'we, the people,' we mean all the people. All the people regardless of race, color, creed, or ethnicity. All the people, regardless of sexual orientation or gender identity. All the people, those with plenty and those with little. The boats at the bottom and the boats coasting on the top. All the people. The least, the last, the lost, the locked in and the left behind. Because we know that our diversity is not our problem. It is our promise.[55]

Throughout the first night of the convention, the stage filled with diverse groups supporting Hillary Clinton interspersed with videos entitled, "Hillary's America" that depicted Clinton's engagement with constituencies, showing her as responsive to their needs. Boston Mayor Marty Walsh opened a segment titled, "Working Americans" and declared Hillary Clinton "the champion American workers need." The presidents of the AFL-CIO, American Federation of State, County, and Municipal Workers, National Education Association, American Teachers Federation, Service Employees International Union, and North America's Building Trades Union completed the endorsement. Clinton's support for communities struggling with addiction epidemics, individuals living with mental illness, and for Americans with disabilities were made personal through testimonials. A segment called, "Keeping Families Together," focused on immigration policy and Trump's threats to deport millions of illegal immigrants. The segment, "Ensuring Equality," featured Clinton's advocacy for the LGBTQ community. Signs throughout the hall reinforced the message, "Stronger Together."

A contrast with Trump was evident in each segment, either through a speaker's challenge or through thematic videos interspersed throughout the evening. Videos entitled "In His Own Words" extracted controversial Trump quotes on an issue. A video, "Trump Exposed," reported in a news style the controversies surrounding Trump University. A series of comedy videos called "Donald Decoded" communicated key ideas through a short humorous exchange between an expert and a comedian. These videos appeared throughout the four days of the convention.

Minnesota Senator Al Franken, who became famous first as a comedian, and Sarah Silverman, stand-up comedian, contributed to the satirical attacks on Trump on the convention's opening night.[56] In fact, Silverman played a key role in pivoting to a major goal in the evening, uniting Sanders supporters behind Clinton. Silverman began her speech identifying as a Bernie Sanders supporter and "the movement behind him." She said, "Bernie showed us that all of America's citizens deserve quality health care and education, not just the wealthy elite." She acknowledged the Clinton campaign's concessions to Sanders issues: "Hillary heard the passion of the people, the people behind Bernie, and brought those passions into the party's platform and that, that is the process of democracy at its very best and it's very cool to see." Silverman then endorsed Clinton and added, "I am proud to a part of Bernie's movement and a vital part of that movement is making absolutely sure that Hillary Clinton is our next president of the United States."

Sanders supporters shouted their displeasure. Franken and Silverman led the crowd in chants of "Hillary!" In one of the few production challenges of the convention, Franken and Silverman were instructed to delay the next introduction and in one of the few unscripted moments in the convention, Silverman said, "Can I just say to the Bernie or bust people, you're being ridiculous." Finally, Franken and Silverman introduced Paul Simon to sing, "Bridge Over Troubled Water," a fitting (or ironic) selection to end the convention's opening.

New Jersey Senator Corey Booker opened the next segment of the evening.[57] He told an American story leading to a more fair and inclusive nation, saying,

> Our founding documents weren't genius because they were perfect. They were saddled with the imperfections and even the bigotry of the past. Native Americans were referred to as savages. Black Americans were fractions of human beings. And women were not mentioned at all. But those facts and

ugly parts of our history don't distract from our nation's greatness. In fact, I believe we are an even greater nation, not because we started perfect, but because every generation has successfully labored to make us a more perfect union.

He contrasted his aspirations for the country with Donald Trump's leadership. He said,

This is the reason why I am so motivated in this election, because I believe this election is a referendum on who best embodies the leadership we need to go far together. Donald Trump is not that leader. We've watched him try to get laughs at other people's expense, try to incite fear at a time we need to inspire courage, try to rise in the polls by dragging our national conversation into the gutter.

Booker reminded the audience of Trump's negative statements and mocking behavior of people with disabilities, immigrants, prisoners-of-war, women, and Muslims. He described Trump as "getting rich" while he "stiffed" those in business with him. He lauded Clinton's record in contrast and called for Democrats and all Americans to unite and "rise together": "Here in Philadelphia, let us declare again that we will be a free people. Free from fear and intimidation. Let us declare, again, that we are a nation of interdependence, and that in America, love always trumps hate."

The final prime time hour featured speeches from First Lady Michelle Obama, Massachusetts Senator Elizabeth Warren, and Democratic Candidate Bernie Sanders. Michelle Obama's speech opened with a very personal account of the responsibility to her own children and to the children of America: "With every word we utter, with every action we take, we know our kids are watching us."[58] And every election, she said, was about "who will have the power to shape our children for the next four or eight years of their lives." Michelle Obama offered a resounding endorsement of Clinton as a champion of children and families, as a devoted public servant, as a person of "grace and guts," as someone with strength and perseverance, and a leader "who will be guided every day by the love and hope and impossibly big dreams that we all have for our children."

Elizabeth Warren followed Michelle Obama and told her life story as emblematic of the American Dream: "The way I see it, I'm a janitor's daughter who became a public school teacher, a professor, and a United

States Senator. America is truly a country of opportunity. Truly."[59]
Warren said the opportunity she and others experienced was slipping away:

> I'm worried that my story is locked in the past, worried that opportunity is
> slipping away for people who work hard and play by the rules. I mean, look
> around, Americans bust their tails, some working two or three jobs, but
> wages stay flat. Meanwhile, the basic costs of making it from month to
> month keep going up, housing, healthcare, childcare, the costs are out of
> sight. Young people are getting crushed by student loans. Working people
> are in debt. Seniors can't stretch a Social Security check to cover the basics.
> And even families who are OK today, worry it could all fall apart tomorrow.
> This is not right. It is not.

Warren's explanation for the stalled American Dream was a "rigged system," one that favors corporations, Wall Street, and the wealthy and does
nothing for working Americans. Donald Trump was among the wealthy
individuals who benefitted from the system: "His whole life has been
about taking advantage of that rigged system. Time after time, he preyed
on working people, people in debt, people who had fallen on hard times.
He's conned them, he's defrauded them and he's ripped them off." She
described Trump's America as intentionally divisive: "An America of fear
and hate, and America where we all break apart. Whites against Blacks and
Latinos. Christians against Muslims and Jews. Straight against gay.
Everyone against immigrants. Race, religion, heritage, gender. The more
factions the better." Hillary Clinton and the Democrats, Warren promised, would challenge the rigged system through increased minimum
wage, fair scheduling, family and medical leave, debt free college,
expanded Medicare and Social Security, environmental policy to fight
climate change, equal pay for equal work and protecting a woman's
right to choose, trade deals that protect workers, and stronger rules for
Wall Street.

Finally, a video tribute ushered Bernie Sanders to the podium. Sanders
thanked his supporters, the voters, and the delegates for creating a political
revolution to transform America. He said, "Election days come and go,
but the struggle of the people to create a government which represents all
of us and not just the 1 percent, a government based on the principles of
economic, social, racial and environmental justice, that struggle continues!"[60] Sanders listed the many issues of his campaign—living wage
and employment, education and debt free college, health care, civil rights,

overturning Citizens United, environment and climate change—and reported a coming together of the Clinton and Sanders positions in the party platform as by far the "most progressive platform in the history of the Democratic Party." Finally, he said, "Hillary Clinton will make an outstanding president and I am proud to stand with her tonight!"

The endorsements of Elizabeth Warren and Bernie Sanders called the most progressive Democrats to join Hillary's cause and unify the party. Michelle Obama aligned Hillary Clinton's life work and service to children and families with generational promise of America, that each generation will have opportunity greater than the one before. And all speakers shared a communal and inclusive message to make America "Stronger Together."

The second might of the Democratic National Convention opened with the nominating speeches for the two candidates followed by the roll call of states. As Hillary Clinton reached the needed delegate count to secure the nomination, Bernie Sanders stepped to a microphone, moved to suspend the rules, and then moved to accept Hillary Clinton's nomination by acclamation. The chair described the motion as "in the spirit of unity." A voice vote supported the motion and a celebration broke out as the Democrats made history, nominating the first woman as a major party presidential candidate. At the same time, Sanders supporters, some with tape over their mouths, walked out of the convention in protest. Others gathered outside the arena to march in opposition to Clinton's nomination while others staged a symbolic sit-in.[61]

Despite the discord, the convention moved forward with speakers, video presentations, and performances to generate energy in the hall, to demonstrate broad support for Hillary Clinton, and to catalogue Clinton's career in support of children, women, and families. Endorsements included Nancy Pelosi, minority leader of the House of Representatives, accompanied by the Democratic women of the House of Representatives; former President Jimmy Carter; New York Senator Charles Schumer; and Donna Brazile, the interim chairwoman of the Democratic National Committee.

Actress Elizabeth Banks served as a guide for the evening's event, providing continuity as she introduced key ideas and speakers. Banks articulated the overarching theme of the evening when she said, "when Hillary Clinton sees a problem, she fights to fix it." Clinton's record of fighting for children, social justice and justice system reform, women's rights, healthcare reform, national security, and her efforts following the

September 11 attack on New York were presented in video, by notable speakers, and by individuals directly affected by Clinton's efforts. Speakers included former Attorney General Eric Holder; Cecile Richards, President of the Planned Parenthood Federation of America; California Senator Barbara Boxer; former Vermont Governor Howard Dean; and former Secretary of State Madeline Albright, among others. Moving testimonials of Clinton's impact came from individuals she had touched, including a mother of an adopted special needs child, a survivor of the 9/11 attacks, and a human trafficking survivor. One of the most moving segments came from members of Mothers of the Movement, an organization of women who lost children to gun violence or to excessive use of force by law enforcement. Their presence embodied the impact of gun violence in America. The women came to give their children a voice, to call for reconciliation and change, and to lend their support to Hillary Clinton's campaign.

The keynote speaker on the second night was former President Bill Clinton in an unusual role for him—as the spouse of the presidential nominee. Bill Clinton's speech conformed to the expectations for a spouse's speech. He told the audience about when he and Hillary first met and about his yearslong quest to convince her to marry him. As he told Hillary's story, he recounted the work described over the course of the evening. He summed up Hillary's approach this way: "She just went out and figured out what needed to be done and what made the most sense and what would help the most people. And then if it was controversial she'd just try to persuade people it was the right thing to do."[62] Bill Clinton addressed Hillary's greatest asset and perhaps her greatest liability as a candidate in 2016. In a year when the American public wanted change, Hillary Clinton was the ultimate insider with decades of political and government service. Bill described Hillary as "a natural leader, she's a good organizer, and she's the best darn change-maker I ever met in my entire life." He continued:

So people say, well, we need to change. She's been around a long time, she sure has, and she's sure been worth every single year she's put into making people's lives better. I can tell you this. If you were sitting where I'm sitting and you heard what I have heard at every dinner conversation, every lunch conversation, on every long walk, you would say this woman has never been satisfied with the status quo in anything. She always wants to move the ball forward. That is just who she is.

Bill Clinton also countered the Republican's characterization of Hillary, what he called a "cartoon alternative" to the "real" Hillary Clinton: "The real one has earned the loyalty, the respect and the fervent support of people who have worked with her in every stage of her life, including leaders around the world who know her to be able, straightforward and completely trustworthy." He said, "Hillary will make us stronger together. You know it because she's spent a lifetime doing it."

The cumulative impact of the evening was a clear depiction of Hillary Clinton's record of service over the course of her career and across a range of issues. The video segments depicted her in direct interaction with constituents: listening, comforting, and advising. Testimony from people she served personalized her policies. Bill Clinton told Hillary's personal and professional story as a lifelong commitment to changing the lives of people for the better. In contrast to the Republican convention, a growing list of Democratic leaders filled the stage in support of their party and their candidate.

The third day of the convention reinforced Clinton's campaign issues with a theme, "Our America." Elected leaders from the Congressional Black Caucus, the Asian Pacific American Caucus and the Women of the Senate, New York Mayor Bill DeBlasio, former New York Mayor Michael Bloomberg, and other elected Democratic leaders spoke on Clinton's behalf. The issues of civil rights, support for and from veterans, and the environment were featured through video and speakers, including Reverend Jesse Jackson. The impact of gun violence was represented through family members of the Sandy Hook Elementary School shooting, survivors of the Mother Emanuel AME Church shooting, gun violence survivor former Arizona Representative Gabby Giffords, and the mother of a victim of the Orlando Night Club shooting that had occurred only a month earlier.

A special segment focused on the president's role as commander-in-chief and Hillary Clinton's record related to veterans, the military, and foreign affairs. A video depicting Republican leaders and others denouncing Trump's fittingness to serve as commander-in-chief reinforced the message of former Secretary of Defense Leon Panetta: "Hillary Clinton is the only candidate who has laid out a comprehensive plan to defeat and to destroy ISIS and keep America safe. She is smart, she is principled, she is tough and she is ready. Hillary Clinton is the single-most experienced and prepared person who has ever run for president of the United States."[63]

Three keynote speakers shared the stage on Wednesday night: Vice President Joe Biden, Vice Presidential nominee Tim Kaine, and President Barack Obama. Symbolically, the Obama administration was "passing the baton" to Hillary Clinton. Throughout the evening, they highlighted Hillary's experience and character, her preparation and fittingness to serve, as they challenged Trump on the same criteria.

The first to speak was Vice President Joe Biden. Biden described, "the Americans he knows," people who when facing hardship "get up, every morning, everyday. They put one foot in front of the other. They keep going. That's the unbreakable spirit of the people of America. That's who we are."[64] He declared that Clinton was the only candidate who understood and would "be there" for American citizens:

> If you worry about your job and getting a decent pay, if you worry about your children's education, if you're taking care of an elderly parent. Then there's only one, only one person in this election who will help you. There's only one person in this race who will be there, who has always been there for you, and that's Hillary Clinton's life story. It's not just who she is, it's her life story. She's always there. She's always been there, and so has Tim Kaine.

In contrast, Biden characterized Trump as a man of "boundless cynicism," without empathy or compassion who exploits fear, who seeks to sow division in America for his own gain, and disorder around the world." He said, "We've had candidates before who attempted to get elected by appealing to our fears, but they never succeeded, because we do not scare easily." Biden declared Americans ready to move forward in the journey of America with Hillary Clinton writing "the next chapter in that journey."

Vice Presidential nominee Tim Kaine carried Biden's theme forward, stating a basic political philosophy developed across his experiences. He said we must "advance opportunity for everybody, no matter where you come from, how much money you have, what you look like, how you worship or who you love."[65] Kaine unified the Democratic Party and its leadership through what he called a simple belief. "Do all the good you can and serve one another. That is what I'm about. That is what you are about. That is what Bernie Sanders is about. That is what Joe and Jill Biden are about. That is what Barack and Michelle Obama are about. And that is what Hillary Clinton is about." Then, first in Spanish and then in

English, he led the delegates in chanting, "Yes We Can," the campaign mantra of President Barack Obama.

Kaine reiterated Clinton's contributions articulated over the course of the convention and then launched a mocking attack on Trump, using one of Donald Trump's frequently repeated phrases, "believe me."

> Trump is a guy who promises a lot but, you may have noticed, he has got a way of saying the same two words every time he makes his biggest, hugest promises. "Believe me." It's going to be great, believe me. We are going to build a wall and make Mexico pay for, believe me. We are going to destroy ISIS so fast, believe me. There is nothing suspicious about my tax returns, believe me.

Kaine continued the litany of Trump's broken promises to contractors, homeowners, charities, and students at Trump University. He said, "It just seems like our nation, it is just too great to put in the hands of a slick-talking, empty-promising, self-promoting one-man wrecking crew." The alternative, a Clinton-Kaine administration, would write the next chapter in a "great and proud story."

> Thomas disclaimed all men were equal and Abigail remembered the women. Woodrow brokered the peace and Eleanor broke down the barriers. Jack told us what to ask and Lyndon answered the call. Martin had a dream and Cesar y Dolores said si se puede. And Harvey gave his life. Bill, Bill built a bridge into the 21st Century and Barack gave us hope. And now Hillary is ready! She is ready to fight! She is ready to win! And she is ready to lead!

The Clinton-Kaine ticket was official with Kaine's speech. Kaine's speech also demonstrated his ability to attack the Trump-Pence ticket in the general election.

Finally, President Barack Obama came to the stage to begin the transition of leadership of the Democratic Party to Hillary Clinton. Obama created a longer vision of the American story, one that started well before his election in 2008 and would continue well beyond the present election. He reflected on his first time speaking to the Democratic National Convention 12 years earlier. While nervous, Obama said he was filled with faith, "faith in America, the generous, bighearted, hopeful country that made my story, that made all of our stories possible."[66] He expressed his optimism based on the achievements of the previous eight years:

overcoming a recession, declaring health care an American right, increasing clean energy production and reducing dependence on foreign oil, bringing troops home from foreign engagements, delivering justice to Osama Bin Laden, shutting down Iran's nuclear weapons program, opening diplomatic relations with Cuba, partnering with 200 nations to protect the environment, protecting consumers from fraud, helping students with loans, and establishing marriage equality.

Obama framed the current dissatisfaction expressed in public opinion within the ongoing work of his administration: "through every victory and every setback, I've insisted that change is never easy, and never quick; that we wouldn't meet all of our challenges in one term, or one presidency, or even in one lifetime. So tonight, I'm here to tell you that yes, we've still got more work to do." Obama challenged Democrats and the American people to stay the course.

He recognized needs within the nation:

> Sure, we have real anxieties about paying the bills and protecting our kids, caring for a sick parent. We get frustrated with political gridlock and worry about racial divisions. We are shocked and saddened by the madness of Orlando or Nice. There are pockets of America that never recovered from factory closures, men who took pride in hard work and providing for their families who now feel forgotten, parents who wonder whether their kids will have the same opportunities we had.

Yet, the response to those problems presented by the Republicans was a "deeply pessimistic vision of a country where we turn against each other and turn away from the rest of the world. There were no serious solutions to pressing problems, just the fanning of resentment and blame and anger and hate. And that is not the America I know." Obama called on Americans to harness their "courage and optimism and ingenuity," and to unite as people of "every party, every background, every faith who believe that we are stronger together, black, white, Latino, Asian, Native American, young, old, gay, straight, men, women, folks with disabilities, all pledging allegiance, under the same proud flag, to this big, bold country that we love." He said only one candidate could bring the future imagined to fruition—Hillary Clinton.

Obama praised Clinton's resilience, intelligence, judgment, discipline, work ethic, experience, and her heart for those who need help. Obama said with confidence that "there has never been a man or a woman, not me, not Bill, nobody more qualified than Hillary Clinton to serve as president of the United States of America." Obama contrasted Hillary Clinton's record to Trump's, saying, "the Donald is not really a plans guy. He's really not a facts guy, either." Obama said Trump offered slogans and fear, "betting that if he scares enough people, he might score just enough votes to win this election." He challenged Trump's record and positions, saying, "America is already great. America is already strong. And I promise you, our strength, our greatness does not depend on Donald Trump." America's greatness, Obama said, rests not on one person but with "what can be achieved by us, together, through the hard and slow and sometimes frustrating, but ultimately enduring work of self-government."

Obama ended his speech with a symbolic transition of leadership and a call to action:

> And now I'm ready to pass the baton and do my part as a private citizen. So this year, in this election, I'm asking you to join me, to reject cynicism and reject fear and to summon what is best in us; to elect Hillary Clinton as the next president of the United States and show the world we still believe in the promise of this great nation. Thank you for this incredible journey. Let's keep it going.

On its final night, the Democratic National Convention focused on the "Stronger Together" theme, encapsulating the arguments from across the convention into an orchestrated summation of the case for electing Hillary Clinton. Their work began through a video presentation devoted to the memory of former New York Governor Mario Cuomo who had died the previous year. The video presented excerpts from many of Cuomo's speeches, including Cuomo's 1984 address to the Democratic Convention in which he described America as two cities, one the shining city on the hill and the other where individuals and families struggle to participate in the nation's opportunity. The video addressed many of the issues before the convention as Cuomo articulated long-standing principles of the liberal tradition in the U.S.

New York Governor Andrew Cuomo, Mario Cuomo's son, then took up his father's message in the 2016 context framing the contrast between the Democrats and the Republicans as the difference between a Democratic vision of promise and prosperity and a backward looking, pessimistic Republican narrative of fear and division. He said, "Republicans say they want to make America great again. They say they want to take us back to the old days, the good old days. I want to know, what good old days do they want to take us back to? Do they want to take us back before the Civil Rights Act? Do they want to take us back before minimum wage and worker protection laws? Or do they want to take us back before Roe v. Wade?"[67] Cuomo said that the Democrats were "going forward" to make America greater than ever before. Cuomo focused on unity, community, and common cause, saying, "She [Hillary Clinton] will unify, not divide. And she will move us forward together as one. That's why we must make Hillary Clinton the next president of these United States of America."

A series of elected officials and citizens, representing an inclusive vision of the Democratic Party, endorsed Clinton. Two speakers represented Republicans for Clinton. Others identified as civil rights activists, as immigrants and children of undocumented immigrants, as veterans, as leaders committed to women's rights, advocates for LGBTQ and transgender rights, as "working Americans," and as environmental activists. Rev. William Barber, a self-proclaimed "theologically conservative liberal evangelical Biblicist," called Christians to support the Democratic cause. Tennessee State Representative Raumesh Akbari summed up the Hillary for America message: "Now, listen, whether you're a Republican, a Democrat, an Independent, whether you are black, white, Latino, or Asian, whether you are gay, straight, or transgendered, whether you run a—whether you run a ranch, a farm, a church, or a beauty shop down in Memphis, Tennessee . . . Secretary Clinton is a fighter for us all."[68]

The fourth day of the convention devoted additional time to the economic challenges Americans faced. Colorado Governor John Hickenlooper and Pennsylvania Governor Tom Wolf told their stories as business owners and contrasted their experiences to Donald Trump's. Hickenlooper said, "I know the true mark of a successful businessman is not the number times you say, "You're fired." It's the number of times you say, "You're hired.""[69] Wolf reminded the audience of Trump's six bankruptcy filings in which Trump "used the process to protect himself and even enriched himself while his employees were left out of luck."[70] Ohio Representative Tim Ryan spoke of the importance of respecting workers, saying, "We are on the side of the worker because we respect the men and women who punch a clock, the ones who shower after they get home from the job. We respect the fighters who go to work early, stay late, and pour their hearts into what they do."[71] Donald Trump, he argued, would not respect workers: "He's been stabbing workers in the back for years. Trump got rich ripping people off, stiffing small businesses and contractors. And now he says he's going to bring our jobs back. Hey, Ohio, we ain't buying it!" Former Michigan Governor Jennifer Granholm voiced the concerns of the American people, saying, "Some people are worried. Some people are angry. I get that. But the answer is not to tear our country down, it's to build our country up, not to build walls that keep out the rest of the world, but to keep building the industries and universities that the rest of the world wishes they could get into."[72] Once again, individuals experiencing economic distress came to the podium to tell their stories and express faith in Hillary Clinton to address their needs.

The next hour focused on "Protecting America" and produced one of the most dramatic moments of the Democratic convention. Basketball star and American cultural ambassador Kareem Abdul-Jabbar shared the story of Captain Humayun Khan, 1 of 14 American-Muslim soldiers who had died in combat since 9–11 and then spoke against Trump's immigration polices directed at Muslims. A "Hillary's America" video featured Hillary Clinton telling Khan's story of bravery and his death in combat, reaffirming the values that led him to serve his country. Following the video, Captain Khan's parents came to the stage, as proud parents and "patriotic American-Muslims." Khizr Khan looked directly into the camera and said, "If—if it was up to Donald Trump, he [Humayun] never would have been in America. Donald Trump consistently smears the character of Muslims. He disrespects other minorities, women, judges, even his own party leadership. He vows to build walls and ban us from this country. Donald Trump, you are asking Americans to trust you with their future. Let me ask you, have you even read the United States Constitution?" Khan pulled a copy of the Constitution from his pocket. "I will—I will gladly lend you my copy. In this document, look for the words … Look for the words "Liberty and equal protection of law."[73]

For the next several minutes, veterans and retired military leaders expressed their support for Hillary Clinton. Medal of Honor winner Florent Groberg and Representative Ted Lieu identified as immigrants and veterans. General John Allen (Ret.) led a contingent of former generals and veterans to the stage accompanied by a military drum cadence. He endorsed Hillary Clinton: "My fellow Americans, I tell you without hesitation or reservation that Hillary Clinton will be exactly—exactly—the kind of commander in chief America needs."[74] Later in the evening, the Democrats included the law enforcement community within the "protecting America" theme. Dallas Sheriff Lupe Valdez honored fallen police officers and introduced three family members of police officers killed in the line of duty. Their message was one of community: "Let us honor all of the fallen officers who weren't named here today, by acting as our officers did, helping others, bridging communities, and building peace."[75] California Representative Xavier Becerra reaffirmed Clinton's support for Mexican immigrants and the children of undocumented workers. Others spoke to the importance of access to education for America's young people. Each speaker elaborated the "Stronger Together" theme.

The momentum of the evening built as the delegates waited for their nominee. The lead in to the culminating hour of the convention was singer Katie Perry's performance of Clinton's campaign anthem, "Fight Song." Then, the announcer introduced Chelsea Clinton.[76] Chelsea, perhaps even more than Bill Clinton, shared a very personal side of Hillary Clinton—as a devoted, caring parent and as a public servant. She described all the special care Hillary Clinton took in parenting—talking about school at dinner, attending school events, being certain she stayed connected with Chelsea whenever she had to be away. While Chelsea did not mention her mother's professional responsibilities explicitly, the audience knew these small and yet significant expressions of care occurred while Hillary Clinton worked as an attorney and served as First Lady. Chelsea shared observations of her mother taking the same care with others:

> I've had a special window into how she serves. I've seen her holding the hands of mothers, worried about how they'll feed their kids, worried about how they'll get them the healthcare they need. I've seen my mother promising to do everything she could to help. I've seen her right after those conversations getting straight to work, figuring out what she could do, who she could call, how fast she could get results. She always feels, like there isn't a moment to lose, because she knows that for that mother, for that family there isn't.

Chelsea drew special attention to her mother's resilience following defeat: "People ask me, all the time, how does she do it? How does she keep going, amid the sound and the fury of politics? Here's how, it's because she never, ever forgets who she's fighting for." Chelsea called her mother "a listener and a doer . . . a woman driven by compassion, by faith, by a fierce sense of justice and a heart full of love." Chelsea introduced the biographical video of Hillary Clinton narrated by Morgan Freeman. Statements from friends, family, and citizens were interspersed with the narration of Hillary Clinton's life story. Hillary Clinton shared key lessons from her life—admonitions to be brave and to do her best. Her actions on behalf of her New York constituents following the attack on 9/11 labeled her a "champion" and a "fighter." One of her constituents even called Clinton a "work horse," a compliment acknowledging her ability to get things done. Toward the end, the narration described the American Dream being passed from generation to generation. Hillary Clinton voiced her commitment to share the American Dream with all Americans and her desire to unify the American people. As the video faded away, Chelsea Clinton returned and introduced "my mother, my hero, and our next President, Hillary Clinton."

After Hillary Clinton took some time to savor the moment, she began her speech acknowledging the legacy of leadership, the mantle she was accepting from Bill Clinton, the "explainer in chief" and the man from Hope; President Barack Obama, "the man of hope"; Vice President Joe Biden, who "spoke from his big heart about our party's commitment to working people as only he can do"; Michelle Obama who "reminded us that our children are watching." She acknowledged her running mate, Tim Kaine, and then offered a special acknowledgement to Bernie Sanders. She pledged to Sanders supporters "your cause is our cause."[77]

Clinton's speech carried forward the themes articulated by Biden, Kaine, and Barack Obama on the previous night. She turned to the symbolism of a Philadelphia meeting, comparing the present election with the revolutionary moment in 1776. She said, "America is once again at a moment of reckoning. Powerful forces are threatening to pull us apart. Bonds of trust and respect are fraying. And just as with our Founders, there are no guarantees. It truly is up to us. We have to decide whether we will all work together so we can all rise together." Donald Trump, she said, "wants to divide us from the rest of the world and from each other. He's betting that the perils of today's world will blind us to its unlimited promise. He's taken the Republican Party a long way from morning in America to midnight in America." "Morning in America" referred to Ronald Reagan's optimistic campaign message in 1984, a touchstone for Republicans since that time. In effect, Clinton accused Trump of undermining, and perhaps even destroying, the vision of an iconic hero of the Republican Party.

Clinton acknowledged the unease among the American people: "We are clear-eyed about what our country is up against.... We know there is a lot to do. Too many people haven't had a pay raise since the crash.

There's too much inequality, too little social mobility, too much paralysis in Washington. Too many threats at home and abroad." While she noted significant progress during the Obama administration, she also said, "none of us can be satisfied with the status quo, not by a long shot." She acknowledged many Americans were "frustrated, even furious." The economy, she said, was not "yet working the way it should. Americans are willing to work and work hard, but right now an awful lot of people feel there is less and less respect for the work they do and less respect for them, period. Democrats, we are the party of working people. But we haven't done a good enough job showing we get what you're going through, and we're going to do something to help. So tonight I want to tell you how we will empower Americans to live better lives." The answer, she said, was to work together, again contrasting a focus on shared responsibility with Trump's philosophy expressed as "I alone can fix it."

She outlined the policy positions and actions she would take as president and contrasted those with Trump's record, with special emphasis on his questionable business practices, his tendency to "lose his cool at the slightest provocation," his statements elevating his knowledge of terrorism beyond that of military leaders. She reminded voters of his "mean and divisive rhetoric," "Like when he called women pigs, or said that an American judge couldn't be fair because of his Mexican heritage, or when he mocks and mimics a reporter with a disability or insults prisoners of war, like John McCain, a hero and a patriot who deserves our respect. Now, at first, at first, I admit, I couldn't believe he meant it either. It was just too hard to fathom that someone who wants to lead our nation could say those things, could be like that. But here's the sad truth: There is no other Donald Trump, this is it."

Clinton called voters to "stand up to bullies" and to "keep working to make things better, even when the odds are long and the opposition is fierce." In the end, she called Americans to continue a hard journey together:

> And though we may not live to see the glory, as the song from the musical "Hamilton" goes, let us gladly join the fight, let our legacy be about planting seeds in a garden you never get to see. That's why we're here, not just in this hall, but on this earth. The Founders showed us that and so have many others since. They were drawn together by love of country and the selfless passion to build something better for all who follow. That is the story of America. And we begin a new chapter tonight.

And, as at the Republican convention, with the end of Clinton's speech, digital fireworks lit up the screen, balloons dropped, and the delegates celebrated. And the general election was underway.

Conclusions

Public perceptions of the two conventions markedly favored the Democrats. Gallup conducted polls to assess reaction in the days immediately following each convention. When asked about the impact of the convention on their image of the party, only 35% viewed the Republican Party more favorably as a result of the convention. More importantly, of those who identified as Republican/Republican Leaning, 13% said they were less likely to vote for Trump as a result of the convention. The Democrats achieved a 44% "more favorable" rating, with 81% of Democrat/Democrat Leaning respondents indicating they were more likely to vote for Clinton as a result of the convention.[78]

Media analysts described the Republican Convention as "a bit more chaotic than usual" and "compelling as a train wreck," making the obvious comparisons to reality television.[79] The marked absence of Republican Party leadership weakened any sense of party unification. The strikingly harsh attacks on Clinton from the podium, encouraging delegates to shout "lock her up" or "liar," contributed to criticism of the Republican convention as dark and angry and reinforced negative perceptions of Trump created throughout the primary season. While Melania Trump and Trump's four adult children countered the negative perceptions of Donald Trump, his own speech invited similar negative audience responses and may have contributed to his speech receiving the most unfavorable rating ever recorded by Gallup, recording the lowest rating ever in the "excellent/good" category and the highest by a significant margin in "poor/terrible."[80] The Republicans also suffered from distractions due to their own mismanagement. The controversy surrounding Melania Trump's speech was embarrassing to the candidate, painful for his spouse, and demonstrated a lack of organizational control within the campaign. Ted Cruz's divisive speech shocked political analysts. Tucker Carlson of Fox News asked, "That does not happen at conventions... How does that happen?"[81] Trump's improvisational, unconventional convention was indicative of his primary campaign and the general election to come.

The Democrats effectively managed and enhanced the communication potential of a nominating convention through strategic and well-orchestrated presentations of Democratic leadership from across the nation representing multiple key Democratic constituencies, testimonials from citizens who embodied issues and concerns central to the campaign message, video presentations both elevating Clinton's image and attacking Trump, and high-profile and highly effective keynote speakers in the critical primetime hours. The key messages of the campaign were evident on each night of the convention. Performances by headliner entertainers, including some produced specifically for the convention, increased interest and attention, both within the hall and for a television audience. The videos attacking Trump were especially effective because many simply presented Trump speaking, in effect inviting audience members to make an independent determination. Video presentation avoided backlash against any individual speaker. The videos also had a life beyond the convention because the short, interesting productions met the demands of Clinton's social media platform. While any number of speakers attacked Trump's experience and character, the videos provided a consistent and sometimes humorous attack on Trump's character and fittingness to serve as president.

The conventions' messages revealed a strikingly similar analysis of national concerns. Both the Democrats and the Republicans spoke directly to the dissatisfaction, frustration, and anxiety of the American people. Financial stress, anxiety about the future for their children, fear for the safety of their families, a feeling of being "left behind" or forgotten, and recognition that the country was increasingly divided all combined to undermine faith in public institutions and the American Dream.

The answer in both cases was a candidate who was not a talker but a "fighter," a doer, a change-maker. Both candidates were described as pragmatic problem solvers who would "have the back" of those who were forgotten or left behind. Both parties promised a leader who recognized and valued the "common person." Both campaigns promised to restore the American Dream, to focus on building a country that would benefit all Americans, especially those who felt the government no longer worked to support their well-being. Both candidates said creating a better world for future generations was a primary motivation of their campaigns.

Of course, the parties offered opposing explanations and responses to the nation's challenges. Republicans blamed ineffectual and destructive policies of the Obama Administration for the nation's sluggish economic, what they perceived as a weak position on the world stage, for crime and violence within the U.S., and for the divisions within the American electorate. Trump summarized the argument simply, "The problems we face now, poverty and violence at home, war and destruction abroad, will last only as long as we continue relying on the same politicians who created them in the first place. A change in leadership is required to produce a change in outcomes." The attacks on Clinton's leadership and character were relentless through the convention. The Republicans called for a "return" to strength, putting American interests before global interests, increasing control of the nation's borders and immigration, protecting American business for unfair trade practices, and supporting American businesses that created jobs in the U.S. The Republicans promised to restore "law and order" both at home and abroad. Trump promised to rebuild the infrastructure, restore the education system, reform the tax code, and repeal Obamacare. He promised to "Make America Great Again," to get the nation back on a track to prosperity and security.

The Democrats, on the other hand, said Clinton would build upon the successes of the Obama administration, leading the country to greater justice, equality, and prosperity through a focus on education, health care, jobs, a path to citizenship for immigrants, and protection of equal rights for all. And while the Democrats claimed to provide positive and optimistic leadership, even President Obama described the work as "hard and slow and sometimes frustrating." Obama reminded voters that he had told us "we wouldn't meet all of our challenges in one term, or one presidency, or even in one lifetime." Obama called for patience and perseverance from a public with immediate frustrations with their current situation. Thus, the Democrats focused on progress through the Obama years and Hillary Clinton's record of "getting things done," fighting the status quo, and serving as a "change-maker."

The Democrats also used the opportunity to respond to the Republican convention effectively. They decried the Republicans as angry and cynical, willing to pit people against one another to achieve their goals, saying Donald Trump had led the party to "midnight in America." They contrasted Donald Trump's statement, "I alone can fix it," to the Democrats vision of the inclusive work of citizenship and democracy. They said Trump's campaign was made up of empty promises, with only his assurances of "believe me" rather than actual plans on which to base his campaign.

Unfortunately, the 2016 nominating conventions reaffirmed a deep concern among the American people, distrust in government. Both conventions reflected the public's perception of the "rigged political system," a broken political process that favored the political elite and power brokers of Washington. On the Democratic side, evidence of the Democratic National Committee's favoritism to Clinton's campaign validated complaints from Sanders. Although he agreed to support Clinton's candidacy in a spirit of unity, primarily in opposition to Trump, the convention represented Clinton's position as the ultimate insider and the heir apparent, an image reinforced when the sitting president explicitly "passed the baton" to her. It raised questions as to the party's commitment to represent "all the people." On the Republican side, Trump, the outsider, overcame all barriers in the primary process to reach the nomination. The refusal of the Republican leadership to participate in his convention reinforced his position as an independent outsider who would challenge a failed system in Washington. Trump's nomination reflected a broader sentiment among the American public. One delegate said it well: "We are really on the road to the new Republican Party. It's cleaning out the establishment, who felt that they are superior to the people. . . . It's allowing people to speak, it's allowing people to vote, it's allowing people to get their true ideas out, because so far most of the elected people have not been paying attention to what we're talking about."[82] Neither campaign fully overcame the anti-elite, anti-Washington sentiment expressed clearly through the nominating conventions nor achieved unity within the party. In the end, neither candidate received a significant convention "bump" in the polls. While Hillary Clinton outperformed Donald Trump in the weeks immediately following the convention, her success at the convention was only in comparison to Trump's less favorable performance. In the end, the candidates entered the general election only slightly better off than when the conventions began.

NOTES

1. Judith S. Trent, Robert V. Friedenberg, and Robert E. Denton, Jr. *Political Campaign Communication: Principles & Practices.* 8th Ed. (Lanham, MD: Roman and Littlefield, 2016), pp. 34–45.
2. Mary E. Stuckey describes political nomination convention discourse as constitutive rhetoric that constitutes American national identity. See Mary E. Stuckey, "One Nation (Pretty Darn) Divisible: National Identity in the 2004 Conventions," *Rhetoric and Public Affairs*, 8, no. 4 (2005). Craig Allen Smith also argues for the constitutive properties of convention rhetoric. See Craig Allen Smith, "Constituting Contrasting Communities: The

2008 Nomination Acceptance Addresses," in *The 2008 Presidential Campaign: A Communication Perspective*, ed. Robert E. Denton, Jr. (Lanham, MD: Rowman & Littlefield, 2009), pp. 48–67.

3. Walter R. Fisher, "Reaffirmation and Subversion of the American Dream," *Quarterly Journal of Speech* 59 (1973): 160.

4. See Robert C. Rowland and John M. Jones, "Recasting the American Dream and American Politics: Barack Obama's Keynote Address to the 2004 Democratic National Convention," *Quarterly Journal of Speech* 93 (2007): 425–448.

5. See "Remarks by Senator Barack Obama (D-IL), Democratic Party Nominee for President, at the 2008 Democratic National Convention," *Federal News Service*, August 28, 2008. Retrieved from Lexis/Nexis Academic database. Obama's articulation of the American promise began in 2004 as analyzed by Rowland and Jones and continued as a central theme in his 2008 address.

6. See Rachel L. Holloway, "The 2012 Presidential—Nominating Conventions and the American Dream: Narrative Unity and Political Division," in *The 2012 Presidential Campaign: A Communication Perspective*, ed. Robert E. Denton, Jr. (Lanham, MD: Rowman & Littlefield, 2014): 1–22.

7. Art Swift, "Americans' Satisfaction With U.S. Drops Sharply." *Gallup*, July 21, 2016. http://www.gallup.com/poll/193832/americans-satisfaction-drops-sharply.aspx.

8. Swift, "Americans' Satisfaction."

9. Matthew Katz, Joyce Lee, and Justin Weiss, "Everything You Need to Know About a Contested Convention," *Time*, May 2, 2016. Accessed at http://time.com/4314188/contested-convention-republican-primary-brokered-results-donald-trump-ted-cruz/; Gregory Kreig, "7 Things You Need to Know About a Contested Convention," *CNN*, March 16, 2016. Access at http://www.cnn.com/2016/03/16/politics/contested-convention-how-it-works-questions.

10. Matt Flegenheimer, "Ted Cruz Suspends His Campaign for President," *The New York Times*. May 3, 2016. Retrieved from Lexis Nexis Academic database.

11. Will Doran, 'Donald Trump Set the Record for the most GOP primary votes ever. But that's not his only record," *Politifact North Carolina*, July 8, 2016. Accessed January 1, 2017 at http://www.politifact.com/north-carolina/statements/2016/jul/08/donald-trump/donald-trump-set-record-most-gop-primary-votes-eve/.

12. Factcheck.org created a comprehensive analysis of the use of the term, "rigged," in the 2016 presidential primaries. See Robert Farley, "Trump's 'Rigged' Claim," *The Wire*, FactCheck.Org. July 12, 2016. Accessed at https://www.factcheck.org/2016/07/trumps-rigged-claim/.

13. Patrick Healy and Jonathan Martin, "Clinton Claims Democratic Nomination," *The New York Times*, June 8, 2016, A1. Retrieved from Lexis/Nexis Academic database; Abby Phillip, Anne Gearan and John Wagner, "Clinton Reaches Magic Number for Historic Nomination," *Washington Post*, June 7, 2016, A1. Retrieved from Lexis/Nexis Academic database.

14. Frank Newport and Andrew Dugan, "One in Four Americans Dislike Both Presidential Candidates." *Gallup*. July 12, 2016. http://www.gallup.com/opinion/polling-matters/187652/one-four-americans-dislikepresidential-candidates.aspx.

15. Justin McCarthy, "Americans' Reactions to Trump, Clinton Explain Poor Images," *Gallup*, July 1, 2016. http://www.gallup.com/poll/193418/americans-reactions-trump-clinton-explain-poorimages.aspx.

16. Fox News Poll. *Fox News*, June 29, 2016. Accessed at http://www.foxnews.com/politics/interactive/2016/06/29/fox-news-poll-june-2-2016/.

17. Description and analysis of the Republican National Convention and the Democratic National Convention, when not otherwise noted, is based on the author's review of digital recordings of the convention proceedings from C-SPAN's live coverage.

18. Julia Jacobo and Veronica Stracqualursi, "Republican National Convention 2016: Schedule, Themes and Headline Speakers," *ABC News*, July 18, 2016. Accessed at http://abcnews.go.com/Politics/republican-national-convention-2016-schedule-themesheadline-speakers/story?id=40388577.

19. Alex Isenstadt, "Hardly anybody wants to speak at Trump's convention." *Politico*, June 27, 2016. Accessed at http://www.politico.com/story/2016/06/hardly-anybody-wants-to-speak-at-trumps-convention-224815.

20. Alec Tyson, "Trump Faces Challenge in Getting a United GOP Behind Him," *Pew Research Center*, July 8, 2016. Accessed at http://www.pewresearch.org/fact-tank/2016/07/08/trump-faces-challenge-in-getting-a-united-gop-behind-him/.

21. Philip Rucker and Robert Costa, "Trump Picks Pence after Last-Minute Hesitation," *Washington Post*, July 16, 2016. Retrieved from Lexis/Nexis Academic database.

22. Ed O'Keefe, "As 'Never Trump' Forces Make a Last Stand, Compelling Scenarios Emerge," *Washington Post*, July 14, 2016. Retrieved from Lexis/Nexis Academic database.

23. Kyle Cheney, "Chaos erupts on GOP Convention Floor after Voice Vote Shuts down Never Trump Forces," *Politico*, July 18, 2016. Accessed at http://www.politico.com/story/2016/07/never-trump-delegates-have-support-needed-to-force-rules-vote-225716.

24. The quotation from Pat Smith is from transcription completed by the author.

25. The quotations attributed to Sheriff David Clarke are from transcriptions completed by the author.
26. The quotations attributed to Darryl Glenn are from transcriptions completed by the author.
27. "Rudy Giuliani, Former New York City Mayor, Delivers Remarks at the 2016 Republican National Convention," *CQ Transcriptions*, July 18, 2016. Retrieved from Lexis/Nexis Academic Database. All subsequent references to Rudy Giuliani's speech are attributed to this source.
28. "Donald Trump Republican Presidential Candidate, Delivers Remarks at the 2016 Republican National Convention," *CQ Transcriptions*, July 18, 2016. Retrieved from Lexis/Nexis Academic database.
29. "Melania Trump Delivers Remarks at the 2016 Republican National Convention," *CQ Transcriptions*, July 18, 2016. Retrieved from Lexis/Nexis Academic database. All subsequent references to Melania Trump's speech are attributed to this source.
30. Christina Wilkie, "Melania Trump Plagiarized Her Convention Speech From Michelle Obama," *The Huffington Post*, July 19, 2016. Accessed at http://www.huffingtonpost.com/entry/melania-trump-speech-plagiarized_us_578da752e4b0a0ae97c33675.
31. "Donald Trump, Jr., Son of Donald Trump and EVP, The Trump Organization, Delivers Remarks at the 2016 Republican National Convention," *Federal News Service*, July 19, 2016. Retrieved from Lexis/Nexis Academic database. All subsequent references to Donald Trump, Jr.'s speech are attributed to this source.
32. "Sen. Shelley Moore Capito, R-W.VA., Delivers Remarks at the 2016 Republican National Convention," *CQ Transcriptions*, July 19, 2016. Retrieved from Lexis/Nexis Academic database.
33. The quotations attributed to Kimberlin Brown are from transcriptions completed by the author.
34. "Gov. Chris Christie, R-NJ., Delivers Remarks at the 2016 Republican National Convention," *Federal News Service*, July 19, 2016. Retrieved from Lexis/Nexis Academic database. All subsequent references to Chris Christie's speech are attributed to this source.
35. "Ben Carson, Neurosurgeon, Delivers Remarks at the 2016 Republican National Convention," *CQ Transcriptions*, July 19, 2016. Retrieved from Lexis/Nexis Academic database. All references to Dr. Ben Carson's speech are attributed to this source.
36. Maeve Reston, "Trump Campaign tries to Move on from Plagiarism Controversy," *CNN*, July 20, 2016. Accessed at http://www.cnn.com/2016/07/20/politics/donald-trump-campaign-organization/.

37. Katherine Faulders, Josh Haskell, and Ryan Struyk, "Ted Cruz's Cleveland Rally Interrupted by Donald Trump's Plane," *ABC News*, July 20, 2016. Accessed at http://abcnews.go.com/Politics/ted-cruzs-cleveland-rally-interrupted-donald-trumps-plane/story?id=40741922.
38. "Laura Ingraham, Radio Host, delivers remarks at the 2016 Republican National Convention," *Federal News Service*, July 20, 2016. Retrieved from Lexis/Nexis Academic database.
39. "Gov. Scott Walker, R-Wis., delivers remarks at the 2016 Republican National Convention," *Federal News Service*, July 20, 2016. Retrieved from Lexis/Nexis Academic database.
40. "Sen. Marco Rubio, R-Fla., delivers remarks at the 2016 Republican National Convention," *Federal News Service*, July 20, 2016. Retrieved from Lexis/Nexis Academic database.
41. "Eric Trump, Executive Vice President of The Trump Organization, delivers Remarks at the 2016 Republican National Convention," *Federal News Service*, July 20, 2016. Retrieved from Lexis/Nexis Academic database.
42. "Newt & Callista Gingrich, Former Speaker of the House and his wife, deliver remarks at the 2016 Republican National Convention," *Federal News Service*, July 20, 2016. Retrieved from Lexis/Nexis Academic database.
43. Quotations attributed to Speaker of the House Paul Ryan are from the author's transcription.
44. "Gov. Mike Pence, R-Ind., delivers remarks at the 2016 Republican National Convention," *Federal News Service*, July 20, 2016. Retrieved from Lexis/Nexis Academic database.
45. Quotations from Rev. Mark Burns speech are from the author's transcription.
46. Peter Thiel, Venture Capitalist, delivers remarks at the 2016 Republican National Convention," *Federal News Service*, July 21, 2016. Retrieved from Lexis/Nexis Academic database.
47. "Tom Barrack, CEO of Colony Capital, delivers remarks at the 2016 Republican National Convention," *Federal News Service*, July 21, 2016. Retrieved from Lexis/Nexis Academic database.
48. "Ivanka Trump, Daughter of Donald Trump and EVP at the Trump Organization, delivers remarks at the 2016 Republican National Convention," *Federal News Service*, July 21, 2016. Retrieved from Lexis/Nexis Academic database. All references to Ivanka Trump's speech are attributed to this source.
49. "Donald Trump, Republican Presidential Candidate, delivers remarks at the 2016 Republican National Convention," *Federal News Service*, July 21,

2016. Retrieved from Lexis/Nexis Academic database. All references to Donald Trump's speech are attributed to this source.

50. At least one group launched a webpage to coordinate its effort. See "Occupy Convention at: https://occupydncconvention.com/about/.

51. Noland D. McCaskill, "DNC apologizes to Sanders for 'Inexcusable Remarks' in Email Leak," *Politico*, July 25, 2016. Accessed at http://www.politico.com/story/2016/07/dnc-apologizes-to-sanders-for-inexcusable-remarks-in-email-leak-226149.

52. Lou Dobbs, Ed Rollins, Michael Goodwin, Dennis Kucinich, Charles Hurt, Monica Crowley, KT McFarland, Fred Barnes, Trish Regan, and Boris Epshteyn, "Democratic National Convention Opens in Discord; Clinton Campaign Manager Accuses Russians of Hacking DNC; Democrats Divided; Elizabeth Warren, Michelle Obama & Bernie Sanders to Speak Later; Trump Holding Campaign Rally in North Carolina," Lou Dobbs Tonight, *CNN*, July 25, 2016. Retrieved from Lexis/Nexis Academic database.

53. John Wagner, Philip Rucker, and Robert Costa, "Doing Great Too Late," *Washington Post*, June 6, 2016. A1. Retrieved from Lexis/Nexis Academic database.

54. David Weigel, "Democrats vote to bind most superdelegates to state primary results, " *Washington Post*, July 23, 2016. Accessed at https://www.washingtonpost.com/news/post-politics/wp/2016/07/23/democrats-vote-to-bind-most-superdelegates-to-state-primary-results/?utm_term=.49570b1b5212.

55. "Rev. Leah Daughtry Delivers Remarks at the 2016 Democratic National Convention," *CQ Transcriptions*, July 25, 2016. Retrieved from Lexis/Nexis Academic database.

56. Gloria Borger, David Axelrod, Anderson Cooper, Michael Smerconish, Jeffrey Lord, Van Jones, Wolf Blitzer, Jake Tapper, and Nia—Malika Henderson, "Live Coverage of Democratic National Convention; Sarah Silverman & Al Franken Introducing Paul Simon; Silverman: Bernie or Bust People are Being Ridiculous; Bill Clinton Attending Convention; Widow Who Spent Thousands on Trump University Speaks. Aired 9-10p ET," CNN Live Event/Special, *CNN*, July 25, 2016. Retrieved from Lexis/Nexis Academic database.

57. "Sen. Cory Booker, D-N.J., Delivers Remarks at the 2016 Democratic National Convention," *CQ Transcriptions*, July 25, 2016. Retrieved from Lexis/Nexis Academic database. All subsequent references to Cory Booker's speech are attributed to this source.

58. "Michelle Obama Delivers Remarks at the 2016 Democratic National Convention," *Federal News Service*, July 25, 2016. Retrieved from Lexis/Nexis Academic database. All subsequent references to Cory Booker's speech are attributed to this source.

59. "Sen. Elizabeth Warren, D-Mass., Delivers Remarks at the 2016 Democratic National Convention," *Federal News Service*, July 25, 2016. Retrieved from Lexis/Nexis Academic database.

60. "Bernie Sanders Delivers Remarks at the 2016 Democratic National Convention," *Federal News Service*, July 25, 2016. Retrieved from Lexis/Nexis Academic database.

61. Matt Flegenheimer and Colin Moynihan, "Angry Bernie Sanders Supporters Protest Hillary Clinton's Nomination," *New York Times*, July 27, 2016. Accessed at http://www.nytimes.com/2016/07/27/us/politics/bernie-sanders-protests.html?_r=0.

62. "Bill Clinton delivers remarks at the 2016 Democratic National Convention." *Federal News Service*, July 26, 2016. Retrieved from Lexis/Nexis Academic database.

63. "Former Secretary of Defense Leon Panetta delivers remarks at the 2016 Democratic National Convention," *Federal News Service*, July 27, 2016. Retrieved from Lexis/Nexis Academic database. All subsequent references to this speech are attributed to this source.

64. "Vice President Joe Biden delivers remarks at the 2016 Democratic National Convention." *Federal News Service*, July 27, 2016. Retrieved from Lexis/Nexis Academic database. All subsequent references to this speech are attributed to this source. All subsequent references to Joe Biden's speech are attributed to this source.

65. "Democratic Nominee for Vice President Tim Kaine delivers remarks at the 2016 Democratic National Convention," *Federal News Service*, July 27, 2016. Retrieved from Lexis/Nexis Academic database. All subsequent references to this speech are attributed to this source. All subsequent references to Tim Kaine's speech are attributed to this source.

66. "President Barack Obama delivers remarks at the 2016 Democratic National Convention," *Federal News Service*, July 27, 2016. Retrieved from Lexis/Nexis Academic database. All subsequent references to President Obama's speech are attributed to this source.

67. "Gov. Andrew Cuomo, D-N.Y., Delivers Remarks at the 2016 Democratic National Convention," *Federal News Service*, July 28, 2016. Retrieved from Lexis/Nexis Academic database.

68. "Tennessee State Representative Raumesh Akbari Delivers Remarks at the 2016 Democratic National Convention" *Federal News Service*, July 28, 2016. Retrieved from Lexis/Nexis Academic database.

69. "Gov. John Hickenlooper, D-Colo., Delivers Remarks at the 2016 Democratic National Convention," *Federal News Service*, July 28, 2016. Retrieved from Lexis/Nexis Academic database.

70. "Gov. Tom Wolf, D-Penn., delivers remarks at the 2016 Democratic National Convention," *Federal News Service*, July 28, 2016. Retrieved from Lexis/Nexis Academic database.
71. "Rep. Tim Ryan, D-Ohio, delivers remarks at the 2016 Democratic National Convention," Federal News Service, July 28, 2016. Retrieved from Lexis/Nexis Academic database.
72. "Former Michigan Governor Jennifer Granholm delivers remarks at the 2016 Democratic National Convention" *Federal News Service*, July 28, 2016. Retrieved from Lexis/Nexis Academic database. All subsequent references to this speech are attributed to this source.
73. "Khizr Khan delivers remarks at the 2016 Democratic National Convention," *Federal News Service*, July 28, 2016. Retrieved from Lexis/Nexis Academic database. All subsequent references to this speech are attributed to this source.
74. "John Allen delivers remarks at the 2016 Democratic National Convention." *Federal News Service*, July 28, 2016. Retrieved from LexisNexis Academic database.
75. "Jennifer Loudon, Wayne Walker, and Barbara Owens deliver remarks at the 2016 Democratic National Convention," *Federal News Service*, July 28, 2016. Retrieved from Lexis/Nexis Academic database.
76. "Chelsea Clinton delivers remarks at the 2016 Democratic National Convention." *Federal News Service*, July 28, 2016. Retrieved from LexisNexis Academic database. All subsequent references to Chelsea Clinton's speech are attributed to this source.
77. "Hillary Clinton delivers remarks at the 2016 Democratic National Convention," *Federal News Service*, July 28, 2016. Retrieved from LexisNexis Academic database. All subsequent references to Hillary Clinton's speech are attributed to this source.
78. Jeffrey M. Jones, "Americans More Positive about Democratic Than GOP Convention." *Gallup*. Accessed at http://www.gallup.com/poll/194084/americans-positive-democratic-gop-convention.aspx.
79. Eric Deggans, "Republican National Convention Parallels Reality Television." *NPR All Things Considered*, July 21, 2016. Retrieved from Lexis Nexis Academic database.
80. Jeffrey M. Jones, "Americans More Positive."
81. "Tucker Carlson: Why Wasn't Cruz's RNC Speech Vetted? *Fox News*, July 20, 2016. Accessed at http://video.foxnews.com/v/5044278235001/?#sp=show-clips.
82. Linda Feldmann, "It's Now Donald Trump's Republican Party," *Christian Science Monitor*, July 22, 2016. Retrieved from Retrieved from Lexis Nexis Academic database.

Rachel L. Holloway serves as vice provost for Undergraduate Academic Affairs at Virginia Tech while maintaining her faculty status in Virginia Tech's Department of Communication. A graduate of Purdue University, Holloway's research interests include political rhetoric and rhetorical approaches to public relations and issue management. Her scholarly work appears in *Rhetorical and Critical Approaches to Public Relations II* (2009, *Studies in Communication Science*, and *Political Communication*. She has coedited two books, *The Clinton Presidency: Images, Issues, and Communication Strategies* (1996) and *Images, Scandal, and Communication Strategies of the Clinton Presidency* (2003), both with Robert E. Denton, Jr.

CHAPTER 3

The Presidential Debates 2016

Ben Voth

THE RHETORICAL SIGNIFICANCE OF PRESIDENTIAL CAMPAIGN DEBATES

Since at least 1960, when Kennedy and Nixon debated in the first televised debate, millions of prospective voters have tuned in to gain a relatively unmediated sense of the political options for the presidency.[1] By comparison, televised presidential debates currently tend to dwarf the political conventions that take place in August and September and exert considerable political persuasion.[2] In 2016, 20–25 million people viewed the Democratic and Republican conventions.[3] This is not the case for the televised presidential debates.[4] In 2016, for the three Presidential debates held in October, the average viewing audience was 73 million (see Fig. 3.1). The first Presidential debate between Hillary Clinton and Donald Trump on September 26 at Hofstra University set a record with 81 million viewers—surpassing the record from the Carter/Reagan debate of 1980.

The debates can make a significant difference for the two contestants. Since 1960, Gallup polling indicates noticeable persuasive effects. Only in

B. Voth (✉)
Southern Methodist University, Dallas, TX, USA
e-mail: bvoth@mail.smu.edu

© The Author(s) 2017
R.E. Denton, Jr. (ed.), *The 2016 US Presidential Campaign*,
Political Campaigning and Communication,
DOI 10.1007/978-3-319-52599-0_3

Table 1

2016 Presidential and VP Debate statistics	Debate 1	Debate 2 VP	Debate 3	Debate 4		Totals
	Hempstead Hofstra University	Farmville, Virginia Longwood	St Louis Washington University	Las Vegas UNLV		
Viewing audience	81 million	37 million	67 million	71 million	*	avg. 73M *
Date	September 26	October 4	October 9	October 19		
Moderator	**Lester Holt**	**Elaine Quijano**	**Anderson/ Raddatz**	**Chris Wallace**		
News network	NBC	CBS	CNN/ABC	FOX		
			910			
			1196			
Percent speaking time	10.83%	10.21%	17.20%	19.04%		14.32%
Estimated time	11m 30s	11m 30s	16m	15m		54m
Words/minute	162.43	162.09	131.625	197.20		163.34
Total words	1868	1864	2106	2958		8796
Democrat	**Clinton**	**Kaine**	**Clinton**	**Clinton**		
Total words	6581	7992	6091	6554	*	6408.67
Percentage	38.15%	46.00%	40.18%	42.18%		41.63%
Time speaking	41m 50s	44m 46s	39m 5s	41m 46s		2h 47m 27s
Words/minute	159	178.53	155.86	156.98		162.59
Moderator interruptions	7	12	12	25		56
Trump interruptions	39	42	13	44		138
CNN ORC poll	62	42	57	52	*	57
Republican	**Trump**	**Pence**	**Trump**	**Trump**		
Total words	8875	8393	6964	6025	*	7288.00
Percent speaking time	51.45%	43.00%	45.93%	38.8%		44.79%
Time speaking	45m 3s	42m 6s	40m 10s	35m 41s		2h 43m 0s
Words/minute	200	199.36	173.41	168.96		185.43
Moderator interruptions	41	11	26	39		117
Clinton interruptions	6	72	1	3		82
CNN ORC POLL	27	48	34	39	*	33.33
Total words	17,249	18,249	15,161	15,537		66,196
					*	* average of presidential debates— excluding VP debate

Fig. 3.1 Statistics for the four General Presidential and Vice Presidential debates of 2016

the 1984 election did the October debates fail to register a change in the polling of the two major candidates (Reagan and Mondale). Poll changes since 1960 range from 12 points for President Bush in 2000 to one point for President Bush Sr. in 1988.[5] Empirical communication studies suggest about 7% of voters change from undecided to a candidate preference on the basis of debates.[6]

Analysts felt and polls indicated that Hillary Clinton won all three debates—winning debate number one most convincingly and Trump coming the closest in the final debate. Exit polls found a rather different story. *Washington Post* analysts Chris Cizilla included this fact in a discussion of surprises in exit interview polling from election-day:

> 13. People didn't think Trump lost the debates as badly as I did
> I named Clinton the winner in each of three presidential debates—and I didn't think any of the three were particularly close. Lots of people who voted Tuesday did not agree with me. Among the 64 percent who said the debates were an "important" part of their vote for president, Clinton won by a narrow 50 percent to 47 percent margin over Trump. Of the 82 percent of people who said the debates were a "factor" in their decision for president, Trump took 50 percent to 47 percent for Clinton. [emphasis added][7]

The Presidential Debates in 2016 were a major factor for 82% of voters and even an important factor for at least 64% of voters. Presidential debates constitute a significant communication opportunity for presidential candidates. Very few communication outlets offer a comparable audience. As a matter of comparison, the *Saturday Night Live* skit about the debates on any following Saturday night will likely attract about 3 million viewers. *Saturday Night Live* drew one of its largest numbers of viewers ever in October 2008 when Sarah Palin joined Tina Fey on the show. The Palin SNL attracted 17 million viewers, which is exponentially larger than the average viewership of the NBC comedy show.[8] Most of the news shows hosted by debate moderators attract between 2 and 8 million viewers.

THE PRINCIPLES OF DEBATE

Presidential debates pose a special analytical problem for academics. Presidential debates are a political communication vehicle offered as an ideal pedagogical tool for voters. It is important to reflect on the well-established academic ideals of debates. The discrepancies between the ideals of debate and the practice of political debate are important in understanding how political communication actually works. Debates represent an ideal form of communication wherein typically two sides have an equal opportunity to present their viewpoints and a reasonably fair adjudication of those views by a relatively impartial party. The four essential ingredients of a debate according to most studies of the topic are:

1. A topic of controversy—typically known as the resolution.
2. Two sides to oppose one another on the topic—typically known as affirmative and negative sides
3. Equal time to speak assigned to both sides.
4. A judge to review and render a decision as to which side won the performed debate.

These four ingredients create a communication context of inherent fairness so that competing ideas on a matter can be reasonably compared. The ideals of debates for purposes of the presidential election are mediated by the respective parties of DNC and RNC and the media organizations who host the events. Incumbent candidates and challengers are not required by law or statute to participate in these debates. In fact, in 1964, 1968, and 1972 there were no presidential debates. In many states, governors do not participate in debates. In fact, incumbents face a peculiar strategic communication burden in that attending a debate with a new challenger will inherently elevate that challenger both in the public imagination and in the polls themselves. Though many were stunned at the loss of President Obama in debate number one during the election of 2012, he followed in a tradition of incumbents stumbling in the first debate. President Bush in 2004 and President Reagan in 1984 both ostensibly lost their first debates while recovering to win re-election. Incumbents face serious risks in agreeing to debate. The 2016 season of debates was energized by the absence of an incumbent. Both debaters needed to convey a challenger role while Hillary Clinton did attempt to carry the mantle of incumbent President Obama.

Presidential Primary Debates 2015–2016

Primary debates do not typically attract the large audiences of general Presidential debates that usually take place one month prior to the election. Primary debates take place more than one year in advance, and the prospects for an audience are therefore much reduced. They can feature more than two candidates. The 2016 election was a blockbuster year for primary debates—especially on the Republican side—and the media was eager to have as many debates as candidates might willingly entertain. For Republicans, the candidates were so numerous that they were originally divided into two slates of candidates who debated at different times—with the leading candidates performing their debates in the prime time viewing schedule while the "undercard" debate was offered earlier in the evening. Democrats began with five candidates but almost immediately were reduced to two candidates: Bernie Sanders versus Hillary Clinton. The winnowing of the Republican field was much slower and, arguably, hindered by the peculiar dynamics of public preference for outsiders such as Ben Carson and Donald Trump. The conventional leaders of the political packs—Scott Walker and Jeb Bush—were never able to establish themselves through the debate process as true frontrunners. The debates played a pivotal role in winnowing the candidates of both the Democratic and Republican primaries.

On October 24, 2015 early in the primary process, the poll leaders as noted by *Real Clear Politics* were: Ben Carson at 28%, Donald Trump at 24%, Marco Rubio at 9.3%, Ted Cruz at 8.7% and Jeb Bush at 5.7% (*Polls: Iowa*, 2016). By November 5, Cruz and Rubio were tied at 12%. Carson and Trump were at 26% and 22%, respectively. Jeb Bush was fifth with 7%. The polling suggests that the debate performances of Rubio and Cruz did improve their polling positions and provided slightly more support for Cruz. In the long march of polling data, it does appear that this debate of October 28 was an important rhetorical launching point for the Cruz campaign that would ultimately lead to his challenge to the dominance of Donald Trump in 2016 and Cruz defeating Trump in the Iowa primary (*Polls: Iowa*, 2016). Cruz was a decisive polling candidate from October 28 until January 5, 2016 when he became the polling leader for Republicans.

The RNC primary debates were also distinctive beyond the large number of candidates. Viewership for these debates was often twice as large as debates held by the DNC. In fact, some commentators complained that DNC debates were scheduled against popular sporting events to discourage viewership.[9] The first two Republican primary debates held by *CNN* and *Fox News* garnered more than 20 million viewers—which is a staggering number for television viewing, especially for primary debating. Even with smaller networks hosting, such as

CNBC, the viewership of the debates broke 14 million.[10] The November 14 debate two weeks after the Colorado debate gained 8.5 million viewers for the Democrats. It was not unusual for Democratic party debates to have roughly half the viewers as Republican primary debates and it contained a signal about national enthusiasm for the arguments of each party. Regardless of party, the primary debates represented real money-making opportunities for networks and financially valuable political advertising for candidates. In many respects, the debates carried out by the Republicans factored into Donald Trump's no personal cash approach to winning the Republican primary, and it drove the paradoxical outcome whereby the cash-laden frontrunner of Jeb Bush was run out of the Republican primary process early. Without the debates, it is unlikely that Jeb Bush would have lost so early and so decisively.

The newest twist was the sharp antagonism between Megyn Kelly and Donald Trump in the first RNC primary debate. Fox stood from its inception as the standard bearer of conservative and Republican politics for television news. The brutal exchanges from the Fox debate were an exigence toward the Colorado debate and created a ripe condition for confrontation with the more traditionally left-leaning CNBC moderator crew. The Harvard Study of news coverage in this election cycle provided this summary:

> Even if metanarratives are not as self-fulfilling as Kovach and Rosenstiel suggest, there is no question that journalists create and apply them as a shorthand way to describe presidential candidates. In 2008, for example, journalists early on embraced the idea that Barack Obama represented hope and change and could deliver it through his charismatic leadership and communication skill. It was a narrative that carried all the way to the November election.
>
> Whether the metanarratives that emerged during the 2016 invisible primary will persist is a yet unanswered question but the outlines of these early narratives was unmistakable. Trump was the shoot-from-the-lip bully, given to braggadocio and insulting and outrageous comments. Yet, he also had a finger on the anger felt by many middle—and lower-class white voters. As regards Clinton, she was the candidate best prepared for the presidency as a result of her experience and detailed knowledge of policy issues. But this positive metanarrative competed with more frequently employed negative ones—that she was difficult to like, overly calculating, and hard to trust. As for Sanders, the storyline was that he means what he says—that he speaks, not from what the polls say is expedient, but from what he believes.[11]

Journalistic Antagonism toward Republicans and Conservatives

The media plays a powerful role in shaping the potential of a presidential candidate. Theodore H. White wrote in *The Making of the President, 1972*, "The power of the press is a primordial one. It determines what people will think and talk about—an authority that in other nations is reserved for tyrants, priests, parties, and mandarins."[12] The media's role has been met with considerable public frustration. Public antipathy toward journalists and a concurrent lack of trust for journalism has grown for over a decade. The public sense of this painful reality is, arguably, a driving factor in present frustration evident in polling regarding institutions. Put simply, public trust of major cultural institutions is at an all time low.[13] When Gallup first began asking about public trust for the television press in 1993, 19% of the public had very high trust in the television press and 16% had very little trust. Today in June of 2016, 8% of the public has very high trust and 38% have very little trust for the television press.[14] Television press are among the least trusted institutions measured in the United States by Gallup and includes institutions such as the military and the church. Gallup measures continued to find plummeting confidence during the election of 2016. A study in September 2016 found that while the long-standing trend of reduced trust continued—among Republicans— it plummeted in one year from 32% to 14%.[15] The drop stands out from a "trend" and constitutes a collapse. It is difficult to overstate the public hostility to journalists and the smaller community of television journalism.

The public believes that the media is profoundly biased, and they believe that journalists dramatically distort the information they receive. Those trends have accelerated to unprecedented levels of public anger. The problem of media bias is well documented and detailed in the excellent work by communication professor Dr. Jim Kuypers, detailing a similar systemic corruption of the journalistic process that is supposed to interrogate the politically powerful in order to prevent abuses of the weak and vulnerable.[16] Kuypers traces a similar trend rooted in the 1960s where journalistic assessment of the Vietnam War embodied in the CBS news anchor Walter Cronkite took an ideological turn. Cronkite's misrepresentations of American military success in Vietnam were decisive in rallying anti-war activist toward further engagement in the cause. These interpretations were vital to the Jacobin insurgencies against the Democrat party convention in 1968 Chicago.

Such trends amplified by journalism schools on college campuses have accentuated the ideological delivery of news in the twenty-first century. Party affiliation of journalists remains decisively one-sided—favoring the democrats by more than 3 to1 in almost all newsrooms.[17] A mutual fantasy theme[18] between the political party of favor (Democrats) and journalists is that this political collaboration is morally justified as part of a broader agenda of protecting the weak from the ravages of inequality. Donald Trump who has a long tradition of supporting the Democratic party—including Hillary Clinton—was helped tremendously in his campaign to be the RNC nominee, against more conservative Republican candidates.[19] These Jacobin-styled arguments seek to displace individual liberty in favor of state managed equality, convinced journalists to approach their craft with a clearer unrepentant ideology that interrogates one party defending established interests (Republicans) and the opposing party (Democrats) as being an inherent insurgency against those established interests. The public is overwhelmingly convinced that this bias is real and destructive to their trust of the original social contract in the First Amendment. For Republicans, an ethical rubicon was crossed and all trust in the media was lost during 2016.

A powerful example of how far off from a free press we have gone can be found in a Republican primary debate of 1996. Not unlike 2016, Republicans had a number of candidates seeking the nomination to run against incumbent president Bill Clinton. Among them was a surprising upstart by the name of Alan Keyes. Keyes is an African-American and in 1996 his oratorical skills were greatly admired and he finished strongly in the Iowa and New Hampshire Presidential Republican caucuses. That set up a televised candidate debate in 1996 at an Atlanta TV station. Keyes was invited to attend by the Atlanta Press Club. About a week before the event, the station had second thoughts about hosting Keyes, but Keyes remain adamant that he had an invitation and other candidates said the original plan should be honored. That set the stage for a rather incredible incident. On the night of the debate, Keyes arrived along with dozens of supporters for the televised debate. As Keyes approached the venue, the station called Atlanta police to the site. In front of television news crews recording the event, Alan Keyes was handcuffed and pushed into the backseat of a police car. He was driven to the edge of Atlanta and released on the top of a parking garage while the television debate went on without him. At no time was Alan Keyes charged with a crime. He was simply handcuffed by officers and forcibly removed from the property of the station and driven away. It sounds like something from a distant authoritarian government. The next day, the democratic major of Atlanta, Bill Campbell, apologized for Keyes mistreatment, saying "this is not usually how we treat our guests in the city." That was the end of the conflict. No lawsuits were filed. No other apologies were made. One of the nation's first serious African-American presidential candidates was handcuffed in Atlanta and kidnapped from a televised public debate. Imagine for a moment if in 2008, Presidential candidate Barack Obama had shown up for a democratic primary debate and instead of entering the studio, was met by police officers, forcibly detained, and driven off-site until the debate was over. America's epistemological communities would have rallied Jacobin forces to powerful results—immediately. Epistemological voices would have thundered against the outrageous racial slur inherent in such actions. It is impossible to reconcile the events that happened to Keyes—and still viewable today on YouTube[20]—without understanding that the journalistic community believes that the concept of racism is an ideograph. Michael Calvin McGee pioneered this important rhetorical notion suggesting that certain terms exert powerful political influence in society despite their compartmentalized wording and symbolism.[21] Alan Keyes could not be a victim of racism because racism is an ideograph that serves only Jacobin ideological interests. It demonstrates rather forcefully that journalism exists as service for these ideological interests and not for the political interests of individual liberty as embodied in Alan Keyes' free political speech rights and political arguments.

Journalism today continues to serve limited political interests. Fox news is derided as "partisan" by our elite while almost all other news outlets are relatively unchallenged as nonpartisan. Fox was not allowed to moderate any of the 2012 Presidential debates. Fox contributor Chris Wallace did moderate the final debate of 2016. The problems between the Republicans and the media extend back to the rivalry that took down President Nixon in the early 1970s. The salience of this argument shows little signs of abating or declining.

The Harvard *Shorenstein* study completed the most comprehensive and probing examination of media coverage for election 2016. Not surprisingly, the study found that Trump got much more negative press coverage than Clinton. More interesting was the sharp uptick in negative coverage as the campaign entered the final phase between August 8 and the election on November 8. The study found that interval dominated by 77% negative coverage and only 23% positive coverage in relation to Trump. In the general campaign, Trump's coverage was almost neutral at 56/44 in the positive/negative ratio.[22] The 21% uptick in negative coverage suggests that the media helped Trump arrive at the nomination during the primary process—defeating more than a dozen Republican rivals and then dramatically increasing negative coverage after the nomination in order to help Hillary in the final push toward the election. In fact, Clinton got 13% more positive coverage in the closing general election phase than Trump. Yet in the overall election coverage Trump had 6% more favorable coverage than Clinton. This is a rather dramatic reversal in coverage between the primary and the election. The negative coverage of Trump in the fall hit a crescendo in the week of October 16 when 96% of the coverage was negative.[23] Of ten different news outlets analyzed, Fox had the most positive tone of coverage for Trump—though more than 70% was negative.

By contrast, Clinton press coverage in the Presidential debate period was relatively positive. In the week of October 2, Clinton's total coverage actually went net positive—which rarely happens in elections. She was close to that same positive mark three weeks later on October 23. Press coverage in the closing month of the election was incredibly positive for the Clinton campaign.[24] The *Los Angeles Times* was her most favorable outlet, while *Fox News* was her least favorable outlet.

Debate press coverage was a key ingredient in this overall problem. Coverage was overwhelmingly positive for Clinton with regard to the debates and overwhelmingly negative for Trump. Sixty-five per cent of stories about the Presidential debates were positive for Clinton, whereas 82% of stories about the Presidential debates were negative for Trump. For the month of October when most of the debates happened, the primary focus of news was the Presidential debates.

Speaking Times at the Presidential Debates

2012 was a difficult debate season for Republicans Mitt Romney and his running mate Paul Ryan. In the course of four debates, their opponents received almost 10% more speaking time. More than nine and half minutes were given to Obama and Biden over the course of the events. One of the most profound changes in 2016 was that over the course of four debates, the two parties received nearly identical amounts of speaking time. There was less than two minutes of total speaking time difference between the two candidates over four debates. The most significant time departure in

2016 was the amount of time consumed by moderators. 2016 moderators consumed almost 15% of all speaking time. 2012 moderators consumed less than 10% of speaking time. This point reflects a common journalistic meme approaching the debates that suggested that moderators needed to function as "fact checkers." Over the primary process and the campaigns, journalists and democrats expressed a concern that candidate Trump was being so wildly inaccurate and nonfactual that he must be challenged by moderators and not allowed to pass opinionated commentary as fact. This more aggressive suggestion for moderators likely led to an increased participation in the debates by moderators. Moreover, the behavior of the moderators from the primary debates to the general election debates suggests that debates are becoming more about the journalists and less about the candidates. This stands in direct contradiction to the prepared statements read by moderators at the beginning of the debates where they state that the debates will be about the candidates and their views and not the moderator. That promise is not observably true in a comparison of 2012 and 2016 data.

The Collusion of the Moderators

One of the more significant stories of the 2016 election was the collusion of journalists to thwart and direct the larger debate process. Both in the general debates of the fall and the earlier primary debates, there is strong evidence that journalists colluded to grant Hillary Clinton an advantage in the debating process. The most significant story in this genre involved former DNC chief Donna Brazille. Brazille was also a CNN contributor. Wikileaks that generated almost daily news stories based on stolen emails, suggested that Brazille leaked primary debate questions to the Clinton campaign in advance of a Townhall-style debate between Clinton and Sanders. Brazille warned the Clinton campaign about an impending question on the Flint water crisis.[25] Clinton appeared incredibly well prepared for the question that did come on the Flint Water crisis. Brazille was questioned about the breach and ultimately relieved of her CNN duties in relation to the breach.[26] This story was part of a larger scandal that shook the DNC with multiple reports of how Bernie Sanders was deliberately defeated by party planners throughout the primary process.

In a pre-debate Townhall event hosted by Matt Lauer shortly before the main debates started in late September, each candidate had half an hour to answer questions from Lauer and the audience. Reports indicate that the Clinton campaign gained an advance concession from Lauer not to discuss the email scandal story that had plagued the campaign throughout the election. Clinton appeared pained when the question emerged from Lauer.

These ruptures contributed to a public unease with the debate process as held within the grip of the journalistic community. These problems likely contributed to the public backlash that would secretly steal the election from Clinton amidst overwhelming polling evidence that she was an inevitable win.

The New Presidential Debate Moderator Paradigm: "Fact-Checking"

As candidate Donald Trump continued to eviscerate the Republican field and threaten the presumed victor and heir apparent to President Obama, a meme began to emerge within the media. Moderators needed to perform a more activist role in the general election debates of late September and October. The essential idea was that Donald Trump was so improvisational in his public abuse of "facts" that he would need moderators who could control him and correct him. Candidate Hillary Clinton would not be capable of fulfilling that task as a debater or candidate. Essentially, the dramatic failure in moderation committed by Candy Crowley in 2012 would now become the institutional norm for moderating the general election debates. A Lexis/Nexis survey of the print journalism usage of the term "fact check" more than doubled from the month of June 2016—when the term was used 153 times—October 2016—when the term was used 341 times. The Christian Science Monitor had a headline that typified the usage of the period in mid-October: "Why Google News is adding a 'Fact Check' label; While pundits are in disagreement about the role the media should play in vetting politicians' statements, readers are bringing record traffic to fact-checking websites like Politifact."[27] The journalistic community that gave 96% of its political donations in 2016 to the Democratic campaign of Hillary Clinton[28] came to a consensus that fact-checking was needed to control the rhetoric of Republican candidate Donald Trump. The consensus behavior was part of a larger agenda of epistemological poisoning designed to insure Hillary Clinton's ascendancy to the Presidency.[29] Journalist moderators interrupted Trump (106 times)—almost 3 times as often as Clinton (44 times). The amount of time and words expended my moderators increased dramatically in debates two and three between Trump and Clinton—despite Clinton's apparent strong victory in the polling taken after debate number one. Trump was always interrupted two or three times as much as his Vice Presidential running mate, Mike Pence (11 times) in the debates. In a significant respect, Trump was debating Clinton and the journalistic moderators of the debate. The data is clear that the four journalistic moderators acted to reduce and control Donald Trump in the three debates and their active participation in the debates increased as the debates went on.

The ability to control "facts" by various fact-checking journalistic outlets was an important ideological control exerted strenuously in campaign 2016 and severely performed in the debates. In 2012, Candy Crowley "fact checked" Republican contender Mitt Romney on the important question of Clinton and Obama's handling of Benghazi mere weeks before the debates. The CNN personality and debate moderator found in favor of Democratic candidate President Obama—eliciting audible applause from his wife despite moderator instructions that audience members were to remain silent. During the 2012 debate, Romney was mocked for alleging that Russia was more of a foreign policy threat than either Secretary of State Clinton or President Obama properly understood. Obama told Romney "that the 1980s are calling and they want their foreign policy back." That humorous jab was scored by the media as proper truth telling.[30] Today, the same media applauds President Obama for denouncing Russia as a major international and national security foreign policy threat that tampered with the 2016 elections, allowing Trump to win.[31] The media does not flinch to score this dramatic reversal as a fact as well. Since the iconic case of Republican President Richard Nixon, journalists have operated within a narrow reactionary ideological view that Republicans lie and Democrats tell the truth. In this view, the only way Republicans can win elections is by propagating falsehoods that journalists have an ethical obligation to catch and call to account. That mythic view of journalism came to a powerful confrontation in the journalistic moderation of the debates in 2016. It is probable that the positive effects Trump derived from all of the debates—primary and general election debates—were derived from an antagonistic but heroic role that many in public derived from his arguments and style in those events. The public trusts journalism less than ever. The public trusts conventional politicians less than ever. Trump was a rhetorical antithesis to these epistemological leaders and he prospered persuasively in every endeavor where he embodied this battle. The debates were an ideal forum for that show because of the debate commission's insistence upon using

journalists as moderators in the debates. The problem was slightly miti-
gated by the 2016 decision to allow a Fox news journalist to moderate the
final debate. Fox is viewed as relatively conservative compared to the other
media outlets that provided moderators.

Why Did Trump's Vulgarity and Offensive Arguments Work?

Throughout the debates and the campaign season, Donald Trump made
offensive statements. Often these statements could be found on twitter. In
the third and final debate, he referred to Hillary Clinton as a "nasty
woman." In a Republican Presidential primary debate, Trump got into
an argument with Marco Rubio about the size of his hands—a clear
innuendo about masculine genitalia and the common psychological anxi-
eties surrounding size. In many instances, Trump's rhetorical behaviors
exceeded known modern registers for analyzing argument. What was
Trump doing? At almost every phase of the 18-month struggle, experts
and pundits predicted that the spectacular nature of these statements and
arguments could not ultimately prevail. Of course in the field of more than
25 candidates for President in 2016, the arguments did not fail. In fact,
Trump pulled off one of the biggest argumentative upsets in modern
history. It is important to seek some modicum of answers for these here-
tofore, inexplicable events.

Initially, the offensive comments and remarks of Trump inverted the
media pattern for diminishing candidates through an attrition of attention. As candidates conventionally adapt to "expected" norms of political
rhetoric—attention from the media declines. The media appears to be
looking for mistakes. Trump's "mistakes" created spectacles that by
almost any account led to billions of dollars in free advertising for his
campaign. That was an important concept that was incorporated in the
RNC primary debates. In those debates, planners held that any candidate
who was attacked during the debates was entitled to an additional 30
seconds of rejoinder to the attack. It is likely that planners thought this
might help the many Republican candidates attacked by Trump. If that
was the logic—it backfired. The rule helped Trump consistently emerge
from the debates with the most speaking time. Ben Carson in one
desperate moment begged one of his rivals to attack him so he could
have more speaking time. The extra speaking time garnered by Trump in
the primary debates was an important factor in clinching the nomination.

For many analysts, this is a sufficient pragmatic explanation for why Trump's argument gambit worked. But the success involved a deeper psychic relationship with the electorate. Though roughly connoted to a notion of "political correctness," there was a deep-seated anger in the public toward the abuse of "-isms" in the public sphere. This went beyond political correctness and toward the management of discrimination claims by an epistemological elite that factored in benefits for this elite and punishment or decline for those outside the political establishment. This pattern of making abusive claims surrounding sexism, racism and homophobia was a long boiling public contention that crossed party lines. Trump brought the ideological hypocrisy of this boil to a head when for debate number two he brought alleged sexual assault victims of President Bill Clinton in front of the media and public.[32] After being publicly humiliated for his remarks about "grabbing female private parts" Trump fought back by showing how elite epistemological communities ignored the claims of direct physical abuse by women such as Juanita Broaddrick and Kathleen Wiley. These victims were in essence embodying the same argument made by Republican social justice activist Sojurner Truth—Ain't I a Woman?[33] America's Jacobin Left had over decades of culture war formulated a simple basis for destroying populist insurgencies by decrying them of one or more of the sacred discriminatory sins: racism, sexism, homophobia. This epistemological establishment built a political economy around discrimination that handed bullhorns of intimidation to key political allies so that political challengers could be consistently silenced. The public was and remains to a large extent outraged at the public crucifixions performed on this altar. Far from approving of Trump's verbal transgressions, the public that endorsed Trump's triumph was rejecting the judge and jury that was conducting the trials on these transgressions. Many Trump voters indicated in exit polls that they remained concerned and disapproving of Trump's character. The radical nature of this Jacobin political economy is expounded by the incredible number of false flag hate crimes that were committed with an eye toward tarring and feathering Trump as a racist, anti-Muslim, hater of all things human. The burning of a black church in Mississippi while spray painting "Vote Trump" on the side of the church was one of many such false flag operations designed to create an overwhelming rhetorical association of Trump the racist.[34] For many analysts, this second feature of Trump's success remains implausible. The exit polls make the point rather clear despite these protests. Trump received dramatically more votes from African-American males than Mitt Romney (+7%). Trump received more Hispanic votes than Mitt Romney (+8%).[35] Trump's argument success should not be read as an endorsement of offensive speech. It should be read as a re-consideration of how charges of offensiveness are made and socially arbitrated by dysfunctional epistemological communities. These re-considerations return us to the deeper ideological problem of blue privilege afflicting our epistemological communities in journalism, entertainment, academia, the Church, and the government. In essence, why are some individuals "allowed" to be offensive while others are not allowed to be offensive? That is the question that allowed Hispanics to vote in greater numbers for someone who said such offensive things against "Mexicans" and why so many women were able to vote for a candidate who said such hurtful things toward and about women. The effort to re-appropriate blue privilege and re-convene Star Chamber-styled discrimination accusations, will not be met with public enthusiasm in future elections if past is indeed prologue.

CONCLUSIONS FROM PRESIDENTIAL DEBATES 2016

1. Moderators took a more aggressive and participatory role in the debates
   Moderators took roughly 50% more time from each of the four 90-minute debates than they did in 2012. Moderators adopted an aggressive fact-checking mode that also sought to counter the unusually aggressive and disruptive style of Republican Presidential candidate Donald Trump. The ideological underpinnings of this aggressive behavior that sought to correct the false statements of Trump appears to have backfired upon the intentions of the journalistic community that embraced this strategy.

2. Both candidates had nearly equal speaking time; unlike 2012 Clinton and Trump both spoke almost identical speaking times.
   Trump interrupted his opponent much more than she did. The more equal speaking time may have allowed the Republican candidate to have a better chance of winning in the final results of the election. This fact points to an increasing measure of fairness with regard to the debate ideal of equal time. More improvements can still be made.

3. Huge audiences watched the debates and voters indicated they influenced their decision
   The largest audience in US history since televised debates began in 1960 watched debate number one between Donald Trump and Hillary Clinton on September 26, 2016. Eighty-one million people watched the debate. The average viewership for all the debates between Clinton and Trump was 73 million viewers. Roughly 125 million voters voted for the two candidates in the end so it is difficult to conceive of a more accessible channel of political communication that influenced these voters. Neither TV ads nor convention programming reached an audience nearly as large as the debates.

4. Voters rejected the polling on the debates and the general sense of winners and losers and elected Trump
   Exit polls suggest that the debates were highly influential but gave almost no margin to Hillary Clinton and actually favored Trump as a final result. These results suggest that the public notion of a "winner" in the debates was opposed to their own private notions of what was best for the nation politically. At the level of argument theory, the Toulmin warrants[36] supplied by voters in interrupting argument norms were quite different than what the voters understood to be the "rules of debate" for political insiders. This result may be the most important lingering result from the study of Presidential debates 2016. Primary debates that operated on an unusual rule that anytime someone was attacked, they got an extra 30 seconds to respond led to an advantage for Trump who in most primary debates got more speaking time than any other candidate. In the general election phase, overly aggressive journalist moderators led to a heightened public backlash against the poll results of the debate showing Clinton winning all three debates.

5. The debates in the primaries and the general election disproved the political maxim that money corrupts and overwhelms the deliberative political process.
   Jeb Bush massively out-spent Donald Trump in the bid to become the Republican nominee. Secretary of State Hillary Clinton spent more than one billion dollars to defeat Donald Trump in the general election. She out-spent her rival by more than 2 to 1.[37] Both of these events defied the logic that was central to Hillary Clinton's campaign and a creed of the establishment Left in America that holds the

Supreme Court decision in *Citizens United* as the death of democracy in 2010. *Citizens United* was a group that in 2008 sought to distribute a political film critical of Presidential candidate Hillary Clinton. The Supreme Court upheld the political speech rights of this small corporation. For Obama, Sanders, Clinton and many on the American Left, *Citizens United* epitomized the current corruption of the American political process whereby money could buy elections. The idea that corporations were worthy of civil rights found in the First Amendment free speech guarantees was derided as ridiculous if not dangerous.[38] President Obama publicly attacked members of the Court in a State of the Union message before Congress. The blue privilege[39] enjoyed by the American Left wherein film makers like Michael Moore made "educational" films attacking Republican Presidents like George W. Bush was institutionalized by the ideological promise of Hillary Clinton at the Democratic national Convention in 2016 to pass a constitutional amendment overturning *Citizens United*. This debate process disproved the underlying logic of money buying elections and demonstrated how the flawed yet essential ideals of debate can allow an outsider to defeat a well-established and deeply funded insider to the political process.

In sum, the Presidential primary debates and general debates will stand out as some of the most interesting in American history. 2016 will establish incredible pretexts to election 2020 that are already too alluring to ignore. Has offensiveness reached a plateau or peak? Will the sensational mold of Donald Trump result in further emulations at state and local levels? Some measure of a political revolution has taken place. Debate was an integral social communicative engine powering that revolution.

NOTES

1. Mitchell McKinney, "Debating Democracy: The History and Effects of the U.S. Presidential Debates," *Spectra*, 48 (3), September 2012.
2. Robert V. Friedenberg, *Rhetorical Studies of National Political Debates, 1960–1992*, 2nd edition, (Santa Barbara, Praeger, 1993).
3. Brian Stelter, "Convention ratings: Democrats beat Republicans, and cable tops broadcast," *CNN Money*, July 27, 2016, http://money.cnn.com/2016/07/27/media/democratic-convention-night-two-ratings/.

4. "Historical TV Ratings For Presidential Debates 1960–2008 Presidential Campaigns," http://uspolitics.about.com/od/elections/l/bl_historical_tv_ratings_prez_debates.htm.

5. Lydia Saad, "Presidential Debates Rarely Game-Changers But have moved voter preferences in several elections," *Gallup*, September 25, 2008. http://www.gallup.com/poll/110674/Presidential-Debates-Rarely-GameChangers.aspx.

6. Mitchell McKinney and Ben Warner, "Do Presidential Debates Matter? Examining a Decade of Campaign Debate Effects," *Argumentation and Advocacy 49*, Spring 2013, 245–6.

7. Chris Cizilla, "The Thirteen Most Amazing Findings in the Exit Polls," *The Washington Post*, November 10, 2016, https://www.washingtonpost.com/news/the-fix/wp/2016/11/10/the-13-most-amazing-things-in-the-2016-exit-poll/?utm_term=.01b23d4e2bee.

8. Leigh Holmwood, "Sarah Palin helps Saturday Night Live to best ratings in 14 years," *The Guardian*, October 20, 2008.

9. Gabriel Debenedetti, "Disappointing debate ratings spark Democratic campaign complaints: The DNC comes under fire for Saturday's low viewership figures," *Politico*. November 15, 2015, http://www.politico.com/story/2015/11/democratic-debates-cbs-clinton-sanders-omalley-215909.

10. Gabriel Debenedetti, "Disappointing debate ratings spark Democratic campaign complaints: The DNC comes under fire for Saturday's low viewership figures," *Politico*. November 15, 2015, http://www.politico.com/story/2015/11/democratic-debates-cbs-clinton-sanders-omalley-215909.

11. Thomas E. Patterson, Research: Media Coverage of the 2016 Election. *Shorenstein Center*, Harvard University, September 7, 2016. https://shorensteincenter.org/news-coverage-2016-general-election/.

12. Theodore White, *The Making of the President, 1972*, New York: Bantam Books, 1973.

13. "Confidence in Institutions," *Gallup*, 2016. http://www.gallup.com/poll/1597/confidence-institutions.aspx.

14. Art Swift, "Americans Trust Mass Media Sinks to New Low," *Gallup*, September 14, 2016, http://www.gallup.com/poll/195542/americans-trust-mass-media-sinks-new-low.aspx.

15. Art Swift, "Americans Trust Mass Media Sinks to New Low," *Gallup*, September 14, 2016, http://www.gallup.com/poll/195542/americans-trust-mass-media-sinks-new-low.aspx.

16. Jim Kuyper, *Partisan Journalism: A History of Media bias in America*, (Lanham, Maryland: Rowman and Littlefield, 2014).

17. Chris Cilliza, "Just 7 Percent of Journalists are Republicans. That's Far Fewer than even a Decade Ago," *The Washington Post*, May 6, 2014,

http://www.washingtonpost.com/news/the-fix/wp/2014/05/06/just-7-percent-of-journalists-are-republicans-thats-far-less-than-even-a-decade-ago/.

18. Ernest Bormann, "Fantasy and Rhetorical Vision: The Rhetorical Criticism of Social Reality," Quarterly Journal of Speech, 58, (1972): 396–407.

19. Thomas E. Patterson, Research: Media Coverage of the 2016 Election. *Shorenstein Center*, Harvard University, September 7, 2016. https://shoreinsteincenter.org/news-coverage-2016-general-election/.

20. "Alan Keyes Barred from Presidential Debate and "Kidnapped" by Atlanta Police—1996," *YouTube*, 2015, https://www.youtube.com/watch?v=SehAtMQPNmQ.

21. Michael Calvin McGee, "The "ideograph": A link between rhetoric and ideology." *Quarterly Journal of Speech, 66*, (1980): 1–16.

22. Thomas E. Patterson, Research: Media Coverage of the 2016 Election. *Shorenstein Center*, Harvard University, September 7, 2016, https://shoreinsteincenter.org/news-coverage-2016-general-election/.

23. Thomas E. Patterson, Research: Media Coverage of the 2016 Election. *Shorenstein Center*, Harvard University, September 7, 2016, https://shoreinsteincenter.org/news-coverage-2016-general-election/.

24. Thomas E. Patterson, Research: Media Coverage of the 2016 Election. *Shorenstein Center*, Harvard University, September 7, 2016, https://shoreinsteincenter.org/news-coverage-2016-general-election/.

25. Hadas Gold, "Brazile under siege after giving Clinton debate question," *Politico*, October 31, 2016, http://www.politico.com/story/2016/10/donna-brazile-wikileaks-fallout-230553; Glenn Kesler, "Donna Braziles Misleading Statements on Sharing Questions with the Clinton Campaign," *The Washington Post*, November 2, 2016, https://www.washingtonpost.com/news/fact-checker/wp/2016/11/02/donna-braziles-misleading-statements-on-sharing-questions-with-the-clinton-campaign/.

26. Marisa Schultz, "CNN Drops Brazile for Feeding Debate Questions to Clinton," *The New York Post*, October 31, 2016, http://nypost.com/2016/10/31/cnn-drops-brazile-for-feeding-debate-questions-to-clinton/.

27. Ellen Powell, *Christian Science Monitor*. "Why Google News is adding a 'Fact Check' label; While pundits are in disagreement about the role the media should play in vetting politicians' statements, readers are bringing record traffic to fact-checking websites like Politifact," October 14, 2016, LEXIS/NEXIS December 30, 2016.

28. Dave Levinthal and Michael Beckel, *Center for Public Integrity*, "Buying the President 2016: Journalists shower Hillary Clinton with campaign cash/ Far fewer making contributions to Donald Trump, analysis shows," October 17, 2016, https://www.publicintegrity.org/2016/10/17/20330/journalists-shower-hillary-clinton-campaign-cash.

29. Robert Denton and Benjamin Voth, *Social Fragmentation and the Decline of American Democracy: The End of the Social Contract*, (Palgrave Macmillan, 2016): 85–112.

30. Molly Moorhead, "Obama: Romney Called Russia Our Top Geopolitical Threat." *Politifact*, October 22, 2012, http://www.politifact.com/truth-o-meter/statements/2012/oct/22/barack-obama/obama-romney-called-russia-our-top-geopolitical-fo/.

31. David Sanger, December 29, 2016, "Obama Strikes Back at Russia for Election Hacking," *The New York Times*, http://www.nytimes.com/2016/12/29/us/politics/russia-election-hacking-sanctions.html?_r=0.

32. Olivia Nuzzi, Donald Trump Brings Five Bill Clinton Accusers to Debate Definitely Not Sorry about Tape," *The Daily Beast*, October 9, 2016, http://www.thedailybeast.com/articles/2016/10/09/donald-trump-brings-five-bill-clinton-accusers-to-debate-definitely-not-sorry-about-tape.html.

33. Ben Voth, "Ain't I a Woman: The Political Economy of Sexism and Racism," *American Thinker*. October 21, 2016, http://www.americanthinker.com/articles/2016/10/aint_i_a_woman_the_political_economy_of_sexism_and_racism.html.

34. Emily Wagster Pettus, "Mississippi church member charged in 'Vote Trump' arson," *The Washington Post*, December 21, 2016, https://www.washingtonpost.com/national/religion/arrest-in-vote-trump-burning-of-mississippi-black-church/2016/12/21/b3641010-c7bd-11e6-acda-59924caa2450_story.html?utm_term=.1eb77d5c21ed; Jonathan Dienst and Ray Villeda, "Muslim Student Who Said She Was Harassed by Trump Supporters Charged With Filing False Report: Sources," NBC News New York, December 15, 2016, http://www.nbcnewyork.com/news/local/Missing-Muslim-Student-Baruch-College-Arrested-False-Alert-Trump-Subway-406606865.html.

35. Karthick Ramakrishnan, "Trump Got More Votes from People of Color than Romney Did Here's the Data," *The Washington Post*, November 11, 2016, https://www.washingtonpost.com/news/monkey-cage/wp/2016/11/11/trump-got-more-votes-from-people-of-color-than-romney-did-heres-the-data/?utm_term=.c40775527717.

36. Stephen Toulmin, 1958, *The Uses of Argument*, Cambridge University Press.

37. Jacob Pramuk, "Trump Spent About Half of What Clinton Did on His Way to the Presidency," *CNBC*, November 16, 2016.

38. David E. Weisberg, "Democrats Complained about Citizens United Until the Cash Rolled In," *The Hill*, December 4, 2016.

39. Ben Voth, "Blue Privilege," *American Thinker*, July 11, 2013, http://www.americanthinker.com/articles/2013/07/blue_privilege.html.

Ben Voth is Associate Professor and Director of Debate and Speech programs in the Communication Studies Division of the Meadows School of the Arts at Southern Methodist University. He is a leading national scholar on debate and the power of the human voice. He is the author of *Social Fragmentation and the Decline of American Democracy: The End of the Social Contract* (with Robert E. Denton, Jr.) (2017) and *The Rhetoric of Genocide: Death as a Text* (2014). He is currently an Advisor to the Bush Institute and the Debate fellow for the Calvin Coolidge Foundation in Vermont. He is an officer in the American Forensics Association and served on the editorial board of *Argumentation and Advocacy*.

CHAPTER 4

Political Advertising in the 2016 Presidential Election

Scott Dunn and John C. Tedesco

Ever since 1952, when the Eisenhower Answers America advertising ushered in televised political advertising as a feature of presidential campaign communication, candidates have embraced political advertising. Prior to candidate web pages and candidate social media accounts, televised political advertisements presented a rare form of communication that allowed candidates to create messages in a distilled form, free from journalistic gatekeeping, framing, or interpretation. In general, campaigns have understood that televised political advertising, since it remains an important candidate-controlled medium, allows the campaign to accomplish presentation of positive messages about their candidate while simultaneously allowing them to attack the image and issue stances of opponents or to rebut or respond to attacks made by the opponent. Even though candidate web pages and social media platforms, such as Facebook and Twitter, offer campaigns additional forms of candidate-controlled messages, evidence of the importance of political advertising

S. Dunn (✉)
Radford University, School of Communication, Radford, VA, USA
e-mail: swdunn@radford.edu

J.C. Tedesco
Virginia Tech Department of Communication, Blacksburg, VA, USA
e-mail: Tedesco@vt.edu

© The Author(s) 2017
R.E. Denton, Jr. (ed.), *The 2016 US Presidential Campaign*,
Political Campaigning and Communication,
DOI 10.1007/978-3-319-52599-0_4

remains. Evidence that campaigns rely on televised political advertising to disseminate their unfiltered messages is found in spending data, which shows that throughout our presidential campaign history, campaigns have outspent previous presidential campaign spending on paid political advertisements.[1]

The 2016 presidential election, while unique for many reasons, stands out specifically when exploring data that show televised advertising spending did *not* exceed the prior election spending. In fact, as data show, spending in the last few election cycles has far outpaced the prior cycle in terms of dollars spent by the major-party candidates, especially when normalized and adjusted for inflation, population growth, and income growth.[2] In addition to the data showing a decrease in spending during 2016, tracking of advertising volume shows decreases when compared to 2012 in a number of advertisement broadcast by the campaigns.[3] In fact, the Wesleyan Media Project, which reports numbers of advertisements aired by candidates, parties and outside groups, shows that between September 16, 2016, and October 13, 2016, 117,000 presidential ads were aired, which is less than half the 256,000 ads aired during the same time during the 2012 presidential election. While the report shows that advertising spending and advertising volume decreased for Clinton when compared to Obama, the numbers are even more significant when Trump is compared to Romney. While most followers of the 2016 election recognized that Trump ran an unconventional campaign, it seemed baffling to most observers that Trump espoused his lack of need for political ads. At a campaign rally in June 2016, before the general election campaign hit full stride, Trump stated the following:

> First of all, I don't even know why I need so much money. You know, I go around, I make speeches. I talk to reporters. I don't even need commercials, if you want to know the truth.[4]

While political observers argued that Trump's statement seemed short-sighted,[5] Trump continued to dominate headlines and the airwaves throughout the general election campaign with his unconventional campaign messages and strategies. And, for much of the general campaign season, the polls seemed to suggest that Trump's strategy was failing him. Although hindsight tells us that polls were not representative of the entire electorate and failed to tap into important pockets of Trump supporters, Clinton enjoyed a seemingly comfortable lead throughout much of the campaign. In fact, strategists were even discussing the possibility that she could win some traditional Republican states, such as Arizona.[6]

Political advertising typically plays a significant role in presidential campaigns by reinforcing attitudes of important base voters for each campaign and swaying low-information voters who are more likely to be influenced by advertising messages. In fact, we tend to agree with those who asserted that the narrative of political campaigns is often driven by the rhetoric of televised ads.[7] But, that was not the case in 2016. Despite the seemingly diminished power of political advertising in the 2016 presidential campaign, in terms of advertising expenditures, advertisement volumes, and prominence of ads in the campaign narrative, we argue that the political advertising remained a significant tool for the candidates in 2016. This chapter reviews the strategies that dominated the candidate's televised advertising messages and discusses some opportunities seized or missed by the campaigns.

POLITICAL ADVERTISING RESEARCH

Researchers, mostly from communication and political science, have applied a broad range of approaches to interpret the content and effects of political advertising.[8] Space does not permit a thorough review of this expansive literature here, but we will highlight some key studies that are directly relevant to the advertising use by the Trump and Clinton campaigns in 2016.

Researchers have tended to analyze political advertisements by differentiating between categories such as positive and negative ads or issue and image ads.[9] A preliminary analysis has shown that in 2016, the ads from both campaigns were overwhelmingly negative and image-focused, with limited attention to issues and few purely positive ads.[10] These types of ad hominem attack ads are nothing new, but up through the 2008 presidential elections they had been balanced by more positive ads and issue-focused ads.[11] However, the 2012 election was characterized by overwhelmingly negative advertising both from the campaigns themselves and from outside groups known as SuperPACs,[12] and the 2016 elections seems to have continued that trend.

Quite a few studies have examined negative advertising over the years. Although negative ads are obviously designed to denigrate the sponsor's opponent in voters' minds, voters generally claim not to like negative advertising, so there is an ongoing concern that there could be a backlash effect that will ultimately harm the sponsoring campaign. Despite that concern, research suggests that negative advertising often has its desired effect,[13] although it is certainly possible that backlash effects can happen in certain contexts. For instance, one study found that negative advertising is more effective for candidates who are leading in the polls and for incumbents.[14]

With the widespread use of negative advertising, it is unsurprising that campaigns have developed a range to strategies for attacking their opponents. In their comprehensive content analysis, Johnston and Kaid identified three purposes of negative ads: attacking the opponent's personal characteristics, attacking the opponent's issues stands or consistency, and attacking the opponent's group affiliations. They also identified four strategies used to achieve those goals: humor or ridicule, negative associations, name calling, and guilt by association.[15] Fear appeals are also popular strategy, as candidates try "to create a suspicion or anxiety about the opponent's beliefs or previous actions."[16]

One way that campaigns try to avoid the potential backlash that can come from negative advertising is by use of comparative ads, which combine as attack on the opponent with a positive message about the sponsoring candidate. Historically, this type of ad has not been as common as purely negative or purely positive ads,[17] so research on comparative ads is somewhat limited. However, experimental research suggests that well-made comparative ads can be effective at damaging the targeted candidate's evaluations without harming the sponsoring candidate.[18]

Preliminary quantitative data show that comparative ads were used frequently in the 2016 presidential race.[19] This use of comparative ads makes intuitive sense for an election in which the two major-party candidates has record-low favorability ratings.[20] Since both candidates were largely disliked (outside of a fervent but relatively small base for each), it would be a tough sell to convince the public that either candidate was the kind of inspiring leader that would make excite voters the way charismatic candidates like John F. Kennedy, Ronald Reagan, or Barack Obama did. A much more realistic approach was for each campaign to convince the public that their candidate was the least bad alternative. While purely negative ads are usually effective for denigrating an opponent, they might not serve much purpose in an election in which both candidates were facing opponents who were already viewed poorly by most voters. Comparative ads offered an alternative that allowed each campaign to further diminish views of the opponent while also attempting to boost views of their own candidates.

This chapter will take an in-depth qualitative approach to further investigate how the Clinton and Trump campaigns, along with the outside groups supporting them, used these strategies to try to make the case for their preferred candidate being the more palatable alternative.

METHOD

For this analysis, the researchers examined all of the general election ads posted on the website of the Political Communication Lab at Stanford University.[21] This archive includes ads from the official Trump and Clinton campaigns, as well as the major outside organizations supporting each candidate (Priorities USA Action PAC for Clinton and Rebuild America PAC, NRA Political Victory Fund, Make America Number 1 PAC, Future 45 PAC, the Republican National Committee and Great America PAC for Trump). In all, there were 38 ads sponsored by the Clinton campaign and 26 ads from Priorities USA, for a total of 64 pro-Clinton ads. There were 24 ads sponsored by the Trump campaign and 54 ads sponsored by the various outside groups supporting Trump, for a total of 78 pro-Trump ads. Both authors watched each ad multiple times to identify the major themes for this analysis. They focused primarily on the campaign-sponsored ads, but also examined the ads from outside groups as a point of comparison.

ANALYSIS

As already noted, both campaigns' advertising was overwhelmingly negative. The campaigns seemed to assume that there was little need to build up their own candidates when they could denigrate the opposing candidate so thoroughly that voters would find him or her to be completely unacceptable. The remainder of the chapter will discuss the negative advertising strategies used by the campaigns.

CLINTON'S CAMPAIGN ADS

The overarching theme of the Clinton campaign's advertising was Trump's unfitness for office due to his temperament and lack of experience. The campaign did run some purely positive ads, most of which focused on Clinton's record of working for children and families.[22] However, these ads were noticeably less common than negative and comparative ads and seemed to be incidental to the overall advertising strategy, which was overwhelmingly focused on painting Trump in a negative light. Some strategies the campaign used included using Trump's own words against him, highlighting Republicans who opposed Trump, and comparing Trump's temperament and experience with Clinton's.

In Trump's Own Words

One strategy that the Clinton campaign used in many ads was to prominently feature Trump's own words. For instance, just before the Republican National Convention, the Clinton campaign started their general election advertising campaign with an ad called "Role Models." This ad features audio of some of Trump's most widely reported controversial statements, including his suggestion that he'd like to see a protester at a rally "carried out on a stretcher," his instruction to a crowd to tell businesses that moved jobs to Mexico "to go [bleep] themselves," his boast that he could "stand in the middle of Fifth Avenue and shoot somebody and I wouldn't lose any voters," his allegation that many Mexican immigrants are rapists who are "bringing drugs [and] crime," his assertion that Fox News anchor had "blood coming out of her wherever" during a Republican primary debate, and his mocking of a reporter with a disability. At the end of the ad, the text on the screen reads, "Our children are watching. What example will we set for them?" The clear implication is that Trump's rhetoric places him outside of the realm of acceptable candidates for president. This focus on character rather than policy would set the tone for Clinton's advertising throughout the rest of the election.

Many of the statements from Trump used in Clinton's "Role Models" ad would be used in multiple Clinton ads throughout the campaign, but later ads were somewhat more specific with their attacks. One ad, titled "Sacrifice," features a series of people who were implied to be veterans or people who had lost loved ones in combat. While these individuals are not named directly, their status as veterans or members of Gold Star families was signified by the presence of prosthetic limbs, a hat reading "U.S. Navy Retired," and a picture of a young man in uniform next to (presumably) his grieving mother. Each of these individuals is watching a clip of Trump making a statement that could easily be interpreted as disrespectful to veterans. These statements include Trump's claims to "know more about

ISIS than the generals do," that he does not believe Senator John McCain is a war hero because "I like people that weren't captured," and that he has made sacrifices similar to those of Gold Star families because he has "built great structures" and "had tremendous success." The tagline at the end of the ad reads, "Our veterans deserve better."

An ad called "Mirrors" uses the exact same format but highlights the effects of Trumps words on a different audience. This ad shows a series of preteen or teenaged girls looking at themselves in mirrors while the audience hears statements from Trump that imply a superficial way of viewing women. These statements include the following: "I'd look her right in that fat ugly face of hers," "A person who's flat-chested is very hard to be a 10," and "I can't say that either" in response to an interviewer asking if he treats women with respect. The final tagline reads, "Is this the president we want for our daughters?" As with the previous ad, the clear message was that Trump's temperament should make him unacceptable to a certain group of voters (in this case, parents with daughters).

An ad called "American Bully" juxtaposes Trump's most hostile statements with clips of famous cinematic bullies, such as Scut Farkus from *A Christmas Story*, Biff Tannen from *Back to the Future*, Nurse Ratchet from *One Flew Over the Cuckoo's Nest*, Mick McAllister from *Teen Wolf*, and Regina George from *Mean Girls*. In some cases, the statements from the films are matched directly with statements from Trump. For instance, the audience sees Nurse Ratchet yell "Sit down!," followed by Trump telling a protester at a rally the same thing. A clip of Mick McAllister saying "Shoot it, fat boy," is paired with Trump saying, "I'd look her right in that fat, ugly face of hers." A clip of Biff Tannen saying, "I don't want to see you in here again" pairs with Trump yelling for security to "Get him [a protester] out of here!" After this montage, the ad cuts to Hillary Clinton taking a question from a young girl at a town hall meeting who asks what she would do to stop bullying. Clinton responds, "I really do think we need more love and kindness in our country, and that's why it's important to stand up to bullies wherever they are and why we shouldn't let anybody bully his way into the presidency." Although Clinton does not offer any policy solutions to curb bullying, the ad makes the clear case that Trump represents the archetypal bully figure that Americans are familiar with from pop culture and that Clinton represents a kinder alternative.

Other ads used Trump's words to set up fear appeals regarding Trump's fitness to serve as commander-in-chief. In an ad titled "Silo," a former nuclear missile launch officer named Bruce Blair testifies, "If the president gave the order, we had to launch the missiles…I prayed that call would never come. Self control may be all that keeps these missiles from firing." This statement is juxtaposed with statements from Trump such as "I would bomb the shit out of them," "I want to be unpredictable," and "I love war." Blair then returns in a voiceover saying, "The thought of Donald Trump with nuclear weapons scares me to death, should scare everyone."

Similarly, in an ad called "Just One," interspersed with statements from Trump such as his claim to "know more about ISIS than the generals do," a voiceover says, "In times of crisis America depends on steady leadership, clear thinking, and calm judgment. Because all it takes is one wrong move. Just one." As the narrator finishes this statement, the sound of a jet flying by is heard in the background. Unlike the previously discussed ads that simply implied that Trump's temperament was disrespectful or set a bad example, these ads imply that Trump's temperament would make him downright dangerous as commander-in-chief.

This focus on Trump's temperament and its implication for national security echoed the fear appeals used against Senator Barry Goldwater when he challenged President Lyndon Johnson in 1964, as best exemplified by the famous "Peace Little Girl (Daisy)" ad.[23] This iconic ad juxtaposed the image of an innocent little girl counting the flowers she pulls from a daisy with the audio of a countdown followed by a nuclear explosion and a mushroom cloud, with the clear implication that electing Goldwater would result in nuclear war. In an interesting allusion to presidential advertising history, the Clinton campaign ran an ad featuring Monique Corzilius Luiz, the actress who played the little girl in the original 1964 ad. The ad begins with a brief visual of Luiz picking petals in the original ad, as the adult Luiz says, "This was me in 1964. The fear of nuclear war that we had as children, I never thought our children would ever have to deal with that again, and to see that coming forward in this election is really scary." As with "Just One" (and other ads), this ad then features statements from Trump himself that would call into question his ability to be a steady hand in overseeing national defense. The explicit connection to the Johnson campaign's attacks on Goldwater provides additional resonance for viewers who are familiar with Goldwater's perceived extremism and the general climate of fear that characterized that period of American history. The message is that, like Goldwater, Trump's temperament and attitude toward nuclear war are outside the realm of what is acceptable in American politics, and may even result in a devastating nuclear war.[24]

One of the most memorable ads from the 2016 presidential campaign did not include direct quotes from Trump, but was a clear response to things that Trump had said. In "Captain Khan," Khizr Khan relates the story of how his son, Army Captain Humayun Khan, who was killed in the process of saving his fellow soldiers from a suicide bomber in Iraq in 2004. The ad's visuals reinforce the sense of loss Khan and his wife feel by showing him reflectively examining his son's uniform, American flag, and photograph. At the end, Khan says, "He was a Muslim-American. I want to ask Mr. Trump, would my son have a place in your America?" While the ad is effective on its own, what makes it really resonate is the way the ad responds to the controversy surrounding Trump's proposal to ban Muslims from entering the United States,[25] Khan's speech at the Democratic National Convention questioning the constitutionality of such a ban,[26] and Trump's response to Khan's speech.[27] As with the ads using direct quotes from Trump, this ad paints the Republican candidate as someone too far out of the mainstream to be an acceptable choice.[28]

Republicans against Trump

Another strategy Clinton used to discredit Trump was to use Republican voices against him. An ad called "Agree" features quotes from prominent Republicans, including the party's previous presidential nominee, Mitt Romney, in addition to four United States Senators (Lindsey Graham, R-SC; Ben Sasse, R-NE; Jeff Flake, R-AZ; and Susan Collins, R-ME) and two Congressmen (Richard Hanna, R-NY; and Reid Ribble, R-WI). All of these leaders are shown condemning Trump's qualifications for the office of president. These statements include Graham calling Trump "a race-baiting, xenophobic, religious bigot," Romney calling him "a phony, a fraud," and Sasse saying that Trump is "not a serious adult." The tagline at the end of the ad reads, "Unfit. Dangerous. Even for Republicans."

Similarly, the Clinton campaign released a series of ads that featured testimonials from ordinary people who all included their identification as Republicans in their statements. One called "The Right Thing" features Jennifer Kohn, a mother of a child with autism, testifying about how Trump's statement mocking a reporter with a disability affected her and her son. She says,

> It's not uncommon for autistic kids to flap their hands, and so when I saw that, that was completely disqualifying. I'm a Republican, but this election is

so much bigger than party. My son Max can't live in Trump World, so I'm crossing party lines and voting for Hillary. I don't always agree with her, but she's reasonable, and she's smart. She can work with people to solve problems. I want to be able to tell my kids that I did the right thing when it really mattered.

Another ad, "Respect," features an Army veteran named Robert Kearney, who testified,

I fought for my country in Kosovo and Iraq, and I've been a Republican all my life, but I'm the father of three girls and I can't stand hearing Donald Trump call women pigs, dogs, and bimbos, and I sure don't want my daughters hearing it. I want my girls to grow up proud and strong in a nation where they're valued and respected. Donald Trump's America is not the country I fought for, so I'm voting for Hillary Clinton.

Whether they featured elected officials or ordinary people, the message of the ads featuring Republicans speaking out against Trump was that Trump's candidacy represented something beyond mere politics. The messages seemed to be that if, in this time of polarization, Republicans cannot bring themselves to support their candidate, that candidate must be patently unqualified, or even dangerous.

Comparative Advertising

As previously noted, campaigns often use comparative ads to attack opponents while minimizing the risk of a backlash against the sponsoring candidate. The Clinton campaign used the comparative approach in a number of ads to contrast Trump's temperament and lack of experience with her own qualifications for the presidency. Traditionally, comparison ads would be split, with roughly the first half of the ad attacking the opponent and the second half acclaiming the sponsoring candidate. Clinton's ads took a different approach by integrating the comparison throughout the ads. Perhaps the best example of this approach is an ad appropriately titled "Example," which features images of smiling, playing children and a voiceover from actor Morgan Freeman. This voiceover states,

Our children, they look up to us, what we value, how we treat others, and now they're looking to see what kind of leaders we choose, who we'll entrust our country and their future to. Will it be the one respected around the world or the one who frightens our allies and emboldens our enemies? The one with the deep understanding of the challenges we face or the one who is unprepared for them? A steady hand or a loose cannon? Common sense and unity or drama and division? A woman who spent her life helping children and families or a man who spent his life helping himself? Our children are looking to us. What example will we set? What kind of country will we be?

This ad hits on a lot of points covered by other Clinton ads, such as Trump's lack of experience, the dangers his temperament could pose for national security, and the bad example Trump's action set for children. In addition, the ad incorporates a positive message painting Clinton as an internationally respected leader "with a deep understanding of the challenges we face," "a steady hand," and "common sense." The ad also emphasizes Clinton's history of advocacy for children, something that her campaign emphasized in its positive ads as well.

In addition to emphasizing her experience, Clinton used comparative ads to make the case that she was more compassionate than Trump. An example of an ad making this case was titled "Sees," and it features a woman named Anastasia Somoza who suffers from cerebral palsy and spastic quadriplegia and who worked for Clinton during her time in the Senate.[29] Somoza relates her experience with Clinton, saying, "I first met Hillary Clinton when I was nine years old, and I could tell that when she looked at me she didn't see disability, she saw someone strong and capable, like I see myself." Then, while watching the well-publicized video of Trump mocking the reporter with a disability, Somoza continues, "Donald Trump doesn't see people like me, he just sees disability. I honestly feel bad for someone with so much hate in his heart. We need a president who sees the best in all of us." While ads like this one do not directly address Clinton's policies or experience, they send the message that her character is stronger than Trump's because of her compassion.

The very last ad the Clinton campaign ran the day before the election (appropriately titled "Tomorrow") illustrates the comparative nature of her campaign's advertising strategy, albeit in a way that is more subtle than the previously cited ads. In many ways, the ad is a typical get-out-the-vote message of the kind you would expect to see toward the end of a campaign. With no accompanying visuals, Clinton addresses the audience directly, saying, "I think we can all agree, it's been a long campaign, but tomorrow you get to pick our next president." She goes on to draw a distinction between Trump and herself by saying, "It's not just my name and my opponent's name on the ballot, it's the kind of country we want for our children and grandchildren. Is America dark and divisive or hopeful and inclusive? Our core values are being tested in this election, but everywhere I go, people are refusing to be defined by fear and division." With this statement, she outlines clear differences between the candidates and attacks Trump for causing "fear and division," all without even mentioning Trump's name. She goes on to give a fairly conventional end-of-campaign message about the importance of unity and how hard she will work as president, but the part of the ad that resonates the most is the subtle dig on Trump during this comparative portion.

Trump's Campaign Ads

As with Clinton's ads, the Trump campaign's ads were largely negative or comparative. The purely positive ads the campaign did run were mostly focused on the idea that Trump was leading "a movement, not a campaign" (as heard in an ad called, appropriately, "Movement"). Again, though, these positive ads were rare and largely tangential to the campaign's overall advertising strategy, which was overwhelmingly focused on denigrating Clinton. Some of the strategies the Trump campaign used included the following.

Allegations of Clinton's Corruption

The overarching narrative told by most of Trump's ads was that Clinton was guilty of engaging in corrupt activities that make her unqualified to be president. A representative ad was titled "Unfit." As visuals of Clinton from over the years appear on the screen, an unnamed narrator alleges,

> Decades of lies, cover-ups and scandals have finally caught up with Hillary Clinton. Hillary Clinton is under FBI investigation again, after her emails were found on pervert Anthony Weiner's laptop. Think about that. America's most sensitive secrets, unlawfully sent, received, and exposed by Hillary Clinton, her staff, and Anthony Weiner. Hillary cannot lead a nation while crippled by a criminal investigation. Hillary Clinton, unfit to serve.

This ad was obviously released in the wake of FBI Director James Comey's late-October revelation that the FBI had become aware of additional emails relevant to the investigation of Clinton's use of a private email server. These emails were reportedly found in the course of investigating allegations that Weiner exchange explicit messages with an underage girl.[30] Of course, the connection to Weiner was largely circumstantial, as Weiner's estranged wife is a longtime aide to Clinton. However, associating the email scandal with "pervert Anthony Weiner," adds a salacious angle, perhaps even implying that there is a sexual aspect to it. This implication might not resonate for many candidates, but considering the history of sexual scandals involving Clinton's husband, it might have more resonance for her.

A similar ad, titled "Betrayed," also focuses on the email scandal. This ad particularly focuses on the question of whether Clinton was truthful in her statements about the scandal to the FBI and Congress. The narrator claims, "Even *The Washington Post* says Hillary Clinton lied, comparing her to Pinocchio." This reference to Pinocchio is based on *The Washington Post*'s use of a scale from "One Pinocchio" ("Some shading of facts") to "Four Pinocchios" ("Whoppers") to rate untrue statements in its fact-checking articles.[31] By focusing on Clinton's dishonesty about the emails in addition to the use of a private server itself, the ad invokes the Monica Lewinsky scandal, in which Bill Clinton was criticized, and ultimately impeached, more for his dishonesty about his sexual relationship with Lewinsky than for the relationship itself.

Other attack ads went a step further and suggested that a Clinton presidency would actually be dangerous for the nation. An ad called "Dangerous" made this point explicitly. Over images of tanks and warring troops, the narrator warns,

> Our next president faces daunting challenges in a dangerous world: Iran promoting terrorism, North Korea threatening, ISIS on the rise, Libya and North Africa in chaos. Hillary Clinton failed every single time as Secretary of State. Now she wants to be president. Hillary Clinton doesn't have the fortitude, strength, or stamina to lead in our world. She failed as Secretary of State; don't let her fail us again.

At the point when the narrator questions Clinton's "fortitude, strength, or stamina," the ad shows an image of Clinton collapsing, presumably from her bout with pneumonia that required her to leave a September 11 memorial service during the campaign.[32] So, while the text of the ad implies only that Clinton's policies and history as Secretary of State provide reasons to be wary of her ability to be an effective president, the ad's visuals also imply that her health is a reason for concern.

In Clinton's Own Words

The Trump campaign was not quite as prolific at using Clinton's words against her as the Clinton campaign was with Trump's words, but they did use this strategy in several ads. One ad, titled "Why," starts with Clinton asking, "Why aren't I 50 points ahead, you might ask?" A narrator replies that Clinton is behind because of lying about her email server, policies that "have allowed ISIS and terrorism to spread," and "because you call Americans deplorable." This last statement is followed by a clip of Clinton's infamous speech in which she claimed, "You could put half of Trump's supporters into what I call the basket of deplorables."[33] At the end of the ad, Clinton is again seen asking why she's not 50 points ahead, and the narrator ask, "Do you really need to ask?" By using both Clinton's initial question and her "deplorables" statement, the ad paints Clinton as out of touch with much of the country, and arrogant enough to believe that voters will not care about the email scandal or her foreign policies.

An ad simply called "Deplorables" zeroes in on that unfortunate comment even more. The narrator opens by saying, "Speaking to wealthy donors, Hillary Clinton called tens of millions of Americans 'deplorable.'" The ad then shows more of Clinton's remarks than the previously discussed ad, including her assertion that the "deplorables" are "racist, sexist, homophobic, xenophobic, Islamophobic, you name it." The narrator comes back in to say, "People like you, you, and you, deplorable! You know what's deplorable? Hillary Clinton viciously demonizing hard-working people like you." Despite the fact that Clinton only said that half of Trump's supporters were deplorable, and went on to say that many had legitimate reasons for supporting him that did not involve racism or other discriminatory beliefs,[34] the ad suggests that Clinton was attacking all Trump supporters. By referring to Trump supporters as "hard-working people," the ad implies that there is a divide between Clinton and her supporters are the kind of "real Americans" that she and her supporters look down on as "deplorable."

An ad called "Predators" extends the attack on Clinton as an elitist who looks down on people who are different from her, but with a different implied target for her ire. The ad shows Clinton making a statement about some young African-Americans being "the kinds of kids that are called 'super predators.' No conscience, no empathy." It then shows Clinton talking about young people who supported Bernie Sanders as "new to politics completely. And they are living in their parents' basement. That is a mindset that is really affecting their politics." Finally, the ad replays the "basket of deplorables" remark. Again, the message is that Clinton thinks she is better than all three of these groups and looks down on them. While it is easy to assume that young African-Americans, Sanders supporters, and Trump supporters are the target audiences for the ad, it is at least as likely that the ad actually aims to engage anyone who is likely to find Clinton to be condescending, even viewers who do not consider themselves a part of any of the groups to which Clinton referred.

Comparative Ads

Like the Clinton campaign, Trump used a lot of comparative advertising in order to attack Clinton without as much risk of a backlash. In fact, his campaign seemed to use this strategy more than hers did. Many of these ads took the form of comparing "Donald Trump's America" to "Hillary Clinton's America." The first of these ads ran soon after Clinton's speech at the Democratic National Convention. The narrator says,

> You heard the speech, but behind the glitter lies this stark truth: In Hillary Clinton's America things get worse. Under her dishonest plan taxes keep rising, terrorism spreads, Washington insiders remain in control, Americans losing their jobs, homes, and hope. In Donald Trump's America, people are put back to work, our families are safe, the American Dream achievable again, change that makes America great again.

Although, like many political ads, this one is thin on policy specifics, it does make a clear distinction between what voters should expect if they elect Clinton as opposed to what they should expect if they elect Trump.

The Trump campaign ran several ads that made a general comparison between Clinton's America and Trump's America, but they also ran some that based the comparison on specific issues. For instance, an ad called "Two Americas: Immigration" narrowed the focus to Trump's signature issue. The narrator reads,

> In Hillary Clinton's America, the system stays rigged against Americans; Syrian refugees flood in; illegal immigrants convicted of committing crimes

get to stay, collecting social security benefits, skipping the line; our border open; it's more of the same, but worse. Donald Trump's America is secure, terrorists and dangerous criminals kept out, the border secure, our families safe. Change that makes America safe again.

As with the more general comparative ads, this ad draws a stark distinction, but in this case it also allows Trump to score some points on an issue that was the centerpiece of his campaign. Again, the policy specifics are vague, but for viewers concerned about illegal immigration and the possible influx of refugees, this distinction surely resonated.

Another approach the Trump campaign took to comparative advertising was to compare his experience in the private sector with Clinton's experience in government. One ad, titled "Deals," makes this point with the following voiceover:

Our economy once dominated the world and our middle class thrived. Today, jobs are gone, factories closed, because of bad trade deals pushed by the Clintons that sent our jobs to other countries. Donald Trump's plan: renegotiate NAFTA, stop foreign nations from cheating us, cut taxes to reopen factories. Donald Trump knows business, and he'll fight for the American worker.

This ad allows Trump to get in an attack on Clinton for her (and her husband's) support for free trade policies that many believe have led to the decline in manufacturing jobs in the United States. It also allows him to make the case that his experience as a businessman gives him a negotiating ability that will be relevant to helping improve the economy. Interestingly, Trump's experience in business was not mentioned frequently in his campaign's advertising, but this is one example where it was used to draw a distinction with Clinton's political experience.

An ad called "Change" uses a similar comparative strategy, but without mentioning Trump's business experience. The voiceover for this ad reads,

Hillary Clinton won't change Washington. She's been there 30 years. Taxes went up, terrorism spread, jobs vanished, but special interests and Washington insiders thrived. Donald Trump will turn Washington upside down, day one. Real change that puts Americans first. A vote for Hillary is a vote for more of the same. A vote for Donald Trump is a vote for change that makes America great again.

In this case, the selling point is not Trump's experience but his lack of experience. For voters who are unhappy with the way things are going, Trump offers an opportunity to see things turned "upside down."

Overall, Trumps comparative ads, and the majority of his spots, sent the message that Clinton is a corrupt career politician who would only offer more of the same policies that were already in place. Of course, many voters presumably were perfectly happy with the way things were, but the Trump campaign bet that enough were not happy that this message would get them to turn out and vote for Trump.

CONCLUSIONS

Our analysis supports the conclusion of an earlier analysis that said, "The takeaway message of the 2016 campaign ads is that *neither candidate is fit to lead*."[35] While loyal supporters of each candidate surely found plenty to like, more ambivalent voters would have had a hard time discerning any compelling reason to vote for either candidate based on the campaign advertising (although they would have found plenty of reason to vote *against* both candidates). Clinton could have capitalized more on some of her successes in public service or her years of dedication to children's issues, which was the topic of one of her positive ads, "Measures." "Measures" is narrated by Clinton herself, in her own voice, and addresses her longstanding devotion to children's issues. Obviously, there are many other sources of information besides advertising, but since advertising tends to be one of the major sources of information for less-engaged voters, it is likely that many voters came away from the campaign accepting this conclusion that neither candidate would make a good president.

One concern about this relentlessly negative advertising is that it might suppress turnout if voters just decide that neither candidate deserve their votes. It is difficult to draw conclusions about the effects of campaign messages based on year-to-year turnout numbers; the data show that turnout dropped slightly compared to 2008 and 2012, but was comparable to the levels seen from 1972 to 2000.[36] It is possible, but my no means conclusive, that the overwhelmingly negative advertising seen in 2016 led some voters to simply stay home on Election Day.

One important question for communication scholars is whether the overtly negative strategies used by both campaigns were effective. It is always tempting to assume that the candidate who won the election did everything right and the losing candidate did everything wrong, but that assumption is especially dangerous when analyzing an election in which the loser actually got many more votes than the winner. Since the two candidates' advertising strategies were largely similar, it's virtually impossible to make conclusive judgments about whose strategy was better. It is, however, possible that both campaigns made a misstep by running such negative campaigns. Perhaps if either candidate had run a few more positive ads to give voters an affirmative reason to vote for them rather than trying to convince voters they were the lesser evil, they could have pulled away and won the election convincingly.

Notes

1. Max Galka, "What Trump and Hillary Spent vs Every General Election Candidate Since 1960," *Metrocosm*, last modified November 7, 2016, http://metrocosm.com/2016-election-spending/.
2. Max Galka, "What Trump and Hillary Spent vs Every General Election Candidate Since 1960," *Metrocosm*, last modified November 7, 2016, http://metrocosm.com/2016-election-spending/.
3. Wesleyan Media Project, "Presidential Ad Volume Less than Half of 2012," last modified October 18, 2016, http://mediaproject.wesleyan.edu/releases/oct-2016/
4. Kathleen Ronayne and Jill Colvin, "In ME, Trump strikes back on US Chamber on Trade," Associated Press, last modified June 29, 2016, http://bigstory.ap.org/article/6517ec1db84c43a99b6070e1e9453d04/me-trump-strikes-back-us-chamber-trade, para. 10.
5. Ed Rogers, "Trump says his campaign doesn't need money or ads. Is he serious?" The Washington Post, last modified July 1, 2016, https://www.washingtonpost.com/blogs/post-partisan/wp/2016/07/01/trump-says-his-campaign-doesnt-need-money-or-ads-is-he-serious/?utm_term=.1c872dc7e60a.
6. McManus, "The best political ads of the 2016 campaign."
7. Doyle McManus, "The best political ads of the 2016 campaign," Los Angeles Times, last modified October 26, 2016, http://www.latimes.com/opinion/op-ed/la-oe-mcmanus-best-ads-20161026-snap-story.html. The quote is from Vanderbilt political scientist, John G. Geer, para 4.
8. Eric Van Steenburg, "Areas of Research in Political Advertising: A Review and Research Agenda," *International Journal of Advertising* 34, no. 2 (2015): 195–231.
9. Anne Johnston and Lynda Lee Kaid, "Image Ads and Issue Ads in U.S. Presidential Advertising: Using Videostyle to Explore Stylistic Differences in Televised Political Ads from 1952 to 2000," *Journal of Communication* 52, no. 2 (2002): 281–300.

10. Prashanth Bhat, Alyson Farzad-Phillips, Morgan Hess, Lauren Hunter, Nora Murphy, Claudia Serrano Rico, Kyle Stephan, and Gareth Williams, "A Report on Presidential Advertising and the 2016 General Election: A Referendum on Character," *Political Advertising Resource Center*, last modified November 7, 2016, https://parcumd.files.wordpress.com/2016/11/parc-report-2016-v-21.pdf.
11. Johnston and Kaid, "Image Ads and Issue Ads in U.S. Presidential Advertising."
12. Erika Franklin Fowler and Travis N. Ridout, "Negative, Angry, and Ubiquitous: Political Advertising in 2012," *The Forum: A Journal of Applied Research in Contemporary Politics* 10, no. 4 (2012): 51–61. John C. Tedesco and Scott W. Dunn, "Political Advertising in the 2012 U.S. Presidential Election," in *The 2012 Presidential Campaign: A Communication Perspective*, ed. Robert E. Denton Jr. (Lanham, MD.: Rowman & Littlefield, 2013).
13. Amy E. Jasperson and David P. Fan, "An Aggregate Examination of the Backlash Effect in Political Advertising: The Case of the 1996 U.S. Senate Race in Minnesota," *Journal of Advertising* 31, no. 1 (2002): 1–12. Spencer F. Tinkham and Ruth Ann Weaver-Lariscy, "A Diagnostic Approach to Assessing the Impact of Negative Political Television Commercials," *Journal of Broadcasting & Electronic Media* 37, no. 4 (1993): 377–400.
14. Hsuan-Yi Chou and Nai-Hwa Lien, "How do Candidate Poll Ranking and Election Status Affect the Effects of Negative Political Advertising?," *International Journal of Advertising* 29, no. 5 (2010): 815–834.
15. Johnston and Kaid, "Image Ads and Issue Ads in U.S Presidential Advertising," 289.
16. Judith S. Trent, Robert V. Friedenberg, and Robert E. Denton, Jr., *Political Campaign Communication: Principles & Practices* (eight edition, Lanham, MD: Rowman & Littlefield, 2016), 122.
17. Fowler and Ridout, "Negative, Angery, and Ubiquitous," 59.
18. Paul W. Clark and Monica B. Fine, "Expanding Direction-of-Comparison Theory and Its Applications for Political Advertising Practitioners," *Journal of Management and Marketing Research* 10 (2012): http://www.aabri.com/manuscripts/111031.pdf. Bruce Pinkleton, "The Effects of Negative Comparative Political Advertising on Candidate Evaluations and Advertising Evaluations: An Exploration," *Journal of Advertising* 26, no. 1 (1997): 19–29.
19. Bhat, Farzad-Phillips, Hess, Hunter, Murphy, Rico, Stephan, and Williams, "A Report on Presidential Advertising and the 2016 General Election."
20. Harry Enten, "Americans' Distaste for both Trump and Clinton Is Record-Breaking," *Fivethirtyeight*, last modified on May 5, 2016, http://fivethirtyeight.com/features/americans-distaste-for-both-trump-and-clinton-is-record-breaking/.

21. Stanford University, "Campaign 2016—Presidential General Election Ads," *Political Communication Lab*, https://pcl.stanford.edu/campaigns/2016/. Unless otherwise noted, all ads quoted here are taken from this site, and the titles used will be those used by the site. The archive's General Election page includes ads released on July 14 or later. Because it was evident that Trump and Clinton were going to be their party's nominees well before this date, both campaigns produced ads attacking each other before the general election could really be said to have begun. These earlier ads are excluded from this analysis because most appear to have been produced for online-only distribution and/or for screening at the parties' conventions. Additionally, these ads seem to have reflected the same themes as in the official general election ads. We will occasionally reference earlier ads in the endnotes when they contribute additional insight into advertising during the election.

22. For examples of such ads, see "For Those Who Depend on Us," "Watch," "Measure," "Children," and "Families First."

23. Trent, Friedenberg, and Denton, *Political Campaign Communication*, Peace Little Girl (Daisy), *The Living Room Candidate*, http://www.livin groomcandidate.org/commercials/1964/peace-little-girl-daisy.

24. The Clinton campaign achieved a similar effect by invoking the classic "Confessions of a Republican" ad from the 1964 campaign. This web-only ad featured the same actor, Bill Bogert, and much of the same language from the original ad. Rebecca Savransky, "Clinton Revisits 'Confessions of a Republican' in New Ad," *The Hill*, July 18, 2016, http://thehill.com/blogs/ballot-box/presidential-races/288115-clinton-releases-confessions-of-a-republican-ad.

25. Donald J. Trump, "Donald J. Trump Statement on Preventing Muslim Immigration," last modified December 7, 2015, https://www.donaldj trump.com/press-releases/donald-j.-trump-statement-on-preventing-mus lim-immigration.

26. Khizr Khan, "Full Text: Khizr Khan's Speech to the 2016 Democratic National Convention," *ABC New*, last modified August 1, 2016, http://abcnews.go.com/Politics/full-text-khizr-khans-speech-2016-democratic-national/story?id=41043609.

27. Steve Turnham, "Donald Trump to Father of Fallen Soldier: 'I've Made a Lot of Sacrifices,'" *ABC News*, last modified July 20, 2016, http://abc news.go.com/Politics/donald-trump-father-fallen-soldier-ive-made-lot/story?id=41015051.

28. For more about why this ad is effective, see Jeremy Stahl, "Hillary's New Humayun Khan Ad Is Brutal to Watch and Devastatingly Effective," *Slate*, last modified October 21, 2016, http://www.slate.com/blogs/the_slat est/2016/10/21/hillary_s_new_khizr_khan_ad_is_brutal_to_watch_and_so_effective.html.

29. Hope Racine, "Who Is Anastasia Somoza? Hillary Clinton's Debate Guest Is Adamantly with Her," *Bustle*, last modified September 26, 2016, https://www.bustle.com/articles/186156-who-is-anastasia-somoza-hillary-clintons-debate-guest-is-adamantly-with-her.
30. Patrick Healy and Jonathan Martin, "Hillary Clinton Assails James Comey, Calling Email Decision 'Deeply Troubling,'" *The New York Times*, last modified October 29, 2016, https://www.nytimes.com/2016/10/30/us/politics/hillary-clinton-emails-fbi-anthony-weiner.html.
31. Glenn Kessler, "About the Fact Checker," *The Washington Post*, last modified September 11, 2013, https://www.washingtonpost.com/news/fact-checker/about-the-fact-checker/?utm_term=.e19d30c86595.
32. Jessie Hellmann, "Watch: Videos Show Clinton Collapse After 9/11 Memorial," *The Hill*, last modified September 11, 2016, http://thehill.com/blogs/ballot-box/presidential-races/295341-watch-clinton-collapses-after-9-11-memorial.
33. Amy Chozick, "Hillary Clinton Calls Many Trump Backers 'Deplorables,' and G.O.P. Pounces," *The New York Times*, last modified September 10, 2016, https://www.nytimes.com/2016/09/11/us/politics/hillary-clinton-basket-of-deplorables.html.
34. Angie Drobnic Holan, "In Context: Hillary Clinton and the 'Basket of Deplorables,'" *Politifact*, last modified September 11, 2016, http://www.politifact.com/truth-o-meter/article/2016/sep/11/context-hillary-clinton-basket-deplorables/.
35. Bhat, Farzad-Phillips, Hess, Hunter, Murphy, Rico, Stephan, and Williams, "A Report on Presidential Advertising and the 2016 General Election," 2. Emphasis in original.
36. Carl Bialik, "Voter Turnout Fell, Especially in State that Clinton Won," *Fivethirtyeight*, last modified November 11, 2016, https://fivethirtyeight.com/features/voter-turnout-fell-especially-in-states-that-clinton-won/.

Scott Dunn is an associate professor in the School of Communication at Radford University. He has conducted research on a variety of topics related to political communication at the state and national levels, but his current research agenda focuses on political engagement among young voters. In addition to teaching at the university level, he regularly teaches a summer class on political engagement for high school students through the Virginia Governor's School for the Humanities. He has served as chair of the Eastern Communication Association's Political Communication Interest Group.

John C. Tedesco is professor of communication and affiliate professor of human-computer interaction at Virginia Tech, where he teaches undergraduate and graduate courses in public relations and political communication. Tedesco's research focuses on political candidate-controlled messages and their effects, public relations campaign content and effects, and electronic government. His research appears in many of the field's leading journals, including *Journal of Advertising, Harvard International Journal of Press/Politics, Communication Studies, Journal of Broadcasting and Electronic Media, Journalism Studies, Argumentation and Advocacy, Journal of Interdisciplinary Research, American Behavioral Scientist, International Journal of Strategic Communication*, and *Government Information Quarterly*. He has received research funding from the U.S. State Department, National Science Foundation, and the British Economic, Social Research Council. Tedesco is a past chair of the Political Communication Division of the National Communication Association and past chair for Political Communication at the Eastern Communication Association. He currently serves as chair for Communication & Technology at the International Academy of Business Disciplines.

CHAPTER 5

The Social Media Election of 2016

John Allen Hendricks and Dan Schill

Social media now play a dominant and integral role in modern American politics. It is not an exaggeration to say that political campaigns today *are* social media campaigns. Without incorporating social and digital media into a political campaign, a candidate has almost no chance of being competitive. Communicating with the electorate is vital for politicians, and to do it proficiently, candidates must go where the voters can be found—online and using social media. Particularly, social media such as Facebook, Instagram, and Twitter are the most viable social media outlets to communicate with voters. More specifically, the Pew Research Center found that 86% of Americans use the Internet and, of those users, nearly 80% use Facebook, 32% use Instagram, 31% use Pinterest, 24% use Twitter, and 29% use LinkedIn.[1] Nearly 75% of all Americans own smartphones and use them to access these social media platforms.[2] *The Hill* observed: "the continued rise of social media in presidential politics is, in many ways, a case of candidates meeting supporters where they have their conversations... As

J.A. Hendricks (✉)
Stephen F. Austin State University, Nacogdoches, TX, USA
e-mail: jhendricks@sfasu.edu

D. Schill (✉)
James Madison University, Harrisonburg, VA, USA
e-mail: schilldk@jmu.edu

© The Author(s) 2017
R.E. Denton, Jr. (ed.), *The 2016 US Presidential Campaign*,
Political Campaigning and Communication,
DOI 10.1007/978-3-319-52599-0_5

Americans continue to make using social media a part of their routines, candidates are as well."[3]

Social media radically upended the traditional campaign norms and practices in 2016. "The 2016 cycle has been categorized by unprecedented unpredictability, not as much from the perspective of technology disruption, but a whole-scale shift in the norms of campaign communications," concluded Michael Slaby, the Chief Integration and Innovation Officer for President Obama's 2012 and 2016 campaigns.[4] These norms, instituted over many years and controlled by political and media elites such as party leaders, business executives, and editors and publishers in the news media, appear to be significantly damaged, if not gone completely. *New York Times* media columnist Jim Ruttenberg summarized these changes: "email, websites, Facebook, Twitter, text messaging, Instagram, Periscope and now Snapchat. It was into this media hurricane that the presidential campaign caravan drove this year, and many of its cars were blown off the road. Experienced strategists and their candidates, who could always work through their election plans methodically—promoting their candidacies one foot in front of the other, adjusting here and there for the unexpected—suddenly found that they couldn't operate the way they always did."[5]

In addition to unpredictability and disruption, the other word that characterizes social media's impact on our 2016 political discourse is blurring. Scholar Michael X. Delli Carpini describes this muddling media ecosystem: "This emerging 'media regime' blurs traditional distinctions between fact and opinion, news and entertainment, information producers and consumers, and mass mediated and interpersonal communication, creating a political landscape that is both 'multiaxial' (i.e., in which control of the public agenda emerges from multiple, shifting, and previously invisible or less powerful actors) and 'hyperreal' (i.e., in which the mediated representation of reality becomes more important than the facts underlying it)."[6] This multiaxial and hyperreal environment was a good fit for Donald Trump: his impulsiveness, his "fire, ready, aim (maybe)" communication strategy, his celebrity status, and his background as a reality television star. Nicholas Carr put it well: "If traditional print and broadcast media required candidates to be nouns—stable, coherent figures—social media pushes them to be verbs, engines of activity."[7] In this formulation, Trump was clearly a verb. In an election postmortem, Marc Fisher made the same point: "More than any other major political figure in the digital era, Trump saw how social media had segregated the nation into almost wholly separate ideological and cultural camps, each with its own attitudes and its own narratives. He saw how Facebook and Twitter had blurred the line between public and private. He took advantage of that shift in culture and turned himself into a human vent, blasting the country with a stream of frustration and anger that many people had either kept to themselves or spewed about only anonymously."[8] And while Donald Trump seemed matched for the moment, Hillary Clinton was the wrong candidate for the social and cultural trends that dominated the 2016 presidential race, despite the technical proficiency of her campaign communications operation. If Trump was a verb in 2016, Clinton was most definitely a noun. Her social media feeds attempted to create a warm-and-fuzzy image with descriptions of her background and fitness for office. For example, her campaign released an official playlist on Spotify, a popular music listening service with social media aspects, full of inspiring and affirming songs, but, as Nicholas Carr criticized, the playlist "sounded like an anachronism in a campaign that [was] more punk than pop."[9] As Ross Douthat pointed out: "all the messaging and advertising produced by the Clinton campaign and the culture industry couldn't persuade millions of voters who feared Trump to vote against him—and that the Hillary campaign's data and turnout operation, staffed by the technocracy's best and brightest, couldn't turn a small but solid polling lead into the electoral vote advantage that they always knew they needed."[10]

Importantly though, just because Americans engage with social media platforms does not mean these platforms will be fertile ground for effectively communicating with the electorate. Cognitive Dissonance and Selective Exposure Theories were exhibited on social media platforms as users displayed tendencies to be very selective about information they allowed themselves to see on their Facebook newsfeeds and Twitter feeds. The Pew Research Center found that during the 2016 campaign four out of ten people blocked social media content they disagreed with and eight out of ten people simply ignored political posts that did not align with their beliefs. As scholars Seth Lewis and Matt Carlson declared: "What we ended up with was a filter bubble election. The decline of shared news, the echo chambers of partisan media, and the algorithms that serve confirmation biases coalesce in frightening ways for the future of the republic."[11] This prompted Laeeq Khan, director of the Social Media Analytics Lab at Ohio University, to normatively assert: "In a pluralistic society, healthy social media engagement should be unafraid of competing views, even welcome them."[12]

Social media usage by politicians not only allows them to go where the voters are having conversations but it also provides politicians the ability to strip away the agenda setting and gatekeeping responsibilities held by traditional news media outlets. Politicians can now deliver their message directly to the electorate in an unfiltered and unanalyzed manner. This requires traditional news outlets to cover what is being tweeted and posted on social media, which dictates what the day's news cycle and news topics will be for viewers and readers. In past elections, this operated in a converse manner. Traditional media coverage of social media also influenced the speed and duration of news stories. Alex Conant, a senior strategist for Marco Rubio, described this change: "There was no news cycle—everything was one big fire hose. News was constantly breaking and at the end of the day hardly anything mattered. Things would happen; 24 hours later, everyone was talking about something else."[13] Trump capitalized on this era of short political attention spans by "realizing that if you're the one regularly feeding the stream, you can forever move past your latest trouble, and hasten the mass amnesia."[14]

The sheer volume of social media followers was astonishing compared to traditional media. As of three months prior to the 2016 election, Trump had access to more than 22 million people between his Facebook, Twitter, Instagram, and Reddit accounts alone, while Clinton had access to more than 14 million people. By wide margins, Trump had far more followers on all social media platforms than Clinton. He had more than 10 million Facebook followers compared to her more than 5 million followers; he had more than 10 million Twitter followers compared to her more than 8 million followers; he had more than 2 million Instagram followers compared to her more than 1 million followers; and he had nearly 200,000 Reddit subscribers compared to her nearly 25,000 Reddit subscribers. An interesting side note, and illustration of the tone of the rhetoric in the 2016 presidential election, was that "Hillary for Prison" subreddit had more than 55,000 subscribers on Reddit.[15] Comparatively, in 2016, *Fox News* averaged 2.4 million prime time viewers each evening,[16] *CNN* averaged 1.2 million prime time viewers each evening,[17] and MSNBC averaged 1.08 million prime time viewers each evening.[18] The television news networks simply could no longer compete with the social media platforms when comparing the number of viewers versus the number of followers. Importantly, traditional media largely provided passive experiences while social media provided active and engaged experiences. Put another way, in an article titled, "How Donald Trump Broke the Media," Nicholas Mirzoeff explained: "We *watch* TV. We *go* online. It's the difference between passive and active that makes new media so disruptive, to use the favorite Silicon Valley word. And the results are, in this case, really transformative."[19]

Indeed, Trump's campaign was transformative because he chose to not spend as much money on television advertising compared to what had been spent on past presidential campaigns. As Issie Lapowsky noted in *Wired*, "Social media was Trump's primary communication channel."[20] Further, his social media presence and his penchant for calling into and appearing on television shows provided his campaign with free airtime that in past elections would have cost candidates millions of dollars. Trump leveraged his experience as a reality TV star on *The Apprentice* and *The Celebrity Apprentice* to his campaign's advantage. Although her name was almost universally known, Hillary Clinton did not have the same advantage and outspent Trump by a tremendous margin. CNBC reported: "[Trump's] campaign committee spent about $238.9 million through mid-October, compared with $450.6 million by Clinton's. That equals about $859,538 spent per Trump electoral vote, versus about $1.97 million spent per Clinton electoral vote."[21] The social media strategy implemented by Trump most certainly made up the difference in traditional television advertising spending compared to his competitors in both the primary and general elections. While, like all campaigns, the 2016 campaign was multidimensional and cannot be explained by a single factor, social media may have been decisive. And at least one Trump staffer saw it being determinative. Brad Parscale, Trump's digital director said after the election: "Facebook and Twitter were the reason we won this thing. Twitter for Mr. Trump. And Facebook for fundraising."[22] Consequently, this chapter examines the social media strategies used by both Donald J. Trump and Hillary Rodham Clinton in the 2016 presidential election and briefly examines social media strategies in the primary elections and caucuses. Particularly, this chapter will compare and contrast the social media strategies used by the two candidates, because as *The New York Times* suggested, Trump may well have "permanently changed the rules of politics . . . discarding the playbook that winning candidates have used for many decades."[23]

HILLARY CLINTON SOCIAL MEDIA USE IN THE 2016 CAMPAIGN

A team of more than 100 staff members comprised Clinton's digital team at the Clinton campaign headquarters in Brooklyn, New York. This group, made up of mostly millennials, developed and wrote content for social media, shot and edited video, managed email outreach, digitally organized, purchased digital advertising, and managed *The Briefing* blog. The Clinton team was a "who's who of the Democratic digital world."[24] Leaders of the team included: Jenna Lowenstein, digital director for the Clinton campaign, Katie Dowd, senior digital advisor, Teddy Goff, chief digital strategist, Elan Kriegel, director of analytics, and Andrew Bleeker, digital marketing advisor. In addition to the content group, a tech team of more than 50 developers and engineers who left lucrative careers at companies like Facebook, Google, and Twitter to help code Clinton's way to the White House.[25]

Clinton's team saw themselves as a media production company. In the words of Clinton's strategist Dowd: "I definitely think we are a production company. We are producing our own content and we are thinking about how to make it viral, how to make it successful."[26] And generate content they did; Clinton cast a wide net on social media—if there was a social media site or platform, her campaign likely maintained a presence. Clinton and her surrogates answered questions on Quora, a question-and-answer platform. On Tumblr, inspirational letters written to Clinton by supporters—largely children—were featured on Letters to Hillary. Recipes from Chefs for Hillary and plenty of grandmother-related content were highlighted on Pinterest. On the emerging publishing platform Medium, Clinton's team posted policy editorials and narrative-driven essays to over 174,000 followers. Independently from the campaign, Clinton supporters even released a specialized emoji keyboard called Hillarymoji that allowed supporters to post cartoon emoji stickers of the candidate, such as Clinton wearing a "The future is female T-shirt" and Clinton dressed like Wonder Woman.[27]

This content was designed to be glowing, inspirational, and ready-made for social media,[28] and Clinton's social media operation, with a staff of dozens producing original content managed by an audience development team, followed the model of digital media startups like Vox and Buzzfeed.[29] For example, in January 2016, a listicle headline appeared in countless Facebook feeds reading: "8 Hollywood women who took a stand for progress and inspired us." At first glance, it appeared to come from a viral media company, like Buzzfeed, but clicking on the link would take users to a post on Clinton's website with photos and information about the 8 celebrities. The tagline at the bottom of the post read, "We couldn't agree more—equal rights, gun safety, racial justice and equality are all issues Hillary is fighting for" and directed readers to a page containing information on Clinton's policy proposals for women and girls.

Headlines on Clinton's website clearly borrowed the attention-grabbing techniques of websites like Buzzfeed and Upworthy.[30] For example, Clinton headlines in 2016 included: "Was this Donald Trump's worst week ever?," "How easy is it for a convicted felon to get a gun?," and "Read the letter this Republican wrote to his daughter about Hillary Clinton."

Clinton's team attempted to humanize the candidate and use humor and personal stories to soften a candidate who was disliked by many.[31] For example, Hillary Clinton's debut Instagram post, an image of a rack of pant suits with the text "Hard choices," employed the title of her memoir to play on gender expectations and poke fun at her stereotypical clothing choices. Clinton's Twitter profile description was similarly self-deprecating: "Wife, grandma, women + kids advocate, FLOTUS, Senator, SecState, hair icon, pants suit aficionado, 2016 presidential candidate." Clinton's website told the story of how Bill and Hillary Clinton fell in love through vintage photos and included a regular series, called "Quick Question" that seemingly caught the candidate spontaneously discussing light topics, like what it is like to watch football in the Clinton household.

Clinton went to great lengths to create this image and uniquely embraced the burgeoning podcast medium with her own podcast titled, "With Her," that topped the iTunes news and politics podcast chart when it launched. On the podcast, host Max Linsky, co-founder of the popular app and website Longform, described himself as "a huge supporter of Secretary Clinton" and warns listeners that he will not be impartial. The podcast was clearly an attempt to make Clinton more relatable. For example, in the first episode, Linsky asked Clinton what an average day is like, what ringtone she uses on her phone, what dinner she likes at the end of a long day, and what she thinks about before falling asleep. In response to the last question, Clinton replied, "Well, probably my grandchildren. I Facetime with them and lots of times on the plane when I just can't think about anything else because I'm just so burnt out, I'll take my phone out and look at all the little videos and the pictures and put a smile on my face and then collapse."

This humanization strategy was not entirely successful and Clinton's digital staff took some time to get their footing. "The team was struggling cultivating a voice for Clinton at the very beginning, as evidenced in her awkward attempt on Twitter last August, asking followers to tell how they feel about their student loan debt in three emojis or less," Yuyu Chen criticized.[32] Likewise, when Clinton released a short Vine video saying, awkwardly and unconvincingly, "I'm just chillin' in Cedar Rapids," Internet commenters attacked with a wave of counter videos and critical posts.

Clinton also struggled to generate emotion and enthusiasm in both the primary and general election. "While stories were legion about the enthusiasm of the Sanders and Trump voters, Hillary Clinton struggled to build deep brand loyalty partly because of a lack of emotion that went right down to the hashtag: #ImWithHer."[33] While the "I'm with her" message is a public statement of support and invokes the gendered nature of the race, it also suggests a concession vote as if to say, "I am with her, but don't love her." Trump's grand message envisioned what he was going to do for the country, Clinton's message emphasized what America would do for her. She presented herself as an upholder of the status quo and a third term of the Obama administration, but this stability messaging was limiting in a contest when many voters were demanding change.

Clinton was perhaps most successful when using social media tools to go on the attack. In June of 2016, for example, after President Obama endorsed Clinton, Trump tweeted "Obama just endorsed Crooked Hillary. He wants four more years of Obama—but nobody else does!" Five minutes later, the Clinton campaign tersely tweeted back "Delete your account," borrowing the popular online expression that is the online equivalent of colloquialism like "kill yourself." Twitter exploded as the post became a globally trending topic on Twitter and users responded with often humorous text-, GIF-, and emoji-filled posts. Ultimately, the "Delete your account" response was retweeted over 550,000 times, gained over 700,000 likes, and kicked off the popular hashtag #DeleteYourAccount. A similar on-the-attack success for Clinton was a Facebook app called TrumpYourself that allowed users to overlay controversial statements from Trump atop their Facebook profile photos. "In its first day and a half, the site had 1.2 million page views from over 800,000 unique visitors. Half of those people authorized their account to be connected to the app—granting access to their data to the Clinton campaign."[34]

There were many ways in which Trump and Clinton diverged in their social media use. Jennifer Stromer-Galley computationally analyzed Trump and Clinton's Twitter and Facebook posts and found there were stark differences in the ways Trump and Clinton used social media.[35] Clinton posted three times as many messages as Trump about issues, such as the economy, education, and women's issues. While Clinton's posts routinely provided facts and backing for her positions, Trump's posts were characterized as broad generalizations or generic claims with little evidence. Additionally, as Issie Lapowsky described, "Where Clinton's team is using scratch-built tools to shave off time for volunteers and staffers and make her ground game more efficient, Trump is running a national strategy, using television and social media to get his message into every household."[36] In the end, the power of Trump's message and his mastery of Twitter, Facebook, and Instagram outperformed Clinton in the electoral college.

DONALD TRUMP SOCIAL MEDIA USE IN THE 2016 CAMPAIGN

After officially announcing his candidacy for the presidency on June 16, 2015, the billionaire real estate mogul and reality television star's campaign began to gain traction and the momentum continued. As the campaign expanded, Donald Trump's son-in-law, Jared Kushner, also a real estate and newspaper mogul with a net worth exceeding $200 million, began playing a prominent role in the campaign overseeing the Republican nominee's campaign strategy. Ever the businessman, Kushner's primary strategy was to focus on the best return on investment (ROI) by getting the most electoral votes for the least amount of money and social media was a key way to achieve that ROI goal. Describing Kushner's strategy, *Forbes* reported: "Unschooled in traditional campaigning, he was able to look at the business of politics the way so many Silicon Valley entrepreneurs have sized up other bloated industries. Television and online advertising? Small and smaller. Twitter and Facebook would fuel the campaign, as key tools for not only spreading Trump's message but also targeting potential supporters, scraping massive amounts of constituent data and sensing shifts in sentiment in real time."[37]

The Trump campaign not only utilized social media, but also utilized big data for fundraising, messaging, and targeting all from a characterless building outside of San Antonio, Texas.[38] Big data combined with social media allowed the campaign insight into issues that mattered most to voters in specific locations around the nation and within specific demographic groups. Interestingly, *Forbes* reported the campaign was able "to map voter universes and identify which parts of the Trump platform mattered most: trade, immigration or change. Tools like Deep Root drove the scaled-back TV ad spending by identifying shows popular with specific voter blocks in specific regions—say, *NCIS* for anti-Obamacare voters or *The Walking Dead* for people worried about immigration. Kushner built a custom geo-location tool that plotted the location density of about 20 voter types over a live Google Maps interface."[39] Kushner and other Trump campaign staff used this system of big data and social media to determine nearly everything for the campaign, including travel, fundraising, advertising, rally locations, and speech topics. *Forbes* succinctly summed up the winning campaign strategy: "For those who can't understand how Hillary Clinton could win the popular vote by at least 2 million yet lose handily in the electoral college, perhaps this provides some clarity. If the campaign's overarching sentiment was fear and anger, the deciding factor at the end was data and entrepreneurship."[40]

SOCIAL MEDIA PLATFORMS AND STRATEGIES IN 2016

Twitter

The brash and braggadocio New York Republican presidential candidate and the 2016 campaign he operated will likely be remembered by the candidate's divisive, damning, and demeaning rhetoric using social media, particularly Twitter, to attack his opponents and anyone else who dared say anything unsupportive of him. His Twitter account, @realDonaldTrump, was created May 4, 2009, many years before his run for the White House. But, once he announced his bid for the presidency, he witnessed an impressive spike in followers as well as an increase in having his posts retweeted.[41] He was not timid about his tweeting prowess declaring, for example: "I understand social media. Maybe better than anybody, ever. Somebody said I'm the Ernest Hemmingway of 140 characters."[42] His campaign will also likely be remembered for the amount of inaccurate information posted to Twitter and other social media sites. *The Guardian* stated: "Trump's main medium is the Internet—and the Internet is a place where lies quite comfortably live."[43]

Accordingly, "fake news" full of misinformation dominated the 2016 presidential election on social media platforms and was "shared" and "liked" and "retweeted" many times perpetuating the inaccurate news. *Wired* reporter, Issie Lapowsky, stated: "this last year in American media has been rougher than most. The election inspired more than the usual amount of tribalism online, and citizens' trust in traditional media fell to an all-time low: just 32 percent told Gallup they have a great deal or fair amount of trust in the media. This lack of trust formed the perfect petri dish in which a plague of misinformation could fester and bloom."[44] The 2016 campaign saw the emergence of extremely partisan websites that focused on publishing content that reinforced people's existing beliefs— whether those beliefs were true or not. This inaccurate information got passed along on social media platforms. As Matt Kapko asserted: "Much of today's political discourse starts on social media, and the medium often amplifies vitriol and slants information."[45] While rumor and innuendo has always been a part of politics, Oxford's Phil Howard hypothesized that the sharing function of social media gave it additional import in 2016: "Social media platforms have provided a structure for spreading around fake news, we users tend to trust our friends and family, and we don't hold media technology firms accountable for degrading our public conversations."[46] The fake news crisis has prompted Facebook to declare that hoax sites will not be permitted to advertise on its platform in the future.[47]

Trackalytics.com reveals that on June 12, 2014, Trump had more than 2.6 million followers and by Election Day, November 8, 2016, he had more than 13 million followers (see Figs. 5.1 and 5.2) compared to Clinton's more than 10 million followers.[48] As noted earlier, he had more followers than television networks had nightly viewers and more

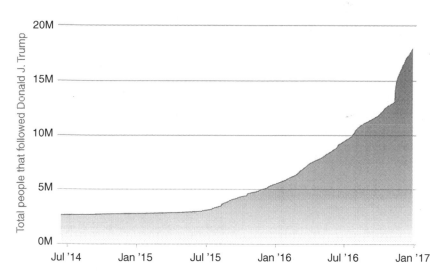

Fig. 5.1   Total people that followed Donald J. Trump on Twitter
Source: Trackalytics

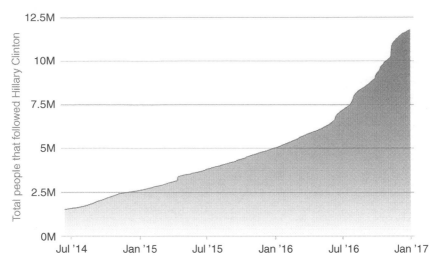

Fig. 5.2 Total people that followed Hillary Clinton on Twitter

Source: Trackalytics

followers than newspapers had daily readers, allowing him to bypass mainstream media altogether. His followers on Twitter were also dedicated as they frequently "liked" and "retweeted" Trump's tweets, thus amplifying his message many times over. *Politico* reported the average number of retweets Trump received in January 2015 was about 79, but only a year later that jumped to more than 2,000 retweets per post. Hence, *Politico* proclaimed, "It's clear Trump's Twitter feed offers him a tool for direct access to voters, who then amplify that access by retweeting him at remarkable rates."[49] With more than 18 million Twitter followers as of December 2016, Trump had a powerful platform to communicate to Americans what his positions were and attack opponents who dared disagree with him.[50]

It is yet to be determined if and how often he personally will tweet as President even though he declares he will continue tweeting. Traditionally, presidents have a team of media experts who handle messaging for the White House. It would be unprecedented to have the leader of the free world carrying around a smartphone posting 140-character missives on a smartphone app. In a postelection interview with the television program

60 Minutes, President-elect Trump declared that he would indeed continue tweeting as President but would "be very restrained." Trump told Lesley Stahl, "I won. I think that social media has more power than the money [his opponents] spent, and I think maybe to a certain extent, I proved that."[51] Intriguingly, at 18.2 million followers as of a month prior to his Inauguration, Donald Trump's @realDonaldTrump account had more Twitter followers than Barack Obama's @POTUS account, which had a little less than 13 million followers (see Fig. 5.3).

Even before declaring his candidacy for the presidency, as early as 2012, Trump used Twitter to promote what would eventually become his campaign slogan—"Make America Great Again" and the accompanying hashtag #MAGA.[52] The same slogan was originally used by Ronald Reagan in 1980 when he successfully ran for president. Trump cleverly used social media to his campaign's advantage by capitalizing on the anger that existed in a large portion of the 2016 American electorate and aggressively promoted a populist agenda. "A vote for Trump was a vote for change back to an America in which working class Americans could make good money, everyone spoke English, law and order prevailed, and the country

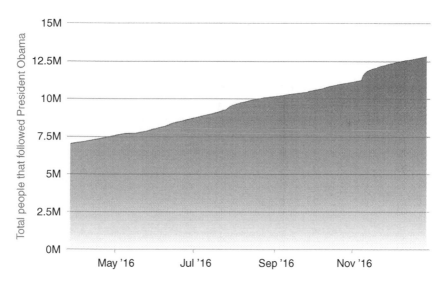

Fig. 5.3   Total people that followed President Obama on Twitter

Source: Trackalytics

was feared and respected around the world," summarized Ken Cosgrove.[53] In fact, he was labeled a "modern social media master."[54] His social media strategy proved to be successful in garnering free media coverage as well as gaining followers who actually planned to vote for the candidate. MediaQuant, an analytics firm, estimated that Trump received more than $3.4 billion in free media coverage with about $372 million alone just from traditional media outlets covering his outlandish, attention-grabbing tweets.[55] Comparatively, Hillary Clinton received only $1.4 billion in free media with only $93 million of free media being generated from her tweets.[56]

The attention-grabbing tweets were frequent and prolific throughout the campaign, often several missives fired off consecutively throughout the day and night containing policy stances as well as personal insults. The "Trump Twitter Archive" indicates that he has tweeted more than 30,000 times since he started his account.[57] *The New York Times* estimated that about 1 in 8 tweets made by the candidate and president-elect were personal insults.[58] Despite not having a computer in his office, Trump asserted he personally does the tweeting in the evenings and during the night, but has "one of the young ladies" working in his office tweet what he "shouts out" during the day.[59] Trump's tweets dominated complete news cycles and, as noted by *Politico*, they were "a surprisingly effective strategy that saw him drive entire news cycles merely by blasting out choppy pronouncements on his Samsung Galaxy smartphone, often at odd hours."[60]

In addition to the staff in Trump's office, Dan Scavino—Trump's former golf caddy who served in that role during high school and college, but later worked his way up through the Trump Organization—oversaw all of the presidential campaign's social media operations. Beginning July 2015, Scavino served as the director of social media for the Trump campaign and served in the same role of the president-elect's transition team.[61] He shadowed Trump and managed all of the social media platforms in the campaign's arsenal. He would average 8–15 Facebook posts a day, 1–3 Instagram posts per day, and many tweets per day that were dictated to him by Trump.[62] In addition to Scavino's role as director of Trump's social media, Justin McConney worked as the director of new media at the Trump Organization and provided guidance on how to best leverage these social media platforms. McConney began serving in that position February 2011 and *Politico* reported: "It is McConney who has pushed the businessman to deliberately build a social-media presence and experiment with new platforms and types of content."[63] Scavino shared with *Breitbart News* that Trump's appeal to voters was the fact that he was not a scripted politician and, instead, was authentic on social media. Scavino said: "People across the country... were looking for someone who was human, not a scripted politician. They got that in Trump, and given the industry-wide failures of the corporate media throughout the election cycle to accurately report the news, Trump's social media operation filled the void."[64]

Although the insults that Trump tweeted at his opponents were unorthodox, the content of many of his tweets did include more traditional information that usually comes from political campaigns such as polling information, pitches to purchase his book, future campaign stops, crowd sizes, upcoming television appearances, and well wishes to victims when terrorist attacks occurred such as those in Paris. Regarding the substance of Trump's tweets, *Politico* reported: "Trump's social media game is a bewildering blend of brash and bland. But overall, his Twitter feed is an astonishing campaign lesson in how to command the world's biggest stage: the Internet."[65] As noted, the Twitter feed of the real estate mogul was full of insults and attacks that a traditional politician would never say publicly, much less post on social media for millions to read. Poignantly, *Politico* reporter Joe Keohane concluded: "The things @realDonaldTrump hits others for are the things the real man is most defensive about: his intelligence, his success, his appearance, his body (be it in terms of stamina or various forms of endowment). By the end of my Trump Twitter immersion, I was sure that the reason @realDonaldTrump uses these insults is that he thinks they are the most hurtful things you can possibly say about another person. And that's because they are the most hurtful things you can say about Donald J. Trump."[66]

Undeniably, Trump's social media strategy was effective in getting *his* message to *his* followers and generating free media coverage for *his* campaign, leading *Politico* to assert, "@realDonaldTrump is a force, a newsmaker, an agitator, an American political phenomenon that combines the high profile of a presidential candidate with the reach and velocity of social media... It is a thing."[67] Moreover, compared to the large social media teams of the 2008 and 2012 presidential campaigns, it was a very small and efficient apparatus. Confirming the Trump social media team was not a large operation, Scavino suggested it capitalized on the work of the campaign's social media followers. *The New York Times* reported: "In the absence of a large, organized online operation, the Trump campaign has leaned on its candidate's huge following on social media, where supporters share links and photos, argue on his behalf and spread his views to friends and family. But if major social media platforms are where Mr. Trump amplifies his pronouncements, sites like Reddit and 4chan have become a sort of proving ground, where an extreme, Internet-amped version of Mr. Trump's message is shared and refined."[68]

Reddit

In addition to Twitter, the Trump campaign utilized other social media platforms, including Reddit. Reddit is a topic or news aggregator that allows its more than 230 million subscribers to post information to the social media outlet that is then voted on by other subscribers. The content on Reddit is organized into subjects and are called subreddits. The topics range from news to movies to technology, but of course also includes political subreddits such as "The Donald," that engaged in activities that allowed them to network, discuss and promote the candidacy of Trump. Pew Research Center surveyed Reddit users and found that while just 4% of US adults are Redditors, seven-in-ten Reddit users say they get news on the site and nearly half (45%) report learning about the election on Reddit each week, a share comparable to Facebook and Twitter users.[69] Reddit users are more likely to be younger (59% are 18–29 years old), male (71%), and liberal (47% compared with just 24% of US adults who consider themselves liberal). Further, Pew content analyzed about 165 million Reddit comments from May, June, and September of 2015, and found that Bernie Sanders was the most frequently discussed candidate with 165,000 total comments, followed by Hillary Clinton (85,000 comments), and Donald Trump (73,000 comments). Active commenting was concentrated among a minority of posters as only a quarter of comments made three or more posts. And while posting in explicitly political forums subreddits, such as /r/Politics or /r/SandersForPresident, four-in-ten comments mentioning the presidential candidates were in nonpolitical forums, such as r/atheism and r/LateShow.

Snapchat

Snapchat was the hot new thing in political tech 2016 with 150 million daily users and their own campaign news team headed by Peter Hamby, formerly of CNN. Snapchat was wildly popular with the coveted and hard-to-reach 18-to-34-year-old demographic. On any given day Snapchat reaches 41% of 18-to-34-year-olds in the United States, according to Nielsen.[70] Snapchat said its data indicated that twice as many 18-to-24-year-olds watched the first Republican debate on its app than watched it on television.[71] Candidates used Snapchat to communicate with hard-to-reach younger and millennial generation voters who have largely shunned newspapers, radio, and television news.

In 2016, Americans shifted their attention to video content—especially videos that were pithy, personal, and humorous—and Snapchat rode that trend. By design, users of the app share photo messages with their friends that last for a few seconds and disappear after being viewed by the recipient. A different feature called "stories" allows users to assemble and share "snaps" that are viewable to all of their friends or to the public for 24 hours after posting. Numerous candidates used Snapchat to post behind-the-scenes "stories" each day and show supporters an informal side to their campaign. For example, Democrat Martin O'Malley teased his May 30, 2015, announcement with a series of snaps around Maryland, his home state.

Also influential in 2016 was the app's "Live Stories" feature, which curated several user-submitted video snippets from events and assembled either by users or Snapchat's own production team, such as Hillary Clinton's announcement speech on Roosevelt Island, a Sanders or Trump rally, or the party nominating conventions. Experiencing a political event on Snapchat was a novel experience. Instead of training the camera on the speaker's lectern or pundit's talking heads, Snapchat live stories curated short, impromptu cell phone video snippets and selfies from throughout the crowd, backstage, and protestors outside the event. Live stories were used extensively. Prior to the Iowa Caucus, for example, Republican candidates Scott Walker and John Kasich used Snapchat's live story feature. Walker's sons would post videos and photos to his Snapchat account when they traveled with their dad on the campaign trail.[72]

Ads and image filters also became popular as the app added features during the campaign. Both Trump and Clinton, in addition to numerous primary candidates, purchased Snap Ads, 10-second full-screen videos that played between other content and Snapchat geofilters, text or images that appeared over pictures taken from within a specific geographic area. To generate a sense of authenticity on an app known more for joking with friends than with political appeals, candidates used humor, cartoons, and catchy slogans in their geofilters to grab the attention of users. For example, on the day of the Iowa Caucuses, a geofilter for the Sanders campaign featured a cartoon caricature of Sanders holding a match with the tagline, "Iowa, Are You Ready to Feel The Burn?" In the same vein, when some commentators said John Kasich's campaign logo looked like bacon, the Kasich campaign paid for a geofilter in New Hampshire that depicted its campaign logo made entirely of bacon.

YouTube

YouTube, the video sharing web site, has over a billion users that accounts for almost a third of all Internet users. YouTube was a destination in 2016 and hosted video that was linked from other social media services. After reviewing YouTube's prominence, Drew Harwell concluded that YouTube "has proven even more spellbinding—and powerful—than political campaigns ever imagined" and that three political ads ranked among YouTube's ten most-watched ads for the first time in history in January of 2016.[73]

On YouTube, there were more than 4 billion views of videos pertaining to the candidates in the last 8 months of the campaign, including over 1.2 billion views in the final month.[74] The tracking firm ZEFR found that Trump dominated YouTube views in the primaries and early general election, with Clinton improving and matching or besting Trump from September to October.[75] The most common uploads were late night comedy clips, commentary videos, news clips, debate uploads, live event footage, and parody and satire clips. Hillary Clinton's channel was a mix of campaign ads, attack videos, and longer, more personal videos. For example, a widely shared video that was viewed over 1.3 million times was a narrative ad of Clinton supporter Khizr Khan, whose son was killed in Iraq while serving in the United States Army, questioning if his son would be welcome in Donald Trump's America. The most viewed video on Clinton's channel was a montage ad of young women looking in mirrors juxtaposed with audio and video clips of Trump's demeaning comments towards women and concluding with the text, "Is this the president we want for our daughters?" Donald Trump's YouTube channel featured numerous attack ads and clips of Donald Trump explaining his policies by talking directly to the camera in his Trump Tower office. For the most part, Trump's YouTube content was less produced than Clinton's and was more likely to be simple clips of speeches or debates.

Instagram

As previously mentioned, Instagram is the second most popular social media service with over 500 million active monthly users and Trump and Clinton intensely fought for votes on this platform. While both campaigns were active, Trump bested Clinton on Instagram with over 1,300 posts and 4.5 million followers, compared to Clinton's 835 posts and 4.5 million followers.[76] And both campaigns mixed Instagram's conventional photo-sharing with their own voice and communication tactics. On the one hand, Clinton's Instagram profile wryly described her as a "Doting grandmother, among other things" and relied on superimposing inspiring quotes and slogans over dramatic campaign photos and videos and historic photos documenting Clinton's long career in public service. On the other hand, while Trump also included pictures of crowds from his rallies, photos of his children, and quotes laid over of him on the stump, and stills from news stories showing him ahead in polls, Trump created a new form of political messaging: the Instagram attack ad. Trump's Instagram account often used harsh and simply produced 15-second barrages against his primary opponents and later Clinton. In the primaries, Trump broke norms on the service by posting campaign-style short videos attacking Jeb Bush's support for the Iraq War and posting a video of Jeb's mother, Barbara, discouraging him from running for president. *National Public Radio's* Sam Sanders asserted: "Instagram, which for national politicians at least, has moved from the app you used to share photos of your food with good friends, to a new forum for political attack videos."[77] These videos were spearheaded by McConney, who would meet with Trump each morning to discuss what video would be posted on social media that particular day and then Trump would write it.[78] The short videos are also posted to Trump's Facebook, Twitter, and Vine accounts.[79]

The photographic style of Instagram and social media in general has influenced the way candidates are visually depicted. Marvin Heiferman considered this change: "Traditional photojournalism once dominated campaign coverage. Candidates strove to appear 'presidential' in staged or stately images, which were then published in weekly picture magazines and daily newspapers or broadcast on the nightly television newscast. With the growth of social media, which offers a round-the-clock stream of information both serious and trivial.... On Instagram, for example, their images pop up among pictures of friends, vacations and pets."[80]

Facebook

Facebook is "the single most important tool of the digital campaign"[81] because of its reach and targeting abilities. Statistica.com and the Pew Research Center reported that nearly 80% of the United States adult population had a social media profile on Facebook.[82] And, Facebook is ubiquitous as more than 123 million users access Facebook via smartphones.[83] Every major contender and significant Political Action Committee (PAC) has a strong Facebook presence and purchased ads on the service in 2016. Facebook actively sought the business of politicians during the 2016 campaign by promoting new tools and capabilities that were beneficial to the political campaigns. *The New York Times* reported: "Since 2012, Facebook has doubled its government and politics team, which includes a political ad sales group, a data communications team and employees devoted solely to Democrats or Republicans."[84] For instance, taking advantage of this, Governor Scott Walker's presidential campaign team worked closely with the representatives at Facebook leading up to his presidential campaign announcement to ensure that all capabilities Facebook had to offer were being employed to maximum effect.[85] Facebook improved its video delivery and question/answer capabilities specifically for political campaigns and there was an explosion of video content on Facebook in 2016. Specifically, when the video viewing capability was introduced to Facebook in 2014, users engaged in a billion video views a day and that number quadrupled by 2016. While Trump did spend less on television advertising, he spent significantly more on Facebook video ads: "Trump's campaign embraced Facebook as a key advertising channel in a way that no presidential campaign has before— not even Clinton's."[86]

Compared to other social media platforms, Facebook is unique in the amount of data it gathers on users, such as gender, age, location, and interests. Through partnerships with big data firms, the site also layers a trove of behavioral information onto Facebook profiles, including shopping habits.[87] Facebook essentially knows everything users do and then attempts to determine what their political preferences are based upon their online activity, which is highly beneficial to campaigns. Most importantly, campaigns can pinpoint individual voters at the most granular of levels and tailor messages to voters based on the issues and appeals that will be most likely to resonate with each individual voter. Describing this microtargeting, Shane Golmacher observed in the *National Journal*: "Candidates can upload their databases of donor emails, find their corresponding profiles on the site, and ask Facebook to spit out ads to a 'look-alike' universe of users whom they haven't yet pitched for money. Or they can take the sign-ups from an event, upload them, and ask to advertise to people who look like them."[88]

As with Twitter and the other social networking services, the Trump campaign also outperformed the Clinton campaign on Facebook. On November 8, 2016, Election Day in America, Trump had 12.2 million Facebook followers compared to Clinton's 8.2 million followers (see Figs. 5.4 and 5.5). Not only did Trump have more Facebook followers but his Facebook page had more "engagement" from his followers than Clinton received from her followers. In October 2016, Trump made 327 posts to Facebook compared to Clinton's 302 posts.[89] Facebook was central in Trump's fundraising operation as Facebook appeals generated the bulk of the campaign's $250 million in online fundraising.[90] Additionally, Trump overpowered Clinton in terms of using Facebook's new Live Video streaming function. Specifically, "Trump used Live to flood voters across the country with notifications about 21 broadcasts in the last four days of the campaign (amassing 45 million views), while Clinton used that Facebook

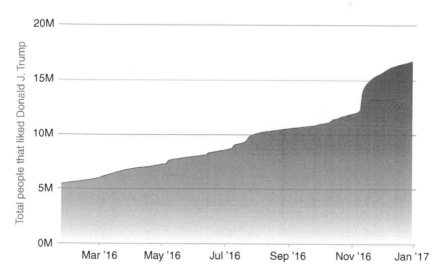

Fig. 5.4   Total people that liked Donald J. Trump on Facebook

Source: Trackalytics

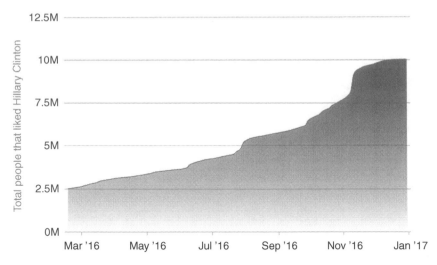

Fig. 5.5   Total people that liked Hillary Clinton on Facebook

Source: Trackalytics

function 3 times in the same stretch (with only 14 million views)."[91] The Trump campaign's social media strategy worked on many platforms, but it especially worked with Facebook. Based upon an analysis of algorithms of the timing of posts and types of posts, *EzyInsights.com* asserted: "It is fair to assume that Trump has personnel with a high level of expertise when it comes to taking advantage of Facebook engagement and reach. The campaign is behaving like a media entity rather than a politician's fan page."[92] Moreover, based upon Facebook analytics, it was determined: "Here is one area where without a doubt, Donald Trump's campaign has utterly trounced Hillary Clinton's."[93]

LinkedIn

The most neglected social media service of 2016 was LinkedIn.[94] In the middle of the primaries, while several of the candidates had pages, they were mostly neglected and incomplete. Ben Carson, for example, had a short page with no picture and just 23 networking connections. Rick Santorum and Rand Paul pages were largely blank other than saying they were running for president and neither had connections. Donald Trump did not use the service at all. The lone exception was Hillary Clinton, who not only had a complete profile on the site, but whose campaign also posted forty-two "LinkedIN Influencer" posts on everything from her plan to improve small businesses to why she campaigned in a bowling alley. User engagement with these posts was relatively small, with each post garnering about two to five thousand views and a few hundred comments. Clinton's Influencer post on the water crisis in Flint, Michigan did break through with nearly half a million views.

CONCLUSION

As this chapter has documented, without doubt, social media and digital communication were critical in the 2016 race for the White House, but it is an overstatement to claim that social media elected Donald Trump. Scholar Daniel Kreiss described it well:

> The Internet did not bring about a 'post-fact' or 'post truth' era, nor did it bring about conspiracy theories, white nationalism, conservative identity and its farcical villains, and the distrust of institutionalized ways of produ- cing knowledge, from journalism to science.... The uptake of social media likely has given broader exposure to the particular mix of racial resentment, conservative identity, populist rhetoric, and economic anxiousness that marked the 2016 U.S. presidential election and afforded it greater visibility, but it did not cause them.... And, while social media might increase the speed of half-truths, rumors, and outright lies, it did not create the cynical public that does not understand, or care to, how knowledge producing institutions work.[95]

The tools of social media *hastened* the transformation in our discourse, but did not *cause* the disruption in isolation. In a democracy, the citizenry, news media, and elected officials work together—including through com- munication—to create and maintain a public sphere. And the type of public talk exhibited on our social media platforms in 2016 emerged because it served instrumental functions for various actors in these groups. Only time will tell if the trends that begun in 2016 continue or if they were a historical aberration having to do with distinct factors in the Trump- Clinton race and the electorate.

Notes

1. Shannon Greenwood, Andrew Perrin and Maeve Duggan. "Social Media Update 2016: Facebook Usage and Engagement is on the Rise, While Adoption of Other Platforms Holds Steady," *Pew Research Center*, November 11, 2016, http://pewrsr.ch/2fiOTBE.
2. Keely Lockhart, "Watch: Why Social Media is Donald Trump's Most Powerful Weapon," *The [London] Telegraph*, September 22, 2016, http://www.telegraph.co.uk/news/2016/09/22/watch-why-social-media-is-donald-trumps-most-powerful-weapon/.
3. David McCabe, "Welcome to the Social Media Election," *The Hill*, August 17, 2015, http://thehill.com/policy/technology/251185-welcome-to-the-social-media-election.
4. Michael Slaby, "The New Normal: Digital Defines Presidential Campaigns," *The Hill*, http://thehill.com/blogs/pundits-blog/presidential-campaign/300535-the-new-normal-digital-defines-and-revolutionizes.
5. Jim Ruttenberg, "In This Snapchat Campaign, Election News Is Big and Then It's Gone," *New York Times*, April 24, 2016, http://nyti.ms/1qKDtsi.
6. Michael X. Delli Carpini, "The New Normal? Campaigns and Elections in the Contemporary Media Environment," *U.S. Election Analysis 2016*, http://www.electionanalysis2016.us/us-election-analysis-2016/section-1-media/the-new-normal-campaigns-elections-in-the-contemporary-media-environment/.
7. Nicholas Cass, "How Social Media Is Ruining Politics," *Politico Magazine*, September 2, 2015, http://www.politico.com/magazine/story/2015/09/2016-election-social-media-ruining-politics-213104.
8. Marc Fisher, "How Donald Trump Broke the Old Rules of Politics—and Won the White House," *Washington Post*, November 9, 2015, http://wpo.st/eN1P2.
9. Cass, "How Social Media."
10. Ross Douthat, "Confessions of a Columnist," *New York Times*, December 31, 2016, http://nyti.ms/2iQmvWb.
11. Seth C. Lewis and Matt Carlson, "The dissolution of News: Selective Exposure, Filter Bubbles, and the Boundaries of Journalism," *U.S. Election Analysis 2016*, http://www.electionanalysis2016.us/us-election-analysis-2016/section-6-internet/the-dissolution-of-news-selective-exposure-filter-bubbles-and-the-boundaries-of-journalism/.
12. Laeeq Khan, "Trump Won Thanks to Social Media," *The Hill*, November 15, 2016, http://thehill.com/blogs/pundits-blog/technology/306175-trump-won-thanks-to-social-media.

13. quoted in Ruttenberg, "In This Snapchat Campaign."
14. Ruttenberg, "In This Snapchat Campaign."
15. Jim Hoft, "Social Media Patterns Show Trump Is Looking at a Landslide Victory," *The Gateway Pundit*, August 7, 2016, http://www.thegateway pundit.com/2016/08/evidence-trump-landslide/.
16. A. J. Katz, "2016 Ratings: Fox News Channel is Cable TV's Most-Watched Network," *Adweek*, December 28, 2016, http://adweek.it/2hOrw15.
17. A. J. Katz, "2016 Ratings: CNN Has Most-Watched Year Ever," *Adweek*, December 28, 2016, http://adweek.it/2hHVVB8.
18. A. J. Katz, "2016 Ratings: MSNBC Weekday Shows Deliver Record Ratings," *Adweek*, December 28, 2016, http://adweek.it/2hx9ODc.
19. Nicholas Mirzoeff, "How Donald Trump Broke the Media," *The Conversation*, March 4, 2016, http://theconversation.com/how-donald-trump-broke-the-media-55693.
20. Issie Lapowsky, "Here's How Facebook Actually Won Trump the Presidency," *Wired*, November 15, 2016, https://www.wired.com/2016/11/facebook-won-trump-election-not-just-fake-news/.
21. Jacob Pramuk, "Trump Spent about Half of what Clinton did on his way to the Presidency," *CNBC*, November 9, 2016, http://cnb.cx/2fCzwT9.
22. Lapowsky, "Here's How Facebook."
23. Maggie Haberman and Jonathan Martin, "Donald Trump Scraps the Usual Campaign Playbook, Including TV Ads," *New York Times*, December 24, 2015, http://nyti.ms/1TjtmU3.
24. Darren Samuelsohn, "Hillary's Nerd Squad," *Politico*, March 25, 2015, http://politi.co/1NhnFSl.
25. Ashley Codianni, "Inside Hillary Clinton's Digital Operation," *CNN.com*, August 25, 2015, http://cnn.it/1IbSmVJ.
26. Ibid.
27. Sara Ashley O'Brien, "Can Hillary Clinton Emojis Win Over the Snapchat Generation?", *CNNMoney*, June 30, 2016, http://cnnmon.ie/298rTTo.
28. Clare Foran, "Clinton's End-Run Around the Press," *The Atlantic*, August 17, 2016, http://www.theatlantic.com/politics/archive/2016/08/hillary-clinton-media-press-conferences/495965/.
29. Heidi M. Przybyla, "Clinton Media Campaign Follows Buzzfeed Model," *USA Today*, January 18, 2016, http://usat.ly/1RwwqyT.
30. Natalie Andrews, "On Social Media, Hillary Clinton and Donald Trump Have Different Styles," *Wall Street Journal*, July 28, 2016, http://on.wsj.com/2ajE0tL.
31. Rebecca Ruiz, "How the Clinton Campaign Is Slaying Social Media," *Mashable*, July 25, 2016, http://mashable.com/2016/07/25/inside-social-media-hillary-clinton/.

32. Yuyu Chen, "#ImWithHer: Inside the Clinton Campaign's Social Strategy, *Digiday*, September 26, 2016, http://digiday.com/brands/imwithher-look-inside-clinton-campaigns-social-strategy/.

33. Ken Cosgrove, "The Emotional Brand Wins," *U. S. Election Analysis 2016*, http://www.electionanalysis2016.us/us-election-analysis-2016/section-2-campaign/the-emotional-brand-wins/.

34. Andrews, "On Social Media."

35. Jennifer Stromer-Galley, "In The Age of Social Media, Voters Still Need Journalists," *U. S. Election Analysis 2016*, http://www.electionanaly sis2016.us/us-election-analysis-2016/section-6-internet/in-the-age-of-social-media-voters-still-need-journalists/.

36. Issie Lapowsky, "Clinton Has a Team of Silicon Valley Stars. Trump Has Twitter," Wired, July 14, 2016, https://www.wired.com/2016/07/clin ton-team-silicon-valley-stars-trump-twitter/.

37. Steven Bertoni, "Exclusive Interview: How Jared Kushner Won Trump The White House," *Forbes*, November 22, 2016, http://www.forbes.com/sites/stevenbertoni/2016/11/22/exclusive-interview-how-jared-kushner-won-trump-the-white-house/.

38. Ibid.

39. Ibid.

40. Ibid.

41. Joe Keohane, "The Cry-Bully: The Sad Mind and Evil Media Genius Behind @realDonaldTrump," *Politico Magazine*, May/June, 2016, http://politi.co/1Wsnhbs.

42. David Sherfinski, "Donald Trump: 'Somebody said I'm the Ernest Hemingway of 140 characters'" *Washington Times*, November 20, 2015, http://go.shr.lc/2hMKaFJ.

43. Hannah Jane Parkinson, "Can Donald Trump's Social Media Genius Take Him all the Way to the White House?" *The Guardian*, December 23, 2015, https://www.theguardian.com/technology/2015/dec/23/donald-trump-social-media-strategy-internet-republican-nomination-president.

44. Lapowsky, "Here's How Facebook."

45. Matt Kapko, "How Social Media Is Shaping the 2016 Presidential Election," *CIO*, September 29, 2016, http://www.cio.com/article/3125120/social-networking/how-social-media-is-shaping-the-2016-presi dential-election.html.

46. Phil Howard, "Is Social Media Killing Democracy," *Culture Digitally*, November 14, 2016, http://culturedigitally.org/2016/11/is-social-media-killing-democracy/.

47. Lapowsky, "Here's How Facebook."

48. *Track Analytics*, "Total People that Followed Donald J. Trump on Twitter," http://www.trackalytics.com/twitter/followers/widget/realdo naldtrump/.

49. Oren Tsur, Katherine Ognyanova and David Lazer, "The Data Behind Trump's Twitter Takeover: Want to Know How @realDonaldTrump became the force it is? We Crunched the Numbers," *Politico Magazine*, April 29, 2016, http://politi.co/21pADWb.

50. @realDonaldTrump, "Donald J. Trump Twitter Account," https://twitter.com/realdonaldtrump.

51. Rebecca Morin, "Trump Says Social Media was Key to Victory," *Politico*, November 11, 2016, http://politi.co/2fmXgMi.

52. Amanda Hess, "How Trump Wins Twitter: Everyone Knows He's the Best on Social Media. Here's Why," *Slate*, February 18, 2016, http://www.slate.com/articles/technology/future_tense/2016/02/donald_trump_is_the_best_at_twitter_here_s_why.html.

53. Cosgrove, "The Emotional Brand."

54. Hess, "How Trump Wins."

55. Darren Samuelsohn, "Trump's Twitter Army: New Data Show the GOP Nominee's Followers are Exactly What the Dems Hoped they Weren't— Reliable Voters," *Politico*, June 15, 2016, http://politi.co/24QmtOC.

56. Ibid.

57. Jasmine C. Lee and Kevin Quealy, "Introducing the Upshot's Encyclopedia of Donald Trump's Twitter Insults," *New York Times*, January 28, 2016, http://nyti.ms/1OSZpJw.

58. Ibid.

59. Samuelsohn, "Trump's Twitter Army."

60. Nolan D. McCaskill, "Donald Trump's Year of Tweeting Dangerously: We Read Every Tweet of his 2015 Campaign. And what we Learned Might Surprise You," *Politico*, January 1, 2016, http://politi.co/1mnXVxB.

61. Erik Sherman, "Two Trump Insiders Behind the Campaign's Social Network Explosion," *Fortune*, March 25, 2016, http://fortune.com/2016/03/25/trump-scavino-mcconney-social-media.

62. Matthew Boyle, "Exclusive—Under the Hood: How Donald Trump Has Cut Around Corporate Media to Reach Millions Directly Online," *Breitbart*, November 29, 2016, http://www.breitbart.com/big-govern ment/2016/11/29/exclusive-how-trump-bypasses-corporate-media-reach-millions/.

63. Ben Schreckinger, "Meet the Man Who Makes Donald Trump Go Viral: Justin McConney Spearheaded This Cycle's Biggest Innovation: The 15-second Instagram Attack Ad," *Politico*, October 1, 2015, http://politi.co/1JFqk5C.

64. Boyle, "Exclusive—Under the Hood."
65. McCaskill, "Donald Trump's Year."
66. Joe Keohane, "The Cry-Bully."
67. Ibid.
68. John Herrman, "Donald Trump Finds Support in Reddit's Unruly Corners," *New York Times*, April 8, 2016, http://nyti.ms/25PvHhe.
69. Michael Bathel, "How the 2016 Presidential Campaign Is Being Discussed on Reddit," Pew Research Center, May 26, 2016, http://pewrsr.ch/1Z2JCf3.
70. Nicole Piper, "Snapchat Lures More Campaign Spending as Candidates Court Young Voters," Bloomberg Technology, August 25, 2016, http://bloom.bg/2bIMcqn.
71. Jim Ruttenberg, "In This Snapchat Campaign, Election News Is Big and Then It's Gone," New York Times, April 24, 2016, http://nyti.ms/1qKDtsi.
72. Philip Rucker, "Snapchat Steps into 2016 Campaign with Iowa 'Live Story' and Kasich, Walker Ads," *Washington Post*, July 16, 2015, http://wpo.st/Er_P2.
73. Drew Harwell, "How YouTube is Shaping the 2016 Presidential Election," Washington Post, March 25, 2016, http://wpo.st/gwUP2.
74. Todd Longwell, "Which Candidate is Winning the Race on YouTube in the Home Stretch?", ZEFR Insights, November 4, 2016, http://blog.zefr.com/which-candidate-is-winning-the-race-on-youtube-in-the-home-stretch/.
75. Ibid.
76. Hillary Clinton Instagram Account, @HillaryClinton, https://www.instagram.com/hillaryclinton/; Donald Trump Instagram Account, @RealDonaldTrump, https://www.instagram.com/realdonaldtrump/.
77. Sam Sanders, "Instagram: The New Political War Room?" NPR Morning Edition, September 3, 2015, https://n.pr/1O997G8.
78. Sherman, "Two Trump Insiders."
79. Parkinson, "Can Donald Trump's Social."
80. Marvin Heiferman, "On the Instagram Presidential Campaign Trail," New York Times, September 15, 2015, http://nyti.ms/1idSfn7.
81. Shane Goldmacher, "Facebook the Vote," *National Journal*, June 12, 2015, https://www.nationaljournal.com/s/25829/is-facebook-holy-grail-political-advertising.
82. *Statista*, "Percentage of U.S. population with a social media profile from 2008 to 2016," https://www.statista.com/statistics/273476/percentage-of-us-population-with-a-social-network-profile/.
83. *Statista*, "Most popular mobile social networking apps in the United States as of November 2016, by monthly users (in millions)," https://www.

statista.com/statistics/248074/most-popular-us-social-networking-apps-ranked-by-audience/.

84. Ashley Parker, "Facebook Expands in Politics, and Campaigns Find Much to Like," *New York Times*, July 29, 2015, http://nyti.ms/1IJnpyK.
85. Ibid.
86. Lapowsky, "Here's How Facebook."
87. Goldmacher, "Facebook the Vote."
88. Ibid.
89. Steve El-Sharawy, "Donald Trump as President? Thank Facebook," *EZY Insights*, November 1, 2016, https://ezyinsights.com/blog/2016/11/01/donald-trump-as-president-thank-facebook/.
90. Lapowsky, "Here's How Facebook."
91. Alan Rosenblatt, "What Did Hillary Clinton Leave on The Social Media Table?", *Huffington Post*, December 12, 2016, http://www.huffingtonpost.com/entry/what-did-hillary-clinton-leave-on-the-social-media_us_58419d99e4b04587de5de94d.
92. El-Sharawy, "Donald Trump as President."
93. Ibid.
94. Eliza Collins, "LinkedIn: The Saddest Social Network of the 2016 Campaign," *Politico*, July 17, 2015, http://politi.co/1MfQWAM.
95. Daniel Kriess, "Social Media Did Not Give Us Donald Trump and It Is Not Weakening Democracy," *U. S. Election Analysis 2016*, http://www.electionanalysis2016.us/us-election-analysis-2016/section-6-internet/social-media-did-not-give-us-donald-trump-and-it-is-not-weakening-democracy/.

John Allen Hendricks has published more than ten books on media/politics, social media, and the broadcasting industry. His most recent books include *Communication and Midterm Elections: Media, Message, and Mobilization* (coedited with Dan Schill) and *Presidential Campaigning and Social Media: An Analysis of the 2012 Campaign* (coedited with Dan Schill). His book *Communicator-in-Chief: How Barack Obama Used New Media Technology to Win the White House* (coedited with Robert E. Denton, Jr.) was the recipient of the National Communication Association's Applied Research Division's 2011 Distinguished Scholarly Book Award. He has been a professor and chairman of the Department of Mass Communication at Stephen F. Austin State University since 2009.

Dan Schill is an associate professor in the School of Communication Studies and affiliate professor in political science at James Madison University, where he teaches courses in advocacy, political communication, research methods, and media and politics. He has published four books on political communication topics, including *Political Communication in Real Time* (with Rita Kirk and

Amy Jasperson, Routledge, 2017), *Communication and Midterm Elections* (with John Allen Hendricks; Palgrave Macmillan, 2015), and *Presidential Campaigning and Social Media* (with John Allen Hendricks; Oxford University Press, 2014). In addition to his academic research, he frequently conducts research for media outlets with frequent collaborator Dr. Rita Kirk. In the 2008, 2012, and 2016 presidential campaigns, he organized and moderated on-air dial focus groups for CNN and provided real-time analysis of debates, convention speeches, and campaign ads.

Studies of Communication in the 2016 Presidential Campaign

Trump as Troll: Personae and Persuasive Inoculation in the 2016 Presidential Campaign

Deronda Baughman and Dennis D. Cali

In one of the most bombastic and startling presidential elections in recent history, Donald Trump was elected President of the United States in November 2016. The transition from self-made billionaire to president of the foremost world power is one that deserves (and, no doubt, will receive) in-depth analyses. However, in contrast to a down-in-the-trenches political scrutiny that other scholars may undertake, the analysis offered here is one that goes to the heart of the political process: the process of communicating the public perception of who the candidates are and what they stand for to the voting public.

Candidate persona performs many functions. It shapes voter perceptions of performance-based traits, positions candidates as scam artist or "good king," provides a terministic screen for viewing candidates, imposes rhetorical constraints, differentiates candidates among rivals, synthesizes characteristics in a symbolic shorthand, and contributes to agenda-setting, among other functions[1]

D. Baughman (✉) · D.D. Cali
Communication Department, University of Texas, Austin, TX, USA
e-mail: dbaughman@uttyler.edu; dcali@uttyler.edu

© The Author(s) 2017
R.E. Denton, Jr. (ed.), *The 2016 US Presidential Campaign*,
Political Campaigning and Communication,
DOI 10.1007/978-3-319-52599-0_6

153

This chapter posits yet another function of presidential campaign persona that issues from the above ones—that of inoculating the candidate from attacks. The inoculation strategy was first described by McGuire in 1964.[2] The idea was that in the same way that a vaccination introduces a weakened version of a virus to produce antibodies that protect against stronger viral attacks, an argument can be introduced into an advertising campaign to preempt imminent negative messages and serve as an antidote or immunity to them.[3] The literature shows that inoculation messages can work more effectively than bolstering messages or image restoration messages in the face of attack messages.[4] Most pertinent to this chapter, inoculation strategies have proven effective in political campaigns in promoting resistance to attack messages.[5] In particular, Chasu and Pfau have shown the efficacy of inoculation strategies in televised political debates.[6]

Pfau and Gorgoon explain the "inoculation effect":

> [I]noculation deflects the persuasiveness of subsequent political attacks in a number of ways: undermining the potential influence of the source of political attacks, deflecting the specific content of political attacks, and reducing the likelihood that political attacks will influence receiver voting intention.[7]

Persona construction of a candidate or the candidate's rivals normally is a straightforward process and hardly worthy of undue scrutiny. The communication of candidate persona typically consists of two primary means: the personae presented by the candidates themselves, and the personae that candidates attempt to assign to their rivals. This presidential election, however, was radically different from the norm in one major way: one presidential candidate was almost exclusively the author of the entire story. The analysis presented here will demonstrate how Donald Trump used persuasive inoculation to imprint his version of the other Republican candidates' personae on the public and to enfeeble the influence from the candidates themselves. To do so, we present first the personae of respective rivals that the rivals presented of themselves and then present the personae that Trump constructed of them that effectively incapacitated those personae and overtook them. Our basic contention is that in the presidential campaign of 2016, while Trump's rivals carefully scripted their own personae, Trump effortlessly and offhandedly destroyed each in turn.

TRUMP AS TROLL

Donald Trump has long contemplated a bid for President of the United States. He first considered a presidential run in 1988 as a Republican, in 2000 for the Reform Party, again in 2012 as a Republican, and finally entered the 2016 race for the Republican party. As Trump began his rise in the campaign, the Republican party was split into factions (which continue today), with one sector hailing him as America's last effort to be "great again"[8] and the other sector bemoaning his volatility and lack of restraint.[9] Donald Trump was never known for reticence, and he habitually threw stones at politicians prior to his bid for the 2016 presidential election. However, his name became associated with vicious political attacks in 2012 when he made his most notorious strike against President Barack Obama. Trump repeatedly challenged Obama's legitimacy as President in 2011 with the claim that he was not born in Hawaii, as Obama claimed, and therefore was not an American citizen and was ineligible for the American presidency. This spurious claim became known as "birtherism,"[10] and brought an astounding response from the public, both pro and con. In fact, according to an August 2016 *NBC News* poll, 72% of the American public still believe that Obama is foreign-born,[11] even though President Obama produced both the short and long forms of his birth certificate in response to public outcry.

This taunting of the President in order to provoke a response is an oft-run play from Trump's playbook. While he does not portray himself as a bully, his mocking and spiteful jabs at his opponents have added an additional layer to his crafted persona:

> He has clearly figured out that this running for president thing has every-thing to do with creating a persona. His jumbo jet, his photogenic family, his boasts, his feuds against powerful people, his efforts to tie himself to Ronald Reagan and John Wayne and Arnold Schwarzenegger, all convey a message. He can handle anything people throw at him. He's a winner, even when he isn't, if only because he's ingrained that word in our heads over and over again.[12]

Trump has been immersed in marketing and branding since he was a child, and he naturally used this experience in his presidential bid. This instinctive and ingrained positioning of his persona resulted in his being the sole persona in the field of Republican candidates that did not alter or shift to deflect his rivals or pacify the voters.

THE REPUBLICAN RIVALS

Trump had many rivals to his nomination as the Republican candidate, of whom the strongest and most long-lived were Chris Christie, Jeb Bush, Marco Rubio, Ted Cruz, and John Kasich. Each of these candidates was seen by the public and/or the political pundits as a strong contender at different times during the election cycle, while Trump himself was widely regarded as the dark horse who would soon be defeated by one of the more conventional candidates. The usual calculus was an intensive analysis of each candidates' political history and voting record, and how the governed public perceived these performances, followed by the candidates' own versions of themselves along with the competing candidates' characterizations. This election, however, was different. While the orthodox candidates' carefully crafted personae were strategically (and sometimes heavy-handedly) deployed, Trump took a shotgun approach towards destroying them. And although his vitriolic characterizations and statements were widely reported and repeated, they were commonly seen as just an entertaining sideshow to the more serious main event of choosing a sobersided contender. This rabble-rouser was good for a sound bite, but his *bon mots* were not regarded by the media or serious analysts as substantively impactful. The candidates seemed to dismiss him, as well, and gave little effort toward rebutting his character assassinations other than patronizing denials or equally patronizing disregard. The public, however, was fascinated: the sobriquets assigned by Trump seemed to stick, and began to be used by disenfranchised Republicans to capture the personae of the candidates. By the time the Republican candidates (and, indeed, the Republican party itself) realized that Trump posed a serious threat to the traditional communication process, it was too late. The Trump personae had battled each candidates' own to victory. Here, we examine the five candidates who fell victim to Trump's taunts in the order they dropped out of the race.

CHRISTIE: OUTSPOKEN EVERYMAN

Chris Christie was elected the Governor of New Jersey in 2010, and announced his candidacy for the Republican nomination in June, 2015. The two-term governor and former chair of the Republican

Governors Association gained a national reputation early in his tenure for his brash demeanor and tendency to say whatever comes to mind,[13] said Kira Lerner of *ThinkProgress.org*. He had a "willingness to revel in conflict and contradiction"[14] and "that combination of centrist positions on social issues and a brash partisan chauvinism was a hallmark of Christie's rise and reelection" as governor.[15] Christie assumed the role of an "anti-politician"[16] as he remained outspoken and, most controversially to fellow Republicans, open to cooperation with the Obama administration. "In an era when elected officials are about as popular as burglars and bank C.E.O.s, the answer is that Christie cleverly created a public persona as a plain-talking, non-ideological Honest Joe."[17] This persona took a beating when Christie was implicated in the Bridgegate scandal, a situation in which two lanes from Fort Lee, NJ to the George Washington Bridge, a major point of entry to New York City, were closed, causing massive backups. Internal documents soon emerged that indicated that the lane closures were in retaliation to perceived slights by the Fort Lee mayor towards Christie, and further evidence suggested that Christie knew about the closures prior to the event. He has long denied knowing about the closures, and he has not been charged with any crime, although a federal jury in Newark returned guilty verdicts against Christie's former deputy chief of staff, Bridget Kelly, and Bill Baroni, former deputy executive director of the Port Authority of New York and New Jersey (each convicted of seven criminal counts, including conspiracy and fraud).[18]

Even after his reputation was tarnished with the events surrounding Bridgegate, Christie continued to project his persona of the outspoken everyman. According to David Horsey of the *Los Angeles Times*, "Christie's appealing persona overrides differences in political views, and that may be the biggest advantage he has... Christie is that classic politician you'd like to have a beer with while a Bruce Springsteen song plays on an old jukebox in the corner of the bar,"[19] and Jonathan Martin observed, "Mr. Christie is trying to turn his persona into something resembling a hybrid of style and substance: He is not only offering hard truths, but doing so on some of the nation's most nettlesome challenges."[20] While this persona was his most important political advantage, it was also his most vulnerable as Trump effortlessly stole his mantle of brashness and outspokenness and the everyman faded into no one.

Trump's Christie: Underbelly of Bridgegate

Throughout the majority of the campaign, Chris Christie was one of the few candidates who refrained from attacking Trump, whether out of respect or out of fear of reprisals, and Trump reciprocated. The fact that Christie and Trump and their wives had been friendly for over a decade when the campaign began[21] fueled speculation that this accounted for the rapprochement early in the campaign. However, the hands-off treatment ended abruptly when Trump felt that Christie had criticized him, and Trump proceeded to retaliate. Christie's first jabs came late in the campaign as he hit the trail in Iowa in December, and were soft and veiled as he only alluded to Trump in his statements that "We do not need reality TV in the Oval Office right now,"[22] and "President of the United States is not a place for an entertainer."[23] These statements, along with Christie's criticism of Trump's proposal to ban Muslims from the United States, were enough to infuriate Trump. Trump responded immediately with a multipronged attack that included an assault on Christie's record on taxes, New Jersey's credit downgrades, and his camaraderie with President Obama after Superstorm Sandy devastated New Jersey in 2012. Speaking at a National Pearl Harbor Remembrance Day campaign rally in South Carolina, Trump said "I've been nice to Christie, but he really hit me today. He really hit me on the whole thing with we have to stop the Muslims until we find out what's going on. . . . So Chris, who's a friend of mine, he hit me hard. And I said, 'I've got to hit him at least once.'"[24] His sharpest barbs were reserved for Christie's still-soft underbelly of Bridgegate: "Look, here's the story: The George Washington Bridge, he knew about it. . . . They're closing up the largest bridge in the world. They never said, 'Hey boss, we're closing up the George Washington Bridge tonight.' No, they never said that. They're talking about the weather, right? So he knew about it. Totally knew about it."[25]

Christie quickly pulled back from direct conflict with Trump and viciously attacked Marco Rubio in the February 2016 debates instead. This strategy also failed, and Christie withdrew from the race shortly after. In an insightful analysis of the Christi/Trump dynamic, Doris O'Brien of the *American Thinker* offered:

> Christie barely rose above the lower single digits once Donald Trump entered the race. Without political chops or even a proper audition, The Donald co-opted the role that had been intended for the governor of New Jersey: a tough,

brash, fearless, plain-talking, no-holds-barred candidate, full of beans and brag-gadocio. What happened in short order was that one of them, dressed impec-cably, was standing at center stage in the GOP debates, while the other, wearing a baggy suit, was leaning on the last lectern in the candidate lineup. And while Trump was exuding a certain celebrity glam and attracting huge audiences, Chris Christie, looking more like a comfortable shoe, was settling for far less.[26]

Rather than representing everyman, Christie seemed to embody failure, and the slick, shiny Trump embodied success. So, in yet another crafty method of establishing his competitors' personae, Trump was able to take over Christie's genuine and hard-earned persona and make Christie look like the imposter.

BUSH: JOYFUL TURTLE

Perhaps the most startling upset of the recent Presidential campaign was that of Jeb Bush, double legacy to the Presidential throne, who sustained "daunting advantages in money and organization"[27] during the beginning of the campaign. Although his name recognition was invaluable, "he [was] dogged by fears of voter exhaustion with a family name indelibly linked to his older brother."[28] Bush seemed to respond to this fear as "the younger Mr. Bush seems to have defined himself as the anti-George W. Bush: an intellectual in search of new ideas."[29] Jeb Bush has long been regarded as the family wonk and has embraced that role enthusiastically. With wonk-dom, however, comes a deep study of the issues and often results in a more nuanced view of policies than is common in today's politics, such as Bush's opinions on educational standards and immigration reform.

Bush has long championed Common Core standards, a divisive topic among Republicans that emerged from the ashes of No Child Left Behind, the Bush-era education reform law that tied federal funding for the nation's schools to new, mandatory standardized tests.[30] Although the standards were developed by state and local officials as a way to measure student achievement nationally, they evolved into a stand-in for federal overreach in education. And not only did Bush support Common Core, his Foundation for Excellence in Education is devoted to promoting national education standards, and he's barnstormed the country to promote the standards.[31] He also promoted a kinder, gentler immigration reform than many of his opponents. In 2014, prior to his bid for Republican nominee, he described economic immigration as an "act of love" when he told *Fox News*

"Yes, they broke the law, but it's not a felony. It's an act of love, it's an act of commitment to your family."[32] Bush continued to maintain this position throughout the campaign. Bush steadfastly maintained his stances on Common Core standards and immigration reform throughout the campaign, and although he recognized that these stances were perceived by mainstream, conservative Republicans as too moderate, he decided to make a bid for the Republican nomination "without shifting his positions or altering his persona to satisfy his party's hard-liners."[33] Unfortunately for him, this insistence on sticking to principles backfired with voters as "Jeb's decision to show general-election swing voters some leg by disagreeing with 'the base' on education standards and immigration policy wound up being a disaster instead of a calculated risk. He squandered one precious asset at precisely the wrong time: his reputation as the only seriously ideological conservative in his family."[34]

Bush endeavored to pivot midway through the campaign as he began to realize that his gloves-on fighting (or, rather, nonfighting) style was woefully ineffective in the race. Bush "emerg[ed] from a weekend confab with family and donors"[35] with his game face on. Where he had once characterized himself as a "joyful tortoise"[36] in the breakneck race for the candidacy, Bush attempted to "reinvent [himself] as a badass"[37] by attacking Trump during the February Republican debate. As noted by Patrick Healy in the *New York Times*, "Mr. Bush aggressively took on Mr. Trump—an imperative for the former governor... Mr. Bush had the look and feel of a man taking his last, best shot to rescue his candidacy and destroy Mr. Trump's."[38] This rescue attempt failed and Bush retracted back into his tortoise shell.

Trump's Bush: Low-Energy Loser

As previously noted, it is not unusual for a candidate to attempt to modify or manufacture a persona in response to what he or she perceives that the public wants. It is, however, extremely unusual for a candidate to gyrate as wildly as did Bush in this attempt. His overall weakness seemed to be, in the words of Kathleen Parker of the *Washington Post*, that "in today's theater of bloviating showmen, viral sound bites and platitudes passing as policy, people like Bush who prefer experience and a more thoughtful approach to complex issues will never be appreciated. He's a Charlie Rose kind of guy trapped in a Donald Trump reality show—miscast in a movie he would have no interest in seeing."[39] Unfortunately, the only guns he stuck to were his early stances on Common Core standards and immigration reform, even though Trump had attacked him in a speech at the Freedom Summit, a conservative gathering: "And I said, say it again. I didn't get—that's one I've never heard of before. I've heard money, I've heard this, I've heard sex, I've heard everything! The one thing I never heard of was love. I understand what he's saying, but, you know, it's out there, I'll tell you."[40]

When his meager and ineffectual effort to be the anti-Trump of joy and intellectualism failed, he awkwardly morphed into a tough guy playing on Trump's playground. Most amazingly, all of these efforts were in response to an early (and persistent) character assessment by Trump: "I don't see how he's electable," Trump said in a town hall meeting in New Hampshire in August 2015. "Jeb Bush is a low-energy person. For him to get things done is hard. He's very low energy."[41] Later, taking questions from the audience, Trump said, "You know what is happening to Jeb's crowd right down the street? They're sleeping."[42] When Trump gauged the overwhelming response this innocuous remark had with the media and the public, he—as usual—used it over and over during the next few months—in talk show appearances, in tweets, and in debates—with devastating effects on the Bush campaign. Say what you like about Trump's methods, as Matt Latimer of *Politico.com* noted, "For all of his faults, the New York businessman has the instinctive talent of getting into his opponent's head."[43] Bush was unable to shake the "low-energy" label, and like a battery drained of its charge, quietly faded from the public's consciousness.

Rubio: The Commoners' Kennedy

Marco Rubio entered the national political scene as a young Senator from Florida in 2010, and quickly capitalized on his smooth good looks and Horatio Alger-esque background to enter the Republican race in 2015. Rubio used his modest upbringing as the son of a maid and a bartender to affirm to the public "the idea that in a free market, anyone can rise without the benefit of connections or wealth. That he did so as the child of Latin American parents who fled an autocratic government...has sent some Republicans swooning."[44] As Sandra Johnson of the *Inquisitor* wrote, "Marco Rubio's diverse background has helped him paint himself as someone who's lived out the American Dream, while his religious ambiguity helps him to appeal to more voters."[45] She went on to note that John F. Kennedy had used a similar strategy when he became the first

Catholic president.[46] In fact, Rubio seemed to purposefully draw comparisons between himself and the handsome, charismatic JFK while stumping for the Republican nomination, as "Rubio presented the 2016 campaign as a generational pivot point, likening his vision for a 'New American Century'—the tagline of his campaign—to Kennedy's 1960 challenge to the nation to embrace a 'New Frontier.'"[47] Chris Christie seemed to see a similar dynamic when he called Rubio "Barack Obama with a Republican pedigree" in an interview with CNN.[48]

Rubio's greatest asset seemed to be his broad appeal within the GOP. More than any other candidate, Rubio had the potential to unite the Republican establishment, and Democrats perceived him as the greatest threat to a Clinton victory in the Presidential race.[49] However, this curious attempt to meld JFK and his modest, minority background into the commoners' Kennedy met with limited success. And although the Republican base initially welcomed him as an antidote to the allegations of prejudice that are routinely leveled against the party,[50] his self-promoted persona was shot down by the public.

TRUMP'S RUBIO: LITTLE MARCO

Trump made several slurs against Rubio during the campaign for Republican nominee, each ridiculing a gaffe or personal characteristic rather than a policy deficiency. These included such terms calling Rubio a "low life," "a nasty little guy," a "basket case," and "a choker who sweated so much he had to put makeup on with a trowel" at campaign rallies.[51] Trump also jabbed Rubio for his embarrassing "water moment" while giving his televised 2013 response to the State of the Union address, when he reached for a water bottle, took a sip, and then ducked to put it back; "Trump even went as far as to send Rubio a gag gift last October of Trump-branded bottled water in order to drive the point home."[52] Rubio attempted to play in Trump's sandbox when, in response to Trump calling him "Little Marco" at a Super Tuesday rally in Columbus, OH, Rubio "conceded that Trump was taller than him. However, the Florida senator suggested Trump had small hands for his height. 'And you know what they say about guys with small hands,' Rubio said with a smile, prompting stunned laughter from the crowd. After a brief pause he added: 'You can't trust 'em!' The crowd responded with applause."[53] As Rubio discovered, efforts to best Trump at Trump's game always failed. Trump confronted Rubio about the implied insult in his usual direct fashion during a

Republican debate when he "noted a recent jab from Rubio that he had small hands. 'Look at those hands,' he said, displaying them for the audience. Then he acknowledged what he apparently believed needed to be spoken: that the size of a man's hands revealed something about the size of another part of his anatomy. 'I guarantee you there's no problem' on that front, he said."[54] Once again, Trump the Troll was successful at imprinting his version of the candidate's persona on the public as "Little Marco" faded from the limelight shrunk into irrelevance.

CRUZ: TEA PARTY TORCH CARRIER

Ted Cruz entered national consciousness as a young superstar, described by Tim Murphy of *MotherJones.com* as "the tea party wonder boy [who] is sweeping the GOP establishment off its feet"[55] in 2012 when he entered national politics as a freshman Senator from Texas. Murphy explained this implausible union thus:

> Cruz...represents an amalgam of far-right dogmas—a Paulian distaste for international law; a Huckabee-esque strain of Christian conservatism; and a Perry-like reverence for the 10th Amendment, which he believes grants the states all powers not explicitly outlined in the Constitution while severely curtailing the federal government's authority to infringe on them. Toss in a dose of Alex P. Keaton and a dash of Cold War nostalgia, and you've got a tea party torch carrier the establishment can embrace.[56]

Cruz carefully crafted a persona that blended confident (some would say arrogant) certitude about the best course for the Republican party with the story of his humble beginnings:

> It's the story of my Mom. Irish and Italian, working class, the first in her family to go to college—she became a pioneering computer programmer in the 1950s. It's the story of my father, imprisoned and tortured in Cuba, beaten nearly to death. He fled to Texas in 1957, not speaking English, with $100 sewn into his underwear. He washed dishes making 50 cents an hour to pay his way through the University of Texas, and to start a small business in the oil and gas industry... He had nothing, but he had heart. A heart for freedom.[57]

This story, along with his credentials, effectively built a bridge between the explosive Tea Party and the GOP aristocrats. Tim Murphy described the process thus: "Cruz ran as an outsider, even though his credentials...did not fit that billing. But, schooled since childhood in its tenets, he spoke the language of the tea party fluently... Cruz's greatest asset is that he lives in both worlds."[58] However, this détente between the Establishment and the upstart did not survive the crucible of national politics. Cruz's true colors began to show shortly after his relocation to Washington. His interest in actually participating in the governing process seemed weak, as Cruz "proposed no major legislation and has shown little interest in changing that"[59] during his first term in the US Senate. In fact, he seemed content accomplishing nothing "because, in Cruz's view of the federal government, nothing *is* the accomplishment."[60] His single notable achievement as a Senator is a case in point: he waged a 21-hour filibuster intended to kill Obamacare. During this filibuster, Cruz "read Dr. Seuss, sang the praises of White Castle hamburgers, did a Darth Vader imitation and quoted from the reality TV show 'Duck Dynasty.'"[61] Instead of trying to constructively lead the country, Cruz chose to burnish his reputation as a Tea Party hard-charger when he waged a "war on the GOP establishment"[62] which resulted in a "reputation as an arrogant, grating, in-your-face ideologue."[63] In fact, his efforts to distinguish himself as a maverick fighting big Government by battling "leaders who [don't] honor their commitments"[64] resulted in a "long running feud"[65] with Speaker of the House of Representatives (and fellow Republican) John Boehner, who described Cruz as "Lucifer in the flesh."[66] Rather than fight this new version of his persona during the campaign for Republican nominee, "Cruz is increasingly embracing his irascible persona, trying to turn what could be a liability into an asset."[67]

TRUMP'S CRUZ: LYIN' TED

As previously noted, Trump made national headlines as a "birther" when he made his claim that President Obama had not been born in America. This tactic was so successful that Trump recycled this tactic with Ted Cruz when Cruz was exploring a bid for the presidency. In a phone interview with a Fox news station, Trump "wondered if the Texan was even eligible to become commander-in-chief. 'It's a hurdle, somebody could certainly look at it very seriously.'"[68] Cruz feebly struck back at Trump during the first Republican debate when he derided Trump for not being representative of the Republican party because he was from Manhattan: "Everybody understands that the values in New York City are socially liberal and pro-abortion and pro-gay marriage, and focus on money and the media."[69]

Trump's most effective attack, however, was an off-the-cuff remark at a Super Tuesday rally: "I call him 'Lying Ted.' The only advantage I have is I have a big speaker out there. We don't have to lie."[70] This bewildering statement was met with great fanfare, and Trump polished this sobriquet a few days later in the Republican debate when he stated, "You're the lying guy up here. You're the one, you're the one. I've given my answer, Lying Ted. I've given my answer."[71] This casual slur from Trump—most typically rendered "Lyin'" Ted, with the "g" dropped—signaled the beginning of the end of Cruz's campaign, as he battled unsuccessfully to turn the focus to other candidates or back to Trump. His passive-aggressive attempt at retaliation was to refuse to endorse Trump at the Republican National Convention, and even this weak punch was met with ridicule:

> It was hard to imagine a more ignominious ending to his 2016 campaign. Standing before the party he had plotted for years to take over, Texas Sen. Ted Cruz stood for 38 seconds as the convention hall booed and jeered his announcement that Republicans should "vote their conscience" this fall, a faintly coded declaration that he did not support nominee Donald Trump.[72]

Trump's characterization of Cruz as a liar ignited the public, and Cruz's self-made firecracker persona was a dud.

KASICH: FOLKSY FAITH-BASED MODERATE

John Kasich, the longest-lived competitor, was one of the few presidential candidates in the 2016 race with substantial political experience, with nine terms in Congress, and two terms as the Governor of Ohio. This experience resulted in a political persona that was strong, if not particularly positive. According to traditional calculations, Kasich's first job would be to negate the negative aspects of this persona and carefully indoctrinate the public with his own version of himself. This election, however, would upturn most traditions on their heads. While he struggled to burnish his reputation and character in the way best designed to replace the negative with his positive, Trump effortlessly destroyed these attempts with a single, minimal effort.

John Kasich entered the Republican Presidential nomination race in July of 2015 in front his alma mater, Ohio State. He gave his speech with the same energy and disposition that he had shown during his 30+ years as a politician, with fairly unanimous negative reviews. As Mark Barabak summarized in the *Los Angeles Times* on July 21, 2015, "the appearance in front of 4,000 cheering supporters distilled the candidate to his essence: It was unscripted, ambitious, scattered and often assertively blunt. Indeed, one of the largest questions surrounding Kasich's candidacy is a personal one: Is he too abrasive to be elected president?"[73] As the stakes of the Presidential game were much higher than any Kasich had previously played for, he chose the strategy to alter these negative perceptions that many politicians do by painting himself as the anti-Kasich: "As Kasich crisscrosses New Hampshire, he is offering himself as the sunny, folksy, fun candidate for president, the alternative to Donald Trump's insults and rage. He's actually calling himself, without a trace of irony, 'the Prince of Light and Hope' and other candidates 'the princes of darkness.'"[74]

This attempt at an about-face was so complete that it was met with disbelief by many of his peers, as the *New York Times* reported on March 28, 2016: "Several of the governor's allies and adversaries said they were watching the newly genial Mr. Kasich, as a presidential candidate, with bewilderment. 'I think a lot of people are kind of scratching their heads saying, "Where did this John Kasich come from?"' said Fred Strahorn, the Democratic minority leader in the Ohio House."[75] This anti-Kasich not only failed to soften his previous persona, it backfired with the electorate. As the *New York Times* reported, "Mr. Kasich's aura of civility, kindness and positivity is so pronounced...that an anxious voter in Worcester, Mass. wondered whether he could summon the combativeness required to be an effective president."[76]

When the result of this attempt to amend his reputation of being "unpleasant, cranky, a jerk"[77] was a total failure, the electorate and pundits alike were left with a nonfeeling for a nonperson: "But who would support Kasich? Say what you will about the other candidates in the race; they at least have some kind of hook....John Kasich is so devoid of personality that he probably gets an erection from watching the Golf Channel. Who'd vote for this walking pile of mulch?"[78] Kasich took this criticism to heart and decided to fill the personality void with his private, authentic persona. This Kasich is a devout Christian who believes in putting his money where his mouth is, and was thereafter seen as the un-Trump[79] candidate as he began to display Christian concern for the down-and-out without overtly referring to his faith. "I have a heart for people who—and, look, I don't question anybody else's, but I just have a heart for people who have been disabled or disadvantaged. And, you know, I care about them."[80] In a further show of his new caring persona he "affirmed he believes marriage should remain between a man and woman [when] he told Matthews that everyone should be 'a bit more tolerant.'"[81] In an address before the 2015 Faith and Freedom Coalition conference, he said "'We know we have to stand for the poor and the bereaved and the widowed,' before launching into a variation of what has become a theme on the stump—that his work in Ohio has managed to both lift the economy and the poor and forgotten."[82] However, this strategy was ineffective as well, as reported in *Politico Magazine*:

> The irony here is not just that the most pious Republican candidate has been largely overshadowed in a campaign for which Christianity is a major calling card. As Kasich makes what could be his last big campaign push to win Ohio's primary on Tuesday, his devout faith might actually be hurting him. The governor's faith appears to drive his politically moderate stances on immigration, climate change and gay marriage—positions that alienate him from mainstream conservatives whose support Kasich needs to have a chance at the nomination.[83]

But while Kasich struggled to find the magic middle ground for his persona, Trump had no such trouble arrowing in on a wholly irrelevant characteristic and making this Kasich's primary persona. Kasich relied on a reinvention of himself as an aw-shucks compassionate conservative to power his persona, but this could not save his candidacy.

TRUMP'S KASICH: STARVING SLOB

Trump largely ignored Kasich as a serious rival for the majority of the race for the Republican nomination, limiting his barbs to relatively innocuous school-yard taunts about his name at a campaign rally in Connecticut: "I'm millions of votes more than Kasich and I don't know how you pronounce his name. Kasich. It's I-C-H. Every time I see it, I say Kay-SITCH. But it's pronounced Kay-SICK. . . . can we ask him to change the spelling of his name?"[84] But it was his ridicule of the candidate's eating habits at a campaign rally in Rhode Island that sparked a fire in the press and with voters: "'Did you see him?' Trump asked. "He has a news conference all the time while he's eating. I have never seen a human being eat in such a disgusting fashion. I'm always telling my young son Barron . . . I'd say, 'children, small little bites.' This guy takes a pancake and he's sticking it in his mouth. Do you want that for your president?"[85] While Kasich's campaign limped along for two weeks longer, this spurious and nonsensical attack, spoken and tweeted along with other equally campy attacks, effectively ended his shot at the nomination. Thus the most tenacious and hungry candidate was dismissed by the voters by one of the most ridiculous taunts of the campaign.

TRUMP'S IMMUNITY

The above profiles of candidate personae bring into relief the orchestration of personae at work in the 2016 Republican presidential primary and reviews how Trump commandeered the personae of his rivals that ultimately led to their demise. We have argued that a primary function that Trump's assignment of persona performed was that it inoculated him from his rivals' attacks on him, serving a refutational pretreatment function.

Other factors ally with the inoculation effect in exercising the peculiar success of this take-down by assignment of persona. In this section, we review a few plausible explanations for the potency of persona in the 2016 Republican primary. One factor is that Trump's persona as that of the tough-talking, hard-hitting, take-no-prisoners candidate can be viewed as characteristic of a type of workplace bully, which has been defined as one who uses "persistent, offensive, abusive, intimidating, malicious or insulting behavior, abuse of power and unfair penal sanctions, making the target feel upset, threatened, humiliated or vulnerable."[86] Although Trump was not in the position to sanction or punish his fellow candidates officially, he co-opted the media to use as a blunt tool to bludgeon his rivals into irrelevance. As a case in point, he proudly touted the fact that whenever one of his Republican rivals had gone after him on the stump, that candidate's poll numbers dropped.[87] His tactics were often characterized as "taunting" by the media, and Trump's taunting of his Republican rivals was quite effective, as are most bullying devices: just as it is well established that a common response of victims of workplace bullying is to leave the organization,[88] Trump's victims/rivals likewise abandoned their campaigns.

Bullying is a complex phenomenon that has received a great deal of attention by numerous researchers in fields of studies ranging from education to psychiatry, from social psychology to public health and from child care to social work. Although research into bullying from a communication standpoint is relatively scarce, one study defines bullying and labeling from a communication perspective as "communication tools of control and domination, wherein the victims are frequently exposed to various negative actions and have hard time defending themselves against the offenders."[89] Another study theorizes that employee-abusive organizations (defined as those in which workers experience persistent emotional abuse and hostile communication they perceive as unfair, unjust, and unwanted) come into being, persist, and change though a confluence of communication flows.[90]

Another factor that could account for the potency of the Trump phenomenon may be the billionaire's penchant for capturing news coverage. Even budding journalists know that news favors that which is new, and Trump's unprecedented and political correctness defying lobs at his rivals met that standard for newsworthiness. Certainly Trump's provocative statement on August 7, 2015, to Fox News Channel anchor Megyn Kelly, who co-moderated a GOP primary debate that evening, rightly drew massive media coverage. His mocking of a disabled reporter likewise circulated across the media. In tweets, during debates, and in television interviews, candidate Trump referred to adversaries—rivals, media outlets, the establishment—variously as "losers," "stupid," "failing," and the like. Such harangues break with political conventions of attacking opponents in more mannerly means.

A third factor accounting for the salience and effectiveness of Trump's wrecking-ball persona follows from the above one. In the lexicon of media ecology, Trump's irreverent persona may have performed an anti-environmental role. If voters viewed the existing political environment as toxic—replete with corruption, political correctness, and ineptitude—they may have built an aching appetite precisely for someone to "drain the swamp." If convention needed to be overturned, someone nonconventional, in ways all too familiar to everyone who followed the campaign, was desired to rid the system of its "reverence." Like abnormal characters in a Tolkien, O'Conner, or Percy novel, an obnoxious Trump character would jar readers and viewers into an awareness that the norm needed repair.

Finally, perhaps cartoonist Scott Adams, creator of the Dilbert comic strip, had it right in predicting a Trump presidency early in the primaries. In a March 21, 2016 interview with the *Washington Post*, the cartoonist outlined the tenets of his persuasion theory that predicted a Trump landslide:

1. Trump knows people are basically irrational.
2. Knowing that people are irrational, Trump aims to appeal on an emotional level.
3. By running on emotion, facts don't matter.

4. If facts don't matter, you can't really be wrong.
5. With fewer facts in play, it's easier to bend reality.
6. To bend reality, Trump is a master of identity politics—and identity is the strongest persuader.[91]

Extrapolating from Adams, we might say that Trump's persona assignment against his rivals operated best at the emotional level, vitiating his opponents with his swamp-draining caricatures of them and raising the capital of his own celebrity billionaire belligerence in the process. Inoculated from counter-punches, he was the hermitic huckster. For the voters who put him in office, he was *their* troll.

NOTES

1. Dennis D. Cali. "Personae in the 2012 Presidential Election," in Studies of Communication in the 2012 Presidential Election, ed. Bob Denton (New York: Lexington Book Series on Political Communication, 2014), 41–70.
2. W.J. McGuire, "The Effectiveness of Supportive and Refutational Defenses in Immunizing and Restoring Beliefs against Persuasion," Sociometry 24 (1961):84–197.
3. J. Compton and M. Pfau, "Spreading Inoculation, Resistance to Influence, and Word-of-Mouth Communication, Communication Theory 19 (2009):9–28.
4. Bobi Ivanov, Michael Pfau, and Kimberly A. Parke, "Can Inoculation Withstand Multiple Attacks?" Communication Research 36 (2009): 655–676.
5. Michael Pfau, H. C. Kenski, M. Nitz, and J. Sorenson, "Efficacy of Inoculation Strategies in Promoting Resistance to Political Attack Messages: Applications to Direct Mail," Communication Monographs 57 (1990): 25–43.
6. An Chasu and Michael Pfau, "The Efficacy of Inoculation in Televised Political Debates," Journal of Communication 54 (2004): 421–436.
7. Michael Pfau and M. Gurgoon. "Inoculation in Political Campaign Communication," Human Communication Research 15 (1988): 91–111.
8. Michael Mathes, "US Republicans Move to Dump Trump," Yahoo!news.com, November 25, 2015, accessed November 28, 2016, https://www.yahoo.com/news/us-republicans-move-dump-trump-234604543.html?ref=gs.
9. "Donald J. Trump," accessed November 28, 2016, https://www.donaldjtrump.com/.
10. Dave Johnson, "The Origins of the Birther Theory," Huffington Post, August 27, 2009, accessed November 28, 2016, http://www.huffingtonpost.com/dave-johnson/the-origins-of-the-birthe_b_245672.html.

11. Josh Clinton and Carrie Roush, "Poll: Persistent Partisan Divide Over 'Birther' Question," NBC News, August 10, 2016, accessed November 28, 2016, http://www.nbcnews.com/politics/2016-election/poll-persistent-partisan-divide-over-birther-question-n627446.
12. Matt Latimer, "Where Jeb Bush Went Horribly Wrong," Los Angeles Times, February 3, 2016, accessed November 28, 2016, http://www.latimes.com/opinion/op-ed/la-oe-0203-latimer-jeb-bush-performance-20160203-story.html.
13. Kira Lerner, "Governor Chris Christie Wants to Be President. Here's How He Hurt New Jersey," ThinkProgress.org, June 30, 2015, accessed November 28, 2016, https://thinkprogress.org/governor-chris-christie-wants-to-be-president-heres-how-he-hurt-new-jersey-f32cba99111a#.cfgy3lxki.
14. J. T. Aregood, "The Last Gasp of the Christie Persona?" PolitikerNJ, March 2, 2016, accessed November 28, 2016, http://politickernj.com/2016/03/the-last-gasp-of-the-christie-persona/.
15. Ibid.
16. John Cassidy, "Joy Behar Is Right: Chris Christie Is 'Toast,'" New Yorker, April 7, 2014, http://www.newyorker.com/news/john-cassidy/joy-behar-is-right-chris-christie-is-toastDaniel Strauss, "Chris Christie Warns Iowans Against Trump," Politico.com, December 5, 2015, accessed November 28, 2016, http://www.politico.com/story/2015/12/christie-trump-iowa-216460.
17. Ibid.
18. Ray Sanchez, "Bridgegate Trial: What's Next for Chris Christie?" CNNPolitics.com, November 4, 2016, accessed November 28, 2016, http://www.cnn.com/2016/11/04/politics/bridgegate-trial-chris-christie/.
19. David Horsey, "Chris Christie Is the Tea Party's Newest Nightmare," Los Angeles Times, November 7, 2013, accessed November 28, 2016, http://www.latimes.com/opinion/topoftheticket/la-na-tt-chris-christie-nightmarc-20131107-story.html.
20. Jonathan Martin, "What Chris Christie Would Need to Do to Win," New York Times, June 30, 2015, accessed November 28, 2016, http://www.nytimes.com/interactive/2015/06/30/us/elections/chris-christie.html?_r=0.
21. Jeremy Diamond, Jake Tapper, Phil Mattingly and Stephen Collinson, "Chris Christie Endorses Donald Trump," CNNPolitics.com, February 26, 2016, accessed November 28, 2016, http://www.cnn.com/2016/02/26/politics/chris-christie-endorses-donald-trump/.
22. Strauss, "Chris Christie Warns Iowans."
23. Ibid.
24. Colin Campbell, "Donald Trump Unloads on Chris Christie with Multipronged Attack," Business Insider, December 7, 2015, accessed November 28, 2016, http://www.businessinsider.com/donald-trump-chris-christie-muslim-immigration-bridgegate-2015-12.

25. Ibid.
26. Doris O'Brien, "Who Needs Christie When We Have Trump?" American Thinker, February 14, 2016, accessed November 28, 2016, http://www.americanthinker.com/articles/2016/02/who_needs_christie_when_we_have_trump.html.
27. Michael Warren, "Jeb's Biggest Problem Is Trump," Weekly Standard, August 24, 2015, accessed November 21, 2016, http://www.weeklystandard.com/jebs-biggest-problem-trump/article/1017735.
28. Ibid.
29. Michael Barbaro, "Jeb Bush Gives Party Something to Think About," New York Times, May 24, 2014, accessed November 21, 2016, http://www.nytimes.com/2014/05/25/us/politics/jeb-bush-gives-party-something-to-think-about.html?ref=todayspaper.
30. Tim Murphy, "Inside the Mammoth Backlash to Common Core," MotherJones.com, September/October 2014, accessed November 30, 2016, http://www.motherjones.com/politics/2014/09/common-core-education-reform-backlash-obamacare.
31. Ibid.
32. Ed O'Keefe, "Jeb Bush: Many Illegal Immigrants Come Out of an 'Act of Love'," Washington Post, April 6, 2014, accessed November 22, 2016, https://www.washingtonpost.com/news/post-politics/wp/2014/04/06/jeb-bush-many-illegal-immigrants-come-out-of-an-act-of-love/.
33. Brett LoGiurato, "Jeb Bush Was Public Enemy No. 1 at One of the Year's Biggest Conservative Gatherings," Business Insider, April 14, 2014, accessed November 22, 2016, http://www.businessinsider.com/jeb-bush-booed-new-hampshire-conservatives-2014-4.
34. Ed Kilgore, "The Problem with Jeb Bush's Brain," New York Magazine, January 21, 2016, accessed on November 21, 2016. http://nymag.com/daily/intelligencer/2016/01/problem-with-jeb-bushs-brain.html.
35. Kathleen Parker, "Jeb's Tough Guy Persona Falls Flat," Newsmax.com, October 28, 2015, accessed November 21, 2016, http://www.newsmax.com/Parker/jeb-bush-2016-trump/2015/10/28/id/699348/.
36. Adam Smith, "Jeb Bush: 'I'm A Joyful Tortoise' in Long, Acrimonious Race," Miami Herald, July 27, 2015, accessed on November 21, 2016, http://www.miamiherald.com/news/politics-government/election/jeb-bush/article29074546.html.
37. Parker, "Jeb's Tough Guy Persona."
38. Patrick Healy, "In Republican Debate, Jeb Bush Attacks Donald Trump," New York Times, February 13, 2016, accessed November 21, 2016. http://www.nytimes.com/2016/02/14/us/politics/republican-debate.html.

39. Kathleen Parker, "Jeb Bush Doesn't Know How to Fight," Washington Post, October 30, 2015, accessed November 21, 2016, https://www.washingtonpost.com/opinions/jeb-bushs-fake-anger-and-real-dilemma/2015/10/30/ab0b3f90-7f40-11e5-b575-d8dcfedb4ea1_story.html?utm_term=.b0b49bb322b2.

40. O'Keefe, "Jeb Bush: Many Illegal."

41. Theodore Schleifer, "Town Hall Throw-Down: Trump, Bush Trade Shots," CNN, August 20, 2015, accessed November 21, 2016, http://www.cnn.com/2015/08/19/politics/donald-trump-mitt-romney-choked-2012/.

42. Ibid.

43. Matt Latimer, "Jeb, the Unluckiest Bush," Politico.com, February 21, 2016, accessed November 21, 2016, http://www.politico.com/magazine/story/2016/02/jeb-bush-family-2016-213666.

44. Jonathan Martin and Ashley Parker, "Marco Rubio's Immigrant Story, and an Aging Party in Search of a Spark," New York Times, May 7, 2015, accessed November 30, 2016, http://www.nytimes.com/2015/05/08/us/politics/marco-rubio-campaigns-on-his-immigrant-story-cautiously.html?_r=0.

45. Sandra Johnson, "Marco Rubio: Republican Candidate Compared to Obama, Kennedy" Inquistr.com, June 3, 2015, accessed November 30, 2016, http://www.inquisitr.com/2141914/marco-rubio-republican-candidate-compared-to-obama-kennedy/.

46. Ibid.

47. Daniel Larison, "Rubio's Weird JFK References," The American Conservative, June 8, 2015, accessed November 21, 2016, http://www.theamericanconservative.com/larison/rubios-weird-jfk-references/.

48. Phil Mattingly and Cassie Spodak, "Christie Attacks Rubio as a 'Boy in the Bubble,'" CNN.com, February 2, 2016, accessed November 30, 2016, http://www.cnn.com/2016/02/02/politics/marco-rubio-attacks-chris-christie/.

49. Sean Illing, "Survey of Dems in Early Primary States Shows They're Terrified of Rubio, Excited About Trump," Salon.com, December 4, 2015, accessed November 30, 2016, http://www.salon.com/2015/12/04/survey_of_dems_in_early_primary_states_shows_theyre_terrified_of_rubio_excited_about_trump/.

50. Martin and Parker, "Marco Rubio's Immigrant Story."

51. Diamond et al., "Chris Christie Endorses Donald Trump."

52. Allen Smith, "Donald Trump Just Dramatically Drank a Bottle of Water in Order to Taunt Marco Rubio," Business Insider, February 26, 2016, accessed November 21, 2016, http://www.businessinsider.com/donald-trump-marco-rubio-water-bottle-2016-2.

53. Alexandra Jaffe, "Donald Trump Has 'Small Hands,' Marco Rubio Says," NBC News, February 29, 2016, accessed November 21, 2016, http://www.nbcnews.com/politics/2016-election/donald-trump-has-small-hands-marco-rubio-says-n527791.
54. Cooper Allen, "Trump Defends Anatomy in Debate's Opening Moments," USA Today, March 4, 2016, accessed November 21, 2016, http://www.usatoday.com/story/news/politics/onpolitics/2016/03/03/donald-trump-hands-rubio-debate/81297208/.
55. Tim Murphy, "Meet Ted Cruz, 'The Republican Barack Obama,'" Mother Jones, November/December 2012, accessed November 18, 2016, http://www.motherjones.com/politics/2012/10/ted-cruz-texas-gop-senate.
56. Ibid.
57. Ted Cruz, "Republican National Convention Speech," accessed November 18, 2016, http://2012.presidential-candidates.org/?news=Ted-Cruz-Speech-At-The-Republican-National-Convention:-Full-Transcript.
58. Murphy, "Meet Ted Cruz."
59. Jason Zengerle, "Ted Cruz: The Distinguished Wacko Bird from Texas," GQ, September 22, 2013, accessed November 21, 2016, http://www.gq.com/story/ted-cruz-republican-senator-october-2013.
60. Ibid.
61. Dan Friedman and James Warren, "Ted Cruz 'Filibuster': After 21 Hours of Anti-Obamacare Talk Mixed with Dr. Seuss and Star Wars, Texas Senator Votes to Consider House Bill," NY Daily News, September 26, 2013, accessed November 18, 2016, http://www.nydailynews.com/news/politics/ted-cruz-filibuster-talks-21-hours-votes-house-bill-article-1.1467344.
62. Jake Miller, "GOP Debate: Trump, Bush, Cruz, Paul, and Rubio Mix It Up," CBS News, August 7, 2015, accessed November 18, 2016, http://www.cbsnews.com/media/gop-republican-debate-august-2015-high lights-analysis/.
63. Scott Bauer, "Abrasive GOP Candidate Ted Cruz Tries to Use Personality to His Advantage," Los Angeles Daily News, Jan 2, 2016, accessed November 18, 2016, http://www.dailynews.com/government-and-poli tics/20160102/abrasive-gop-candidate-ted-cruz-tries-to-use-personality-to-his-advantage.
64. Miller, "GOP Debate."
65. Bill Hoffman, "Boehner Blasts Cruz: 'Lucifer in the Flesh,'" Newsmax.com, April 28 2016, accessed November 21, 2016, http://www.newsmax.com/Politics/John-Boehner-Blasts-Cruz-Lucifer/2016/04/28/id/726229/.
66. Ibid.
67. Bauer, "Abrasive GOP Candidate."

68. Leslie Larson, "Donald Trump Is a Ted Cruz Birther," Business Insider, March 23, 2015, accessed November 21, 2016, http://www.businessinsi der.com/donald-trump-is-a-ted-cruz-birther-2015-3/.
69. Ted Cruz, "Transcript of Republican Presidential Debate," New York Times, January 15, 2016, accessed November 21, 2016 http://www. nytimes.com/2016/01/15/us/politics/transcript-of-republican-presiden tial-debate.html.
70. Donald Trump, "Super Tuesday Rally, Columbus, OH," The Hill, March 1, 2016, accessed November 21, 2016, http://thehill.com/blogs/ballot-box/presidential-races/271298-trump-swaggers-way-through-ohio-rally-on-super-tuesday.
71. Ben Kamisar, "Trump Digs at Cruz, Calling Him 'Lying Ted,'" The Hill, March 3, 2016, accessed November 21, 2016, http://thehill.com/blogs/ballot-box/presidential-races/271746-trump-digs-at-cruz-calling-him-lying-ted.
72. Zeke Miller, "How the Establishment Beat Ted Cruz and Never Trump," Time, July 21, 2016, accessed November 21, 2016, http://time.com/4417656/republican-convention-ted-cruz-speech-behind-scenes/Mark Barabak, "Ohio's John Kasich Enters GOP Race, Bringing Heat, Intrigue," Los Angeles Times, July 21, 2015, accessed November 18, 2016, http://www.latimes.com/nation/la-pn-kasich-2016-20150721-story.html.
73. Mark Barabak, "Ohio's John Kasich Enters GOP Race, Bringing Heat, Intrigue," Los Angeles Times, July 21, 2015, accessed November 30, 2016, http://www.latimes.com/nation/la-pn-kasich-2016-20150721-story.html.
74. Erick Trickey, "How Mean Old John Kasich Became Mr. Nice," Politico. com, February 3, 2016, accessed November 18, 2016, http://www.poli tico.com/magazine/story/2016/02/john-kasich-mean-became-nice-new-hampshire-213589.
75. Thomas Kaplan, Michael Barbaro, and Steve Eder, "Soft and Cuddly? John Kasich's Old Colleagues Don't Recognize Him," New York Times, March 25, 2016, accessed November 18, 2016, http://www.nytimes.com/2016/03/26/us/politics/john-kasich-campaign.html.
76. Ibid.
77. Trickey, "How Mean Old John Kasich."
78. Matt Forney, "The Unbearable Blandness of John Kasich," Righton.net, March 20, 2016, accessed November 18, 2016, https://www.righton.net/2016/03/20/the-unbearable-blandness-of-john-kasich/.
79. Jennifer Rubin, "John Kasich Is the Un-Trump," Washington Post, August 17, 2015, https://www.washingtonpost.com/blogs/right-turn/wp/2015/08/17/john-kasich-is-the-un-trump/?utm_term=.a8a97c04478d.
80. Ibid.

81. Andrew Rafferty and Kailani Koenig, "John Kasich Supports 'Moving On' from Gay Marriage Debate," NBC News, April 15, 2016, accessed November 22, 2016, http://www.nbcnews.com/politics/2016-election/john-kasich-supports-moving-gay-marriage-debate-n556086.
82. Jessica Wehrman, "Gov. John Kasich Talks of Faith at Conference," Columbus Dispatch, June 20, 2015, accessed November 22, 2016, http://www.dispatch.com/content/stories/local/2015/06/19/Gov-john-kasich-talks-of-faith-at-conference.html#.
83. Laura Turner, "How Kasich's Religion Is Hurting Him with Conservatives," Politico Magazine, March 15, 2015, accessed November 22, 2016, http://www.politico.com/magazine/story/2016/03/john-kasich-2016-religion-213735.
84. Reena Flores, "After Promises of Change, Trump Attacks Cruz, Kasich," CBS News, April 23, 2016, accessed November 18, 2016, http://www.cbsnews.com/news/donald-trump-john-kasich-name-ted-cruz-citizenship-change-promises-election-2016/.
85. Tim Hains, "Trump Mocks Kasich for Giving Interviews While Eating Pancakes: 'Disgusting,'" RealClearPolitics.com, April 25, 2016, accessed November 18, 2016, http://www.realclearpolitics.com/video/2016/04/25/trump_mocks_kasich_for_giving_interviews_while_eating_pancakes_disgusting.html#
86. M. Pörhölä, S. Karhunen, and S. Rainivaara, "Bullying at School and in the Workplace: A Challenge for Communication Research," in Communication Yearbook, ed. P.J. Kalbfleisch (Manway, NJ: Erlbaum), 256.
87. Strauss, "Chris Christie Warns Iowans."
88. Pamela Lutgen-Sandvik and Virginia McDermott, "The Constitution of Employee-Abusive Organizations: A Communication Flows Theory," Communication Theory 18 (2008): 304.
89. Paul Elovitz, "A Psychobiographical and Psycho-political Comparison of Clinton and Trump," Journal of Psychohistory 44 (2016): 100.
90. L. Quine, "Workplace Bullying in NHS Community Trust: Staff Questionnaire Survey," British Medical Journal 318 (1999): 228–232.
91. Michael Cavna, "Comic Riffs: Donald Trump Will Win in a Landslide. The Mind Behind 'Dilbert' Explains Why," Washington Post, March 21, 2106, accessed November 30, 2016, https://www.washingtonpost.com/news/comic-riffs/wp/2016/03/21/donald-trump-will-win-in-a-landslide-the-mind-behind-dilbert-explains-why/?utm_term=.8ae76247371e.

Deronda Baughman is an instructor in the Speech Communication Department at the University of Texas at Tyler.

Dennis D. Cali is professor and chair of the Communication Department at the University of Texas at Tyler, where he has been awarded the President's Scholarly Achievement Award. He has authored or edited two other books, and his research appears in book chapters and in journals, including *China Media Research, Communication Studies, Critical Studies in Media Communication, Explorations in Media Ecology*, and the *Journal of Mass Media Ethics*, among others.

CHAPTER 7

Issues of Gender in the 2016 Presidential Campaign

Robert E. Denton, Jr.

In 2008, history was made in a dramatic fashion. The first African-American not only became the Democrat nominee for president, Barack Obama became the first African-American president. The presidential election of 2016 was destined to be historic once again. All indications pointed to the real possibility of America's first woman would be elected president. In fact, it appeared virtual certainty just days before the election. However, the nomination fight was surprisingly challenging for Hillary Clinton. And election night was simply shocking. In the aftermath, Clinton acknowledged in her concession speech that her effort fell short but maintained her hope and belief that a woman would indeed become president, sooner rather than later. "And to all the women, and especially the young women, who put their faith in this campaign and in me, I want you to know that nothing has made me prouder than to be your champion. Now, I know we have still not shattered that highest and hardest glass ceiling, but some day someone will and hopefully sooner than we might think right now."[1]

Exit polls revealed that although women voted against Trump by one of the largest margins in history, noncollege women voted for Trump

R.E. Denton, Jr. (✉)
Department of Communication, Virginia Tech., Blacksburg, VA, USA
e-mail: rdenton@vt.edu

© The Author(s) 2017
R.E. Denton, Jr. (ed.), *The 2016 US Presidential Campaign*,
Political Campaigning and Communication,
DOI 10.1007/978-3-319-52599-0_7

179

two to one and he carried married and evangelical white women by double digits. It also appeared that many women who voted for Clinton did so with some degree of ambivalence. And younger women, "third-wave feminists" largely stayed home compared to previous elections. Naomi Riley pondered the notions of "sisterhood" and "female solidarity" in the 2016 presidential campaign. "Sisterhood is dead. If the left learns nothing else from this election, perhaps they should understand that there's no such thing as female solidarity—not, at least, as they envision it."[2]

Nearly a century after women secured the right to vote in 1920 and 241 years after the county's founding, there has not been a woman president of the United States. In terms of global ranking of women in government, the United States ranks 97. Of the 175 current heads of state around the world, eighteen or just over 10 percent are women. Most global female leaders tend to serve less than four years.[3] In the Americas, women have been elected as heads of state in Canada, Brazil, Argentina, Chile, Peru and Jamaica. Only Mexico and the United States lag behind. Both nations have a more masculine political culture. Women hold 19 percent of elected government offices in the United States.[4]

Yet, according to a 2016 Rasmussen poll, 78 percent of men and 79 percent of women said they could vote for a woman for president. Interestingly, only 4 percent of all Americans think they should vote for a woman because of being female. For women, it is double that of 8 percent.[5]

There are many studies and books documenting the challenges women face in political campaigns and governing. Camille Paglia argues there are numerous "systemic factors, arising from the Constitution, popular tradition, and our electoral process, that have inhibited American women from attaining the highest office in the land." At the heart of the challenges is the need to combat gender stereotypes and sexism. The long and vicious electoral process itself drives many talented women politicians from running for president.

The 2008 presidential campaign brought issues of race, gender and age to the forefront. The candidacies of Hillary Clinton, Barack Obama, John McCain and Sarah Palin provided the context and dynamics for charges of racism, sexism and ageism. Kristina Sheeler and Karrin Anderson characterized Clinton's 2008 nomination run dominated by the four C's: cleavage, cackle, crying and conniving.[6] Not surprising, most of the gender characterizations and portrayals noted in the 2008 race appeared in the 2016 contest as well.

A recent series of studies by Princeton professor Susan Fiske found that women who represent traditional feminine traits or roles, such as housewife are generally viewed as warm, but not competent. In contrast, women considered less traditional feminine traits or roles such as lesbians, athletes or working-women are viewed as competent but not warm and inviting. The latter, according to Fiske, face more antagonistic form of sexism. Thus women are seldom perceived as warm and competent, which puts them in a "catch 22 situation."[7]

Theodore Sheckles and his colleagues identified several criteria and areas especially important to potential female candidates for President from analyzing nine women and the barriers they faced in campaigns.[8] They must, of course, have the appropriate credentials. So do men, however, women are expected to have more experience as elected officials than men. It is also important for women candidates to have foreign policy experience. All candidates must be able to raise significant amount of money to finance a campaign. Historically, women such as Elizabeth Dole have had trouble raising the funds compared to male candidates. Women candidates have a more difficult time than males appearing to be dynamic and charismatic while not appearing to be too aggressive or assertive. Sheckles and his colleagues also note how media will focus on aspects of dress, looks, stature that are not part of coverage for male candidates. Women candidates are caught in a double bind between looking "presidential" historically in masculine terms and "attractive" according to cultural feminine terms. They also noted in 2012, that women who aspire to run must not have "a spouse problem." The spouse must be well in the background or shadows of public attention. Finally, they suggest that potential women candidates need to be aware of the complexity of women voters. As an audience, they too represent "waves of feminism" and life experiences. As will become apparent, all of these areas of concern played a role in the 2016 campaign.

In this chapter, space only allows an overview of how issues of gender played out across the primaries, general election and postelection phases. Over 200 newspaper, magazine, media and political website articles and postings were reviewed to identify common themes and issues related to gender in the 2016 presidential campaign.

PRIMARY SEASON

Hillary Clinton

In 2008, Hillary Clinton downplayed her gender and the historic nature of the candidacy. In that campaign, Clinton believed she needed to project an image of strength and experience in order to convince voters she could be the first woman to serve as commander-in-chief—a "kind of tough single parent" rather than a "first mama," as her chief strategist Mark Penn described at the time.[9] According to Gail Sheehy, "In 2008, Clinton allowed her husband and her chief strategist, Mark Penn, to run her as an alpha male commander-in-chief. From the start of the presidential campaign, she came across as brittle and overbearing. No wonder voters sensed an authenticity problem."[10]

However, in this campaign, she embraced gender as a strategic appeal. As Sheehy observed, "this time, though, Clinton is not running as a made-over man. She is in a new stage of life, having become the kickass grandma with a cackle and a fierce new brand of feminism."[11] For Sheehy, "for the first time Hillary seems comfortable in her own skin—not just with her age but also with her gender."[12] Clinton's gender wasn't something she needed to explain or defend. Rather, her potential to make history as the nation's first female president became one of her biggest applause lines. She often ended speeches by invoking an America where a father can tell his daughter, "Yes, you can be anything you want to be, even president of the United States."

Clinton's strategy for women was threefold. First was to note the historic nature of being the first woman president. Second was to confirm her feminist credentials and finally to speak to issues most important to women such as education, gun control, equal pay for equal work, abortion rights, etc.[13]

There was a clear assumption in the Clinton campaign that Clinton's candidacy would have a strong appeal to all women. And women vote in larger numbers than men in general. Many of the older women's rights advocates viewed the election of Clinton as the next logical step in the women's rights movement. They viewed Clinton as the best chance to finally have a woman president. However, it became clear very early in the primary season that millennial women were not enamored with the Clinton campaign and that gender was less important in voting than issues. A generational clash emerged among feminists. Clinton did well among first- and second-wave feminists. It was the third-wave feminists that initially rejected the Clinton candidacy and strongly favored Bernie Sanders.

Clinton came to age during the middle years of second-wave feminism. The first wave started in mid-1800s with women's suffrage battle. The second wave, according to scholars, was in the 1960s to the early 1980s. Betty Friedan book, *The Feminine Mystique* published in 1963 is credited in starting the second wave. The work called for women to seek opportunities beyond family and home. Second-wave feminists proclaimed that the "personal is political" meaning that personal life informs political and social realities. However, criticism mounted that this wave of feminism addressed primarily middle-class white women. Many say a third wave of feminism emerged in 1989 with the term "intersectionality." The term references the connections between all the forms of oppression and social justice—not just based upon gender. Feminist philosophy should address concerns of women of color, lower socioeconomic class and other marginalized groups. Thus, racism may incorporate issues of poverty, sexism, etc.

Today's generation of feminists thus viewed Clinton's feminism as more traditional, outdated, limited and were less likely to support views that are only gender based. Clinton appears to empower women who are already powerful. Reproductive rights and equal pay are on par with criminal-justice reform, police brutality, environmental issues, etc. Today's young women discuss relevant issues well beyond the classroom within social media outlets and the blogosphere. According to Molly Mirhashem, "as young women's notions of feminism evolved and broadened, so did their idea what constitutes 'women's issues' in the political arena. In essence, from the intersectionality perspective, concerns are well beyond how any one specific policy issue affects women."[14] For many millennial young women, Clinton was a symbol of an "older generation of women more concerned with female empowerment—in particular with white, middle-class, American female empowerment—than with broader issues of social and economic justice."[15]

The generational divide intensified throughout the primary season. Many millennial women expressed resentment of the notion they should actually feel "obligated" to vote for Clinton simply because she is a woman. Some argued that given Sanders' views on income inequality, free college, more regulation on environmental issues actually made him the "more feminist candidate."[16] He appeared more bold and revolutionary. As Jill Abramson observed, "many younger women do not think 'voting with your uterus' is as important as income disparity and social justice issues."[17] For others, voting for Hillary was anti-feminist. "No one should imagine that there is honor in voting for Clinton *because* she's a woman. Wasn't that the key point of feminism, after all, that women are more than biology?"[18]

As one millennial, Holly Scheer, wrote in an op-ed for The Federalist website, "Should the sisterhood of all women dictate that when one of us steps up, the rest need to fall in line to support her?"[19] Scheer did not trust Clinton and "she lies, repeatedly, and for her own benefit."[20] For Scheer, voting based on gender runs counter to genuine feminism, where men and women are equal. Women are just as smart and capable of making a voting decision based upon issues. "Women fought for the vote to make their own choices, based on their understanding of the issues and the possible solutions."[21] Scheer concludes, "It's not sexism making young women flee Clinton—it's simply that she doesn't represent us."[22]

During the primary season, Clinton made direct appeals to millennial women. Lena Dunham, creator and star of HBO's "Girls," and singer Demi Lovato introduced Clinton at rallies. In addition to media interviews with women celebrities, Clinton did interviews with Refinery 29 and The Skimm, trendy websites aimed at young women. She made use of the new media to target messages such as an emoji-animated Snapchat video supporting Planned Parenthood. Clinton also started focusing on issues such as college affordability, social justice and measures to reduce sexual assault.

Some questioned Clinton's authenticity as a feminist. Hillary's entire career is based on her husband Bill Clinton. Her status and opportunity were a direct result of being married to Bill Clinton. Camille Pagilla, one of the major critics of Clinton throughout the election, argued "She's been handed job after job, but primarily due to her very un-feminist association with a man...Her public prominence has always been based not on any accomplishment of her own but on her marriage to a charismatic politician, now in his dotage."[23]

Clinton was also attacked how she defended her husband during allocations of sexual assault referring to Lewinski as a "narcissistic loon" and assault victims as "trash," "floozy," "bimbo," and "stalker." Past accusers like Paula Jones and Juanita Broaddrick reemerged during the primary season.

According to Amy Chozick, for some younger women, it's difficult to reconcile the comments by the Clintons in the 1990s in discrediting women who said former President Bill Clinton had sexually assaulted them. Many friends of the Clintons and prominent women disparaged his accusers. When one of the first women to come forward, Connie Harmzy, during the 1992 presidential campaign, Hillary Clinton told then aid George Stephanopoulos, "We have to destroy her story." When Gennifer Flowers came forward, according to Carl Bernstein, Hillary Clinton undertook an "aggressive, explicit direction of the campaign to discredit Flowers."[24]

Again, critic Camille Paglia asserted, "the horrible truth is that the feminist establishment in the U.S., led by Gloria Steinem, did in fact apply a double standard to Bill Clinton's behavior because he was a Democrat. The Democratic president and administration supported abortion rights, and therefore it didn't matter what his personal behavior was."[25]

A critical aspect of Caitlin Flanagan's feminism is "the idea that when a woman came forward to report that she had been raped we would believe her—publicly and unanimously."[26] For her, Paula Jones' story of work-place sexual harassment by Bill Clinton was believable. She was surprised by the reactions of fellow feminists. They tended to believe that "a woman could lie about sexual harassment for personal gain."[27] Flanagan felt the same way about Juanita Broaddrick' story. She believed her. For her, Clinton lacked credibility when saying, "every survivor of sexual assault deserves to be heard, believed and supported."[28] "As Democrats, as women, we must ask ourselves: Do we stand with the women who report sexual assault—all women: big-haired, 'slutty,' trailer-park, *all* of them— or do we stand, once again, with the Clinton machine and its Arkansas *droit du seigneur*?"[29]

In November 2015 on Twitter, Hillary wrote, "Every survivor of sexual assault deserves to be heard, believed, and supported."[30] In town hall sessions, audience members questioned Hillary about whether Bill Clinton's accusers should be believed. She generally responded with yes, until the evidence suggest otherwise.

Naturally, Trump inserted himself into the debate. When Clinton attacked Trump for his "penchant for sexism," he accused her of hypocrisy given her husband treatment of women. He went so far to say that Clinton " is not a victim. She was an enabler."[31] Trump's attacks challenged the perception that Hillary was a strong feminist and was an "apologist for a predator."[32] The general thought at the time was if Clinton calls Trump sexist, then former President Bill Clinton's behavior was legitimate game for commentary and questions. For some, Clinton's characterizations of sexism against Trump were viewed as Clinton playing "the woman card." An editorial in *The Wall Street Journal* argued that Clinton wanted to use her gender as both a shield and a sword. The Clinton campaign calls virtually any criticism sexist. They also, especially in the primary season, continually accused the Republican Party as conducting a "war on women."[33] This broader issue carried forward in a more dramatic fashion during the general election.

As part of her stump speech and town hall meetings, Clinton articulated the clear benefits of having a woman in the White House. She said she could make a difference to family and women's issues. She also highlighted her work on health care, paid sick leave, affordable childcare and universal preschool. At one rally Clinton was asked, "what are the merits of a female leader? What does a female leader bring that a man doesn't?" Women, she responded, "have a very different life experience, I think it's fair to say," to a burst of female applause. Women, she argued, live through things like family, finances, sickness and aging "in a much more real, day-to-day way, and I will bring all of those feelings and experiences with me to the White House."[34]

Clinton often acknowledged the double standard "where women are just expected to combine traits and qualities in a way that men are not. And it does make running for office for a woman a bigger challenge . . . I just think there are some areas where our own life experiences really prepare us to be more receptive. I do think there is something in the governing or organizing approach. I just think women in general are better listeners, are more collegial, more open to new ideas and how to make things work in a way that looks for win-win outcomes."[35]

An interesting tactic frequently used during the primaries was Clinton talking about being a mother and grandmother. Liza Mundy thought this would ultimately help Clinton in the campaign. "She deployed her new role much as grandfatherly politicians have long done—as testament to her experience, her family values, and her stake in the future."[36] Mundy muses that in a more "elderly" time of her life, Clinton could perhaps be perceived as warm without losing her reputation for competence.

For Amy Chozick and Yamiche Alcindor, "She uses gender as a way to overcome the perception that she is the establishment candidate and to counter questions about her age. In an exchange with CBS News, Clinton expressed, "I cannot imagine anyone being more of an outsider than the first woman president. I mean, really, let's think about that."[37] And she often related, "I'll be the youngest woman president in the history of the United States."[38]

Some of the personality and gender behavior concerns raised in 2008 were raised again during the primary season. As in previous campaigns, Clinton was regularly scrutinized for her hairstyles and fashion choices. Those topics were more pronounced in the general election phase. Clinton was especially criticized for her tone of voice and being shrill. Many elected women senators thought such comments were a sure sign of continued sexism and being judged by a double standard. Bob Woodward received some noted criticism for commenting on MSNBC's "Morning Joe," "She shouts. There's something unrelaxed about the way she is communicating." Joe Scarborough responded, "I was watching her and I said to myself, 'has nobody told her how the microphone works?"[39] Peggy Noonan complained that Clinton's voice becomes "loud, flat and harassing to the ear" when she emphasizes applause lines. "She lately reminds me of the landlady yelling up the stairs that your kids have left their bikes in the hall again," she wrote.[40] *Fox News* commentator Geraldo Rivera compared Clinton to former Democratic presidential candidate Howard Dean, whose 2004 campaign went down in flames after his infamous scream after the Iowa caucuses. Fox News host Sean Hannity on the same program said Clinton "looked angry, she sounded angry" during her remarks after finishing in a virtual tie with Sanders in Iowa.[41] This became one of the primary narratives of the entire campaign. However, Bryce Covert viewed this as sexism, pure and simple. He argued there are reasons people did not favor Hillary during the primaries having nothing to do with policy. "It's her voice, which becomes 'screaming' when she raises it, even though Sanders' natural speaking voice characterized as a yell (to say nothing of Donald Trump's). It's her personality; she's both boring and inauthentic at the same an emasculating ball buster."[42] For him, "telling women that there is no sexism in the hatred Clinton inspires denies the water we all swim in."[43]

Thus, unlike the nomination run in 2008, Clinton embraced her gender and the historic nature of her potential candidacy to the White House. Unexpected was the generational debate about the nature and even definition of feminism. Millennial women rebelled against the idea that gender alone provides the justification to vote for Clinton. Many outright questioned her feminist credentials in several ways, not the least was her prominence based on being married to Bill Clinton. Also in the mix was the debate about covering up, avoiding and attacking the accusers of Bill

Clinton's sexual assault allegations. Clinton made direct appeals to the millennial women through endorsements, issue appeals and heavy use of social media. The question became, if she won the nomination, would they support her candidacy? Finally, there were the same media portrayals and questions related to her dress, hair and voice. Trump, as we will see, also had issues related to gender during the primary season.

Carly Fiorina

There was another female running for the presidency. Carly Fiorina gained notoriety after the first second tier debate. Subsequently, she was on the main stage with her Republican opponents. Early on many feminists were generally favorable to Fiorina's candidacy. Amy Chozick quoted one saying, "Carly Fiorina is the candidate that I wanted Hillary Clinton to be."[44] However, over the course of the primary campaign and debates, Fiorina's policies were the most troubling to many women in terms of opposing abortion, raising the minimum wage, federally mandated paid maternity leave and the Affordable Care Act. Commenting on Fiorina's comment in a debate about Plan Parenthood and the secret videos, Gloria Steinem responded, "If you thought Republicans could find no woman more damaging to the diversity and needs of the female half of this country than Sarah Palin, take a good look at Carly Fiorina and what she stands for."[45]

Throughout Fiorina's bid for the nomination, she declined to treat biology as a credential for high office. Elections should not be based on "identity politics [or] what you look like, she says, telling journalists she won't let Clinton 'play the gender card'."[46] Fiorina stated on Fox News Sunday, "Frankly, I'm tired of being insulted by liberal feminists who talk about women's issues when the reality is every issue is a women's issue, from the economy to ISIS to Russia to health care to education to the national debt. Women care about all of that."[47] For some Republican women, the rejection of Fiorina was hypocritical. For them, why couldn't a woman who opposes abortion and align on the conservative side of issues be accepted as a feminist?

Carrie Lukas argued that in general, most Liberals dismiss conservative women as tokens, less than smart and lightweights. Lukas admired Fiorina's detailed knowledge of public policy and going head-to-toe with left leaning media interviewers such as George Stephanopoulos or Andria Mitchell. In contrast, for Lukas, Clinton's campaign was very scripted, only giving speeches to safe crowds and interviews to friendly media outlets. Another contrast for Lukas is in addressing the role of gender in the campaign. For Clinton, it is about time for a woman president and need for historic vote. For Fiorina, the election would be a story of women's steady progress. "She can tell jaw-dropping anecdotes about the sexism she faced in the business world, but offers a decidedly positive vision of the United States as a country making strides toward becoming a more perfect union."[48] In a speech, Fiorina put it this way, "Here in this country, where women have more opportunities than any-where else on the earth, we still can make our country a better place by fully tapping the potential of every woman."[49] Fiorina argued women should live the life they chose to live, whether it is to be a stay-at-home mom or corporate CEO. For Lukas, Fiorina's perspective was one of "true tolerance and respect for women's choices."[50]

Donald Trump

To say that issues of gender dominated the Trump campaign during the primary season is an understatement. His attack on Megyn Kelly, Carly Fiorina, Cruz's wife and previous comments and characterizations of women dogged him throughout the primary season. Trump called Fox News anchor Megyn Kelly a "bimbo" and said she had "blood coming out of her wherever" after she challenged him during a debate.

Trump called Clinton "shrill" and used a vulgar variation of a Yiddish term to describe her 2008 loss to Barack Obama. At one point Trump re-tweeted, "If Hillary Clinton can't satisfy her husband what makes her think she can satisfy America?" He continually accused Clinton of playing the "woman's card."

He insulted fellow White House contender Carly Fiorina by saying, "Look at that face! Would anyone vote for that? Can you imagine that, the face of our next president?" A super PAC released a picture of Trump's wife from a photo shoot in GQ magazine. The copy read: "Meet Melania Trump. Your next first lady. Or, you could support Ted Cruz on Tuesday." Then Trump threatened to "spill the beans" on Cruz's wife. He posted on Twitter an unflattering image of Mrs. Cruz next to a glamor shot of his wife. He concludes: "The images are worth a thousand words."

Of course Trump did little to endure himself to women voters. He vowed to "punish" women who have abortions if they are made illegal and defended his campaign manager after he was accused of manhandling a female reporter. Polls continued to reveal that in general, women were very concerned about Trump's bullying nature and volatile temperament. Throughout the primary season, Clinton held a 20-point lead over Trump among women. Even among Republican women over a third did not favor Trump winning the nomination.

Clinton early on accused Trump of being "sexist." Trump was quick to note the hypocrisy given Bill Clinton's behavior. As already noted, this was a major issue even among Democrat women.

There were some women who came to Trump's defense. According to Emma Roller, women who defended Trump express, "He's not sexist, he's just not politically correct. He's not a career politician, so he doesn't stick his finger in the wind before he says something. He believes in treating women as tough as he treats men. The news media has distorted his message with cherry-picked sound bites. If he were sexist, would he have promoted so many female executives, including his daughter within his own company?"[51] Female supporters make the argument that he hires more women in his executive positions than men.

There was speculation that some of Trump's retorts related to women were strategic. *Washington Post* editorial writer Dana Milbank argued that part of Trump's strategy is gender resentment. The argument is that among males there is a perceived societal threat to male identity and masculinity thus leading to increased support for Trump among men. This strategy was designed to boost support among conservative and even evangelical Christian men.[52]

It was very clear that Trump had a "woman's problem" during the primary season. But so did Clinton, but among her own target constituencies. However, Clinton enjoyed a solid lead among women voters in general and mostly among Democrat women.

GENERAL CAMPAIGN

Most of the same issues and themes related to gender in the primary season emerged during the general election campaign. However, issues of gender were prevalent daily in media coverage, commentary and by both candidates. This was, without question, the most "gendered" presidential campaign in American history. Of course, this was not surprising because Clinton was the first woman to be nominated by a major party to run for president. Thus, gender would inevitably be an election issue. Jackson Katz proclaimed that the election was a watershed, "It's as close to a national referendum on the state of women's advancement as you could possibly get."[53] Katz argues that the slogan "Make America Great Again" is actually code "for white men who feel betrayed by the system."[54] However, Donald Trump made gender an issue, intentionally and by design. His masculinity was evident and on display.

According to Julie Sedivy, Trump has been one of the most masculine candidates for president in recent times. He constantly asserted his maleness in statements and actions. Ironically, according to Sedivy, the way Trump "speaks and the actually words he uses makes for a distinctly feminine style. In fact, his speaking style is more feminine by far than any other candidate in the 2016 cycle, more feminine than any other presidential candidate since 2004."[55]

In general, research demonstrates that the more feminine a speaker's style, the more likable and trustworthy they seem to be. Jennifer Jones created an index that captures the ratio of "feminine" to "masculine" words and applied it to several dozen political candidates over the last decade. She found that Clinton's language is more feminine than George W. Bush but less so than Barack Obama. Surprisingly, the most feminine candidate by far is Donald Trump with the next most feminine speaker being Ben Carson. The least feminine candidate was Democrat candidate Jim Webb.[56] For Jones, the key for Trump is not what he talks about, rather how he says it. The feminine style reflects language that is more socially oriented, expressive and dynamic. Masculine language is more impersonal, long-winded and unemotional. Sedivy suggests that perhaps Trump's well above average feminine style countered some of the portrayals of him being domineering and lack of concerns for others.[57]

Margaret Talbot argued that Clinton had been judged "as a woman" since she appeared on the national stage. Clinton had been criticized "for using her maiden name, for her decision to continue working as a lawyer after her husband became governor of Arkansas, her lack of interest in cookie baking, for her hair, her ankles, her clothes, her smile, her laugh, and her voice."[58] There were also suspicions that she was a lesbian and even responsible for the death of deputy White House Counsel Vince Foster. Finally, as already mentioned, some argued Clinton was not an authentic feminist because she obtained national prominence because of her husband, stood by him during an affair in the White House and even lied about it. Interestingly, Talbot notes that Clinton gets the most public sympathy and approval when suffering humiliation. Her approval ratings went up during the Monica Lewinsky episode and when she tiered up at a rally in 2008.[59]

Somewhat prophetic, Gail Sheehy wrote that as far back as 1994 Clinton expressed her frustration in not being able to appeal to working-class white men: "It's not me they hate, it's the changes I represent. I'm the wife who went back to college ... " Sheehy indicated they both knew what she meant. Clinton was the wife who did get a degree and maybe get a better job than the husband. Men become threatened at the loss of their "cultural predominance." For Sheehy, men view Trump as "their savior, an action hero. He takes big risks. He talks a big game. Men like that."[60]

Talbot claims that Trump encouraged a lack of mutual respect by encouraging people at his rallies to chant "lock her up," and such references to invoking a newswoman's menstrual period, calling some women "fat pigs," commenting on their looks and even suggesting sexual assault on women revealed in a leaked tape.[61] Trump, on a daily basis accused Clinton of "playing the woman card," she didn't have a "presidential look" or the "stamina" to be commander-in-chief.

As in the primary phase, debates provided fodder for clashes over gender. As already noted, there are risks of males debating women generating the appearance of "chauvinistic bullying" and for women to appear competent while avoid being called shrill. In the first presidential debate, Trump interrupted Clinton 25 times in the first 26 minutes. Trump had 27 interruptions, 24 interjections and seized the floor from Clinton three times. In contrast, Clinton had only 5 interjections. During the entire debate, Trump had a total of 73 interruptions.[62]

Towards the end of the first debate Clinton attacked Trump for his treatment of women and specifically former Miss Universe Alicia Machado calling her "Ms. Piggy" and "Ms. Housekeeping." Trump withheld direct response by saying, "I was going to say something extremely rough to Hillary, to her family and I said to myself, I just can't do it. It's inappropriate. It's not nice." Trump had to spend several days defending himself against the charges reinforcing his demeaning comments on women's rights and looks. However, Trump surrogates pointed to this statement and response as being respectful and with a "big heart" while also making the argument that Clinton was "phony as a feminist." Clinton took money from countries that stoned women, imprison women and attacked those who claim husband Bill Clinton sexually assaulted. Some of Trump supporters noted that during the debate, Trump treated Clinton the same way he treated his primary opponents. As was often stated, "Trump was being Trump."[63]

Perhaps the most poignant episode was the release of the "Access Hollywood" tape where Trump was most crass and suggested an act of sexual assault. Trump apologized for the remarks noting that it was simply "locker room talk" between two guys. The comments alone were most alarming and the "boys will be boys" argument implied that this how men speak and act. While outrage was expressed among partisans on both sides, the comments did little to dissuade Republican women. One Republican strategist, Liz Mair, said of Trump that he comes across as "the kind of guy every woman out there has rolled her eyes at and turned down flat at least a couple times in her life."[64] After the video became public, 73 percent of Republican women indicated they would still support Trump. For Clare Malone, this was a rational choice about issues. "Republicans and Republican women are, by virtue of the person they have nominated, sacrificing a certain amount of respect in service to their concern for particular issues."[65]

Trump was very much aware of the "gender gap" in terms of support. He directly proclaimed his support and respect for women and related issues at every rally. In late August of 2016, the Trump campaign hired Kellyanne Conway, a longtime Republican pollster. Most of her career had been providing advice to politicians and marketers on how to appeal to women. She was clearly part of the strategy to win back women. It was her influence that he expressed explicit regret of his remarks on the tape as well as his appeals to Black voters. Not questioning Trump's motives, but strategically his appeal to Black voters in very white towns and crowds was successful attempting to demonstrate that he was not a bigot after all. In addition, Conway was a great spokesperson for the Trump campaign. She softened Trump's rhetoric and made him more disciplined. She created a message focused on a stronger economy and national defense. But Conway would equally attack Clinton. In one interview, she asked "You think you would know who Hillary Clinton is if she wasn't married to Bill Clinton?" Conway also faced down a hostile national press without losing her cool. She would often remind viewers she was a mother of four young children and clearly understood the issues and challenges of women today whether at home or in the workforce.[66]

Tara Golshan noted an interesting phenomenon during the campaign. Golshan argues that there was a new brand of "feminist media" that approached political and policy issues. "In the past decade, publications have shifted from a period of fluff election coverage in the early phases to a platform for impactful political content."[67] She thought women's media would help mobilize young female voters. During the campaign most women's magazines joined the #OurVoteCounts initiative to increase voter registration. The Clinton campaign recognized the power of women's magazines with the millennial women voters. Actually, it was in 2014 when *Cosmopolitan* magazine decided to cover the mid-term elections and only endorse pro-choice candidates did other women's media follow suit. The difference now is that women's publications are pushing a pro-women agenda.

Early in the campaign, Clinton made frequent references to the historic nature of her becoming the first woman president. However, moving into the general campaign she shifted appeals focusing more on children, women and families. Michelle Obama, Elizabeth Warren, Senator Amy Klobuchar and others joined Clinton on stage at rallies. What Alex Wagner found notable that pairs of women on the stage without a man. The "pairs of powerful women," who earlier times were somewhat at odds, were united on the campaign trail. There was true demonstration of sisterhood.[68]

With a month to go before the election, both campaigns made strong appeals to female voters. For Clinton, it was the well-educated white women in the suburbs and for Trump married white and evangelical women primarily in the final battleground states. Given Trump's appeal to white men, Clinton needed to exceed Obama's share of the women's vote.

In the final stretch, Clinton used spots aimed at women. The ad "Mirrors" had girls looking at their reflections listening to Trump talking "crudely" about women's bodies. For Trump, he featured his daughter, Ivanka, mother of three small children, who said her father "understands the needs of a modern workforce" and committed to laws that support women with children. His ad was an attempt to change the attention away from Trump's temperament and character to portraying him as a change agent. After analyzing the Clinton campaign advertising, the Trump campaign found that the Clinton campaign had failed to talk about the issues of health care and education. Thus, the Trump campaign began addressing those issues in speeches and media interviews.[69]

The day before the election, Alex Wagner predicted, "America will be no more post-gender in a Clinton Administration than it was post-racial under President Obama." The Clinton campaign was virtually certain of a victory.

POSTELECTION

When women got the vote in 1920, suffragists thought there would be a transformation to cleaner government, better education, safer housing and better quality of lives for American families. However, in fact, it seemed that women voted like their husbands based on their ethnicity, economic class, or geographic location. It was in the 1980s that campaigns began to notice a gender gap in terms of voting.[70] Republicans benefited from married white women and white evangelical women. Democrats received more votes from minority and younger women. The gap between the way men vote and women vote hit low double digits in 1984. The largest gap was in 2000 when it was a 22-point difference followed by 2012 with an 18-point difference. Throughout the summer, most polls showed more than a 20-point gap between men and women voters. Some believed a new record would be established. The question remained were there enough male voters for Trump to make up for the women's vote in Clinton's favor.[71]

According to exit polls, Clinton got 54 percent of the women's vote compared to 42 percent for Trump. Yet Trump received 53 percent of the white women's vote and 62 percent of white noncollege women's vote. Clinton received 51 percent to Trump's 45 percent of white college graduate women. Trump received 89 percent of Republican women's vote compared to Clinton's 90 percent of Democrat women's vote.[72] Although winning the women's vote overall, Clinton still got one percent less of the vote than Obama did in 2012. In fact, the majority of white women voted for Romney, McCain and George W. Bush twice. Even among the groups she won, such as poor women, young women and black women, turnout was disappointing. For example, Clinton won black women by two percentage points less than Obama in 2012 and eight points lower among Latina women.[73] A Pew Center poll showed that 28 percent of millennial women were voting "against" Trump rather than "for" Clinton at just 17 percent.[74]

Naomi Riley argues that "neither the fact that Hillary is a woman nor the fact that Donald Trump insults women seemed to have much of an effect."[75] As a group, women do not have much in common from an electoral perspective. "Their experiences in life and their views on policy issues tend to be shaped more by whether they went to college, whether they live in a city or suburb or rural area, whether they live in a blue state or red state, how much money they make and how they identify them-selves racially and ethnically."[76] Riley asserts that women's issues are really not much different from anyone else's issues. As noted, marital status appears to be a better indicator of one's life experience and ideological perspectives. Riley claims that Democrats will always do well with single women "because they're the ones—having no second adult to help support a family—who are most interested in and dependent on government assistance for income, retirement, childcare, etc."[77] Thus, Democrats will get their vote but not because they are women.

Lisa Featherstone also challenges the notion of "the unity of female identity." For her, "by banking on the idea that women would support a female presidential candidate, feminism made a terrible mistake. Strangely, given feminism's history of ignoring minorities, the group they misunderstood the most is white women, who usually vote Republican."[78] Indeed, gender alone does not overcome issues of mobility, poverty, jobs, law and order, etc. "Feminism has to mature beyond childish appeals to female unity, and recognize our many differences."[79]

John Judis echoes the same sentiment and argues the reason Clinton did so poorly among the core constituencies of minorities, millennials and single women is because the campaign overestimated the influence of identity politics. She underperformed in the critical groups.

> Millennials, it turns out, care about more than the relief of their student debts. Hispanics don't necessarily rate immigration reform first among their concerns, and many of them are as leery of illegal immigration as one of Trump's so-called deplorables. They want a larger vision of the future. In this year's election, Clinton didn't give it to them, and for that reason her vote fell short even among the groups she relied on.[80]

In the aftermath of the election, Tina Brown questioned the role liberal feminists played in Clinton's demise. She claims "the two weeks of media hyperventilation over grab-her-by-the-pussygate, when the airwaves were saturated with aghast liberal women equating Trump's gross comments with sexual assault, had the opposite effect on multiple women voters in the Heartland."[81] For most women, especially in the workplace, "boorish men are an occupational hazard, not an existential threat." The Clinton campaign thought "America's women would all be as outraged as the ones they came home to at night. But pink slips have hit entire neighborhoods, and towns. The angry white working-class men who voted in such strength for Trump do not live in an emotional vacuum. They are loved by white working class women—their wives, daughters, sisters and mothers, who participate in their remaindered pain."[82] Trump was seen as a tough boss and businessman who would bring jobs back "and with it the manhood of the sad guy they love."[83]

It seemed that, in comparison, women who voted for Trump were equally less happy with his behavior as were feminists who supported Bill Clinton about his behavior. It came down to policy choices and concerns. Actually, this perspective is no different from Evangelicals who supported Trump because of his positions on the Supreme Court and religious freedom who still very were concerned about his behavior and demeanor.

Just a couple of weeks before the election, Shikha Dalmia suggested that it would be better for the feminist movement if Clinton "had lost to a good man rather than won against a bad one."[84] At the heart of her argument is that by "brushing her flaws under the rug, whatever the political exigency now, won't be good for the feminist movement in the long run."[85] She thought at the time it would have been better for feminism is if it had taken a pass on Clinton's candidacy. To vote for Clinton while ignoring issues of national security, the Clinton Foundation and contradictions on sexual assault and harassment validates the impression that women were simply voting for Clinton because she was a woman. For Dalmia, "real feminist don't airbrush Hillary Clinton's flaws."[86]

CONCLUSION

From the beginning of the political season, there was no question that gender was going to be a major consideration in this presidential campaign. Clinton started her campaign talking about her mother, the struggles of women and how fathers should be able to tell their daughters that they too could become president of the United States.

Women certainly voted against Trump by one of the largest margins in history. Yet, noncollege women voted for Trump two to one and he carried married and evangelical white women by double digits. It appears that those who voted for Clinton did so with some degree of ambivalence.

The challenges women face in political campaigns are well documented. As noted throughout this chapter, most of the gender characterizations and portrayals noted in the 2008 race also appeared in the 2016 contest. However, there were two very unexpected aspects to the campaign. First were the reactions of third-wave feminists and younger women to the candidacy of Clinton. The milestone of having a women represent a major party running for president and the potential of the first woman serving in the role of president was not motive enough to guaranteed support. In fact, Clinton was an anathema of some of the core values of younger feminists. Turnout among young women and minorities were lower than in 2012.

The second unexpected gender element in this election were simply the statements, attitudes and behavior Trump displayed towards women throughout the campaign, not to mention much of his life. There has never been such public and blatant sexism in a presidential campaign. The sexism and misogyny were recognized on a daily basis.

The lasting impact of this campaign in terms of gender is less than certain. However, it did raise the focus and national discussion of gender in politics and beyond.

Notes

1. "Hillary Clinton's Concession Speech (full text), CNN, November 9, 2016, http://www.cnn.com/2016/11/09/politics/hillary-clinton-concession-speech/, accessed November 9, 2016.
2. Naomi Riley, "Killing the 'Sisterhood': Why Identity Politics Didn't Work for Clinton," *New York Post*, November 13, 1016, http://nypost.com/2016/11/13/killing-the-sisterhood-why-identity-politics-didnt-work-for-clinton/, retrieved November 14, 2016.
3. Dinesh Sharma, ""America's Exceptional Lack of a Female President," *New Republic*, May 12, 2016, https://newrepublic.com/article/133463/americas-exceptional-lack-female-president, retrieved May 13, 2016.
4. Ibid.
5. "Should Women Vote First for Women?" Rasmussen Reports, February 11, 2016, http://www.rasmussenreports.com/public_content/politics/general_ ... source=newsletter&utm_medium=email&utm_campaign= DailyNewsletter, retrieved February 11, 2016.
6. Kristina Sheeler and Karrin Anderson, *Woman President* (College Station: Texas A&M University Press, 2013).
7. Allyson Hobbs, "Why Aren't We Inspired by Hillary Clinton?" *The New Yorker*, September 23, 2015, http://www.newyorker.com/news/news-desk/why-arent-we-inspired-by-hillary-clinton, retrieved September 25, 2015.
8. Theodore Sheckles, Nichola Gutgold and Diana Carlin, *Gender and the American Presidency* (Lanham, MD: Lexington Books, 2012), 169–175.
9. Lisa Lerer, "Clinton Embraces 'First Mama' Role in Second White House Run," Real Clear Politics, June 22, 2015, http://www.realclearpolitics.com/articles/2015/06/22/clinton_embraces_first_mama_role_in_second_white_house_run_127070.html
10. Gail Sheehy, "Hillary's Sixties Surge," *Politico Magazine*, June 14, 2015, http://www.politico.com/magazine/story/2015/06/hillary-clinton-grandmother-in-chief-118978_full.html?print#.VYA4_mCsk2w, retrieved June 16, 2015.

11. Ibid.
12. Ibid.
13. "Hillary Clinton's Problem with Men," National Journal, October 7, 2015, http://www.nationaljournal.com/next-america/workforce/5-key-health-disparities-between-blacks-whites?mref=scroll, retrieved October 8, 2015.
14. Molly Mirhashem, "What Young Feminists Think of Hillary Clinton," *National Journal*, May 18, 2015, http://www.nationaljournal.com/maga zine/2016-hillary-clinton-feminists-20150515, retrieved May 18, 2015.
15. Ibid.
16. "Clinton Looks to Sisterhood, but Votes May Go to Sanders," *The Washington Post*, February 7, 2016, https://www.washingtonpost.com/politics/2016/02/07/8c73740c-c50a-11e5-a4aa-f25866ba0dc6_story.html, retrieved February 8, 2016.
17. Jill Abramson, "'Hillary, Can You Excite Us?': The Trouble with Clinton and Young Women," *The Guardian*, January 26, 2016, http://www.the guardian.com/us-news/commentisfree/2016/jan/24/hillary-clinton-young-women-voters-jill-abramson, retrieved January 26, 2016.
18. Jeff Jacoby, "Gender Is No Credential for the White House," *The Boston Globe*, May 7, 2015, http://www.bostonglobe.com/opinion/2015/0506/biology-credential-for-white-house/YQY5aECzldAAs4BxbjMTGK/story.html/, retrieved May 7, 2015.
19. Holly Scheer, "Women Have Good Reasons for Not Supporting Hillary," TheFederalist.Com, March 12, 2016, http://thefederalist.com/2016/03/11/women-have-good-reasons-for-not-supporting-hillary/, retrieved March 12, 2016.
20. Ibid.
21. Ibid.
22. Ibid.
23. Camille Pagilla, "Sexism Has Nothing to Do with It," Salon.com, February 11, 2016, http://www.salon.com/2016/02/11/sexism_has_nothing_to_do_with_ ... steinem_and_why_new_hampshire_women_broke_for_ber nie_sanders/, retrieved February 11, 2016.
24. Amy Chozick, "'90s Scandals Threaten to Erode Hillary Clinton's Strength with Women," *The New York Times*, January 20, 2016, http://www.nytimes.com/2016/01/21/us/politics/90s-scandals-threaten-to-erode-hillary-clin tons-strength-with-women.html?_r=0, retrieved January 20, 2016.
25. David Daley, "Camille Paglia: How Bill Clinton Is Like Bill Cosby," Salon.Com, July 28, 2015, http://www.salon.com/2015/07/28/camille_paglia_how_bill_clinton_is_like_bill_cosby/, retrieved July 30, 2015.
26. Caitlin Flanagan, "Why This Democrat Won't Vote for Hillary Clinton," *Time*, January 21, 2016, http://time.com/4177436/hillary-clinton-jua nita-broaddrick/?xid=homepage, retrieved January 25, 2016.

200   R.E. DENTON, JR.

27. Ibid.
28. Ibid.
29. Ibid.
30. Amy Chozick, "'90 s Scandals Threaten to Erode Hillary Clinton's Strength with Women."
31. Ibid.
32. Ibid.
33. "The Clinton War on Women," *The Wall Street Journal*, December 29, 2016, http://www.wsj.com/articles/the-clinton-war-on-women-1451432109, retrieved December 30, 2016.
34. Heather Wilhelm, "A Woman President? Who Cares?" Real Clear Politics, October 8, 2015, http://www.realclearpolitics.com/articles/2015/10/08/a_woman_president_who_cares_128336, retrieved October 8, 2015.
35. Jay Newton Small, "Exclusive: Hillary Clinton on Running and Governing as a Woman," *Time*, January 7, 2016, http://time.com/4166539/hillary-clinton-woman-governing-campaigning/?xid=homepage, retrieved 1/7/16.
36. Liza Mundy, "Playing the Granny Card," *The Atlantic*, June 2015, http://www.theatlantic.com/magazine/archive/2015/06/playing-the-granny-card/392105/, retrieved May 19, 2015.
37. Amy Chozick and Yamiche Alcindor, "Moms and Daughters Debate Gender Factor in Hillary Clinton's Bid," *The New York Times*, December 12, 2015, http://www.nytimes.com/2015/12/13/us/politics/moms-and-daughters-debate-gender-factor-in-hillary-clintons-bid.html, retrieved January 22, 2016.
38. Ibid.
39. Alexander Bolton, "Frustrated Female Senators Say Clinton Is Victim of Sexism," *The Hill*, February 15, 2016, http://thehill.com/news/senate/269341-frustrated-female-senators-say-clinton-is-victim-of-sexism, retrieved February 16, 2016.
40. Ibid.
41. Ibid.
42. Bryce Covert, "Of Course Hillary Clinton Is a Victim of Sexism," *New York Daily News*, February 10, 2016, http://www.nydailynews.com/opinion/bryce-covert-hillary-victim-sexism-article-1.2525978, retrieved February 10, 2016.
43. Ibid.
44. Amy Chozick, "Liberal Feminists Ponder Friends, Foes and Carly Fiorina," *The New York Times*, September 28, 2015, http://www.nytimes.com/2015/09/29/us/politics/carly-fiorina-both-repels-and-enthralls-liberal-feminists.html?_r=2, retrieved September 29, 2016.

45. Andrew Tavani, "Gloria Steinem Eviscerates Carly Fiorina with Scathing Post on Facebook," *New York Times*, September 23, 2015, http://nylive.nytimes.com/womenintheworld/2015/0921/gloria-steinem-eviscerates-carly-fiorina-with-scathing-post-on-facebook/html, retrieved September 23, 2015.
46. Jeff Jacoby, "Gender Is No Credential for the White House."
47. Andrea Peyser, "Hillary and Carly Are Putting on a Pathetic Estrogen Spectacle," *New York Post*, November 6, 2015, http://nypost.com/2015/11/06/hillary-and-carly-are-putting-on-a-pathetic-estrogen-spectacle/, retrieved November 6, 2015.
48. Carrie Lukas, "Why Carly Fiorina's Feminism Flummoxes Liberals," *New York Post*, June 30, 2016, http://nypost.com/2015/06/30/why-carly-fiorinas-feminism-flummoxes-liberals/, retrieved July 2, 2016.
49. Ibid.
50. Ibid.
51. Emma Roller, "The Women Who Like Donald Trump," *The New York Times*, May 10, 2016, http://www.nytimes.com/2016/05/10/opinion/campaign-stops/the-women-who-like-donald-trump.html?ref=opinion&_r=0, retrieved May 11, 2016.
52. Dana Milbank, "Trump's Calculated Misogyny," *The Washington Post*, April 29, 2016, https://www.washingtonpost.com/opinions/trumps-calculated-misogyny/2016/04/29/c063a984-0e03-11e6-bfa1-4efa856caf2a_story.html, retrieved May 1, 2016.
53. Ann Kingston, "How Hillary Turned the U.S. Election into a Showdown Over Gender," Maclean's.com July 19, 2016, http://www.macleans.ca/politics/washington/how-hillary-turned-the-u-s-election-into-a-showdown-over-gender/, retrieved July 24, 2016.
54. Ibid.
55. Julie Sedivy, "Donald Trump Talks Like a Woman," POLITICO Magazine, October 25, 2016, http://www.politico.com/magazine/story/2016/10/trump-feminine-speaking-style-214391, retrieved October 26, 2016.
56. Ibid.
57. Ibid.
58. Margaret Talbot, "2016's Manifest Misogyny," *The New Yorker*, October 16, 2016, http://www.newyorker.com/magazine/2016/10/24/2016s-manifest-misogyny, retrieved October 16, 2016.
59. Ibid.
60. Gail Sheehy, "Can She Do It? Hillary's Latest Incarnation: America's Tough But Kind Grandmother," *New York Daily News*, July 31, 2016, http://www.nydailynews.com/opinion/gail-sheehy-hillary-gender-politics-article-1.2731560, retrieved July 31, 2016.
61. Talbot, "2016's Manifest Misogyny."

62. Ben Schreckinger and Daniel Strauss, "Did Trump Come Off as Sexist?" *Politico*, September 27, 2016, http://www.politico.com/story/2016/09/trump-women-sexism-debate-clinton-228759?lo=ap_e2, retrieved September 27, 2016.

63. Ibid.

64. Ibid.

65. Clare Malone, "For Many GOP Women, Party Loyalty Trumps Personal Affront," FiveThirtyEight.com, October 14, 2016, http://fivethirtyeight.com/features/for-many-gop-women-party-loyalty-trumps-personal-affront/, retrieved October 15, 2016.

66. Ibid.

67. Tara Golshan, "Don't Underestimate *Cosmo*: Women's Magazines Are Taking on Trump," VOX.com, September 30, 2016, http://www.vox.com/policy-and-politics/2016/9/30/13089842/feminist-women-magazines-trump-clinton-election, retrieved October 2, 2016.

68. Alex Wagner, "Ladies First," *The Atlantic*, November 5, 2016, https://www.theatlantic.com/politics/archive/2016/11/ladies-first/506546/, retrieved November 7, 2016.

69. Phillip Rucker, "Trump Has a Challenge with White Women: 'You Just Want to Smack Him'," *The Washington Post*, October 1, 2016, https://www.washingtonpost.com/politics/trump-has-a-challenge-wit...ck-him/2016/10/01/df08f9ee-875b-11e6-a3ef-f35afb41797f_story.html, retrieved October 2, 2016.

70. Gail Collins, "The Glass Ceiling Holds, *The New York Times*, November 11, 2016, http://www.nytimes.com/2016/11/13/opinion/sunday/the-glass-ceiling-holds.html?ref=opinion&_r=0, retrieved November 12, 1016.

71. Geoggrey Skelley, "Venus vs. Mars: A Record-Setting Gender Gap?" Crystal Ball, July 7, 2016, http://www.centerforpolitics.org/crystalball/articles/venus-vs-mars-a-record-setting-gender-gap/, retrieved July 13, 2016.

72. "Exit polls: National President," CNN.Com, November 9, 2016, http://www.cnn.com/election/results/exit-polls, retrieved November 10, 2016.

73. Liza Featherstone, "Feminists Misunderstood the Presidential Election from Day One," The Guardian, November 15, 2016, https://www.theguardian.com/commentisfree/2016/nov/15/feminists-election-misunderstood-women-voters, retrieved November 15, 2016.

74. Susan Page, "For Clinton, Sisterhood Is Powerful—and Trump Helps," *USA Today*, July 11, 2016, http://www.usatoday.com/story/news/politics/elections/2016/07/10/hillary-clinton-women-voters/86793244/, retrieved July 12, 2016.

75. Naomi Riley, "Killing the 'Sisterhood': Why Identity Politics Didn't Work for Clinton," *New York Post*, November 13, 1016, http://

nypost.com/2016/11/13/killing-the-sisterhood-why-identity-politics-didnt-work-for-clinton/, retrieved November 14, 2016.

76. Ibid.
77. Ibid.
78. Liza Featherstone, "Feminists Misunderstood the Presidential Election from Day One."
79. Ibid.
80. John Judis, "Why Identity Politics Couldn't Clinch a Clinton Win," *The Washington Post*, November 11, 2016, https://www.washingtonpost.com/opinions/why-identity-politics-cou ... n-win/2016/11/11/ed3bf966-a773-11e6-8fc0-7be8f848c492_story.html, retrieved November 13, 2016.
81. Tina Brown, "My Beef Over Hillary Clinton's Loss Is with Liberal Feminists, Young and Old," The Guardian, November 13, 2016, https://www.theguardian.com/commentisfree/2016/nov/12/hillary-clinton-liberal-feminists, retrieved November 13, 2016.
82. Ibid.
83. Ibid.
84. Shikha Dalmia, "Real Feminists Don't Airbrush Hillary Clinton's Flaws," The Week.com, October 23, 2016, http://theweek.com/articles/656616/real-feminists-dont-airbrush-hillary-clintons-flaws, retrieved October 23, 2016.
85. Ibid.
86. Ibid.

Robert E. Denton, Jr. holds the W. Thomas Rice Chair in the Pamplin College of Business and is professor and head of the Department of Communication at Virginia Tech. He is the author, coauthor, or editor of 26 books, several in multiple editions, on the presidency and political campaigns. His most recent volume is entitled *Social Fragmentation and the Decline of American Democracy: The End of the Social Contract* (with Ben Voth, 2017) and *Political Campaign Communication: Principles and Practices, 8th Edition* (with Judith Trent and Robert Friendenberg).

CHAPTER 8

The Dark Power of Words: Stratagems of Hate in the 2016 Presidential Campaign

Rita Kirk and Stephanie A. Martin

> If liberty means anything at all it means the right to tell people what they do not want to hear.
>
> (George Orwell. *The Freedom of the Press* 1945)[1]

Highly charged elections with offensive tactics and crude language are nothing new in the United States. Whether in state and local elections[2] or races for the White House,[3] campaigns use negative tactics to win. Those negative strategies occasionally boil over into the realm of hate speech, and with great effect. Among the many peculiarities of the 2016 presidential campaign, the most noxious may have been the way it normalized deeply divisive speech in public discourse, including hate speech. Alarming, even

R. Kirk (✉)
Department of Corporate Communication and the William F May Endowed Director of the Maguire Ethics Center, Southern Methodist University, Dallas, TX, USA
e-mail: rkirk@smu.edu

S.A. Martin
Department of Corporate Communication, Southern Methodist University, Dallas, TX, USA
e-mail: samartin@smu.edu

© The Author(s) 2017
R.E. Denton, Jr. (ed.), *The 2016 US Presidential Campaign*,
Political Campaigning and Communication,
DOI 10.1007/978-3-319-52599-0_8

the candidates engaged this kind of speech, articulated sentences and speeches to incendiary effect. This discourse loosened the boundaries of civil discussion, essential to democracy and self-governance, and likely increased already deep divisions and partisan divides among citizens. There is little doubt that the new media climate encouraged and promoted these most base forms of speech. Already, many scholars have begun to take on this important analysis, and likely will continue to do so. Our project here is slightly different. In this chapter, we take up the speech of the candidates themselves – Donald J. Trump and Hillary Clinton – and show how they contributed bad speech, even hate speech, during the 2016 campaign. Sometimes they did this on purpose; sometimes it came as a slip of the tongue. Sometimes an already bad situation was made worse when one of these two candidates refused to issue an honest apology. In either case, we argue that the result was the same: A coarsened discourse that was about the candidates and not the people, and that ultimate left little room for important policy discussion in the campaign.

First, we must make clear the distinction between highly critical attacks that constitute legitimate political commentary and hate speech, as well as the difference between incendiary speech in the political arena – what very nearly acts like hate speech – and what *is* hate speech as a legal matter. In legal terms, "hate speech" may be technically defined: It refers to written or verbal attacks on an individual or group's race, ethnicity, or gender. Moreover, hate speech, explains Jae-Jin Lee, is "abusive, insulting, intimidating, and harassing. And it may lead to violence, hatred, or discrimination."[4] However, the injury need not be corporeal. "In addition to physical violence, there is the violence of the word," writes Mari Matsuda, a critical race theorist who argues that hate speech legislation should be written so that those who engage in it can be criminally charged and punished. "Racist hate messages, threats, slurs, epithets, and disparagement all hit the gut of those in the target group."[5] That the effects of such messages are intangible does not make them less real for this concourse of theory.

Nonetheless, the United States, largely because of the First Amendment, has few restrictions on political speech, even when it comes to hate speech. And this is why it appears in discourse, in politics, and even in presidential campaigns. In earlier writing on the topic of hate speech in election bids, Kirk (then Kirk-Whillock) argued campaigns sometimes go so far as to develop stratagems of hate that are actively deployed as electoral tactics against an opponent. A stratagem is more than a political strategy, it is a device or trick of war, and it is meant to destroy.[6] By contrast, negative attacks are simply mean-spirited, absent of policy claims, and lack any substantive contrast between candidate positions. In negative attacks, claims are made through implication and innuendo. With stratagems, claims are made using epithets, threats, and baseless lies.

To pundits and ordinary voters, alike, the 2016 campaign felt like no other. For example, on October 5, *Washington Post* columnist Stuart Rothenberg released a column with the headline, "The unusual, unexpected, strange, weird and now bizarre presidential election." In it, Rothenberg noted, among other things, the race featured a Democratic nominee who had begun as "a prohibitive favorite for her party's nomination... but ended up as a rather narrow winner after a lengthy fight with a 75-year-old socialist who has few accomplishments on Capitol Hill and isn't even a Democrat." For Republicans, there was Donald Trump, a political novice with no real accomplishments in public service and whose main appeal appeared to be denigrating "the disabled, Mexicans, women, Americans of Hispanic ancestry, Gold Star families and a Republican senator who was tortured by his captors and is widely admired as a war hero."

"And if that wasn't bad enough, it took him five years to accept that Barack Obama was born in the United States. Oh, and the GOP nominee is also the favorite candidate of the KKK."[7] Both parties were astonished at the tumult within their ranks, but in Trump's case, it was the hate-filled accusations that branded his candidacy.

The appeal of Trump that Rothenberg describes in this excerpt exemplifies political stratagems based in hate. These stratagems worked as corrosives in the 2016 campaign, causing deep divisions among families and friends. They set a coarseness of language that many felt was inappropriate for children to hear, particularly on news channels or in primetime. And it reduced the power of arguments to provocative soundbites or tweets.

Indeed, the election of 2016 stands out for its volume of hate-filled messages. Simple Google searches return results with headlines that include, "This election is a referendum on hate," "How Americans are handling post-election hate," and "Please stop the hatred that this election has unleashed."[8] Each of these easy to find examples demonstrates that the discourse this time was different – different in the conversations and divisions it produced around dining room tables, water coolers, classrooms, soccer field sidelines, and more. Different in the kinds of articles and columns media pundits felt compelled to pen. And different because the candidates themselves toed the line as they edged toward of hate.

This, then raises the question: Why are these kinds of appeals, these hate-based stratagems, even permitted in campaigns? Most scholars argue that political speech is the most essential form of free speech, and they posit this based in the belief that the people's right to self-govern is the most sacred freedom contained in the First Amendment. To this way of thinking, a democratic society depends on wide and open debate, where decisions are not made a priori as to who is right or which arguments should win, but constitutes an arena where all ideas – even bad or unwholesome ideas – are welcomed, so that the best ones will eventually prevail. For the most part, the Supreme Court has used this logic in its decisions with regard to political speech in the public sphere, as well. Indeed, they afford the *most* protection to people running for office. An important case for understanding this line of logic is *Bond v. Floyd*, which the Supreme Court decided in 1966. In this case, Julian Bond, a duly elected representative of the Georgia House of Representatives, opposed the war in Vietnam. In response, the House tried to deny him his right to take the oath of office. That position was overturned by the courts. The one person who must always have an unfettered right to speak is an individual who has been duly elected by the people. In fact, elected representatives, while acting in an official capacity, have an unqualified privilege against being sued for libel, a shield that regular citizens do not enjoy. This points to how seriously the founders, and the Court, take the need elected leaders have for being allowed to engage in wide open and robust debate and speech, without fear of retaliation. And while the Court has permitted regulation of time, place, and manner for free speech issues, content cannot serve as a reason for censorship.[9]

But free speech has its cost. While many uphold freedom of expression as the highest of political ideals, the truth is that it does not always enhance the reputation of the speaker. In the 2016 election, we witnessed a race to the bottom. Both Trump and Clinton had high negative ratings. And while the reason for these high negatives was related to many factors besides the things that each said, their discourse probably did not help. *Real Clear Politics' Poll of Polls* showed that on election day, Clinton's favorable ratings were 41.8 percent compared to her unfavorable rating of 54.4 percent. Similarly, Trump had a favorable rating of 37.5 percent and an unfavorable rating of 58.5 percent.[10] While we cannot determine causal effect, the level of hostility between the candidates likely tended to drive down favorable public opinion resulting in the lowest favorability ratings of any general election candidates since polling began.

To merely provide a list of all the hateful things said and done during the election is unsatisfactory to scholars and students of free speech issues and jurisprudence. Instead, it is important for communication researchers to scrutinize how stratagems of hate speech functioned in the 2016 campaign, and what effect these stratagems had, in order to better understand the arc of the discourse as it developed. We argue that this, in turn, will help us to see into the kinds of responses these stratagems encouraged, especially in voters, and how they prevented discussion of policy issues during the general election campaign. To do this, we describe with detailed examples of how enmity-filled discourse was deployed (intentionally or not) by both the Trump and Clinton campaigns, and how the media reported these discourses. We then conclude by evaluating the impact of hate speech on civil discourse, the media, and self-governance.

As a precaution, remember that hate speech is not confined to one party ideology or the other, as the reader will see in this analysis. This may offend the reader who would prefer us to take sides in the election. But that is not the point of this chapter. Neither do we claim that the candidates used these stratagems equally. Clearly, Trump mastered their use in the campaign. Rather, the purpose is to uncover hate appeals and to learn more about how they work, with the hope of finding better, more effective ways to communicate. Hate groups and their leaders, long suppressed and delegitimized, demonstrated new momentum and gained stronger voice in the presidential election of 2016. Our focus is to describe how hate stratagems became normalized in 2016, in the hope that we can de-naturalize them once again to the betterment of the public discourse. Presidents come and go, politicians will rise and fall, but the use and systematic understanding of the hate stratagem is essential for regaining control of the public sphere toward discussion of the issues and the policies that need attention given the constantly changing, complex nature of the twenty-first century, and the global and the global and economic challenges that will require the best problem-solving skills in us all.

HATE AS A STRATAGEM IN THE 2016 ELECTION

Few people will doubt that hateful speech factored into the 2016 election. Some of that speech moved from words into action. Noting that the Bureau of Justice Statistics estimates that two-thirds of hate crimes go unreported to law enforcement, the Southern Poverty Law Center (2016) counted at least 867 incidents of hate crimes that were called-in to police in the 10 days following the election.[11]

In addition, the election changed the climate for discourse throughout our society. There were far more instances reported of hate speech that appeared in public areas that are widely viewed as "safe spaces" meant for respecting human dignity and human life in all its forms and for all its differences, particularly the safe spaces in public schools. In one study released a few weeks after the election's end, "Over 2,500 educators described specific incidents of bigotry and harassment that can be directly traced to election rhetoric. These incidents include graffiti (such as swastikas), assaults on students and teachers, property damage, fights and threats of violence."[12] The message seems clear: behaviors that children see modeled from outside the school system became manifest within it. Certainly, the coarseness of comment escalated on Twitter, Facebook, and other social media sites. It also manifested in news reporting when invited guests lost their typical verbal filters, particularly when it came to responding to Trump's sex tape where he described grabbing women's genitalia. Hate speech is not easy to research, write, or read about. It is coarse and uncomfortable.

Yet, this sudden rupture of speech and behavior directly linked to the election is important and begs the question as to what communication specific appeals were at issue. This section looks at four specific kinds of appeals that carried overtones of hate in the 2016 presidential campaign – stratagems of hate that took root in the campaign, first identified in Kirk's earlier work on hate speech in the political realm.[13] Each of these played a role in the contest between Clinton and Trump. First, were those appeals that worked to inflame the emotions of the followers of one of the two candidates. Second, were those appeals that worked to denigrate the outclass. Third, were those appeals that sought to inflict permanent harm on the opposition. And fourth, were those appeals whose only aim was to conquer. Each of these appeals is outlined in the following.

APPEALS THAT INFLAME EMOTION

In his book, *A Rhetoric of Motives*, Kenneth Burke wrote that identification is fundamental to persuasion. Persuasion, of course, is essential for political candidates, because they need as many of their supporters as possible to be moved both to vote, and to become activists who will try to convince others to back the campaign. Put simply, identification refers to a feeling of having something in common: If A likes chocolate ice cream, and B does, too, then

A can likely be made to identify with B about this dessert. The more deeply A identifies with B – that is, the more important the topic of the identification, or the fiercer the emotional connection, even on a less weighty topic – the greater the sense of unity, and so the greater the sense of identification. For Burke, identification between parties could be particularly potent when it came to topoi of enmity.[14] In critiquing Adolf Hitler's tome *Mein Kampf*, Burke observed that "men [*sic*] who unite on nothing else can unite on the basis of a foe shared by all."[15] This kind identification through unification depends on the existence of a common enemy, even if this enemy must be rhetorically conjured or otherwise created, because it allows for a transference of blame and a corresponding affirmation that others share a particular point of view. Appeals to those who have experienced loss such as a job, a lifestyle, or a dream of the future are ripe for appeals that argue that the fault or blame resides with others.

Take this example. There is no doubt that many Americans, particularly those residing in the Rust Belt region, have been devastated by the loss of US manufacturing jobs over the past 30 years.[16] These job losses have been frequently blamed on Mexico, China, and other nations involved in what candidates from Ross Perot to Donald Trump contended were bad trade agreements, including NAFTA, even though the actual economic data does not fully corroborate this claim. Adding injury to insult, many of those most affected by this initial pattern of deindustrialization were especially hard hit by the 2008 economic recession, and slower to show signs of recovery, as well.[17] This pattern of financial struggle placed these voters at the center of much of the economic conversation in the 2016 campaign. Both Clinton and Trump advanced arguments about (white) working-class life that drew on stratagems of discord, if not outright hate, in an effort to build identification, and perhaps even enthusiasm, for their candidacies with the wider public. To make matters worse, the media sometimes failed to cover the full context of a candidate's incendiary quote, while talking endlessly about the worst parts, adding fuel to the fire.

In fact, from the beginning, Trump engaged rhetoric that used division as a form of identification. In his announcement speech, he situated winning on one side, and losing on the other, which became an important theme of his campaign to "Make America Great Again." On his side were winners; on the other side were losers. This is obviously true in any campaign, where one side gets the most votes and takes office, and the other does not and so goes home. However, right from the onset, Trump expanded his definition of winning and losing, and suggested that countries and constituencies beyond American borders (or, in the case of people, those most stereotypically "American") were unfairly triumphing, and that anyone who supported those outside constituencies were losers, as well. To this end, in his *very first remarks,* he averred: "Our country is in serious trouble. We don't have victories anymore . . . When was the last time anybody saw us beating, let's say, China in a trade deal? They kill us," he said. "When did we beat Japan at anything? They send their cars over by the millions, and what do we do? . . . They beat us all the time."[18]

But he saved some of the most striking rhetoric for Mexico and for Mexican immigrants in the United States. In so doing, he suggested that Mexico was economically ahead of the United States, and that most Mexican immigrants were both the antithesis of his supporters, and the among the worst humans a person could encounter. "They're (Mexico) beating us economically. They are not our friend, believe me," he said. Next, Trump gestured to the crowd gathered in front of him at Trump Tower in New York City, mostly comprised individuals who appeared to be of white, European descent, and said, "Thank you. It's true, and these (the people in front of him) are the best and the finest. When Mexico sends its people, they're not sending their best." That is, if Mexico were sending its best, they would be sending those individuals like the gathered crowd, fit and ready to fight for Team Trump. Instead, Trump continued:

"They're sending people that have lots of problems, and they're bringing those problems with us. They're bringing drugs. They're bringing crime. They're rapists. And some, I assume, are good people.

But I speak to border guards and they tell us what we're getting. And it only makes common sense . . . They're sending us not the right people."[19]

For the first day or two, these remarks were not the lead of the story, but only merited brief mention at the end most reports. This is because most early media reports did not take the Trump candidacy seriously. The *New York Times* report of his announcement speech, for example, described the New York billionaire as a "garrulous real estate developer" with little chance of winning the nomination, since all he had to offer voters were "his wealth and fame." It wasn't until near the bottom of the story that the *Times* reporter, Alexander Burns, brought up Trump's remarks against Mexicans, writing that "he vowed to build a 'great wall' on the Mexican border to keep out rapists and other criminals, who he said were sneaking into the United States in droves."[20] Other media outlets, including the *Washington Post*, immediately began fact checking Trump's speech, zeroing in on his claim about Mexican immigrants. *WaPo's Fact Checker* awarded Trump's claim that Mexican immigrants were mostly a criminal element "four Pinocchios" – its strongest signal to readers that a statement was meritless; an utter falsehood.[21] In explanation, Michelle Ye Hee Lee, a *Post* fact checker wrote:

> It's difficult to connect any crime with illegal immigration, by its nature. Drug smuggling and violent crimes do exist, but the cases are not indicative of larger trends in the immigrant population...
>
> Trump's statements underscore a common public perception that crime is correlated with immigration, especially illegal immigration. But that is a misperception; no solid data support it, and the data that do exist negate it.[22]

This kind of fact checking should be useful to voters. The 2016 campaign, because the race was plagued by innuendos, false allegations, and so-called fake news, was not.[23] However, in these kinds of fact checks, reporters tended to do little parsing, or holistic readings of candidate statements, which we claim was to the detriment of the overall discourse. To wit, included in Trump's remarks about Mexican immigrants was the phrase, "And some, I assume, are good people." However, in the days following Trump's speech, reporters and commentators who talked to him about his announcement bid typically only asked him about his most incendiary remarks. There was not time for nuanced conversation about the candidate's overall impression of Mexico, its people, or Mexican immigrants to America. Rather, the questions centered on whether Trump would apologize for what he had said – probably made worse by the candidate's ongoing refusal to do so. Nonetheless, the media's failure to acknowledge that Trump had not called *all* Mexicans "rapists and murderers" likely frustrated voters on the right who already doubt that *any* Republican could get a fair shake from the so-called liberal press – including Donald Trump. This left the AltRight, numerous right-wing websites and online news outlets to become more trusted sources for Trump supporters than the mainstream media. This was a difficult needle for the political press corps to try to thread in Trump's case, but in hindsight, their failure to have tried to do so may have made it easier for Trump to defy media convention in the ways that he did, because he could tell his supporters the media were all crooks who could not be trusted and his supporters could point to a specific case for proof. In addition, this perceived oversight may have made these same Trump supporters numb to the very fact check sources like the *Washington Post* who were providing analysis about Trump's most dubious and incendiary claims throughout the campaign.

This, in turn, allowed the real estate mogul to fuel the race-based discourse as a campaign stratagem because he refused to dial back his comments and – again, against all fact checks – insisted they were true.[24] This may have had two effects. First, it increased discord between Trump and the press corps. Second, it likely helped create and then reinforce a sense of rhetorical identification between Trump and his core followers. Just as these voters felt attacked by economic upheaval and demographic shifts, so Trump was besieged by the media. And so, together, they would take the country back – even if doing so required using hateful language to put their message out. To them the problem wasn't the language, after all. It was the politically correct culture that prevented them from speaking the truth.[25] Indeed, this identification between Trump and these economically disenfranchised voters would prove especially poignant for the New York billionaire when Hillary Clinton made a verbal slip early in the fall of the general election campaign.

There is little doubt that Donald Trump and his campaign used incendiary speech as a stratagem more than did Hillary Clinton and her campaign. Even so, Clinton was not immune from stooping low. On Friday, September 9, with a lead of just over three percentage points in the national polls,[26] Hillary Clinton attended a fundraiser in New York City. In a jocular mood, appearing after Barbra Streisand, Clinton took to the stage to speak. It was then that she would make one of her worst statements of the campaign, with reckless, off the cuff, remarks aimed at Trump and – more problematically – his supporters:

> You know, to just be grossly generalistic, you could put half of Trump's supporters into what I call the 'basket of deplorables'. Right? The racist, sexist, homophobic, xenophobic, Islamaphobic – you name it. And unfortunately there are people like that. And he (Trump) has lifted them up . . .

> He tweets and retweets their offensive hateful mean-spirited rhetoric. Now, some of those folks – they are irredeemable, but thankfully they are not America.

Trump and his team immediately seized on Clinton's remarks, calling them "insulting" and "slander." On Saturday, Clinton apologized for her remarks, but only in part. She refused to retract the statement in full, but rather said that it was "too generalistic" to say that "half" of Trump's supporters were deplorable. In part, Clinton likely did this because she was trying to point to the second half of her comment, which was receiving less attention:

> But [there is another] basket... of people... who feel that the government has let them down, the economy has let them down, nobody cares about them, nobody worries about what happens to their lives and their futures, and they're just desperate for change... They don't buy everything he (Trump) says, but he seems to hold out some hope that their lives will be different. They won't wake up and see their jobs disappear, lose a kid to heroin, feel like they're in a dead-end. Those are people we have to understand and empathize with, as well.[27]

For Clinton, this second "basket" of voters made up the largest portion of Trump's base – those white, working class voters in the Rust Belt and rural America, who Clinton hoped she could convince to vote for her instead of the New York billionaire. However, her refusal to fully apologize for her remarks, because she wanted to hang on to this second part of her statement and, with luck, reach this second group of voters, meant that the "deplorables" comment remained in the newscycle. All three Sunday shows on September 11 folded the remarks into their main talking points.[28] However, there was almost no discussion of the second part of Clinton's quote, but only attention to how much the comment would hurt her standing with voters. By Monday, Donald Trump's team had a new advertisement up in battleground states, called "Deplorables." It showed images of voters from all walks of life gathered at Trump rallies, using Clinton's voice for part of the voiccover. No one cared that Clinton was trying to point to Trump's appeal to white supremacists and those with anti-Semitic tendencies.

In the end, it seems likely that Clinton's speech did almost nothing to reach individuals in the so-called second basket, but instead only increased their identification with Donald Trump. That is, her speech ultimately worked to his advantage. Once again, this identification was probably helped along by a media system that lacks both the time and the structure to paint a holistic picture of what a candidate actually says. More than ever, campaigns depend on soundbites, pundits, and advertisements for messaging. In 2016, this meant that when stratagems of hate infiltrated the marketplace of ideas, they could be neither retracted nor explained. Clinton *meant* to call *some* of Trump's supporters deplorable; there is little doubt about that. But her unartful expression meant that she lost control of the conversation, as it spiraled into pathological discourse.

Inflaming the emotions results in the diminished use of reason. It is also the siren call to respond to those feelings by striking back, often by denigrating others.

APPEALS THAT DENIGRATE THE OUTCLASS

A second element of the hate stratagem is the denigration of the outclass. The outclass may be a minority viewpoint or a characterization of "others" that paints them in a negative light. Often, disparate people become coalesced through unfavorable association. The thinking behind this stratagem is that "it is more effective to give voters one good reason to vote against an opponent than a host of reasons to vote for the candidate you want them to support."[29] One of the easiest ways to do this through hatred and blame. If a candidate can situate an opponent and her or his supporters as the source a "voter's misfortune," then that voter will likely join the candidate's side.[30] Donald Trump is a master of this stratagem, and he may have learned how to execute it, at least in part, through his association with professional wrestling.

One of Trump's greatest assets as a politician is that he can command a stage, and he knows how to work a crowd. He is also not above using name-calling as a tactic to generate headlines and fire up an audience. He likely learned and honed this skill during the time that he was most active with World Wrestling Entertainment (WWE). He is still a member of the WWE, and is even enshrined in their Hall of Fame. He is credited with saving wrestling as entertainment when audiences began flagging, but he is remembered best for actually participating himself once in the "Battle of the Billionaires," and aptly playing "the heel." Within the wrestling world, "the heel" is the villain, the insulter, the one who says outrageous things, is rude, and is expected to cheat in order to win. Importantly, it's the heel's job to "make the crowd angry" and to taunt the good guy – called the "face."[31] Spectators love booing the heel and cheering the face.

In many ways, this is just what happened during the 2016 election. Trump played the heel as he dispatched with one election opponent after another who tried to emerge as the good guy, "the face." To do this, Trump gave his opponents wrestling names, but ones that branded by implication and innuendo and so evaded response: "Low-Energy Jeb," "Crazy Bernie," "Lyin' Ted," "Little Marco," and, finally, "Crooked Hillary." Such names did, indeed, denigrate the outclass, and so made it easier for others to engage in name-calling as well. Lost in this political name-calling, however, was the awareness that "[w]restling is first and foremost a morality play between the faces and the heels."[32] While Trump seemed content to play the heel, none of these opponents became a suitable face with an ethical claim to lead, branding the entire slate of candidates as losers. Or, maybe, Trump was the only one who knew the rules of the new game, and so was the only candidate in either the primary or general election who understood that the wrestling model permits heels to turn to faces and then go back again. Thus, political opponents and the media had difficulty pinning him to any set of issues. While many political commentators suggested that Trump is a narcissist,[33] and that this should have proved disqualifying to voters, the character of the narcissist is a wrestling typology role he played well, and to his advantage. He used it to both mock his opponents *and* identify them as enemies worthy of derision and hate. He broke all the rules of political discourse, all the while accusing his opponents of doing the same thing, and said the system was rigged against him, right up until the system awarded him the presidency – the ultimate political prize.

His supporters might say that Trump did little harm with his name-calling; of his many sins in speaking, rough talk aimed at his opponents is the easiest to forgive. However, denigrating the opponent in wrestling is entertainment, but name calling in politics is different. People may not know that it's just designed to spur attention. For the voter, those who believe that "outsiders" are responsible for their lost jobs may conclude that eliminating the out-group will resolve the problem, or at least help prevent future pain. That is, Trump's wrestling discourse and crowd performances filtered into the spaces beyond the arenas. Thus, statements like "Make America White Again" begin to have resonance. In rhetoric, an idea is resonant because it's always been this way; and it's always been this way because it always was.[34] When it comes to racism and hate speech, an idea that is resonant can be quite a dangerous idea, indeed. At Trump rallies, there were many expressions of outrage at the perception of a white culture under attack. Other expressions of distrust of dissimilar others included signs at rallies with expressions like, "Hijab wearing b**ch." "It's our nation now. Get the f*** out." "Die He She." "Trump Nation: Whites Only." In moments of public discourse where it becomes safe or acceptable to denigrate members of the outclass, social filters crumble.

No doubt, appeals such as these inflamed the emotions of many voters on both sides. Words wound, and they sometimes also lead to action. After all, as Anthony Cortese so nicely notes, "Hate speech is seldom an invitation to politely chat."[35] Instead, it has a kind of silencing effect, which makes it nearly impossible to engage further discussion. This brings us to our next stratagem of hate.

Appeals that Inflict Permanent Harm on the Opposition

One marker of the presence of hate speech is the absence of evidence or analysis. In his evaluation of what went wrong with the election in general, *Washington Post* reporter Chris Cillizza noted that "the campaign was almost totally devoid of issues."[36] Instead, the campaigns seemed to be running on gamesmanship, a kind of reality TV full of cliffhangers and surprises. For example, in the days leading up to the debates, there were all sorts of rumors from both sides as to "special guests" that might be invited to the family boxes. The idea was to unsettle to opponent, to get inside of his/her head so the opponent would falter on stage. Senator Clair McCaskill had been invited by Clinton to sit in the family box, but the Presidential Debate Commission forced the campaign to find another seat for Missouri senator. Similarly, Mark Cuban, the Texas billionaire who was an outspoken critic of Trump, was seated on the front row.[37] The thrust and parry were clearly designed as psychological tactics to unnerve the opponent. These kinds of stunts might make for great debate ratings and build debate intrigue, but they lose sight of what these kinds of campaign events are supposed to be about: Candidate discussions regarding substantive issues that give voters a chance to see where the candidates really stand, what kinds of decisions they would make as president, and what sort of leaders they aspire to be.

These kinds of tactics move toward the realm of hate speech when the purpose becomes inflated and the intent is to inflict permanent and irrevocable harm to the opposition. Trump invited three women who accused Bill Clinton of unwanted sexual advances to his family box for the last debate. The plan was for the women to confront President Clinton in front of a national audience as the two family groups entered the hall.[38] Here, too, the Presidential Election Commission found out about the confrontation and so denied the guests access to the family box, seating them in the audience instead. Trump settled for holding a press conference with the women just prior to the debate. The clear intention of the planned confrontation was to inflict permanent and irreparable harm to Clinton's campaign. The event would not only have played out on national television, it may well have shifted the debate's focus from policy arguments to one of salacious personal attacks, while also doing the same to the news-cycle. This, in turn, would have been a disservice to voters who tuned in to the debates looking to hear substantive discussion between the two candidates. In addition, the impact of forcing Hillary to relive without warning, and at her opponent's behest, what was almost surely one of the most difficult times of her life, and to do so on a debate stage, would have had the potential to unfairly frame her as weak or incompetent. It was also disingenuous of Trump – to put it mildly – as the stunt was put together in the aftermath of the so-called Access Hollywood tape, where Trump was heard bragging about kissing women against their will and being unable to resist grabbing female genitalia.

Such stratagems do not end when the event does. When played on the national political scene, they set an election's tone. Others, both within and outside the campaign, join in the drama. For example, on October 6, 2016, the InfoWars website offered rewards of up to $100,000, in $1,000 to $5,000 increments, to try to entice individuals to wear an "Infowars 'Bill Clinton Rape' shirt on television for at least 5 seconds" or to "Anyone who can be vocally heard saying 'Bill Clinton is a rapist' while wearing the shirt or displaying similar imagery."[39] Sure enough, on November 2, 2016, a heckler was able to get close enough to the podium to be heard shouting the phrase while holding up a sign with the required words and the InfoWars logo.[40] To an observer not aware of the bounty, it might seem as if another voter had strong opinions about the issue rather than mere interest in a financial reward. Nevertheless, not only did the act make the news, it appeared to have rattled Clinton who responded, "I'm sick and tired of the negative, dark, divisive, dangerous vision and behavior of people who support Donald Trump." Again, an average citizen – who might not have been aware of the InfoWars incentive or the story behind Clinton's remarks – might have been left with the impression that the Democratic nominee meant to label all Trump supporters as divisive and dangerous. Either way, Clinton was harmed and left with little ground for effective response.

Manifestations of these events were also apparent when voters appeared at Trump rallies holding signs that included phrases like "WHORE" or "Trump vs. Tramp." How does a person respond to a value statement where one is judged to be immoral? There is no valid response. And, indeed, this is the problem with stratagems of hate – they foreclose debate and so invite silence. They promote schism over conversation; pugilism over policy. The point of hate speech is not the search for truth or the democratic good, as those who believe in robust freedoms of speech believe, but rather winning at all costs.

Appeals whose Only Aim is to Conquer

For many, the idea of conquer is a term of battle. In the 2016 election, the battle was not merely ideological. When confronted by a protestor at one of his rallies in February, Trump said to the crowd that he would like to "punch him in the face" rather than allow for dissent or merely stay on his own message.[41] At another rally, Trump invited the audience to participate: "If you see somebody getting ready to throw a tomato, knock the crap out of them, would you? Just knock the hell – I promise you, I will pay for the legal fees. I promise. I promise." One North Carolina supporter was arrested shortly after this statement for punching a protester, and so seemed to take Trump up on his offer.[42]

Protestors pushing the lines of decency against Hillary in particular, and Democratic ideas in general, became a regular feature of Trump rallies, leaving little room for doubt that Trump's rhetoric had provocative effect. However, some progressives also pushed the envelope of violence and hate. Noting that they, too, felt marginalized and left out, various groups on the left joined under the "People for Bernie" moniker and decided to confront Trump protestors directly. (The Sanders campaign insisted it had nothing to do with organizing this showdown.) The "People for Bernie's" Facebook page had over 11,600 people RSVP to a Trump event in Chicago and, according to NBC, the gained site 1.5 million followers, in all.[43] In the end, the Trump campaign had little choice but to shut down the event due to safety concerns.

This episode makes clear that using words and technology to provoke the threat of violence is not limited to one party or ideology or another. CNN reported on an edited tape by an undercover operation investigating a group supposedly working indirectly for the DNC – and, it was alleged, perhaps Clinton, herself. In the video, produced by *Project Veritas Action*, Scott Foval, National Field Director at Americans United for Change, seemed to encourage others to try to incite Trump supporters to violence. He says on the tape: "I mean honestly, it is not hard to get some of these assholes to pop off. It's a matter of showing up, to want to get into the rally, in a Planned Parenthood t-shirt. Or, Trump is a Nazi, you know. You can message to draw them out, and draw them to punch you."[44]

Campaigns have become expert at using hate stratagems to foment outrage. And those techniques now have names such as "bird-dogging."[45] A bird-dogging technique places an opponent's supporters near the head of the entrance line to an event. Once in, they are encouraged to boo or speak out or act in a way that draws media attention. The media becomes the tool that spreads the word to a broader audience.

In the conquering mentality, there is no middle ground or room for compromise. Indeed, finding common ground or settling issues for the common good is beside the point. Rather, the issues at stake are always framed as winner-take-all. In part, this is because conquerors mean to rule over the conquered, as they vanquish an illegitimate foe. Moreover, at the end of battle, conquerors rarely extend their hands in a gesture of peace. Rather, there is a discourse of triumphant haranguing – a kind of "I told you so" in victory that lacks the traditional conciliatory speech that recognizes an opponent for having run a race of dignity that was well fought. For example, even after winning his party's nomination, Trump defied convention and refused to concede that his primary opponents were patriots who had served the United States well. Speaking to a cheering crowd in Bismarck, North Dakota, he said, "Politicians have used you and stolen your votes. They have given you nothing. I will give you everything. I will give you what you've been looking for 50 years. I'm the only one."

The "only one" theme seemed to become a kind of mission statement for Trump during the general election. He didn't just want to win at the polls on election day. He wanted to win in a way that would destroy Clinton. At the Republican National Convention, Trump's first solo opportunity on the national stage, a plane flew overhead with the sign "Hillary for Prison" on it. This was the first welcome most people had to the convention site. Signs in the convention hall also echoed the theme.

Then, in the second debate, Trump threatened that if he were elected he would appoint a special prosecutor to investigate Hillary, even though the FBI had already cleared her of any criminal wrongdoing in the email scandal that had plagued her campaign. Shortly after the debate, signs began showing up and the rally chants returned: Lock her up! This continued even after the election on Trump's so-called victory tour. Commentators were quick to opine that the United States had begun to sound like a third-world country where victors shoot or imprison their former opponents.[46] As such, as the election wound down and the

American people looked to resume life under a new administration, many were left to wonder whether public discourse about the public's business had been irrevocably changed.

Conclusion

At the outset of this chapter, we noted two things. First, we said that free speech is valued as among the highest of democratic goods in the United States because it is regarded as essential to self-government. In order to discover democratic truth, the thinking goes, citizens must engage in robust debate, and listen to ideas both wonderful and ghastly. This was the argument of Alexander Meikeljohn, a foremost thinker in First Amendment thought, and a proponent of a free speech absolutism. This is clear in his text *Free Speech and Its Relation to Self-Government*, when he writes:

> Shall we, then, as practitioners of freedom, listen to ideas which, being opposed to our own, might destroy confidence in our form of government? Shall we give a hearing to those who hate and despise freedom, to those who, if they had the power, would destroy our institutions? Certainly, yes! Our action must be guided not by their principles, but by ours. We listen, not because they desire to speak, but because we need to hear. If there are arguments against our theory of government, our policies in war or in peace, we the citizens, the rulers, must hear and consider them for ourselves. That is the way of public safety. It is the program of self government.[47]

Meikeljohn's position is one that privileges speakers, and democracy, and the idea cherished by Enlightenment thinkers and the American founders, alike, that reason and debate necessarily, eventually, yield the public good.

But the 2016 election throws this certainty into doubt. The second thing we noted at the outset of the chapter is that the most recent presidential contest felt different to most – politicians, pundits, and voters, alike. In part, this was because there was little to no discussion or media coverage of policy, including the policy positions of candidates, during the campaign. For example, Andrew Tyndall who monitors the nightly broadcasts of ABC's *World News Tonight*, *CBS Evening News*, and *NBC Nightly News* found that through early October of 2016, the three networks had devoted just 32 minutes to policy coverage – topics like, healthcare, climate change, terrorism, foreign policy, LGBTQ issues, and more. By contrast, in 2008, the last time there was not an incumbent running for the presidency, the big three networks devoted 220 minutes to stories related to the candidates' policy positions.[48]

A Harvard University study reached similar conclusions about the media coverage of the 2016 campaign. These researchers, whose main focus was the news coverage during the convention period of July, found that the:

> leading "mediality" of the 2016 campaign [was] Clinton's emails...What Clinton might do in the Middle East or with trade or with the challenge of income inequality could reasonably be anyone's guess, given how little attention her policy statements have received in the news.
>
> [The other thing journalists love to cover is polls.] No aspect of the campaign meets journalists' need for novelty more predictably than does the horse race. Each new poll or disruption gives journalists the opportunity to reassess the candidates' tactics and positions in the race.[49]

We contend that this prioritization of scandal and horse race in a campaign that featured candidates who were willing to engage tawdry speech led to a race full of discursive transgression, which, in turn, left the voters almost entirely out of the discussion. Trump, in particular, seemed to take delight in blowing past red lines of normative taste and goodwill, but as we have shown, Clinton also played a role in the downward spiral of discourse.

For their part, the voters appear to be registering their disapproval with how poorly both the candidates and the media performed in this campaign. On November 19, 2016, just 11 days after election day, Liz Spayd, public editor for the *New York Times*, wrote that the newspaper was receiving record levels of calls and emails from readers, "five times the normal level," a volume among "the largest since Sept. 11." And while many of those who were contacting the paper were making general comments about the election, many others were "venting about *The Times's* coverage."[50] Among other things, these readers were upset that the paper had emphasized on its web homepage its statistically driven poll that gave Hillary Clinton an 80 percent chance of winning; had seemed to stereotype all Trump supporters as "homophobic, racist or anti-Muslim," and about a perceived overall liberal bias in coverage. Spayd, who as public editor is responsible for taking a holistic look at coverage and responding as such, noted that many factors were to blame, and that even progressives were frustrated with the paper somewhat surprising ways:

> Few could deny that if Trump's more moderate supporters are feeling bruised right now, the blame lies partly with their candidate and his penchant for inflammatory rhetoric. But the media is at fault too, for turning his remarks into a grim caricature that it applied to those who backed him. What struck me is how many liberal voters I spoke with felt so, too. They were Clinton backers, but, they want a news source that fairly covers people across the spectrum.[51]

At the end of the day, and at the risk of ending this chapter on a maudlin note, democracy is for these "people across the spectrum" – not those far to the left, far to the right, in the vaunted middle, or even those most hurt by job loss, recessions, or anything else. In taking up the question of hate speech and the problem of the inflammatory rhetoric that Spayd points to in her assessment of the 2016 campaign, we go back to our first tenet in this chapter: Free speech is for democracy, because democracy is for the people. However, free speech only works when there is a hearer to go along with a speaker. Listening is the hard part. This is because, "[w]ords," as Ursula K. Le Guin once wrote, "are meant to transform both speaker and hearer; they feed energy back and forth and amplify it."[52] When words work best in a democratic society, we are changed not only through speaking, but through hearing.

The problem, however, as was evident in the 2016 campaign, is that not all kinds of speech encourage listening or engagement. Hate speech, in particular, more often works to frighten, to intimidate and to silence, and hence to limit the participation of the "other" in discourse. This effectively renders moot the idea set forth by Justice Brandeis in writing in dissent in *Whitney v. California* (1927) that "[i]f there be time to expose through discussion the falsehood and fallacies, to avert the evil by the processes of education, the remedy to be applied is more speech, not enforced silence."[53] And in an era of declining public service, public participation, and even public interest in the events of the public square the question is raised: If, indeed, the election of 2016 has normalized stratagems of hate in campaigns, have we now entered an era where candidates will speak in ways that work to silence through injury and so squash the very voice of the people?

NOTES

1. George Orwell, "The Freedom of the Press," in *Animal Farm* (London: The Times Literary Supplement, 1972).
2. David Slayden Rita Kirk Whillock, ed. *Hate Speech* (Thousand Oaks, California: SAGE Publications, Inc.,1995).
3. Alex Sproveri Daniel M. Shea, "The Rise and Fall of Nasty Politics in America," *Cambridge Core* 45, no. 3 (2012). Catherine H. Zuckert Michael P. Zuckert, *Leo Strauss and the Problem of Political Philosophy* (Chicago: The University of Chicago Press, 2014).
4. Jae-Jin Lee, "Understanding hate speech as a communication phenomenon: Another view on campus speech code issues," *Communications and the Law*, (Volume 19, Issue: 2, 1997), p. 55.
5. Mari J. Matsuda, "Public Response to Racist Speech: Considering the Victim's Story," *Michigan Law Review*, (August, 1989), p. 2320.
6. Whillock, "The use of hate as a stratagem for achieving political and social goals," in *Hate Speech*, (Thousand Oaks, California: SAGE Publciations Inc., 1995), p. 29.
7. Stuart Rothenberg, "The Unusual, Unexpected, Strange, Weird and Now Bizarre Presidential Election," The Washington Post, https://www.washingtonpost.com/news/powerpost/wp/2016/10/05/the-unusual-unexpected-strange-weird-and-now-bizarre-presidential-election/?utm_term=.3fe3f6ff8950.
8. David Corn, "This Election Is a Referendum on Hate," Mother Jones, http://www.motherjones.com/politics/2016/11/this-election-is-a-referendum-on-hate-donald-trump-hillary-clinton; Patrik Jonsson, "How Americans Are Handling Post Election Hate," The Christian Science Monitor http://www.csmonitor.com/USA/Society/2016/1112/How-Americans-are-handling-post-election-hate; DP Opinion, "Please Stop the Hate That This Election Has Uneashed" The Denver Post, http://www.denverpost.com/2016/11/16/please-stop-the-hate-that-this-election-has-unleashed/.
9. *Bond v. Floyd,* 385 U.S. 116 (1966).
10. Real Clear Politics, "Real Clear Politics' Poll of Polls," (2016), http://www.realclearpolitics.com/elections/2016/#!.
11. "Ten Days After: Harassment and Intimidation in the Aftermath of the Election," Southern Poverty Law Center, https://www.splcenter.org/20161129/ten-days-after-harassment-and-intimidation-aftermath-election.
12. "The Trump Effect: The Impact of the 2016 Presidential Election on Our Nation's Schools," Southern Poverty Law Center, https://www.splcenter.org/20161128/trump-effect-impact-2016-presidential-election-our-nations-schools.

13. Whillock.
14. Kenneth Burke, *A Rhetoric of Motives* (Los Angeles University of California Press, 1969), 19-21.
15. Kenneth Burke, *The Philosophy of Literary Form: Studies in Symbolic Action* (Los Angeles: University of California Press, 1974); ibid.; Thomas E. Patterson, "Harvard Study: Policy Issues Nearly Absent in Presidential Campaign Coverage," The Conversation, https://theconversation.com/harvard-study-policy-issues-nearly-absent-in-presidential-campaign-coverage-65731.
16. Derek Thompson, "Donald Trump and the Twilight of White America," The Atlantic, http://www.theatlantic.com/politics/archive/2016/05/donald-trump-and-the-twilight-of-white-america/482655/.
17. Tim Henderson, "Fewer Manufacturing Jobs, Housing Bust Haunt Many U.S. Counties," The Pew Charitable Trusts, http://www.pewtrusts.org/en/research-and-analysis/blogs/stateline/2016/01/22/fewer-manufacturing-jobs-housing-bust-haunt-many-us-counties.
18. TIME Staff, "Here's Donald Trump's Presidential Announcement Speech," TIME, http://time.com/3923128/donald-trump-announcement-speech/.
19. Ibid.
20. Alexander Burns, "Donald Trump, Pushing Someone Rich, Offers Himself," The New York Times, http://www.nytimes.com/2015/06/17/us/politics/donald-trump-runs-for-president-this-time-for-real-he-says.html?_r=0.
21. Michelle Ye Hee Lee, "Donald Trump's False Comments Connecting Mexican Immigrants and Crime," The Washington Post, https://www.washingtonpost.com/news/fact-checker/wp/2015/07/08/donald-trumps-false-comments-connecting-mexican-immigrants-and-crime/?utm_term=.967220e8ebe7.
22. Ibid.
23. Amy Mitchell and Jesse Holcomb Michael Barthel, "Many Americans Believe Fake News Is Sowing Confusion," Pew Research Center, http://www.journalism.org/2016/12/15/many-americans-believe-fake-news-is-sowing-confusion/.
24. Lee, Michelle Ye Hee. "Donald Trump's False Comments Connecting Mexican Immigrants and Crime," *Washington Post*, https://www.washingtonpost.com/news/fact-checker/wp/2015/07/08/donald-trumps-false-comments-connecting-mexican-immigrants-and-crime/?utm_term=.607dae048f07.
25. Clive Hamilton, "Political Correctness: Its Origins and the Backlash against It August 30, 2015," *The Conversation* (August 30, 2015), https://theconversation.com/political-correctness-its-origins-and-the-backlash-against-it-46862.
26. Real Clear Politics, "Real Clear Politics' Poll of Polls."

27. Katie Reilly, "Read Hillary Clinton's 'Basket of Deplorables' Remarks About Donald Trump Supporters," TIME, http://time.com/4486502/hillary-clinton-basket-of-deplorables-transcript/.
28. "Meet the Press-Sept. 11, 2016," NBC News, http://www.nbcnews.com/meet-the-press/meet-press-sept-11-2016-n646441. "09/11/16: September 11th, 2001 and the Impact on Today's World," ABC. "Face the Nation Transcript September 11, 2016: Brennan Nunes," CBS News, http://www.cbsnews.com/news/face-the-nation-transcript-september-11-2016-brennan-nunes/.
29. Rita Kirk Whillock, ed. *Hate Speech*, 39.
30. Ibid, 30.
31. TVTropes.org, "Heel," TV Tropes, http://tvtropes.org/pmwiki/pmwiki.php/Main/Heel.
32. Amit Praseed, "What Does Turning Heel in Wrestling Mean?" Quora, https://www.quora.com/What-does-turning-heel-in-wrestling-mean.
33. Dan P. McAdams, "The Mind of Donald Trump," The Atlantic, http://www.theatlantic.com/magazine/archive/2016/06/the-mind-of-donald-trump/480771/; Adam Gopnik, "Donald Trump: Narcissist, Creep, Loser," The New Yorker, http://www.newyorker.com/news/news-desk/donald-trump-narcissist-creep-loser; Amy Ellis Nutt, "Is Donald Trump a Textbook Narcissist?" The Washington Post, https://www.washingtonpost.com/news/the-fix/wp/2016/07/22/is-donald-trump-a-textbook-narcissist/?utm_term=.2e0da63603f0; Jeffrey Kluger, "The Truth About Donald Trump's Narcissism," TIME, http://time.com/3992363/trump-narcissism/.
34. Linda Kintz, *Between Jesus and the Market: The Emotions That Matter in Right-Wing America* (Durham, NC: Duke University Press, 1997).
35. Anthony Cortese, *Opposing Hate Speech* (Westport, CT: Greenwood Publishing Group, 2006), 1.
36. Chris Cillizza, "Think This Election Is as Bad as It Gets? Just Wait," The Washington Post, https://www.washingtonpost.com/news/the-fix/wp/2016/10/27/hate-this-election-just-wait.
37. Dan Balz Robert Costa, Phillip Rucker, "Trump Wanted to Put Bill Clinton's Accusers in His Family Box. Debate Officials Said No," The Washington Post, https://www.washingtonpost.com/news/post-politics/wp/2016/10/10/trumps-debate-plan-to-seat-bill-clintons-accusers-in-family-box-was-thwarted/?utm_term=.ab6c89d3d570.
38. Ibid.
39. Infowars, "Expose Rapist Bill Clinton, Win $5 k," InfoWars, http://www.infowars.com/expose-rapist-bill-clinton-win-5k/.
40. Laura Bult, "Clinton Lashes Out at Heckler Who Called Husband a Rapist," New York Daily News, http://www.nydailynews.com/news/national/clinton-lashes-heckler-called-bill-clinton-rapist-article-1.2855092.

41. Jeremy Diamond, "Donald Trump on Protestor: 'I'd Like to Punch Him in the Face'," CNN, http://www.cnn.com/2016/02/23/politics/donald-trump-nevada-rally-punch/.

42. Philip Bump, "Donald Trump Reverses Course on Paying Legal Fees for Man Who Attacked Protester: But Could He Do It?" The Washington Post, https://www.washingtonpost.com/news/the-fix/wp/2016/03/10/trump-once-said-he-would-pay-legal-fees-for-people-who-beat-up-protesters-now-that-its-happened-can-he/?utm_term=.94049ea8b74f.

43. Alex Seitz-Wald, "How Bernie Sanders Supporters Shut Down Donald Trump's Rally in Chicago" NBC News, http://www.nbcnews.com/politics/2016-election/how-bernie-sanders-supporters-shut-down-donald-trump-s-rally-n537191.

44. Daniella Diza and Drew Griffin. 18 October 2016. Dem operative 'stepping back' after video suggests group incited violence at Trump rallies" http://www.cnn.com/2016/10/18/politics/project-veritas-action-robert-creamer-donald-trump-rallies/.

45. Karen M. McCormack A. Javier Trevino, ed. *Service Sociology and Academic Engagement in Social Problems* (New York: Routledge, 2016), 289.

46. Joshua Berlinger, "Trump Threatened to Jail Clinton If Elected. These Countries Might Do the Same," CNN, http://www.cnn.com/2016/10/10/politics/countries-that-jail-opposition-second-presidential-debate/; Benjamin Freed, "The Race between Clinton and Trump Looks Like a Third-World Election," Washingtonian, https://www.washingtonian.com/2016/10/12/veteran-republican-pollster-says-race-clinton-trump-looks-like-third-world-election/; Charlie Savage, "Threat to Jail Clinton Smacks of 'Tin-Pot Dictators,' Experts Say," The New York Times, http://www.nytimes.com/2016/10/11/us/politics/donald-trump-hillary-clinton-special-prosecutor.html?_r=0.

47. Alexander Meiklejohn, *Free Speech and Its Relation to Self-Government* (Lawbook Exchange Ltd., 2001), pp. 65–66. Originally published in 1948.

48. Eric Boehlert, "Study Confirms Network Evening Newscasts Have Abandoned Policy Coverage for 2016 Campaign," Media Matters, http://mediamatters.org/blog/2016/10/26/study-confirms-network-evening-newscasts-have-abandoned-policy-coverage-2016-campaign/214120.

49. Patterson, "Harvard Study: Policy Issues Nearly Absent in Presidential Campaign Coverage." Also see Thomas E. Patterson, "News Coverage of the 2016 National Conventions: Negative News, Lacking Context," Harvard Kennedy School Shorenstein Center of Media, Politics and Public Policy, https://shorensteincenter.org/news-coverage-2016-national-conventions/.

50. Liz Spayd, "One Thing Voters Agree On: Better Campaign Coverage Was Needed," The New York Times, http://www.nytimes.com/2016/11/20/public-editor/one-thing-voters-agree-on-better-campaign-coverage-was-needed.html.
51. Ibid.
52. Ursula K. Le Guin, *The Wave in the Mind: Talks and Essays on the Writer, the Reader, and the Imagination* (Boston: Shambhala, 2004), 199.
53. *Whitney v. California*, 274 U.S. 357 (1927).

Rita Kirk is a Meadows Distinguished Professor in the Department of Corporate Communication & Public Affairs and William F May Endowed Director of the Maguire Center for Ethics & Public Responsibility at Southern Methodist University. She is the author of several award-winning books and articles, including *Political Empiricism: Communications Strategies in State and Regional Elections; Hate Speech*, a book analyzing implications for hate discourse in public communication, with coeditor David Slayden; and *Solo Acts: The Death of Discourse* in a Wired World. She frequently serves as a media commentator and has served as an analyst for CNN during presidential election debates over the past ten years. She consults with national and multinational corporations on public policy and leadership.

Stephanie A. Martin is an assistant professor of political communication in the Division of Corporate Communication and Public Affairs at Southern Methodist University. Her research centers on conservative discourse in the United States, and especially how white, evangelical voters discursively frame their economic and social political interests, as compared to how political elites imagine such interests. She has also written about presidential rhetoric regarding the American economy. She has edited one book and a growing collection of refereed articles and book chapters on both of these topics. She holds PhD in communication from the University of California, San Diego.

CHAPTER 9

From Benghazi to E-Mails: Two Sides of the Same Scandal

David R. Dewberry

INTRODUCTION

In the second Democratic primary debate of 2015, the participants were asked, "Soon after your inauguration, you will face a crisis. All presidents do. What crisis have you experienced in your life that suggests you've been tested and can face that inevitable challenge? Secretary Clinton, you first."[1] Clinton paused and humorously replied, "Well, there are so many, I don't know where to start." Even though it was a lighthearted reply, there was some truth to it. During her political career—from First Lady of Arkansas and then of the United States, to US senator, to secretary of state, with two campaigns for president in the mix—Clinton had dealt with a great deal of controversy and scandal.

Clinton followed her lighthearted comment with a response that would earn her the most political capital: her role in going after Osama bin Laden. However, her most pressing crisis at the time was dealing with a Republican-led congressional inquiry, which started by investigating the 2012 attack on the American consulate in Benghazi where four Americans were killed. At the time of the debate, there had been over

D.R. Dewberry (✉)
Rider University, Lawrence Township, NJ, USA
e-mail: ddewberry@rider.edu

© The Author(s) 2017
R.E. Denton, Jr. (ed.), *The 2016 US Presidential Campaign*,
Political Campaigning and Communication,
DOI 10.1007/978-3-319-52599-0_9

six investigations into Benghazi, but it became apparent that the most recent congressional committee was more interested in her e-mails.

Even though the shift to Clinton's e-mails was something new at the time, the thematic narrative of what some have called "e-mailgate" is not.[2] As the noted political scientist Lance Bennett once observed, "It is difficult to watch the development of political issues without experiencing a powerful sense of déjà vu."[3] This observation, I have found, applies quite well to American political scandals. I have argued elsewhere that many political scandals share many of the same constitutive elements and play out with slight variations on a theme as they unfold.[4]

This chapter argues that the Benghazi and e-mail scandals are no exception to the American political scandal narrative in our political culture. To make this argument, I first describe the American political scandal narrative and then recount the Benghazi attack. Next, I focus on how scandals related to Benghazi followed the scandal narrative in the 2012 and then the 2016 presidential elections. In describing how the scandals unfolded in these two campaigns, I suggest that political scandals are political weapons, which is an argument I address at the end of the chapter.

The American Political Scandal Narrative

The American political scandal begins during a time of relative prosperity, which is disrupted by the press's publicity of misconduct. Next, politicians attack the alleged wrong doer, who, alongside his/her supporters, dismiss those accusations and respond in what can best be described as partisan rhetoric. To gain legitimacy and credibility, the accusers attempt to officialize themselves by assuming the proper role and setting. In response, the accused attempts to deofficialize the accusations by continuing to discredit the accusatory discourse as nothing more than partisan rhetoric.

Critical testimony and/or the potential for shocking evidence revealed by a smoking gun then reengages the public's attention, but often there is a battle for control of that evidence. Consequently, the heightened attention is lost as the scandal goes to the courts, where there often is little comment by those involved due to "ongoing litigation" or because the accused asserts his or her Fifth Amendment rights.

Finally, the scandal concludes with the confirmation of wrongdoing, the vindication of the accused, or abdication. This is the basic thematic narrative of the scandal, and many large and small scandals throughout

American political history can be described with this narrative with slight variations on the themes. Two recent and related scandals, although some question their status as such, originated out of an attack on a diplomatic compound in Benghazi, Libya.

THE ATTACK ON BENGHAZI

On September 9, 2012, US ambassador to Libya, J. Christopher Stevens, arrived in Benghazi to meet with local businessmen. He was well known and respected for his work in the area. Nevertheless, for obvious safety reasons, Stevens held all meetings inside the US diplomatic compound in Benghazi two days later on September 11.

That evening packs of heavily armed men stormed the compound. Interior defenses included five-armed diplomatic safety officers, who quickly located Ambassador Stevens and Sean Smith, a computer specialist, and placed them in a safe room. During the attack, a call for reinforcements was sent out to a nearby CIA annex for assistance, but there were delays of 30 minutes at the annex. During this first attack, Smith had been killed and Stevens went missing.

Eventually, reinforcements arrived and the decision was made to move everyone to the nearby CIA annex, where they endured waves of attacks throughout the night that resulted in the deaths of two former Navy Seals. With both compounds under attack, all US personnel prepared to make their way to the airport to leave Benghazi in the morning. Ambassador Stevens was still unaccounted for.

Hours after the attack began, the US embassy in Tripoli received a call from a hospital. A handful of Libyan citizens had apparently found the badly injured ambassador and rushed him to the hospital where doctors attempted to resuscitate him for almost an hour, but Stevens ultimately succumbed to smoke inhalation.

SCANDAL IN THE 2012 ELECTION

THE NEWS BREAKS

In September 2012, Republican Mitt Romney and President Barack Obama were in a close race, with Obama in a slight lead. With only two months left in the election, it was inevitable that Romney would make the most of any political opportunity, and he did on September 11. A YouTube video, which depicted the Prophet Muhammad as "a fool, a philanderer and a religious fake," sparked a significant uprising in Egypt on September 11, 2012.[5] Consequently, the US embassy in Cairo released a statement that condemned those who made the video and expressed concern that they were abusing "the universal right of free speech to hurt the religious beliefs of others."[6] If the statement was an attempt to calm the uprising, it did not work.

Protestors later stormed the Cairo embassy, destroyed the American flag, and replaced it with an Islamic flag. Later that night came the attack on Benghazi. The Associated Press reported at 7:45 p.m. that one American had been killed in Benghazi. News of the other three American deaths came the next day, September 12. Nevertheless, seemingly wanting to make the most of the opportunity fast, Romney responded shortly after 10:00 p.m. on September 11 to what he knew then.

After the news breaks in a scandal, the first major stage is, as Richard Nixon once said, for the opposition to make a "little thing" into a "big thing."[7] Certainly, the death of a US ambassador (and, as later reported, three government workers, who were all military veterans) is no little thing. Nixon's point, however, was that the opposition attempts to focus on a transgression (i.e., the "little thing," such as a break-in) of some standard (e.g., legal, moral, ethical, etc.) and make it into a "big thing," which often results in a full-blown scandal that involves some type of perceived cover-up. The discovery of a cover-up, revealed by a smoking gun, is so significant that it can lead to impeachment, resignation, and even prison as Secretary of the Interior Albert Fall learned at the end of the Teapot Dome scandal. These are significant outcomes, and they can be desirable outcomes, at least for members of the opposition.

Partisan Rhetoric and Dismissals

Mitt Romney attacked his opponent by saying, "It's disgraceful that the Obama administration's first response was not to condemn attacks on our diplomatic missions, but to sympathize with those who waged the attacks."[8] Romney then characterized the embassy's statement as an apology numerous times during his remarks. The nature of Romney's attacks dovetailed nicely with his overall campaign strategy that he, unlike Obama, would issue no apology for America.[9]

Romney did try to make a little thing (i.e., the embassy's statement) into a big thing that Obama apologizes for America. However, there were a number of concerns. First, the embassy's statement was not approved by anyone in Washington and did not reflect the views of the US government; consequently, the statement was later removed from the embassy's website. Second, the embassy's statement came out several hours before it was breached and many hours before the attack on the diplomatic compound and CIA annex in Benghazi. Third, the embassy's statement in no way apologized for anything; it condemned the makers of the video.

While it was later evident that his facts and timeline were wrong, Romney's biggest issue was that he failed to properly consider the *kairos* (i.e., the timing) and decorum of his remarks. An Obama campaign spokesperson responded to Romney's attacks stating that when American lives are lost abroad, any attempt to politicize that tragedy are met with heavy disdain. Other republicans and the press echoed this sentiment. Romney's running mate, Paul Ryan "appeared to undercut him with noticeably more conciliatory and somber responses... [by saying] 'This is a time for healing. It's a time for resolve'" at a campaign stop.[10] The *Washington Post* believed that Romney "would do well to consider the example of Republican former secretary of state Condoleezza Rice, who issued a statement Wednesday lamenting 'the tragic loss of life at our consulate,' praising Mr. Stevens as 'a wonderful officer and a terrific diplomat.'"[11]

In the American political scandal narrative, after attacks and responses on a number of issues related to a perceived transgression, there is often a stalemate. The partisan and accusatory tone coming from political candidates and the subsequent dismissal of such accusations create confusion about whom to believe. In situations where there is confusion, accusers attempt to officialize their attacks to gain legitimacy and credibility.

OFFICIALIZATION AND DEOFFICIALIZATION

Proper officialization requires the proper role and setting to accuse individuals of wrongdoing. In other words, an opportunistic political candidate on the campaign trail does not have the legitimacy of a congressionally appointed investigation that follows formal rules and has an aura of "pomp and spectacle."[12] These congressional investigations often commence quickly when Congress and the presidency are controlled by opposing parties.

A month after the attack and a month before the election, Rep. Darrell Issa, chairman of the House Oversight and Government Reform Committee, began an investigation. While Republicans attempted to officialize the accusations—these now being that the Obama administration had failed to ensure the safety of American officials in Benghazi—Democrats attempted to deofficialize the proceedings, which is when one challenges the attempt to legitimize the accusations via officialization. One way in which arguments of deofficialization can be neutralized is for the investigation to be bipartisan. However, the controlling party of Congress usually holds a majority of the seats on the investigative committee, which still leaves the opportunity for the minority party and/or the accused to deofficialize.

The cycle of officialization and deofficialization goes on until there is the discovery of a smoking gun, which results in two significant moments. First, the discovery of a smoking gun is a powerful argument that the investigation was not partisan and that there was, in fact, wrongdoing. Second, the discovery of a smoking gun confirms the very real possibility that there was a cover-up, which would propel any simmering controversy into a bona fide scandal. For example, Nixon's campaign broke into the DNC offices, but he covered it up. It was the cover-up that did him in, not the break-in. Bill Clinton had an extramarital affair, which was not a crime, but lying about it to a congressional investigation was. It was the lie—the cover-up—that ultimately caused his impeachment.

Consequently, Republicans needed to discover a cover-up to fully officialize their criticisms. They found an opportunity with the comments by then UN Ambassador Susan Rice, who appeared on five different Sunday morning political talk shows. She stated that the attacks were the result of a spontaneous demonstration in response to the YouTube video about Muhammad. Rice's story, Republicans believed, was an attempt to cover up the administration's failures to provide extra security to the Benghazi compound despite Ambassador Stevens's numerous requests. The bipartisan Senate Intelligence Committee later concluded that extra security would have helped prevent the attacks but that the initial description of the attack as a spontaneous demonstration was not an attempt to cover anything up. Other investigations reached similar conclusions.

RESPONSIBILITY AND REPORTS

Ultimately, scandals end when the accused is vindicated or has properly atoned for the wrongdoing. Such atonement can happen via scapegoating (e.g., Oliver North in Iran-Contra) but is often more successful via mortification. Just as Republicans began to officialize via congressional investigation, then Secretary of State Clinton claimed full responsibility. On October 15, 2012, she said, "I take responsibility. I'm in charge of the State Department's 60,000 people all over the world at 275 posts."[13] While an admission of responsibility, such statements often do not properly atone for any perceived transgressions. Claiming responsibility generally suggests that the speaker was not involved in any particular transgression but is grandiosely taking responsibility nonetheless.

The next day, President Obama and Romney debated, with one particular relevant exchange. Romney attempted to point out that there was a political cover-up. Now Romney and others believed that the Obama administration had changed its story from the attack being the result of a spontaneous demonstration spawned by an anti-Muslim video to calling it an act of terror some two weeks later. Obama's critics claimed he had a political incentive to not call the attacks an act of terror for as long as possible or until the election.

Some Republicans theorized that if Obama had called the attacks in Benghazi an act of terror, it would question his campaign's characterization of him as being tough on terror. Furthermore, Obama's critics believed that his campaign had created a narrative that he had ended terrorism with the death of bin Laden. Covering up the terror aspect of Benghazi, the theory goes, and focusing on spontaneous demonstrations would have avoided such a challenge to the Obama campaign's characterization and narrative of his presidency.

Based on this theory, Romney's debate strategy, it seemed, was to point out Obama's political cover-up and create a "gotcha" moment. Romney, however, simply had the facts and timeline wrong. Obama did call it an act of terror the day after the attack. At worst, Romney failed miserably. At best, he looked ill informed.

During the debate, Obama, like Clinton the previous day, said, "I am ultimately responsible for what's taking place there."[14] With two high-level officials taking general responsibility, with the primary accuser wrong on the facts, and with Obama's reelection, the public interest in Benghazi had waned significantly by the end of November.

As the election spotlight dimmed, numerous congressional investigations began, and most issued their final reports as early as November 2012 or as late as September 2014. While each investigation focused on a different aspect of attack, the reports outlined similar findings. Generally, there was clear evidence of a deteriorating security situation, requests for extra security were denied, and once the attacks had begun, not much could be done to stop them.

There were two reports that were critical of President Obama and Secretaries of State Clinton and Kerry. One was the House Committee on Foreign Affairs, which issued a report that was critical of the State Department's failure to hold anyone fully accountable for failing to provide security. The second report was a combination of several House investigations (i.e., Armed Services, Judiciary, Intelligence, Foreign Affairs, and Oversight and Government Reform). This report's worst criticism was that the Obama administration "willfully perpetuated a deliberately misleading and incomplete narrative that the attacks evolved from a political demonstration caused by a YouTube video."[15]

Two points are worth noting about these two reports. First, these reports were authored by the majority party, which happened to be the Republicans, who seemingly disagreed with everything related to Obama's administration. The bipartisan reports, despite noting failures to respond to requests and to properly assess the failing security situation, were far less critical of Obama and Clinton. Despite attempting officialization, the majority reports seemed partisan compared to the more balanced bipartisan findings. Second, no report found any evidence of a cover-up. But the reports found that, as the saying goes, mistakes were made.[16]

Moving Forward

This section has argued that the political discourse of the 2012 campaign regarding the attacks in Benghazi was consistent with the American political scandal narrative. However, the attempt at creating a scandal failed. This failure was due to less-than-accurate accusations, the success of the accused in portraying the accusations as partisan, the absence of a cover-up or even the appearance of one, the accused's taking general responsibility, and a number of investigations that found no explicit wrongdoing. Consequently, Benghazi fell from the public's attention.

But public attention was piqued slightly again on May 8, 2014, when 225 House Republicans and 7 Democrats voted to create the US House Select Committee on Benghazi; 186 Democrats voted against the measure. The seven Democrats who supported the investigation "were all moderate to conservative party members who face tough re-election campaigns."[17] In other words, partisan politics were at play.

The inevitable cycle of officialization and deofficialization was again in full swing. House Minority Leader Nancy Pelosi claimed that the Republicans were "unending" in their efforts to exploit the deaths of the four Americans killed in Benghazi and that "our nation deserves better than yet another deeply partisan and political review."[18] The partisan discourse did not intrigue many, but that changed just as the next election season started in 2015.

CLINTON'S E-MAIL SCANDAL

RELATIVE PROSPERITY

Political scandals typically rise out of a time of relative prosperity. For Hillary Clinton, she had left her position as secretary of state in early February 2013. It was the first time in over 30 years that she was not in public office. Clinton would be free from, as she described it, "the high wire of American politics and all of the challenges that come with that."[19] She had ended her time in public office with a reputation as "a loyal, hard-working, hard-nosed secretary of state."[20] The issue of Benghazi featured prominently at the end of her career as head of the State Department, but that did not affect her reputation. Her future seemed bright and strong. There were coy denials of rumors about a potential presidential run, which concerned Republicans.

PUBLICITY OF MISCONDUCT

The next stage in the American political scandal is that the relative prosperity is disrupted by the press's publication of misconduct. That happened on March 2, 2015, when the *New York Times* reported that Clinton had used a personal e-mail account to conduct government business.[21] The initial major concern was that there were no governmental records of her e-mails.

The State Department had recently begun improving its record keeping and had requested records and e-mails from all secretaries of state since Madeleine Albright. In response, Clinton's staff had reviewed "tens of thousands of pages of her personal emails and decided which ones to turn over to the State Department."[22] Clinton's personal e-mails that did not address public matters were not turned over. In the end, she submitted over 55,000 pages of e-mails.

However, there were two big unknowns. First, it was unclear as to whether she had used any security measures or encryption on her private e-mail servers, which would have been essential due to her high-level position and the sensitive nature of her job as the US top diplomat. Second, and perhaps most important to her critics, it was unknown what process Clinton's aides followed in making their decisions about what was private and what was public.

Such concerns resonated with past criticisms of both Clintons "for a lack of transparency and inclination toward secrecy."[23] Her opponents thought she might be covering something up.

A Clinton spokesperson defended her actions by saying that she had followed the law and that there were copies of every e-mail regarding State Department business in her recipients' government inboxes. Moreover, the *Times* acknowledged that former secretaries of state such as Colin Powell had used their own private e-mail accounts, but current laws had not been in place then. Current federal law requires that correspondence by government officials be kept as public records so that historians, the media, and congressional committees can review them.

The House Select Committee asked the State Department for Clinton's e-mails in February and received about 300 that were related to the attacks. Perhaps thinking that hiding information from a congressional investigation could be severely damaging, the day after the *Times* broke the story, Clinton tweeted, "I want the public to see my email. I have asked State to release them. They said they will review them for release as soon as possible."[24] At this point, Clinton had turned over the e-mails to the State Department, which was going through them to determine if anything was classified or relevant to the requests from the committee.

PARTISAN RHETORIC AND DISMISSALS

Not even a week after the news about the e-mails became public, partisan rhetoric began to appear. Rep. Trey Gowdy, the Republican in charge of the Select Committee, criticized Clinton for her evasiveness and said, "It's not up to Secretary Clinton to decide what's public record and what's not."[25] Sen. Mitch McConnell, the Republican majority leader, expressed concern over the security of her e-mail. Not missing their cue, senior Democrats rallied to support Clinton. Sen. Charles Schumer said, "The bottom line is she's a national figure, a potential presidential candidate. People are going to shoot at her."[26]

The next week Clinton responded to the accusations. She repeated that she had turned over some thirty thousand e-mails to the Obama administration and deleted roughly the same number. The deleted e-mails involved matters such as her daughter's wedding, yoga, and her mother's funeral. She admitted that it would have been "better" and "smarter" to use a government e-mail, but her choice was simply a matter of convenience: "I thought it would be easier to carry just one device for my work and for my personal emails instead of two."[27]

Clinton's remarks were directed at clarifying her actions and dismissing charges of any perceived wrongdoing, but her responses were met with skepticism. The *New York Times* reported her remarks about her e-mails but also contextualized them by reminding readers of what Clinton had said the previous month at a technology conference. There Clinton had said that she used multiple devices, such as two iPads, an iPhone, and a Blackberry. The *Times* also reminded readers that in 2007, then senator and presidential candidate Clinton had attacked the Bush administration for using "secret White House email accounts."[28]

OFFICIALIZATION AND DEOFFICIALIZATION

As mentioned earlier, when there are contradictory accusations and responses, there is an attempt at officialization so as to legitimize the credibility of the accusers. However, this was not the first attempt at creating a scandal with regard to Benghazi, and officialization had already begun. The House Select Committee was already investigating the Benghazi attack but had now focused on Clinton's e-mails and requested her e-mail servers. This shift in focus is called a "second-order transgression where attention is shifted from the original offense to a series of subsequent actions, which are aimed at concealing the offense."[29]

COVER-UP AND SMOKING GUN

It is important to recognize this shift in the inquiry. As mentioned previously, what empowers Congress beyond their powers of investigation is the discovery of a cover-up. Clinton had turned over e-mails, but not all of them by her own admission. If congressional investigators could find evidence that she did not turn over any Benghazi-related e-mails, they would be in a good position to discredit her with suggestions of covering up. After all, political history provides too many examples of when the cover-up, the second-order transgression, seals a politician's fate.

The well-known example is Watergate. It was not the break-in that led to Nixon's resignation. It was, coincidentally enough, private recordings that he refused to give up, and then when he did surrender the tapes, one of them had a section of eighteen-and-a-half minutes that were "accidentally" erased anywhere from five to nine times.[30] Although Clinton had willfully submitted her e-mails to the State Department, she only handed over the ones she thought were relevant. She deleted all her e-mails regarding private matters and then had her e-mail servers wiped clean. If the Republican-led investigation could find a smoking gun, which might reveal a cover-up, it would have found something that the numerous previous Benghazi investigations had missed. It would be significant for the House Select Committee. Their investigation would have been legitimized in the face of accusations of being a political witch hunt.

While Republicans were seemingly on the hunt for a smoking gun, Democrats on the committee were questioning the shift of focus to the e-mail. The ranking Democrat, Rep. Elijah Cummings, claimed that demands for Clinton's e-mail "seem designed to spark a fight with a potential presidential candidate rather than following the standard practice in congressional investigations."[31] Another Democratic committee member said that Clinton had already turned over her e-mails and that the State Department had provided the House Select Committee with the Benghazi-related e-mails.

If Republicans were looking for a smoking gun in Clinton's e-mails, they found none in the 300 e-mails related to the Benghazi attack. Clinton's critics, however, still thought she was hiding something. For them, it did not seem unreasonable to suppose that there was more to her e-mails. After all, Clinton had turned over thirty thousand pages of e-mails and deleted just as many, and the committee had received only 300 of them.

As March turned into April, Gowdy requested the Clinton testify before his committee. Clinton was reluctant to testify as she had turned over information and had addressed the issue at a news conference. She also formally announced her well-known plans that she would be running for president. After her announcement, the *New York Times* noted that "her resilient poll numbers suggest that the email affair does not yet pose a challenge to her primary campaign."[32]

Notwithstanding her strong start, Clinton's campaign did not cease deofficializing the House Select Committee as being an attack on the new presidential candidate. Her campaign chairman offered this assessment of the House Select Committee:

> There have already been 21 congressional hearings, five independent or bipartisan reports, and millions of tax dollars spent in the process of investigating this three-year-old tragedy. This investigation would now be longer than the investigations of Iran-Contra, the Kennedy assassination, Watergate and 9/11.[33]

Nevertheless, if Republicans were skeptical as to whether they had received all of Clinton's Benghazi-related e-mails, those concerns were substantiated not long after her presidential announcement. A longtime aide to both Clintons, Sydney Blumenthal, turned over e-mails that he had sent to Secretary of State Clinton related to Benghazi. Some of those e-mails were compared to the ones Clinton had turned over, and there was a discrepancy. Blumenthal had submitted Benghazi-related e-mails he had sent to Clinton that the State Department had not turned over to the committee. Gowdy believed that the State Department was trying to protect Clinton and slow their investigation down. The State Department said it had turned over e-mails related specifically to the Benghazi attack, not every e-mail related to Libya. Moreover, they were still going through her e-mails. Two weeks later, however, the State Department said that 15 of Blumenthal's e-mails sent or received by Clinton were not found in what she had given the agency.

It is easy to believe that while sorting through some 60,000 pages of e-mails, a scant 15 might be skipped over, but when you are a former senator, a former secretary of state, a presidential candidate, a polarizing national figure, and your last name is Clinton, the concern is that you are hiding something, not that there had been an oversight.

A few days later in July, the State Department released a trove of Clinton's e-mails. If the House Select Committee was expecting to find a smoking gun in those e-mails, they were disappointed as the disclosures were anticlimactic. The e-mails did address a few international matters, but not Benghazi. Many e-mails, however, concerned scheduling and appointments. Some dealt with simple office politics at the White House, as she now worked for Obama, who had narrowly defeated her in the long and competitive 2008 Democratic primary. One e-mail asked for an iced tea, another about a broken fax machine, and one asked an aide to find out about the carpets in the room where she met with leaders from China.

If July started humorously, it ended seriously. The *New York Times* reported that the Justice Department was asked to begin a criminal investigation to determine if classified or sensitive information was mishandled with respect to Clinton's use of her personal e-mail account. The headline read, "Criminal Inquiry Sought in Clinton's Use of Email."[34] The *Times* received heavy criticism because the probe was not criminal and it was not aimed at Clinton. Although a correction quickly followed and the article was changed online, the phrase "criminal investigation of Hillary Clinton" from the original article already had a foothold in Republican circles and was frequently brought up in the republican primaries and general election.

RELUCTANT PARTICIPATION

When there are two competing statements in the context of a scandal, the accusers attempt to officialize their accusations, as described earlier in the chapter, with "pomp and spectacle."[35] The accused attempts to deofficialize, but when the suspicion and/or evidence is too great to overcome with simple counteraccusations of partisan politics, the accused must participate in the officialization. In past major US scandals, the accused have claimed that they will participate and cooperate with the investigation, but they do so reluctantly. These scandals, as we know in retrospect, have demonstrated that such reluctance is often a sign that the accused has covered up their initial misconduct.

While Clinton early on had expressed eagerness for the State Department to turn over her e-mails, she was reluctant to testify because she had turned over the e-mails and addressed the issue at several news conferences. However, despite there being no clear evidence of wrongdoing, there were growing revelations, inconsistencies, and suspicions that compelled Clinton to participate in the officialized investigation.

MORE PARTISAN RHETORIC AND DISMISSALS

Scandals do have a beginning, middle, and end, and the thematic elements that constitute them do generally follow that order. However, scandals do not always have distinct separation between each thematic element. For example, there can be partisan accusations and responses throughout the scandal. This happened in the months between Clinton's announcement that she would testify and her actual appearance. The participants in the Republican primary went after Clinton in stump speeches, campaign ads, and the debates. Donald

Trump called her a "criminal," Gov. Chris Christie repeatedly proclaimed that he would call upon his experience as a US attorney to prosecute her, and former Jeb Bush mentioned Clinton's name with Bradley Manning and Edward Snowden, two figures well known for releasing classified and embarrassing information about the United States.[36] Attacks from the multitude of Republican presidential candidates were to be expected. But it was what another Republican said that was quite unexpected.

Rep. Kevin McCarthy, the House republican majority leader, was the potential next speaker of the house. However, the potential ended when he said, "Everybody thought Hillary Clinton was unbeatable, right? But we put together a Benghazi special committee, a select committee. What are her numbers today? Her numbers are dropping."[37] McCarthy tried to backtrack his comments, but he had confirmed what Clinton supporters already knew. The use of a personal e-mail account was at worst a mistake, but the investigation of them was partisan.

ATONEMENT

Scandals conclude when the accused is vindicated or properly atones for his or her misconduct. When the news about the e-mails first broke, Clinton said she could have been "better" and "smarter" but was now stating that she had made a mistake. And, as her appearance before the House Select Committee came closer, she did what few accused do: she said she was sorry. However, one apology is not always enough to calm a scandal. Sometimes the accused, like Bill Clinton, had to apologize several times before it seemed that he was genuinely remorseful. Hillary's aides confirmed that she would need to work on her approach. She also received some help from an unlikely source.

In the first Democratic primary debate, Sen. Bernie Sanders displayed his typical "damn the politics" approach and told the truth as he saw it. Clinton was asked about her e-mails, and Sanders chimed in. In a rare move of supporting one's opponent, he said, "Let me say something that may not be great politics, but I think the secretary is right, and that is that the American people are sick and tired of hearing about your damn emails."[38] With a wide smile, Clinton grabbed Sanders's hand and thanked him. The audience responded with thunderous applause. Later, Republican presidential candidate Donald Trump offered the following unsolicited advice to Sanders: "When you're losing that badly, you have to go a lot stronger."[39]

A week later, Clinton testified before the House Select Committee. It was the critical moment of the committee's investigation that had been long in the making. Republican members of the committee aggressively questioned Clinton for eight hours, and the result was little more than what had already been found by the numerous previous investigations. During the long day, Clinton remained composed, focused, and, according to one commentator, presidential. Perhaps due to the statements made by McCarthy and criticisms that the committee was engaging in a partisan witch hunt, there was little questioning focused on the e-mails. Editorialists noted that what was supposed to be the critical moment of the investigation "produced no damning evidence, elicited no confessions and didn't succeed in getting an angry reaction from Mrs. Clinton."[40]

Three weeks later at the second debate, Sanders repeated his thought on Clinton's e-mails. Sanders said that it was time to move on to the issues facing America, and Clinton happily agreed. The investigations, however, continued and the State Department released more e-mails.

More Partisan Discourse

As the State Department released her e-mails, there was speculation, primarily from her political opponents, that her e-mails contained classified information and being on a private server were vulnerable to hackers and enemies of the United States. While there was no immediate and direct evidence that the server was ever hacked by anyone, it was clear that some e-mails contained classified information. However, that information was not necessarily classified at the time it was sent.

Shortly thereafter Sanders was asked about the controversy. He replied, "There is a legal process taking place, I do not want to politicize that issue. It is not my style."[41] Republicans, however, continued to speculate throughout the first half of 2016 about the extent and possible consequences of, what they believed was, her extreme nefariousness and maliciousness. At the forefront was Trump who not only called her actions criminal but also said that he would advocate for an indictment of Clinton.

These partisan attacks and defenses continued as the investigators went about their business and did their best to stay out of the partisan rancor. Attorney General Loretta Lynch said that the Justice Department's investigation would be based on facts and the law. Congressional Democrats called on the State Department inspector general to depoliticize his investigation.

However, the controversy continued as a blood sport for partisans even though the details of the whole situation were well known.

No Confirmation of Wrongdoing and Repeated Apologies, but No End of Scandal

Despite Clinton's admission that she had made a mistake and would have done things differently, the partisan discourse continued to make her e-mails a primary issue in the campaign. There was hope from Clinton's camp and her supporters that the official reports, once released, would put an end to the ordeal. But that did not happen.

At the end of June 2016, members of the House Select Committee on Benghazi released their reports. On June 27, the democratic minority of the committee released their report to preempt the republican majority report, which would be released the next day. The minority report found that the entire investigation was "a politically motivated crusade that wasted time and money."[42] The next day, the majority report included an outline of seven major findings, which did not include any new findings that others had not already uncovered. Clinton acknowledged that the committee had become partisan, and it was time to move on.

In early July 2016, the FBI's investigation into the e-mails took center stage. There were hopes that the Justice Department's report would be seen as far more officialized and not as partisan as the congressional inquiries. Prior to the release of the House Select Committee's reports, Attorney General Lynch had promised that the Justice Department's investigation into Clinton's e-mails would be no different than any other. Moreover, the e-mail investigation was being handled by "career agents and lawyers" and not partisan actors motived by their own political self-interest.[43] These assurances were shattered on July 1 when Bill Clinton had what was described as an unplanned social meeting with Lynch at the Phoenix airport.

The meeting between the two quickly fueled speculation that President Clinton, who appointed Lynch as an US attorney in 1999, talked to her about the investigation into his wife's e-mails. Although Lynch described the meeting as purely social, the meeting itself questioned the legitimacy and credibility of the Justice Department's work. The day after the meeting, Hillary Clinton voluntarily submitted to an interview with the FBI for three-and-a-half hours. Clinton later said that she hoped that her cooperation would bring the investigation to a conclusion.

Clinton's interview apparently did help conclude the Justice Department's investigation, but it did not stop the controversy over her e-mails. On July 5, 2016, FBI Director James Comey reported the findings and recommendations. He said that the investigation found that Clinton did not try to violate the law, she and her colleagues were "extremely careless" with classified information.[44] Comey continued with his recommendation, "Although there is evidence of potential violations of the statutes regarding the handling of classified information, our judgment is that no reasonable prosecutor would bring such a case." Comey qualified his remarks saying that people in similar situations could face security or administrative sanctions, but his recommendation is that the Department of Justice was that no charges be filed against Clinton. Clinton's campaign quickly tweeted that they were happy with the recommendations.

As Comey concluded, he reassured the public that the "investigation was done competently, honestly, and independently. No outside influence of any kind was brought to bear." However, Clinton's political opponents did not readily accept this characterization. Trump suggested that Clinton bribed Lynch, that Clinton was getting "away with murder," and that she was "guilty as hell."[45]

The perceived criminality and lack of trust of Clinton was apparent at the Republican National Convention. Gov. Chris Christie, a former US attorney, a former presidential candidate, and, at the time, a rumored frontrunner for Attorney General should Trump win, spoke with "a prosecutorial zeal" against Clinton at the convention.[46] After each point, he asked the massive crowd, "Guilty or not guilty?" The republican crowd clearly found her guilty on all counts. But others stood with shaking fists, chanting, "Lock her up!"[47] When the crowd chanted "lock her up!" during Trump's remarks at the convention, he waved off the chant and simply said, "Let's beat her in November."[48] After the convention, however, Trump quickly changed his mind and said, "I've been saying let's just beat her on November 8th. But you know what, I'm starting to agree with you."[49] This would not be the last time Trump changed his mind about Clinton and her e-mails.

Despite the officialized reports, the focus on Clinton's e-mail continued but not with the same intensity as before. During the first presidential debate, her e-mails were brought up only briefly. Clinton attacked Trump about his refusal to release his tax returns. He responded that he would release them when she released her deleted e-mails. Later, the moderator asked if Clinton would like to address her e-mails, and she responded simply by saying, "I made a mistake using a private e-mail. And if I had to do it over again, I would, obviously, do it differently. But I'm not going to make any excuses. It was a mistake, and I take responsibility for that."[50]

In the second debate, Trump attacked Clinton about the e-mails to a greater extent, but it was not a major aspect of the debate. Clinton reiterated that she took responsibility for her mistakes, but contested Comey's characterization of being "extremely careless" with classified information. There was one heated exchange in the second debate where Trump ominously stated, "If I win, I am going to instruct my attorney general to get a special prosecutor to look into your situation, because there has never been so many lies, so much deception."[51] Shortly thereafter in the debate, Clinton said it would be a good thing that Trump would not be in charge of the laws of the country. Trump interrupted with "Because you'd be in jail."

By comparison, her e-mails were hardly addressed in the third debate, but they would make one more prominent reappearance days before the election. On October 28, 11 days before the election, Comey notified Congress that the FBI had discovered new Clinton e-mails, which were found during an investigation of Anthony Weiner's sexting scandal. The FBI found a laptop belonging to Weiner and his wife, Huma Abedin, who was a top advisor to Hillary Clinton. Clinton immediately called for all information to be released. Trump immediately praised the FBI's decision.

Comey's actions have been called scandalous in their own right and have even started a feud within the FBI. Senior officials in the Justice Department described Comey's actions as inconsistent with past practices within the Department.[52] A week later, the FBI said that the review of the new e-mails does not change the conclusion that she should not be charged.

Nevertheless, in the early morning hours of November 9, it was announced that Donald Trump was elected president. The next day, Christie and former New York City Mayor Rudy Giuliani, who both were considered as candidates for attorney general in a Trump administration, softened their once hardline position that Clinton be prosecuted.

Almost two weeks later, President-Elect Trump said that he was no longer focusing on investigating Clinton and that he does not want to "hurt the Clintons."[53] The about-face is telling. At one point, Trump threatened his rival, who by nearly all accounts was likely to win the presidency, with prosecution and prison. But then reversing himself once he attained victory tells us much about the political nature of scandals, which is the focus of the next section.

IMPLICATIONS OF THE SCANDAL NARRATIVE

Throughout this chapter, I have suggested that scandals are political weapons waged by one party over another. This understanding of scandal is based on how the scandal narrative plays out. When the news of a scandal breaks, there are charges of wrongdoing, mainly by members of the opposite party. Members of the accused's party rally to the defense or try to diminish the accusations. To legitimize their accusations, the accusers attempt officialization, which is met with deofficialization. It is important to note at this point that Congressional officialization is focused on investigation. What really empowers Congress to take decisive action in a scandal is to catch someone obstructing justice. To catch someone obstructing justice requires a trap.

American political scandals reflect the Ancient Greek notion of scandal, σκανδάλου, which means "the stick in a trap on which the bait is placed, and which springs up and shuts the trap at the touch of an animal."[54] Think of an inverted box with one side of the box propped up by a vertical stick, with another stick attached to it that has some bait on it. When the animal walks under the box and grabs the bait, the movement dislodges the two sticks, thereby dropping the box and capturing the animal. This is the nature of American political scandals.

In other words, the bait is the initial allegation of wrongdoing, which creates an exigence to which the accused must respond to avoid harm to his or her reputation. These responses must be rhetorically sound. Just as the animal needs to be extremely careful about how it works the bait to escape unharmed, so must the accused. The accused must not admit guilt or misrepresent the truth in any way whatsoever. But yet the accused must protect their political life. If the responses to accusation are later found to be even slightly misleading, they could suggest a cover-up. That cover-up could be proven by the discovery of a smoking gun, which reveals inconsistencies between the accused's responses and the truth. Consequently, the allegations of the original misconduct are overshadowed by the more serious charges of covering up, which is obstruction of justice when in the context of a congressional investigation.

When a member of the executive branch is found to be obstructing justice in a congressional investigation, Congress, which previously could only investigate, then becomes empowered to impeach, which is the most severe punishment Congress can give. If the accused is no longer in office, as is the case with Clinton, impeachment is no longer an option. However, Congress can discredit the accused, the entire administration and/or party he or she was a member of, and whatever future plans the accused may have.

We can see the Greek notion of scandal in the 2012 and 2016 campaigns. Romney tried to trap Obama in the debate by claiming that the president was engaging in a cover-up by attributing the Benghazi attack to a spontaneous protest, not an act of terror. Romney wanted Obama to repeat what he had just said in the debate so that Romney could compare it to what Obama had said immediately after the attacks in order to reveal Obama's supposed inconsistencies. It did not work. Obama saw Romney building a faulty trap, and when the governor invited the president to enter the trap, Obama coolly responded, "Please proceed, governor."[55] Romney's trap fell, ensnaring only himself.

It is telling that Obama has not been a primary focus of the Benghazi investigations after his reelection in 2012, but when his former secretary of state ran for president in 2016, she became a target of the investigations. And when those investigations came up empty handed in regards to Benghazi, they focused on her e-mails. At least until she lost the electoral college. Then the matter became no longer relevant or important.

Clinton's critics have built many traps for her. The first was whether she had turned down requests for extra security at the Benghazi compound. Second, her critics tried to catch her by claiming that she had stalled reinforcements that would have been able to intervene in the attack. The third were the attempts to catch her with regard to her e-mails. While it appears that she has done nothing illegal, the e-mail controversy followed her throughout her campaign and ended with her loss in the 2016 election. Thus, scandalous accusations, whether they are based on the facts or insinuations, are merely political means to achieve political ends.

CONCLUSION

This chapter has offered a reading of two attempts to create scandal out of the 2012 attacks on Benghazi, one with presidential candidate Governor Mitt Romney challenging President Obama in the last months of the 2012 campaign, and the other with Congress investigating Hillary Clinton leading up to and during the 2016 campaign. The chapter has argued that both attempts at scandal unfolded in a similar manner as other prominent political scandals within our political culture, such as Teapot Dome, Watergate, Iran-Contra, and the Clinton-Lewinsky scandal (and smaller, more recent scandals including Chris Christie's Bridgegate and Anthony Weiner's sexting scandal), which I have addressed in detail elsewhere. While both attempts at scandal ultimately failed to reveal a cover-up via a smoking gun, the chapter concluded by addressing the nature of the narrative as reflecting the use of scandals as a discursive political weapon.

NOTES

1. "Election 2016: Democratic Debate Transcript: Clinton, Sanders, O'Malley in Iowa," CBS News, November 14, 2015, accessed December 18, 2015, http://www.cbsnews.com/news/democratic-debate-transcript-clinton-sanders-omalley-in-iowa.
2. Margaret Hartmann, "Could Hillary Clinton Face Criminal Charges over Emailgate?," *Daily Intelligencer*, August 21, 2015, accessed December 18, 2015, http://nymag.com/daily/intelligencer/2015/08/hillary-clinton-legal-emailgate.html.
3. W. Lance Bennett, "Myth, Ritual, and Political Control," *Journal of Communication* 30 (1980): 166–179, 166.
4. David R. Dewberry, *The American Political Scandal: Free Speech, Public Discourse, and Democracy* (Lanham, MD: Rowman & Littlefield, 2015).
5. Barbara Goldberg and Chris Francescani, "Maker of Anti-Islam Film Goes into Hiding: Report," Reuters, September 12, 2012, accessed December 18, 2015, http://www.reuters.com/article/us-usa-libya-film-hiding-idUSBRE88B0XK20120912.
6. "What They Said, Before and After the Attack in Libya," *New York Times*, September 12, 2012, accessed December 18, 2015, http://www.nytimes.com/interactive/2012/09/12/us/politics/libya-statements.html.
7. Hugh Rawson and Margaret Miner, *The Oxford Dictionary of American Quotations* (Oxford: Oxford University Press, 2006), s.v. "Watergate."
8. "What They Said, Before and After the Attack in Libya," *New York Times*, September 12, 2012, accessed December 18, 2015, http://www.nytimes.com/interactive/2012/09/12/us/politics/libya-statements.html.
9. Mitt Romney, *No Apology: The Case for American Greatness* (New York: St. Martin's, 2010).
10. Phillip Rucker, "Romney Repeats Sharp Criticism of Obama after Benghazi, Cairo Attacks," *Washington Post*, September 12, 2012, accessed December 18, 2015, https://www.washingtonpost.com/politics/decision2012/romney-repeats-sharp-criticism-of-obama-on-libya-egypt-attacks/2012/09/12/31074af4-fcdf-11e1-b153-218509a954e1_story.html?hpid=z2.

11. "The Death of an Ambassador," *Washington Post*, September 12, 2012, accessed December 18, 2015, https://www.washingtonpost.com/opi nions/the-death-of-an-ambassador/2012/09/12/ed3b719e-fcfa-11e1-b153-218509a954e1_story.html.

12. Bruce Gronbeck, "The Rhetoric of Political Corruption," *Quarterly Journal of Speech* 64 (1978): 155–172, 165.

13. Elise Labott, "Clinton: I'm Responsible for Diplomats' Security," CNN, October 16, 2012, accessed December 18, 2015, http://www.cnn.com/2012/10/15/us/clinton-benghazi.

14. Michael Pearson, "What the Obama Administration Has Said about the Libya Attack," CNN, May 9, 2013, accessed December 18, 2015, http://www.cnn.com/2013/05/08/politics/libya-attack-statements-2013.

15. Rep. Howard P. "Buck" McKeon, Rep. Ed Royce, Rep. Bob Goodlatte, Rep. Darrell Issa, and Rep. Mike Rogers, *Interim Progress Report for the Members of the House Republican Conference on the Events Surrounding the September 11, 2012 Terrorist Attacks in Benghazi, Libya*, accessed December 18, 2015, https://goodlatte.house.gov/system/uploads/229/original/Libya-Progress-Report.pdf.

16. William Safire, *Safire's Political Dictionary* (Oxford: Oxford University Press, 2008), s.v. "Mistakes Were Made".

17. Bradley Klapper and Donna Cassata, "House Votes to Start New Benghazi Investigation," Associated Press, May 9, 2014, accessed December 18, 2015, http://bigstory.ap.org/article/house-set-approve-select-benghazi-investigation.

18. Bradley Klapper and Donna Cassata, "House Votes to Start New Benghazi Investigation," Associated Press, May 9, 2014, accessed December 18, 2015, http://bigstory.ap.org/article/house-set-approve-select-benghazi-investigation.

19. Steve Holland, "Hillary Clinton Leaving World Stage, But for How Long?" *Reuters*, January 16, 2013, accessed December 18, 2015, http://www.reuters.com/article/us-usa-politics-hillary-idUSBRE90F0A820130116.

20. Ibid.

21. Michael Schmidt, "Hillary Clinton Used Personal Email Account at State Dept., Possibly Breaking Rules," *New York Times*, March 2, 2015, accessed December 18, 2015, http://www.nytimes.com/2015/03/03/us/poli tics/hillary-clintons-use-of-private-email-at-state-department-raises-flags.html.

22. Ibid.

23. Ibid.

24. Michael Schmidt, "Hillary Clinton Asks State Department to Vet Emails for Release," *New York Times*, March 5, 2015, accessed December 18, 2015,

http://www.nytimes.com/2015/03/06/us/politics/hillary-clinton-asks-state-dept-to-review-emails-for-public-release.html?ref=politics&_r=0.

25. Alan Rappeport, "As Hillary Clinton Stays Quiet about Private Emails, Republicans Seize Moment to Criticize Her," *New York Times*, March 8, 2015, accessed December 18, 2015, http://www.nytimes.com/2015/03/09/us/politics/as-hillary-clinton-stays-quiet-about-private-emails-republicans-seize-moment-to-criticize-her.html.

26. Ibid.

27. Zeke Miller, "Here's Everything Hillary Clinton Said on the Emails," *Time*, March 10, 2015, accessed December 18, 2015, http://time.com/3739541/transcript-hillary-clinton-email-press-conference.

28. Ibid.

29. John B. Thompson, *Political Scandal: Power and Visibility in the Media Age* (Cambridge: Polity Press, 2000), 17–25.

30. Dewberry, *The American Political Scandal*, 97.

31. Michael Schmidt, "House Benghazi Committee Requests Hillary Clinton Email Server," *New York Times*, March 20, 2015, accessed December 18, 2015, http://www.nytimes.com/politics/first-draft/2015/03/20/house-benghazi-committee-requests-hillary-clinton-email-server.

32. Nate Cohn, "Huge Head Start for Hillary Clinton, but the Big Race Is Far from Won," *New York Times*, April 12, 2015, accessed December 18, 2015, http://www.nytimes.com/2015/04/13/upshot/huge-head-start-for-clinton-but-the-big-race-is-far-from-won.html.

33. Joseph Cameron and Adam Edelman, "Release of Benghazi Panel Final Report Delayed until 2016," *Daily News* (New York), April 22, 2015, accessed December 18, 2015, http://www.nydailynews.com/news/politics/release-benghazi-panel-final-report-delayed-2016-article-1.2194246.

34. Michael Schmidt, "Criminal Inquiry Sought in Clinton's Use of Email," *New York Times*, July 24, 2015, A1.

35. Gronbeck, "The Rhetoric of Political Corruption," 165.

36. Katie Habermas and Ashley Parker, "While Some Republicans Seize Chance to Attack Hillary Clinton, Others Refrain," *New York Times*, July 26, 2015, accessed December 18, 2015, http://www.nytimes.com/2015/07/27/us/politics/while-some-republicans-seize-chance-to-attack-hillary-clinton-others-refrain.html; "Transcript: Republican Presidential Debate," *New York Times*, December 15, 2015, accessed December 18, 2015, http://www.nytimes.com/2015/12/16/us/politics/transcript-main-republican-presidential-debate.html; Ashley Killough, "Jeb Bush Steps Up Attacks of Hillary Clinton over Emails," CNN, August 12, 2015, accessed December 18, 2015, http://www.cnn.com/2015/08/12/politics/jeb-bush-hillary-clinton-email-server.

37. David Weigel, "Boehner's Likely Successor Credits Benghazi Committee for Lowering Hillary Clinton's Poll Numbers," *Washington Post*, September 30, 2015, accessed December 18, 2015, https://www.washingtonpost.com/news/post-politics/wp/2015/09/30/boehners-likely-successor-credits-benghazi-committee-for-lowering-hillary-clintons-poll-numbers.

38. Michael Barbaro and Amy Chozick, "Hillary Clinton Turns Up Heat on Bernie Sanders in a Sharp Debate," *New York Times*, October 13, 2015, accessed December 18, 2015, http://www.nytimes.com/2015/10/14/us/politics/hillary-clinton-turns-up-heat-on-bernie-sanders-in-a-sharp-debate.html.

39. Jason Easley, "Donald Trump and Jeb Bush Throw a Tantrum after Bernie Sanders Defends Clinton on Emails," PoliticusUSA, October 14, 2015, accessed December 18, 2015, http://www.politicususa.com/2015/10/14/donald-trump-jeb-bush-throw-tantrum-bernie-sanders-defends-clinton-emails.html.

40. "Hillary Clinton and the Benghazi Gang," *New York Times*, October 22, 2015, accessed December 18, 2015, http://www.nytimes.com/2015/10/23/opinion/hillary-clinton-and-the-benghazi-gang.html.

41. Jeremy Diamond, "Sanders: Clinton Emails 'Very Serious Issue,'" *CNN*, January 31, 2016, accessed October 28, 2016, http://edition.cnn.com/2016/01/31/politics/bernie-sanders-hillary-clinton-emails-iowa/index.html.

42. David M. Herszenhorn, "House Democrats Release Benghazi Report to Blunt Republican Inquiry," *New York Times*, June 27, 2016, accessed October 28, 2016, http://www.nytimes.com/2016/06/28/us/politics/house-democrats-benghazi-report.html.

43. Tom LoBianco, "Lynch: Clinton Email Probe Handled the Same as Any Other," *CNN*, June 19, 2016, accessed October 28, 2016, http://www.cnn.com/2016/06/19/politics/loretta-lynch-hillary-clinton-email/.

44. "Statement by FBI Director James B. Comey on the Investigation of Secretary Hillary Clinton's Use of a Personal E-Mail System," FBI, July 5, 2016, accessed October 28, 2016, https://www.fbi.gov/news/pressrel/press-releases/statement-by-fbi-director-james-b-comey-on-the-investigation-of-secretary-hillary-clinton2019s-use-of-a-personal-e-mail-system.

45. Sean Sullivan, "'Bribe,' 'Murder' and the 'Rigged' System: How Trump Describes Hillary Clinton's email Case," July 6, 2016, accessed October 28, 2016, https://www.washingtonpost.com/news/post-politics/wp/2016/07/06/bribe-murder-and-the-rigged-system-how-trump-describes-hillary-clintons-email-case/.

46. Michael D. Shear and David E. Sanger, "Chris Christie Made a Case Against Hillary Clinton. We Fact-Checked," *New York Times*, July 20, 2016, accessed October 28, 2016, http://www.nytimes.com/2016/07/20/us/politics/chris-christie-rnc.html.

47. Peter W. Stevenson, "A Brief History of the 'Lock Her Up!' Chant by Trump Supporters Against Clinton," *The Washington Post*, November 22, 2016, accessed November 22, 2016, https://www.washingtonpost.com/news/the-fix/wp/2016/11/22/a-brief-history-of-the-lock-her-up-chant-as-it-looks-like-trump-might-not-even-try/.
48. Ibid.
49. Jeremy Diamond, "Trump on 'Lock her up' Chant: 'I'm Starting to Agree,'" *CNN*, July 29, 2016, accessed October 28, 2016, http://www.cnn.com/2016/07/29/politics/donald-trump-lock-her-up/.
50. Aaron Blake, "The First Trump-Clinton Presidential Debate Transcript, Annotated," *The Washington Post*, September 26, 2016, accessed October 28, 2016, https://www.washingtonpost.com/news/the-fix/wp/2016/09/26/the-first-trump-clinton-presidential-debate-transcript-annotated/.
51. "Transcript of the Second Debate," *New York Times*, October 10, 2016, accessed October 28, 2016, http://www.nytimes.com/2016/10/10/us/politics/transcript-second-debate.html.
52. Sari Horwitz, Tom Hamburger, and Ellen Nakashima, "Justice Officials Warned FBI that Comey's Decision to Update Congress was not Consistent with Department Policy," *The Washington Post*, October 29, 2016, accessed November 21, 2016, https://www.washingtonpost.com/world/national-security/justice-officials-warned-fbi-that-comeys-decision-to-update-congress-was-not-consistent-with-department-policy/2016/10/29/cb179254-9de7-11e6-b3c9-f662adaa0048_story.html.
53. "Donald Trump's *New York Times* Interview: Full Transcript," *New York Times*, November 23, 2016, accessed November 25, 2016, http://www.nytimes.com/2016/11/23/us/politics/trump-new-york-times-interview-transcript.html.
54. Henry George Liddell and Robert Scott, *A Greek-English Lexicon* (Oxford: Oxford University Press, 1940).
55. Bob Cesca, "Obama's Epic Debate Performance and Romney's Implosion," *Huffington Post*, October 17, 2012, accessed December 19, 2015, http://www.huffingtonpost.com/bob-cesca/obamas-epic-debateperfor_b_1974555.html.

David R. Dewberry is an associate professor of communication at Rider University. He is the author of *The American Political Scandal: Free Speech, Public Discourse, and Democracy*, which serves as the basis for his chapter in this volume. Additionally, he has served as the editor of *First Amendment Studies* and the *Communication Law Review*. He would like to thank Alisa and Robert for their help on this chapter.

The 2016 Presidential Election

CHAPTER 10

Campaign Finance and Its Impact in the 2016 Presidential Campaign

Cayce Myers

In his seventh annual address to Congress in 1907, President Theodore Roosevelt was clearly concerned about the role of money in political campaigns. He said:

> It is well to provide that corporations shall not contribute to Presidential or National campaigns, and furthermore to provide for the publication of both contributions and expenditures. There is, however, always danger in laws of this kind, which from their very nature are difficult of enforcement; the danger being lest they be obeyed only by the honest, and disobeyed by the unscrupulous, so as to act only as a penalty upon honest men.[1]

Nearly 110 years later U.S. presidential elections have become a billion dollar business. The past election cycles have become longer, and, as a result, the money needed to sustain national campaigns has grown exponentially. Compounding the issue of the expense of presidential campaigns is the rise of so-called super-political action committees (super-PACs), political committees that can raise large amounts of money. In fact, fears over the role of money in elections have resulted in the idea that the best-funded candidate is the automatic winner. However, 2016 seems to reject

C. Myers (✉)
Department of Communication, Virginia Tech., Blacksburg, VA, USA
e-mail: mcmyers@vt.edu

© The Author(s) 2017
R.E. Denton, Jr. (ed.), *The 2016 US Presidential Campaign,*
Political Campaigning and Communication,
DOI 10.1007/978-3-319-52599-0_10

the conventional wisdom that money is the best predictor of campaign success. Donald Trump won the presidency even though his opponent's campaign was better funded. However, it should be noted that both the 2016 presidential candidates were well financed. Both had millions in support of their candidacy, and both spent money on conventional campaign expenditures such as advertising, staff, and campaign events.

This chapter explores the campaign finance issues in the 2016 presidential election. Because understanding campaign finance requires a grasp of federal election laws, this chapter provides a brief overview of campaign finance law. Next, this chapter discusses the campaign expenditures and impact the hotly contested presidential primaries meant for the general election campaign. This chapter concludes with an analysis of the campaign fundraising and expenditures of the Clinton and Trump campaigns, joint fundraising committees and super-PACs, and provides some analysis of why Donald Trump lost the money contest, but won the presidential election in 2016.

OVERVIEW OF U.S. CAMPAIGN FINANCE LAWS

The role money plays in politics has been a major issue in the U.S. for a century. The question centers on the larger First Amendment issue of how money relates to speech. U.S. Supreme Court jurisprudence has struggled with if and how campaign contributions are directly related to speech. It is through these contributions that donors express their views, concerns, and support for individual candidates or causes. Equating speech with money is not without its problems. Critics of U.S. campaign finance laws argue that too much money in the political system has a corrupting influence; it gives voice to those whose pocketbooks are the largest, which, in turn, means that those donors' issues are the ones voters are most aware of and influenced by. In short, it leads to the general axiom of campaigns that those candidates with the most money win.[2] Balancing the interests of donors with the influence money has on elections is one of the biggest challenges for courts. Examining the history of campaign finance law in the U.S. shows that this balance has been in a state of flux with current legal trends favoring corporations' right to engage in political speech.

Early campaign finance issues in the U.S. coincided with the rise of corporations and industrialization. At the turn of the twentieth century, corporations had grown in power and structure making these inanimate entities influential in American life.[3] According to Justice Felix Frankfurter's history of U.S. campaign finance law, individual states led the effort to track campaign finance contributions in the 1890s with the idea being that public disclosure of corporate campaign contributions would actually discourage corporate participation in elections.[4] However, campaign disclosure requirements did not deter corporate contributions. This importance of business became an issue during the presidential election of 1904. In response President Theodore Roosevelt was highly critical of corporate money in national federal elections. The Joint Committee of the New York Legislature also investigated the role of corporate donations, specifically from insurance agencies, in elections. In its 1906 report it concluded that corporate money was problematic for elections and said:

> Whether made for the purpose of supporting political views or with the desire to obtain protection for the corporation, these contributions have been wholly unjustifiable. In the one case executive officers have sought to impose their political views upon a constituency of divergent convictions, and in the other they have been guilty of a serious offense against public morals. The frank admission that moneys have been obtained for use in State campaigns upon the expectation that candidates thus aided in their election would support the interests of the companies, has exposed both those who solicited the contributions and those who made them to severe and just condemnation.[5]

The result of this campaign finance reform movement was the Tillman Act of 1907, the first federal campaign finance law, which provided some punishment for violations of federal campaign finance law. The Tillman Act was strengthened by the Federal Corrupt Practices Act (FCPA), which was passed in 1910 and amended in 1911, to include mandatory contribution reporting, caps on spending limits, and a ban on candidate promises of federal employment. The 1910 amendment required that there should be mandatory disclosure of campaign contributions equal to or greater than $100 and "recipients of expenditures of $10 or more."[6]

The FCPA and its 1911 amendment sought to regulate the previously ungoverned nature of campaign finance. It provided for mandatory disclosure of campaign finance by political parties and candidates. However, the power of the FCPA was challenged, and the U.S. Supreme Court in 1921 struck down many of the 1911 disclosure requirements under the rationale that Congress had no power to enforce such requirements under

Article I of the U.S. Constitution.[7] Four years later in 1925 the FCPA was amended to include new campaign expenditure caps and disclosures.[8]

By World War II other campaign finance laws were passed that focused on labor unions. In 1943 the Smith-Connally Act, also known as the War Labor Disputes Act, banned the contributions of any union, congressionally created corporation, or corporation to federal political campaigns.[9] As a result, the Congress of Industrial Organizations (CIO) formed the first PAC, which is a group that is formed to make political donations from pooled money. Later in 1947 Congress passed the Taft-Hartley Act, known officially as the Labor Management Relations Act of 1947, which banned unions and corporations from making donations in federal elections.

The 1970s was a watershed decade for campaign finance laws. It saw the rise of the Federal Elections Commission (FEC), and the battle over corporate political donations. While the older FCPA did attempt to regulate campaign finance, it did not provide a comprehensive regulation of campaign finances. In 1971 Congress passed the Federal Election Campaign Act (FECA), which replaced the FCPA beginning in 1972. The 1971 FECA required a greater amount of disclosures. However, in the wake of the Watergate scandal, U.S. campaign finance reform was a popular political issue leading to the 1974 amendments to the FECA.[10] These amendments provided for an increased level of disclosure and provided for campaign contribution limits for individuals ($1,000 per candidate and no more than $25,000 in total contributions per election cycle). The amendments also included caps on spending in elections and the establishment of the Federal Elections Commission (FEC), which is in charge of enforcing laws related to campaign finance. The board is bipartisan with six total members in which there cannot be more than three members of the same political party. This means that the decisions made by the FEC, which requires at least four votes, should be bipartisan.[11]

However, these amendments to FECA were challenged, and the U.S. Supreme Court upheld and struck down parts of the FECA in the landmark 1976 base *Buckley v. Valeo*. In a per curium opinion, the U.S. Supreme Court upheld the campaign contribution limits for individual contributions per candidate, committees per candidate, and limits on individual contributions in a given calendar year. The court's rationale for finding these provisions constitutional in the FECA is summed up in the following statement:

These limitations [on contributions], along with the disclosure provisions, constitute the Act's primary weapons against the reality or appearance of improper influence stemming from the dependence of candidates on large campaign contributions. The contribution ceilings thus serve the basic governmental interest in safeguarding the integrity of the electoral process without directly impinging upon the rights of individual citizens and candidates to engage in political debate and discussion.[12]

The court pointed out that limiting an individual donor's ability to contribute to a particular candidate did not necessarily involve a restriction on his or her speech:

A contribution serves as a general expression of support for the candidate and his views, but does not communicate the underlying basis for the support. The quantity of communication by the contributor does not increase perceptibly with the size of his contribution, since the expression rests solely on the undifferentiated, symbolic act of contributing. At most, the size of the contribution provides a very rough index of the intensity of the contributor's support for the candidate.[13]

The court also used a corruption rationale in justifying why individuals should be subject to campaign contribution limitations. Disclosure requirements were also found constitutional so long as they were "narrowly construed."[14]

However, the U.S. Supreme Court held that caps on campaign expenditures were unconstitutional. These expenditure caps included both expenditures made by the candidate and "independent expenditure[s]" made by individuals unrelated to a campaign.[15] These independent expenditures legally were not allowed to be associated with a campaign, but it arguably allowed for surreptitious funding for campaigns. However, the U.S. Supreme Court struck down this type of cap holding that independent expenditures were not necessarily associated with a particular campaign:

Unlike contributions, such independent expenditures may well provide little assistance to the candidate's campaign and indeed may prove counterproductive. The absence of prearrangement and coordination of an expenditure with the candidate or his agent not only undermines the value of the expenditure to the candidate, but also alleviates the danger that expenditures will be given as a quid pro quo for improper commitments from the candidate.[16]

Because of its approach to expenditure caps, the U.S. Supreme Court set forth a legal standard that provided for more expensive elections.[17]

The decision in *Buckley v. Valeo* settled some of the constitutional questions surrounding FECA's campaign finance regulations. However, later cases examined who could individually contribute, and if there was a way to cap certain types of money from entering into the election process. In 1978 the U.S. Supreme Court held that corporations had First Amendment speech rights in *First National Bank of Boston v. Bellotti*.[18] In that case Massachusetts state law banned corporations from making contributions that would "for the purpose of . . . influencing or affecting the vote on any question submitted to the voters, other than one materially affecting any of the property, business or assets of the corporation."[19] Writing for the majority of the court Justice Lewis Powell defended the role of corporations to be able to be heard on referendum issues:

> If the speakers here were not corporations, no one would suggest that the State could silence their proposed speech. It is the type of speech indispensable to decisionmaking in a democracy, and this is no less true because the speech comes from a corporation rather than an individual. The inherent worth of the speech in terms of its capacity for informing the public does not depend upon the identity of its source, whether corporation, association, union, or individual.[20]

The issues surrounding corporate contributions to campaigns and political issues continued into the 1980s. The U.S. Supreme Court again considered the contours of corporate political speech in 1986 in *FEC v. Massachusetts Citizens for Life*.[21] In that case the U.S. Supreme Court held that certain types of political corporations that had no shareholders and were not part of a business or union were not subject to FECA's ban on "independent spending" in campaigns.[22] In 1990 another case, *Austin v. Michigan Chamber of Commerce*, stepped back from allowing corporations to use funds in political elections. Writing for the majority Justice Thurgood Marshall held that Michigan law banning corporate use of money for independent expenditures supporting or opposing specific political candidates was constitutional and did not violate the First Amendment.[23]

The 1990s saw the rise of concerns over the so-called use of soft money in elections. Part of the concern with soft money is that it did not adhere to the FEC's regulations on fundraising. Soft money was raised under state regulations in a manner that was not subject to federal oversight. This was legal because soft money is not used at the federal level and not directly associated with federal candidates, but instead used for "grass-roots activities" that incidentally helped federal candidates.[24] Because of this the soft money was subject to less restrictions. This prompted the passage of the Bipartisan Campaign Reform Act of 2002 (BRCA), popularly known as the McCain-Feingold Act.[25] The new law largely banned soft money from being used in federal elections, and banned corporations and unions from making certain ads within 30 days of a primary and 60 days of a general election.[26] After the U.S. Supreme Court upheld the challenge to the BCRA in *McConnell v. FEC*, some political groups used alternative means to introduce soft money in the campaign through 527 s.[27] After the U.S. Supreme Court upheld the challenge to the BCRA in *McConnell v. FEC*, some political groups used alternative means to introduce soft money in the campaign through 527 s. Commonly referred to as 527 s because they fall under tax-exempt status under 26 U.S.C. §527, these organizations are technically PACs. However, in popular use of the term 527 refers to an organization that does not raise money under FECA requirements because they do not expressly advocate for a candidate or party.

By 2010 the U.S. Supreme Court was poised to dramatically change campaign finance laws, and elections, in the United States. The decision in *Austin v. Michigan Chamber of Commerce* is the basis for one of the most controversial U.S. Supreme Court decisions—*Citizens United v. FEC*.[28] The decision in *Citizens United v. FEC* overturned the decision in *Austin v. Michigan Chamber of Commerce*. However, the *Citizens United* decision had a large impact on the way political campaigns would be conducted. The U.S. Supreme Court's ruling meant that corporations and unions were able to make independent expenditures in candidate elections. The decision in *Citizens United v. FEC* coupled with the U.S. Court of Appeals for the D.C. Circuit's decision in *SpeechNow.org v. FEC* gave rise to the super-PAC, an independent expenditure committee that can raise large sums of money from individuals, corporations, and unions.[29] By 2014 U.S. campaign finance law was changed by the U.S. Supreme Court in *McCutcheon v. FEC*, which ultimately struck down the cap on the aggregate amount an individual could contribute in a calendar year.[30]

The legal issues surrounding campaign finance have caused concern in political and academic circles.[31] Campaign finance laws going back to FECA may have an impact on the mechanics of races, such as when U.S.

Senators retire.[32] Another focus of campaign finance research is donors' ideological beliefs and how those beliefs influence campaigns.[33] However, much of the current discussion involves the impact of campaign money and the lack of spending caps on elections. In his examination of the themes of campaign finance debate, Ryan Penick found that the debate goes beyond merely issues limited campaign spending versus unlimited campaign spending; something that Penick calls the "libertarian" versus the "egalitarian" theory of campaign spending.[34] Rather, he found that the campaign finance debates look at a three main themes: "corruption based positions," "equal opportunity for political influence," and "leveling the playing field."[35] Penick argues that each of these positions is subject to major criticisms each of which create competing values that occur in democracy. However, legal analysis of current campaign finance focuses on the impact of vast amounts of corporate money in the election cycle. This signaled to some that the U.S. Supreme Court under Chief Justice John Roberts would be increasingly critical campaign finance regulation.[36]

However, there is some evidence that the influx of campaign funds post-*Citizens United* do not have the same impact on election results that some feared. It is true that candidates with the most money do not automatically win elections, and that sometimes a candidates' gaffes or past indiscretions can sink an otherwise well-funded campaign.[37] In a longitudinal study of state elections from 1968 through 2008 looking at incumbent reelection and rate of Republican election in state legislatures, Raymond Raja and Brian Schaffner found that caps on campaign spending by corporations have little effect on election outcome.[38] Similarly, Robert Mutch found that in the beginning stages of the 2016 presidential primaries, super-PACs support did not correlate with electoral success.[39] However, the issue of campaign finance may not be the money itself, but how the campaign contributions result in political access or political results.[40] Despite this, Bauerly and Hallsrom argue that the influence of super-PACs and campaign finance may be unknown because the reporting requirements and voter confusion.[41]

What this system of election law has created is a very complex set of regulations that require disclosure and reporting. Studies indicate that the true impact of money varies, but is not exclusively an indicator of election success. There also seems to be an issue between donations and spending. While donations have historically been curbed by the corruption rationale articulated by *Buckley v. Valeo*, the spending caps have proved to be constitutionally problematic. Reporting requirements have increased to ensure a greater degree of transparency. The result is that election campaigns are costly. The 2016 presidential election is no exception. Interestingly, despite that candidates' continual fundraising the 2016 election showed that campaign finance not only is a political necessity, it is now a political issue.

CAMPAIGN FINANCE IN THE 2016 PRESIDENTIAL PRIMARIES

Donald Trump and Hillary Clinton agreed on very few issues, but one thing they had in common was their criticism of money in the political process. Both used the issue of campaign finance to distinguish themselves as a candidate. Trump used the campaign finance issue to cast himself as a more unencumbered candidate who was not beholden to the special interests that controlled Washington. He pointed to Clinton's backers as evidence of her own Washington insider status and her loyalty to her donors' interest. Clinton addressed the issue of campaign finance reform in a more traditionally political way that presented herself as against corporate political power. Her criticism of corporate power and influence in the presidential election centered on the U.S. Supreme Court's holding in *Citizens United v. FEC*, and her political solution for this issue was her ability to appoint justices to the high court.

Before Trump was the Republican Party's nominee, he made campaign finance an issue in the campaign. He criticized the role of money in politics and he vowed that he would not be controlled by special interests. Trump was particularly critical of super-PACs, the vast money making committees created by the U.S. Supreme Court's ruling in *Citizens United v. FEC*. In fact, in an interview on CNN he referred to PACs as a "horrible thing" and called for campaign finance reform.[42] His criticism of super-PACs also revolved around the lack of separation of them and the candidates associated with them. Criticizing Jeb Bush, who was funded by super-PAC Right to Rise in the Republican primaries, Trump claimed that Bush's relationship with the PAC was too close. He also mentioned that the funding candidates receive from donors creates conflicts of interest when the candidate becomes the officeholder. Commenting on the influence donors have on candidates Trump said, "They [the candidate] owe them. And by the way, they may therefore vote negatively toward the country."[43]

Early on the media recognized that campaign expenditures did not necessarily correlate with campaign success. Trump spent significantly less on his primary campaign compared to Cruz and Rubio in January 2016.[44] POLITICO noted that this could be the sign of a new type of campaigning where campaign funds were not the ultimate predictors of campaign success. Certainly compared to his three closest rivals, Rubio, Cruz, and Bush, Trump underperformed in January fundraising from individual contributions. As Table 10.1 shows, from January 1 through January 30, 2016, Trump's campaign had raised only $941,007 in individual contributions compared to the $4.8 million raised by Rubio, $7.5 million raised by Cruz, and $1.5 million by Bush. This trend continued throughout the primary when the Republican challengers to Trump winnowed down significantly. In February 2016 (the month Trump won the New Hampshire Republican primary), Trump had an increase in individual contributions, slightly more than $2 million, but he still trailed behind Rubio (slightly under $9.5 million) and Cruz ($11.8 million).

Table 10.1 Trump, Rubio Cruz, and Bush's total individual contributions January–June 2016[***]

Month	Trump	Rubio	Cruz	Bush
January	$941,007	$4.8 million	$7.5 million	$1.5 million
February	$2 million	$9.4 million	$11.8 million	$759,965[*]
March	$2.7 million	$2.3 million[*]	$12.4 million	$601
April	$1.7 million	–$5,858	$10.8 million	–
May	$3.1 million	–$5,149	$2.6 million[*]	–
June	$19.8 million	$442	–$21,719	$300[**]

[*]Indicates Month Candidate Suspended Campaign.
[**]Jeb Bush began filing only quarterly reports after March 2016.
[***]These figures do not include party committee, other committee, or candidate contributions. "Report Summaries Donald J. Trump For President Inc.," U.S. Federal Election Commission, accessed December 27, 2017, http://www.fec.gov/fecviewer/CandidateCommitteeDetail.do?candidateCommitteeId=P80001571&tabIndex=1; "Report Summaries Marco Rubio for President," U.S. Federal Election Commission, accessed April 2, 2017, http://www.fec.gov/fecviewer/CandidateCommitteeDetail.do?candidateCommitteeId=P60006723&tabIndex=1; "Report Summaries Cruz for President," U.S. Federal Election Commission, accessed December 27, 2016, http://www.fec.gov/fecviewer/CandidateCommitteeDetail.do?candidateCommitteeId=P60006111&tabIndex=1; "Report Summaries Jeb 2016, Inc.," U.S. Federal Election Commission, accessed December 27, 2016, http://www.fec.gov/fecviewer/CandidateCommitteeDetail.do?candidateCommitteeId=P60008059&tabIndex=1.

Trump made up for lower individual contributions by providing his campaign loans. After the Republican primaries Trump forgave the loans, meaning that he did not seek to be repaid by the campaign, for approximately $47 million.[45]

Similar to Trump, Democratic candidate Bernie Sanders used campaign rhetoric that criticized the role of corporate money in elections. In October 2015 at the Democratic Candidates Debate held in Las Vegas, Nevada, Sanders specifically mentioned *Citizens United* as an example of how money was corrupting the political system. He said:

> As a result of this disastrous Citizens United Supreme Court decision, our campaign finance system is corrupt and is undermining American democracy. Millionaires and billionaires are pouring unbelievable sums of money into the political process in order to fund super PACs and to elect candidates who represent their interests, not the interests of working people.[46]

Sanders made a point that he would not have a super-PAC, and claimed that his donations were made from regular Americans.[47] After his victory in the New Hampshire primary Sanders said:

> I do not have a Super PAC, and I do not want a Super PAC. I am overwhelmed, and I am deeply moved far more than I can express in words by the fact that our campaigns [sic] financial support comes from more than one million Americans who have made more than 3.7 million individual contributions. That is more individual contributions than any candidate in the history of the United States up until this point in an election. And, you know what that average contribution was? $27 dollars.[48]

However, Sanders outraised Clinton in individual contributions during the Democratic primary. As Table 10.2 shows, Sanders continued to raise millions even going into the Democratic National Convention in July.

Even though he formally endorsed Clinton in July 2016, he also raised over $1 million in individual contributions that month.[49] In his endorsement of Clinton at the convention, Sanders made one more denunciation of campaign finance in the U.S. election. When detailing the impact the 2016 presidential election he said, "This election is about overturning Citizens United, one of the worst Supreme Court decisions in the history of our country."[50]

Table 10.2   Clinton and Sanders' total individual contributions January–June 2016*

Month	Clinton	Sanders
January	$13.1 million	$21.2 million
February	$23.3 million	$43.3 million
March	$22.3 million	$44.7 million
April	$20.2 million	$26.2 million
May	$19.5 million	$15.6 million
June	$23.6 million	$5.9 million

*These figures do not include party committee, other committee, or candidate contributions. "Report Summaries Hillary for America," U.S. Federal Election Commission, accessed December 27, 2016, http://www.fec.gov/fecviewer/CandidateCommitteeDetail.do?candidateCommitteeId=P00003392&tabIndex=1; "Report Summaries Bernie 2016," U.S. Federal Election Commission, accessed December 27, 2016, http://www.fec.gov/fecviewer/CandidateCommitteeDetail.do?candidateCommitteeId=P60007168&tabIndex=1.

CAMPAIGN FINANCE AS A POLITICAL ISSUE IN THE 2016 PRESIDENTIAL GENERAL ELECTION

Campaign finance was both a practical and political issue in 2016. Practically both candidates spent a lot of time raising money and spending on their campaigns. However, politically campaign finance became a larger issue that each candidate used to distinguish themselves from their opponent. It is interesting that as combined political fundraising reached over $1 billion both Trump and Clinton criticized the role money in politics and categorized it as a corrupting force in Washington.

Similar to the primary contests campaign money was a major issue in the general election. However, Trump took on the mantle of criticizing the role of money in the election process by tying Clinton to corporate and Wall Street donors. In his acceptance speech at the Republican National Convention in Cleveland, Ohio, Donald Trump tied Hillary Clinton to the problems of campaign finance saying:

> Big business, elite media and major donors are lining up behind the campaign of my opponent [Hillary Clinton] because they know she will keep our rigged system in place. They are throwing money at her because they have total control over everything she does. She is their puppet, and they pull the strings.[51]

Similarly, Hillary Clinton specifically mentioned campaign finance and big business in her acceptance speech at the DNC in Philadelphia. Trying campaign finance issues to the U.S. Supreme Court's decision in *Citizens United v. FEC* she said:

> I believe our economy isn't working the way it should because our democracy isn't working the way it should. That's why we need to appoint Supreme Court justices who will get money out of politics and expand voting rights, not restrict them. And if necessary, we'll pass a constitutional amendment to overturn Citizens United![52]

These statements show how each candidate took a position that criticized the growing amount of money in politics. Yet both of them raised millions of dollars in campaign donations, benefitted from super-PACs, and rejected federal funding for their campaigns presumably so they could raise greater amounts on their own.[53]

Donald Trump used the campaign finance issue as political fodder early on in his campaign. His self-contributions and personal loans coupled with his declaration that he turned down political donations during the primary races were part of a strategy to emphasize his outsider status. In August 2015, CBS' Face the Nation host John Dickerson asked Trump whether he would finance his entire presidential campaign into the general election. Trump responded by criticizing the role of money in politics:

> I have been a very big contributor to many, many people of all size [sic] for many, many years. I don't want lobbyists. I don't want special interests, but certainly people . . . I actually like the idea of investing in a campaign, but it has to be no strings attached. I don't want any strings attached. You know, these lobbyists come in. I turned down $5 million last week from a very important lobbyist, because there are total strings attached to a thing like that.[54]

Money, of course, was a major issue in all three debates, particularly the money given to the Clinton Foundation during Hillary Clinton's time as Secretary of State and the issues of the U.S. economy. However, in the debates campaign finance was mentioned specifically in the second and third debates. This discussion of money in politics was used by both Trump and Clinton to demonstrate the problems corporate money and large donors caused in American politics. In the second presidential debate on October

10, 2016, Trump and Clinton used campaign donations and the politics of campaign contributions to distinguish themselves from each other. Clinton spoke directly of campaign finance reform and the role cases like *Citizens United v. FEC* played in American politics. She said, "I would want to see the Supreme Court reverse Citizens United and get dark unaccountable money out of our politics. Donald doesn't agree with that."[55] Equating money with disproportionate political power Clinton also said that the U.S. Supreme Court was best equipped to limit the excesses of wealth and political power.

Trump took a different approach toward campaign finance and power. Rather than criticizing courts and campaign finance law he linked the campaign finance issues directly with Clinton. Her relationship with large donors was portrayed as emblematic of the larger political problems in Washington. He also used the campaign finance issue to cast himself in the mold of the Washington outsider who was not beholden to wealthy donors. In a response to his decision to not disclose his tax returns, Trump attacked Clinton's donors arguing that her biggest donors took advantage of the American tax system. He said:

> Many of her friends took bigger deductions. Warren Buffett took a massive deduction. Soros, who's a friend of hers took a massive deduction. Many of the people that are giving her all this money that she can do many more commercials than me—took massive deductions.[56]

Trump later juxtaposed his campaign fundraising strategy to Clinton arguing that his self-contributions to the campaign and acceptance of small donations showed his rejection of big money in campaigning. He said:

> Now, Hillary mentioned something about contributions just so you understand. So I will have in my race more than $100 million put in— of my money, meaning I'm not taking all of this big money from all of these different corporations like she's doing. What I ask is this. So I'm putting in more than—by the time it's finished, I'll have more than $100 million invested. Pretty much self-funding money. We're raising money for the Republican Party, and we're doing tremendously on the small donations, $61 average or so. I ask Hillary, why doesn't—she made $250 million by being in office. She used the power of her office to make a lot of money. Why isn't she funding, not for $100 million, but why don't you put $10 million or $20 million or $25 million or $30 million into your own campaign?[57]

Clinton did not directly answer this question at the debate, and the moderator moved on to the next question.

TRUMP AND CLINTON'S FUNDRAISING IN 2016 PRESIDENTIAL ELECTION

Despite the criticism of campaign finance and money in politics in the primaries and general election, both Trump and Clinton actively raised money after their formal nominations. Clinton outraised Trump in individual contributions throughout the general election cycle from July through November. As Table 10.3 shows, Trump's individual contributions only exceed $20 million in the Post-General report from October 20 through November 28, 2016. Clinton's individual contributions remained above $20 million from July, in which the Democratic National Convention was held, onward making her campaign well funded throughout the general election.

Of course, these figures do not include the party contributions, super-PAC money, or the individual candidate's donations to their own campaign.

As shown in Table 10.4 Trump's campaign also consistently trailed Clinton in cash on hand, which is the amount ending cash a campaign has in its account to spend at the end of a reporting period. The FEC monthly filings indicate that Clinton not only had more cash on hand from July through November but that her totals increased toward the end of the

Table 10.3 Trump and Clinton total individual contributions July 1–November 28, 2016*

Month	Trump	Clinton
July	$19.6 million	$31.2 million
August	$18.3 million	$26.8 million
September	$17.3 million	$41 million
Pre-general	$13.4 million	$28 million
Post-general	$26.2 million	$47.3 million

*"Report Summaries Hillary for America," U.S. Federal Election Commission, accessed April 1, 2017, http://www.fec.gov/fecviewer/CandidateCommitteeDetail.do?candidateCommitteeId=P00003392&tabIndex=1; "Report Summaries Donald J. Trump For President Inc.," U.S. Federal Election Commission, accessed December 27, 2016, http://www.fec.gov/fecviewer/CandidateCommitteeDetail.do?candidateCommitteeId=P80001571&tabIndex=1.

Table 10.4 Trump and Clinton ending cash on hand July 1–November 28, 2016*

Month	Trump	Clinton
July	$38.4 million	$58.4 million
August	$50.2 million	$68.4 million
September	$34.7 million	$59.6 million
Pre-general	$15.9 million	$62.4 million
Post-general	$7.6 million	$838,649

*"Report Summaries Hillary for America," U.S. Federal Election Commission, accessed December 27, 2016, http://www.fec.gov/fecviewer/CandidateCommitteeDetail.do?candidateCommitteeId= P00003392&tabIndex=1; "Report Summaries Donald J. Trump For President Inc.," U.S. Federal Election Commission, accessed December 27, 2016, http://www.fec.gov/fecviewer/ CandidateCommitteeDetail.do?candidateCommitteeId=P80001571&tabIndex=1.

campaign cycle. According to FEC filings from April 2, 2015 through November 28, 2016, Trump donated $18.6 million to his campaign (both in-kind and money contributions). Clinton contributed $1.45 million from April 1, 2015, through November 28, 2016 (in-kind contributions).[58]

Table 10.5 shows that Clinton's campaign had higher operating expenditures during the campaign. Campaign expenditures from July through November increased up until November (Table 10.5).

Fundraising for parties, joint fundraising committees, and super-PACs mirrored that for the campaign committees for Trump and Clinton. The Democratic National Committee and the Clinton Joint Fundraising

Table 10.5 Trump and Clinton campaign operating expenditures July 1–November 28, 2016*

Month	Trump	Clinton
July	$18.4 million	$37.8 million
August	$29.8 million	$49 million
September	$70 million	$82.1 million
Pre-general	$49.1 million	$49.6 million
Post-general	$94 million	$130.7 million

*"Report Summaries Hillary for America," U.S. Federal Election Commission, accessed December 27, 2016, http://www.fec.gov/fecviewer/CandidateCommitteeDetail.do?candidateCommitteeId= P00003392&tabIndex=1; "Report Summaries Donald J. Trump For President Inc.," U.S. Federal Election Commission, accessed December 27, 2016, http://www.fec.gov/fecviewer/ CandidateCommitteeDetail.do?candidateCommitteeId=P80001571&tabIndex=1.

Committees out raised Republicans. Looking at Democratic and Republican National Committee totals the Democrats had a slight edge in fundraising with the DNC's total receipts equaling $350.6 million to the RNC's $343.3 million between January 1, 2015, through December 31, 2016.[59] The sample of joint fundraising committees, shown in Table 10.6, show that both Trump and Clinton raised millions in these committees that are comprised of at least two candidates, committees, or PACs.

This campaign totals do not factor in the role of super-PACs in the campaign. Technically campaigns officially cannot have contact with their super-PAC, and theoretically a super-PAC can produce content or spend money even if the campaign does not endorse what the super-PAC does. The legal restrictions between a campaign and super-PACs are supposed to be so limited that a campaign could not stop a super-PAC from campaigning on its behalf. In fact, in October 2015 Trump sent notices to nine super-PACs asking them to stop fundraising on his behalf and to return all money donated.[60]

The amount of money these super-PACs raise and spend is reported to the FEC. However, not all super-PACs are created equally, and some have more money and therefore more campaign expenditures than others. In 2016 the major super-PACs for Trump included Future45, Great America

Table 10.6 Total joint fundraising committee contributions April 1, 2016 through December 31, 2016**

Joint Fundraising Committee Name	Total Contributions
Trump Make America Great Again Committee	$263.7 million
Trump Victory	$108.3 million
Hillary Victory Fund	$526.5 million*
Hillary Action Fund	$46.5 million

*This total is from July 1, 2015 through December 31, 2016.
**These total contributions include itemized individual contributions, unitemized individual contributions, party committees' contributions, and other committees' contributions. "Financial Summary Make America Great Again Committee," U.S. Federal Election Commission, accessed April 2, 2017 http://www.fec.gov/fecviewer/CandidateCommitteeDetail.do?candidateCommitteeId=C00618371&tabIndex=1; "Financial Summary Trump Victory Committee," U.S. Federal ElectionCommission, accessed April 2, 2017, http://www.fec.gov/fecviewer/CandidateCommitteeDetail.do?candidateCommitteeId=C00618389&tabIndex=1; "Financial Summary Hillary Victory Fund," U.S. Federal Election Commission, accessed April 2, 2017, http://www.fec.gov/fecviewer/CandidateCommitteeDetail.do?candidateCommitteeId=C00586537&tabIndex=1; "Financial Summary Hillary Action Fund," Federal Election Commission, accessed April 2, 2017, http://www.fec.gov/fecviewer/CandidateCommitteeDetail.do?candidateCommitteeId=C00619411&tabIndex=1.

Table 10.7   Total super-pac receipts January 1, 2015 through December 31, 2016**

Super-PAC	Viewpoint	Total Receipts
Future45	Pro-Trump	$24.9 million
Great America PAC	Pro-Trump	$28.6 million
Rebuilding America Now	Pro-Trump	$22.6 million*
Priorities U.S.A. Action	Pro-Clinton	$192 million
American Bridge 21st Century	Pro-Democrat	$19.8 million
Correct The Record	Pro-Clinton	$9.7 million

* This total is from April 1, 2016, through December 31, 2016, 2016.
** "Financial Summary Future45," Federal Election Commission, accessed April 2, 2017, http://www.fec.gov/fecviewer/CandidateCommitteeDetail.do?candidateCommitteeId=C00574533&tabIndex=1, "Financial Summary Great America PAC," Federal Election Commission, accessed April 2, 2017, http://www.fec.gov/fecviewer/CandidateCommitteeDetail.do?candidateCommitteeId=C00608489&tabIndex=1; "Financial Summary Rebuilding America Now," Federal Election Commission, accessed April 2, 2017, http://www.fec.gov/fecviewer/CandidateCommitteeDetail.do?candidateCommitteeId=C00618876&tabIndex=1, "Financial Summary Priorities USA Action," Federal Election Commission, accessed April 2, 2017, http://www.fec.gov/fecviewer/CandidateCommitteeDetail.do?candidateCommitteeId=C00495861&tabIndex=1; "Financial Summary American Bridge 21st Century," Federal Election Commission, accessed April 2, 2017, http://www.fec.gov/fecviewer/CandidateCommitteeDetail.do?candidateCommitteeId=C00492140&tabIndex=1; "Financial Summary Correct the Record," Federal Election Commission, accessed April 2, 2017, http://www.fec.gov/fecviewer/CandidateCommitteeDetail.do?candidateCommitteeId=C00578997&tabIndex=1.

PAC, and Rebuilding America Now. Clinton also enjoyed significant super-PAC support including Priorities U.S. Action, American Bridge Twenty-First Century, and Correct the Record. Table 10.7 provides a sample of total receipts of super-PACs supporting Clinton and Trump.

However, these are but a small listing of super-PACs that made expenditures during the 2016 election cycle. Candidate also may have benefitted from other super-PACs that were focused on party, down ballot, or ideological issues that created ancillary benefits for the presidential candidates.

Conclusions and Implications for Future Campaigns

The presidential election of 2016 stands out for its unexpected results. Part of the reason for this surprise election was that money was not an accurate indicator of campaign success. If money is the best indicator for victory, then Trump should have lost the primary to Bush, Rubio, or Cruz. Moreover, in the general election Clinton outraised Trump, as did her supporting joint fundraising committees and super-PAC support. However, Trump still prevailed and won a historic victory.

What does this say about campaign finance, and, more importantly, does this mean that campaign finance does not matter in winning elections? While this chapter cannot provide a definitive answer to these questions it can provide some insights. First, money does matter. Both Clinton and Trump raised millions of dollars, and the election saw massive spending by super-PACs and both parties. Second, campaign money's influence is limited. A victorious campaign is the result of an amalgam of factors including financing, candidate message, candidate image, and public mood. What the 2016 presidential election shows is that although money is a necessary ingredient for success it is not the only thing needed. Although it is outside the scope of this chapter, it is important to note that Trump's victory was in part due to his message and public sentiment toward his opponent, and the public's view of the political and economic status quo of the United States. While money can amplify or expose these issues public sentiment represents an intangible factor that money cannot complete control. Third, campaign strategy matters, especially the use of free media. One of the most unusual aspects of the 2016 election was that both candidates had a large amount of celebrity the day they announced their campaigns. Because of that they did not have to engage in a strategy to boost name recognition. Trump's candidacy also generated free media attention, which he used at times for his benefit. Perhaps most importantly social media, which is a free medium, allowed for both candidates to engage with the public. It may be Trump's use of social media and the corresponding free media it garnered that allowed him to make up the campaign finance deficit between him and Clinton.

This campaign also signals some significant consequences for campaign finance law. The presidential election in 2016 seems to indicate that public financing of presidential elections is all but over. Both Clinton and Trump opted out of public funding, and it is difficult to imagine a successful campaign agreeing to limit its fundraising abilities, especially if their opponent chooses to refuse funding. Similarly, it seems that super-PACs are not necessarily producing the type of results that detractors anticipated. While they certainly play a role in campaigns, they have not produced a reality where the best-financed candidate is the automatic victor. In fact, political criticism of super-PACs and corporate financing of campaigns seem to have some traction with the public, and as both Trump and Clinton's campaign rhetoric indicates it seems to be a political issue both parties want to use to their advantage. U.S. Supreme Court cases are typically difficult to predict as are potential outcomes. It may be that by 2020 there are limitations on corporate spending and super-PACs may be eliminated. However, like all things in American law those issues remain to be seen, and, if the past is any predictor, they will be addressed at a glacial pace.

Examining campaign finance in the 2016 presents one overriding questions. Is the presidential election in 2016 the exception or the new rule? As with anything future elections will answer this question. However, it is important to note that the 2016 presidential election, like all elections, had factors that are unique. Both candidates were celebrities, one candidate was a billionaire political neophyte, one candidate was a well-established political figure, and the U.S. was experiencing political issues concerning economy, jobs, and security. It is also significant that this election was one with new campaign finance and media realities. Super-PACs were highly engaged in the election, social media was heavily used, and online fundraising reached a greater degree of sophistication. All of this shows that even though 2016 had certain idiosyncrasies, this election may be a signal of a new technological, media, and financial campaign reality.

NOTES

1. Theodore Roosevelt: "Seventh Annual Message," December 3, 1907. Online by Gerhard Peters and John T. Woolley, *The American Presidency Project*. http://www.presidency.ucsb.edu/ws/?pid=29548.
2. Robert E. Mutch, *Campaign Finance: What Everyone Needs to Know* (Oxford University Press, 2016), 5. This is usually true for candidates who raise the most money. However, if a candidate uses his or her own money to self-finance there is a more mixed outcome. Mutch points out that Michael Bloomberg won the New York City's mayor's race using self-funding while Meg Whitman lost her largely self-funded bid for California's Senate.
3. Alfred Chandler, Jr., *The Visible Hand: The Managerial Revolution in American Business* (Cambridge: Belknap Press, 1977), 145–203.
4. U.S. v. UAW-CIO, 352 U.S. 567 (1957). In this case Justice Felix Frankfurter detailed the history of campaign finance up until the 1950s. This history has been criticized for providing a false historical narrative of campaign finance laws that places the U.S. Congress in a positive light and ignores historical contextualization of campaign finance reform history. See Allison Hayward, "Revisiting the Fable of Reforms," *Harvard Journal on Legislation* 45(2) (2008): 421–470.
5. U.S. v. UAW-CIO, 352 U.S. 567, 573 (1957).
6. Buckley v. Valeo, 424 U.S. 1, 61 (1976).

7. Newberry v. U.S., 256 U.S. 232 (1921). This case is interesting because of the fact that the case involved a dispute over Truman Newberry's expenditures used in his 1918 bid to become the U.S. Senator from Michigan. Michigan law only allowed for a candidate to spend 25 percent of his future annual salary as a Senator during the Senate campaign. Newberry spent over $100,000 for his campaign to defeat the great American industrialist Henry Ford in the Republican primary.
8. This version of the FCPA was challenged as well and upheld by the U.S. Supreme Court in two cases Burroughs v. U.S., 290 U.S. 534 (1934) and U.S. v. Classic, 313 U.S. 299 (1941).
9. 50 U.S.C. App.§§ 1501-1511(2010). This law was passed with a Congressional override of President Franklin Roosevelt's veto.
10. Mutch, *What is the Campaign Finance Problem?*,14–15. According to Mutch the campaign finance issue in Watergate emerged because the Committee to Reelect the President did not disclose campaign finance information in compliance with the FECA. This issue was compounded by the fact that portions the presidential campaign in 1971 occurred at a time of transition between the FCPA and FECA.
11. "About the FEC," Federal Election Commission, accessed December 20, 2016, http://www.fcc.gov/about.shtml In the original FECA Congress, not the President of the United States, was tasked with appointing FEC Commissioners. However, the U.S. Supreme Court struck down this appointment scheme in Buckley v. Valeo, 424 U.S. 1 (1976).
12. Buckley v. Valeo, 424 U.S. 1, 58 (1976).
13. Buckley v. Valeo, 424 U.S. 1, 21 (1976).
14. Buckley v. Valeo, 424 U.S. 1, 61 (1976).
15. Buckley v. Valeo, 424 U.S. 1, 47 (1976).
16. Buckley v. Valeo, 424 U.S. 1, 47 (1976).
17. The provision on election expenditure caps was created in part because by the 1970s election costs had increased. In their argument to the United States Court of Appeal for the D.C. Circuit the appellees noted that in the twenty-year period between 1952 and 1972 the cost of federal elections had increased 300 percent.
18. First National Bank of Boston v. Bellotti, 435 U.S. 765 (1978).
19. First National Bank of Boston v. Bellotti, 435 U.S. 765, 768 (1978) (citing Mass. Gen. Laws Ann., ch. 55 § 8 (West Supp. 1977)).
20. First National Bank of Boston v. Bellotti, 435 U.S. 765, 777 (1978). It is important to note that the issue in this case did not involve corporate money used in a political campaign, but in a ballot initiative that concerning state income tax.
21. FEC v. Massachusetts Citizens for Life, 479 U.S. 238 (1986).

22. FEC v. Massachusetts Citizens for Life, 479 U.S. 238, 241 (1986). The U.S. Supreme Court noted that this category of corporation was rare, and that the criteria required to be a corporation like Massachusetts Citizens for Life meant very few corporate entities would fall into this special category.
23. Austin v. Michigan Chamber of Commerce, 494 U.S. 652 (1990).
24. Mutch, *Campaign Finance: What Everyone Needs to Know*, 104. Mutch notes that the reason this soft money was allowed was that at the time FECA applied to federal candidates. This permitted the more lax state fundraising to occur for state and local offices.
25. Bipartisan Campaign Act of 2002, Public Law 107–155.
26. Bipartisan Campaign Act of 2002, Public Law 107–155 §203. This provision was at issue in FEC v. Wisconsin Right to Life, 551 U.S. 449 (2007). In that case the U.S. Supreme Court held that issue ads paid for by unions or corporation could not be banned by the BRCA.
27. McConnell v. FEC, 540 U.S. 93 (2003).
28. Citizens United v. FEC, 558 U.S. 310 (2010).
29. SpeechNow.org v. FEC, 599 F.3d 686 (2010).
30. McCutcheon v. FEC, 134 S.Ct. 1434 (2014).
31. Cynthia L. Bauerly and Eric C. Hallstrom, "Square Pegs: The challenges For Existing Federal Campaign Finance Disclosure Laws in the Age of the Super PAC," *Legislation and Public Policy 15* (2012): 329–362, 356–361; Richard L. Hasen, *Plutocrats United: Campaign Money, the Supreme Court, and the Distortion of American Elections* (New Haven: Yale University Press, 2016); Marcus Cayce Myers and Ruthann Weaver Lariscy, "Corporate PR in a post-Citizens United world," *Journal of Communication Management* 18(2) (2013): 146–157. 152–156; Ryan Penick, "The Anatomy of Debate about Campaign Finance," *The Journal of Politics,* 78(4) (2016): 1184–1195), 1184–1189.
32. David Karol, "Forcing Their Hands?: Campaign Finance Law, Retirement Announcements and the Rise of the Permanent Campaign in U.S. Senate Elections," *Congress & the Presidency* 42 (2015): 79–94, 91–92.
33. Brittany Bramlett, James Gimpel, and Frances E. Lee, "The Political Ecology of Opinion in Big-Donor Neighborhoods, *Political Behavior* 33 (4) (2011): 565–600, 589–591; Raymond J. La Raja and David L. Wiltse, "Don't Blame Donors for Ideological Polarization of Political Parties: Ideological Change and Stability Among Political Contributors, 1972–2008, *American Politics Research* 40(3) (2012): 501–530, 519–523.
34. Penick, "The Anatomy of Debate about Campaign Finance," 1184.
35. Penick, "The Anatomy of Debate about Campaign Finance," 1186, 1187, 1188.
36. Breanne Gilpatrick, "Removing Corporate Campaign finance Restrictions in Citizens United v. Federal Election Commission, 130 S.Ct. 876 (2010),

Harvard Journal of Law & Public Policy 34 (Winter 2011): 405–420, 417. Gilpatrick notes that the U.S. Supreme Court under Chief Justice Roberts has found other campaign finance laws unconstitutional such as in Davis v. FEC, 554 U.S. 724 (2008). In Davis v. FEC the U.S. Supreme Court held that certain provision in the McCain-Feingold Act, commonly referred to as the "Millionaire's Amendment" was unconstitutional.

37. Hasen, *Plutocrats United*, 41.
38. Raymond J. La Raja and Brian F. Schaffner, "The effects of campaign finance spending bans on electoral outcomes: Evidence from the states about the potential impact of *Citizens United v. FEC*," *Electoral Studies* 33 (2014): 102–114, 110. The authors make note that this study looks at success through the lens of incumbency and election of Republican candidates.
39. Mutch, *Campaign Finance*, 87–88.
40. Hasen, *Plutocrats United*, 37–59
41. Bauerly and Hallstrom, "Square Pegs," 356–361.
42. Gregory Krieg, "Best of 'State of the Union': Trump, Clinton, and Sanders," cnn.com, January 17, 2016, http://www.cnn.com/2016/01/17/politics/hillary-clinton-bernie-sanders-donald-trump-sotu/.
43. Bradford Richardson, "Trump open to campaign finance reform," *The Hill*, January 17, 2016, http://thehill.com/blogs/ballot-box/presidential-races/266189-trump-open-to-campaign-finance-reform.
44. Kenneth P. Vogel & Isaac Arnsdorf, "Trump rewrites campaign cash rules," POLITICO, February 21, 2016, http://www.politico.com/story/2016/02/super-pac-fec-campaign-spending-2016-219579.
45. Erik Sherman, "Donald Trump Cranked Up Fundraising in June, Forgave $47 million," *Fortune*, July 21, 2016, http://fortune.com/2016/07/21/donald-trump-fec-fundraising/.
46. Presidential Candidates Debates: "Democratic Candidate's Debate in Las Vegas, Nevada," October 13, 2015, The American Presidency Project. http://www.presidency.ucsb.edu/ws/index.php?pid=110903.
47. This rejection of super-PACs by Sanders is debatable. See Michelle Ye Hee Lee, "Sanders's claim that he 'does not have a super-PAC,'" *The Washington Post*, February 11, 2016, https://www.washingtonpost.com/news/fact-checker/wp/2016/02/11/sanderss-claim-that-he-does-not-have-a-super-pac/?utm_term=.09762dc8cfff.
48. Bernie Sanders: "Remarks in Concord Following the New Hampshire Primary," February 9, 2016. Online by Gerhard Peters and John T. Woolley, *The American Presidency Project*. http://www.presidency.ucsb.edu/ws/?pid=117511.
49. "Report Summaries Bernie 2016," U.S. Federal Election Commission, April 2, 2017, http://www.fec.gov/fecviewer/CandidateCommitteeDetail.do?candidateCommitteeId=P60007168&tabIndex=1.

50. Bernie Sanders: "Remarks to the Democratic National Convention in Philadelphia, Pennsylvania," July 25, 2016. Online by Gerhard Peters and John T. Woolley, *The American Presidency Project*. http://www.presidency.ucsb.edu/ws/?pid=118045.

51. Donald J. Trump: "Address Accepting the Presidential Nomination at the Republican National Convention in Cleveland, Ohio," July 21, 2016. Online by Gerhard Peters and John T. Woolley, *The American Presidency Project*. http://www.presidency.ucsb.edu/ws/?pid=117935.

52. Hillary Clinton: "Address Accepting the Presidential Nomination at the Democratic National Convention in Philadelphia, Pennsylvania," July 28, 2016. Online by Gerhard Peters and John T. Woolley, *The American Presidency Project*. http://www.presidency.ucsb.edu/ws/?pid=118051.

53. The federal matching fund provision is part of the FECA. However, since 2012 no presidential nominee of a major party has accepted the funds. Some view the acceptance of matching funds a severe limitation on fundraising.

54. "Face the Nation transcript August 23, 2015: Trump, Christie & Cruz," last modified on August 23, 2016. http://www.cbsnews.com/news/face-the-nation-transcripts-august-23-2015-trump-christie-cruz/.

55. Presidential Candidates Debates: "Presidential Debate at Washington University in St. Louis, Missouri," October 9, 2016. Online by Gerhard Peters and John T. Woolley, *The American Presidency Project*. http://www.presidency.ucsb.edu/ws/?pid=119038.

56. Ibid.

57. Ibid.

58. "Two Year Summary Hillary for America," U.S. Federal Election Commission, accessed December 27, 2016, http://www.fec.gov/fecviewer/CandidateCommitteeDetail.do?candidateCommitteeId=P00003392 &tabIndex=1; "Two Year Summary Donald J. Trump For President Inc.," U.S. Federal Election Commission, accessed December 27, 2016, http://www.fec.gov/fecviewer/CandidateCommitteeDetail.do?candidateCommitteeId=P80001571&tabIndex=1 See note 46 for more on Trump's campaign loan forgiveness.

59. "Financial Summary Democratic Services Corp./Dem. Nat'l Committee," U.S. Federal Election Commission, accessed April 2, 2017, http://www.fec.gov/fecviewer/CandidateCommitteeDetail.do?candidateCommitteeId=C00010603&tabIndex=1; "Financial Summary Republican National Committee," U.S. Federal Election Commission, accessed April 2, 2017, http://www.fec.gov/fecviewer/CandidateCommitteeDetail.do?candidateCommitteeId=C00003418&tabIndex=1 These totals are based on the number of Total Receipts.

60. Donald J. Trump: "Press Release—Donald J. Trump Calls on All Presidential Candidates to Return Dark Money Sent to Super PAC's," October 23, 2015. Online by Gerhard Peters and John T. Woolley, *The American Presidency Project*. http://www.presidency.ucsb.edu/ws/?pid= 113863.

Cayce Myers is an assistant professor in the Department of Communication at Virginia Tech. Dr. Myers' s research focuses on laws that affect communication practice and the historical development of American public relations. His work has appeared in *Public Relations Review, American Journalism, Journalism History, Media History, Journal of Communication Management*, and *Journal of Information Policy*. He holds a Ph.D. and M.A. from the University of Georgia Grady College of Journalism and Mass Communication, LL.M. from the University of Georgia School of Law, J.D. from Mercer University Walter F. George School of Law, and B.A. in political science and history from Emory University.

CHAPTER 11

Explaining the Vote in the Election of 2016: The Remarkable Come from Behind Victory of Republican Candidate Donald Trump

Henry C. Kenski and Kate M. Kenski

The 2016 election continued the spirited clashes between Republicans and Democrats that characterized the presidential elections of 2000, 2004, 2008, and 2012. From 1968 through 1988 Republican candidates dominated presidential elections, with the exception of 1976 when Jimmy Carter won a narrow victory, but in 1992 and 1996 Democrat Bill Clinton won twice. George W. Bush won two elections for the Republicans in 2000 and 2004 and Obama two elections for the Democrats in 2008 and 2012. In 2016, GOP candidate Donald Trump won and returned the Republicans to the White House.

The study of political campaign communication focuses on the political environment messengers, the messages, the channels of communication (print, radio, television, social media, etc.), the audience, and the effects. The purpose of this chapter is to explain the presidential vote in 2016, and it

H.C. Kenski (✉) · K.M. Kenski
University of Arizona, Tucson, AZ, USA
e-mail: HKenski@aol.com; kkenski@email.arizona.edu

© The Author(s) 2017
R.E. Denton, Jr. (ed.), *The 2016 US Presidential Campaign*,
Political Campaigning and Communication,
DOI 10.1007/978-3-319-52599-0_11

draws upon key factors in the political communication to explain it. We focus on: (1) the overall political environment, (2) the rules of the game and the electoral college, (3) the salience of party identification, (4) the messengers, (5) the messages and campaign strategies, (6) the channels of communication, and (7) and the audience or the regional/state and demographic bases of the presidential vote, with special attention to the roles of gender and race-ethnicity in recent elections and the 2016 campaign. We begin first with observations on the overall political environment.

The Overall Political Environment

The overall political environment has become even increasingly polarized since Bush's reelection in 2004. This polarization continued through Bush's second term and the Obama administration. As Obama finished his term, he left a competitive political situation in which both parties could have won in 2016.

In 2016 the Democrats selected former Secretary of State Hillary Clinton as their nominee. She has had a prolific and visible record in politics since the early 1990s, including service as Senator from New York. Despite a national record, her candidacy carried two dead weights for the presidential race. Sondermann notes that (1) she was the consummate establishment candidate in the ultimate outsider year and (2) her tendency to get involved in questions of ethical improprieties. The fear at the outset of the campaign was that she could overcome one of the objections, but the combination of the two would be too heavy.[1] In the 2016 presidential contest, Clinton dealt with these problems and built on Obama's political base and utilized the gender factor more extensively in forming her own coalition.

Donald Trump was a business and media celebrity without any electoral or military experience. He overcame many obstacles to become the Republican nominee. Trump sought to put Washington on a different course. In dramatic contrast to Clinton's progressive economic approach, Trump promised "to repeal Obama Care, nullify all of President Obama's executive orders and memoranda, begin a wall along the border with Mexico and begin deporting illegal immigrants convicted of crime, cut individual and corporate tax rates, kill the Iran nuclear deal, deregulate energy production, and start negotiations to rewrite trade treaties."[2] The Trump candidacy made for a presidential election with stark contrasts.

Clinton sought a continuation of Obama policies with an emphasis on inclusion and tolerance. Trump offered major change with dramatic language. Among other things, Trump

> characterized Mexicans who immigrated illegally as rapists and murderers, mocked a disabled New York Times reporter, insulted Sen. John McCain (R-Ariz.) for his time as a prisoner of war, suggested a female debate moderator had been tough on him because she was having her menstrual period, and tangled with the Muslim parents of a U.S. soldier who was killed the Iraq War.[3]

The two candidates provided vivid contrasts in both personalities and policies. Clinton struggled throughout the campaign to provide a simple rationale for her running. After considering 85 possibilities, the Clinton campaign settled on the slogan "Stronger Together." It was adequate but did not match the simple power of Trump's pledge to "Make America Great Again."[4]

RULES OF THE GAME: THE ELECTORAL COLLEGE AND THE POPULAR VOTE

Americans do not vote directly for president, but instead cast their ballots for a slate of electors committed to a presidential ticket. Each state has a number of electoral votes equal to its representation in Congress. California, for example, has 53 representatives and 2 senators and therefore has 55 electoral votes. A small state like Wyoming has only one House member and two senators for three electoral votes. The District of Columbia (DC) has three electoral votes as a result of a constitutional amendment. There are 538 total electoral votes, and these votes in most states are counted on the basis of a "winner take all" rule; the ticket winning the state's popular vote receives all of the state's electoral votes. There are two exceptions—Maine (four electoral votes) and Nebraska (five electoral votes). Both award the ticket winning the state's popular vote two electoral votes and then give one electoral vote for each of the state's congressional districts. It takes a majority or 270 electoral votes to win the presidency. Prior to 2008, no candidate had captured a single electoral vote by winning a congressional district while losing a state until Obama carried a Nebraska congressional district while losing the state and earning one electoral vote in 2008. The norm is for all of a state's electoral votes to be awarded to one candidate.

In presidential elections, Democrats historically are consistently stronger in the East and the Pacific West, while Republicans have had an edge in the South, the Mountain West, and the rural Midwest. The larger Midwestern states are often competitive and historically battlegrounds for both party tickets. These Midwestern states again proved to be the battleground in 2016.

Recent political conditions and demographic factors have changed so that it is now easier for the Democratic Party to forge an Electoral College majority. After the 2008 election, Democratic strategist Mike Berman observed that the "Democrats have carried 18 states plus D.C. in five straight presidential elections totaling 248 electoral votes, just 22 short of the 270 to win. In contrast, Republicans have carried 13 states in five straight elections, totaling a mere 95 electoral votes." The Democrats have won the popular vote in six of the past seven elections from 1992 to 2016, including their electoral loss in 2016.[5]

Victory is a steeper climb for Republican candidates to win the Electoral College vote. Given the clear electoral propensity of so many states, both party tickets focus on battleground or potential swing states. The list of swing states changes a little, from election to election, of course, depending on the candidate matchups, issues of the day, and the existing political environment.

The political landscape in 2016 was such that 11 states were considered competitive or swing states. The final list included Colorado, Florida, Iowa, Michigan, Nevada, New Hampshire, North Carolina, Ohio, Pennsylvania, Virginia, and Wisconsin. The list of 11 competitive states was constructed by Real Clear Politics during the campaign. Many of these states have appeared on the most competitive list in past presidential elections. All states and electoral votes are important, but the swing states are the most important because they are more influential in determining electoral outcomes. This was particularly true in 2016 because of Trump's focus on states like Michigan and Wisconsin that were routinely won by the Democratic candidate in previous elections.

PARTY IDENTIFICATION AND THE PRESIDENTIAL VOTE

A central factor in voting is party identification, a psychological concept that is measured by asking respondents if they think of themselves as a Democrat, Republican, Independent, or something else. Usually about

25–30% select Independent, although about a half or three-fifths have partisan leanings. About 70% of the electorate identifies with one of the two major parties, and as the exit surveys in the past four presidential elections reveal, the partisan identifiers cast close to 90% of their vote for their party's candidate. Party identification involves voter perception of their leanings at the present time. It should not be confused with party registration. Sometimes people register with one party but do not bother to change their registration, or simply stay registered with the party to which their families historically have belonged. This is more of a problem in the South, where some older southerners think of themselves as Alabama Democrats or Mississippi Democrats and continue to identify as Democrats while voting Republican in presidential elections because the Democratic candidate may be viewed as too liberal.

Because of the potency of party identification, the two parties conduct massive registration drives in order to have an advantage over the other party. Because partisans vote 90% for their party's candidate, and Independents often split, an edge in party identification is money in the electoral bank. It is an important step before addressing the candidate choices and issue menu in a given election. Because of the Republican image problems so evident in the election of 2006 and in many polls in 2007 and 2008, Obama encouraged Democrats to run up strong advantages in new party registrations to increase Democratic Party identification. Massive party registration drives were successful in swing states, which created a Democratic edge.

The focus on party identification continued in both the Bush and Obama administrations and has remained competitive, with a slight Democratic edge. The voters who are Independent are increasingly more important in the vote. In the presidential election in 2012, Democratic identifiers were 38% of the electorate and voted 92% to 7% for Obama. Republicans were 32% of the vote and only 6% chose Obama. Independents were 29% of the vote and gave a slight 50% to 45% edge to Romney (Table 11.1).

The historical record shows that the Republican candidate received a majority of the Independent vote from 1952 to 2016. The exceptions were 1964 with Independents favoring Johnson and 1992 and 1996 when Bill Clinton won by pluralities (39% to 30%, and 43% to 35%). John Kerry, the Democrat, narrowly won the Independent vote 49% to 48% in 2004, while Barack Obama captured Independents comfortably 52% to 44% in 2008. It is notable that while McCain won Independents in

Table 11.1 Swing states 2012 and 2016 national exit poll profiles: Comparison of all voters (%) and independents (%)

	2012			2016		
	% of the vote	Obama	Romney	% of the vote	Clinton	Trump
All voters						
Nat'l	100	51	48	100	48	46
CO	100	51	47	100	47	44
FL	100	50	49	100	48	49
IA	100	52	46	100	42	52
MI	100	54	45	100	47	48
NV	100	52	46	100	48	46
NH	100	52	46	100	48	47
NC	100	48	51	100	47	51
OH	100	50	48	100	44	52
PA	100	52	47	100	48	49
VA	100	51	48	100	50	45
WI	100	53	46	100	47	48
Independents						
Nat'l	29	45	50	31	42	46
CO	37	45	49	43	42	45
FL	33	50	47	34	43	47
IA	34	55	41	35	38	51
MI	30	48	49	29	36	52
NV	34	43	50	36	37	50
NH	43	52	45	44	45	45
NC	29	42	57	33	37	53
OH	31	43	53	29	37	51
PA	20	45	50	20	41	48
VA	29	43	54	26	43	48
WI	31	49	47	30	40	50

Sources: 2012 figures retrieved December 30, 2016, from http://elections.nbcnews.com/ns/politics/2012/all/president/#.WGYpL1MrJaQ. 2016 figures retrieved December 30, 2016, from http://www.cnn.com/election/results/president.

11 of 13 southern states, there were four states where Obama won the Independents. They were the heavily contested swing states of Florida, Iowa, New Hampshire, and Wisconsin.

The 2012 exit data show more partisanship in the national vote and even less crossover voting, as Obama won 93% of the Democrats and Romney only 7%. Romney took 93% of the Republicans compared to 6%

for Obama. Romney did win the Independents by a small 50% to 45% margin, although the percentages were disappointing for Republicans as some preelection polls had Romney with double-digit leads with this group (Tables 11.1 and 11.2).

The 2016 data underscore the country's continuity on party identification. In 2016 Democrats were 36% of the electorate and voted 89%

Table 11.2 Swing states: 2012 and 2016 national exit poll profiles: Comparison of Democratic and Republican voters (%)

	2012			2016		
	% of the vote	Obama	Romney	% of the vote	Clinton	Trump
Democrats						
Nat'l	38	92	7	36	89	8
CO	34	96	3	32	87	9
FL	35	90	9	32	90	8
IA	33	95	4	31	88	10
MI	40	95	4	40	88	9
NV	38	96	4	36	90	8
NH	30	96	4	28	93	5
NC	39	91	8	35	90	8
OH	38	93	7	34	87	12
PA	45	91	9	42	87	11
VA	39	94	6	40	92	6
WI	37	95	4	35	91	7
Republicans						
Nat'l	32	6	93	33	8	88
CO	29	5	94	24	8	88
FL	33	8	92	33	8	89
IA	33	7	93	34	6	90
MI	30	4	96	31	7	90
NV	28	7	93	28	8	88
NH	27	6	94	28	7	89
NC	33	4	96	31	4	94
OH	31	5	94	37	7	90
PA	35	7	93	39	9	89
VA	32	5	94	33	6	88
WI	32	5	95	34	6	90

Sources: 2012 figures retrieved December 30, 2016, from http://elections.nbcnews.com/ns/politics/ 2012/all/president/#.WGYpL1MrJaQ. 2016 figures retrieved December 30, 2016, from http://www. cnn.com/election/results/president.

Clinton and 8% Trump. The 33% of Republicans were a close image with 88% Trump and 8% Clinton. Independents were 31% of the vote and favored Trump narrowly by a 46% to 42% margin. The 2016 election data suggest that Republicans had a slight edge in partisan voting, as well as a small advantage with Independents.[6]

Table 11.1 contains data on both the overall vote and the Independent vote in the 11 swing states in 2016, with data for how these states voted in both 2012 and 2016. The data underscore that Obama dominated Romney and captured 10 of the 11 states overall. Romney won only North Carolina. Romney did have a national edge with Independents by a 50% to 45% margin, and led Obama among Independents in 7 of these 11 swing states. He topped Obama in Colorado, Michigan, Nevada, New Hampshire, Ohio, Pennsylvania, and Wisconsin. Obama did hold the Independent edge in four states, including Florida, Iowa, New Hampshire, and Wisconsin. Romney's performance was not strong enough with Independents to make serious inroads against the Obama advantage in party identification. To make a serious run at the incumbent, Romney needed to carry all 11 swing states with a double digit edge among Independent voters.

Table 11.2 summarizes the vote in the 11 swing states for both Democratic and Republican identifiers. The partisan vote was strong overall with 92% of the Democrats favoring Obama in 2012 and 89% endorsing Clinton in 2016. Conversely, nationally Romney had 7% of the Democrats in 2012 and Trump won 8% in 2016. The proportion of Democratic identifiers who voted dropped slightly in nine of the 11 states in 2016, with Michigan even with 40% for both, and Virginia recording a slight Democratic increase of 1%. In 2016, 36% of the electorate consisted of Democratic partisans, and they favored Clinton over Trump by 89% to 8%. While Clinton's numbers were good, they were slightly lower than Obama's had been. The vote of Democratic identifiers was heavily Democratic, but slightly lower in 2016 in ten of the states with Florida at parity with a 90% vote in both elections. Overall, Democratic partisan voting was strong in both elections, but Clinton's Democratic support numbers were slightly lower than Obama's percentages. Lower Democratic percentages help the Republican candidate in a close election, as was the case in 2016.

Table 11.2 also contains data on Republican identifiers for the nation and the 11 swing states. Republican identification was slightly higher overall in 2016 (32% to 33%), and slightly higher in 9 of the 11 states. It was slightly lower in Colorado and North Carolina. The vote for Trump among Republicans was slightly lower both nationally (88% compared to 93% for Romney) and in all 11 states. These data suggest that the 2016 Republican candidate Donald Trump, a more controversial Republican, was not able to exploit Republican partisan party identification voting to any great extent. In partisan voting, the Republicans have an advantage with the Independent voters.

There have been recent examples, however, of successful partisan mobilization by George W. Bush in 2004 and Barack Obama in 2008. In 2004, Bush focused on increasing the vote of white evangelicals more likely to support him and added 3.2 million Republican voters to the electorate. In 2008, Barack Obama concentrated on increasing the number of African American voters and added 3.5 million Democrats to the list of Democratic partisans.[7]

THE MESSENGERS

At the heart of every campaign communication are the messengers or candidates and their messages, and the issues and candidate traits they invoke to persuade the audience or voters to support them. Analysts frequently draw too strong a line between issues and personality/character in campaigns when the reality is that American elections have always been "image-oriented/issue involved." The two concepts are like two overlapping concentric circles. Candidates use issues, for example, to demonstrate personal qualities like commitment to change, experience, competence, leadership, vision, trust, and empathy. Voters may lack detailed issue knowledge themselves, but they can observe campaign behavior and assess how candidates fare on important personal traits. Alternatively, voters may focus on the issues identified by the candidate to assess if he or she really cares about people like themselves or is biased towards other groups. We analyze messengers and candidate issues separately.

In a 2012 book entitled *The Candidate: What It Takes to Win and Hold The White House*, Popkin explores in great detail many past campaigns and what it takes to be an effective presidential candidate. Among the most desirable traits he identifies are possessing the ability to persuade voters he or she is one of them, convincing voters he or she understands their lives and shares their values, showing vision on how he or she would lead the country the next four years, stating how he or she would lead us there with a demonstration of ability to oversee a large campaign, and showing people how he or she could command the ship of state.[8]

Before voters respond to a message, they develop a gut appraisal of the messenger. If they have serious reservations about the messenger, they are unlikely to be persuaded by the campaign messages. The election of 2016 was no different, and once again voters expressed concern about candidate traits and issues. Much of the empirical data used to make observations comes from past election exit surveys.

First, at the heart of the communication process dating back to Aristotle is the fact that both the messenger and the message are important. There has to be source credibility for individuals to accept the message sent. It is readily tapped by favorability ratings or job performance ratings. For example, the 2004 exit survey shows that voters by 53% to 46% had a favorable view of Bush, but by 51% to 47% unfavorable view of Kerry.[9] Bush was viewed as the better messenger. This question was asked in the 2012 exit survey, and 53% had a favorable opinion of Obama and 46% were unfavorable. By contrast, 50% had an unfavorable opinion of Romney with 47% favorable.[10] Voters thus gave a higher rating to Obama over Romney as a messenger.

Second, the 2012 exit survey data show that Obama had a strong advantage in 2012 as a messenger compared to Romney.[11] We previously mentioned his edge in voter perceptions of favorability. After struggling to reach majority approval most of the year, Obama's job approval exit poll rating was 54% favorable and 45% unfavorable. At the national level, the question of "who is in touch with voters like you?" found voters favoring Obama 53% to 43% over Romney. This illustrates Popkin's observation that the candidate perceived as one of us and one who shares our values has an edge. Some 53% blamed Bush and only 38% Obama for "who is to blame for current economic problems?" despite Obama's weak economic record as the incumbent.

The 2016 election did not single out either Clinton or Trump as exceptional messengers.

Obama's approval ratings in the 2016 exit poll were 53% approve and 45% disapprove. Compared to Obama, both Clinton and Trump were perceived negatively as messengers. Hillary Clinton's ratings were 43% favorable and 55% unfavorable. Donald Trump fared even worse with 38% favorable and 60% unfavorable. Trump, however, had an important advantage in that the 18% of voters who saw them both as unfavorable supported Trump by a 47% to 30% margin in the trial heat, with 23% undecided or no opinion. No definitive explanations have been given, and it might well be that the electorate was simply more oriented to change. The candidates did not fare well on whether they were honest and trustworthy with 36% yes and 61% no for Clinton, and 33% yes and 64% no for Trump. On the question of having the temperament to be president, the respondents said 55% yes and 44% no for Clinton and 35% yes and 63% no for Trump. On the trait of whether they were qualified for president, 52% recorded a yes and 47% no for Clinton, while 38% said yes and 61% no for Trump. Some 48% felt Trump would better handle the economy to 46% for Clinton, while 53% thought Clinton would better handle foreign policy compared to 42% for Trump. There was an almost even split on who would make a better commander in chief with voters favoring Clinton by a 49% to 46% margin.[12] While Clinton had a slight edge on candidate traits, the percentages for both overall did not suggest that the winner of the election would win because of advantageous traits. There was no Barack Obama running in this election.

MESSAGES AND CAMPAIGN STRATEGIES

Messages are an essential component of the communication process. They are essential in presenting the overall campaign narratives as well as positioning candidates on the issues. In 2012 there was much media discussion as to whether this campaign would be a referendum on Obama or whether it would be seen as simply a choice between two candidates. In reality all campaigns are a mixture of both, but particular campaigns may be weighted more heavily to one of these campaign frames with less support for the other. The 2012 challenger Romney sought to make it a referendum on Obama's record, while Obama tried to discredit Romney as an acceptable alternative so that it would be seen as a choice between two candidates.

Dan Balz emphasizes that Obama wanted to make the 2012 election a choice but not one on his record. He sought to discredit Romney as a wealthy candidate who favored the rich and destroyed jobs while at Bain Capital, etc. Some Democrats said that even before the convention, the Obama campaign had done a good job drawing sharp contrasts with Romney. Obama's support of the auto bailouts, his decision to send the Seals team to kill Osama bin Laden, and his claims that he had helped to set the foundation for economic recovery were all part his narrative on accomplishment claims. His weakness was an economic record of unemployment at 8% or higher for 42 consecutive months.[13]

The narrative Obama chose to deal with the state of the economy involved blaming Bush for the bad economy (tax cuts for the rich, etc.) and stressing that he had inherited a terrible economic situation and still needed more time to deal with it. Although the message was heavily criticized as ineffective, Obama nevertheless used the argument that things could have been worse. He even went so far to claim that if he had not done what he did, the country could have plunged into a depression. What hurt politically was the persistence of unemployment and slow economic growth. One Democratic strategist said in early September "his most convincing defense of his economic record is contrast and comparison with the other side's proposals moving forward. If he is defending his record, he is not doing what he needs to do."[14] Obama tended to follow this advice and did not opt for refutation, but rather a counterargument that involved a compare and contrast between the two candidates.

Obama was on the attack in early spring and all summer with his advertising, his messages of the day, his conference calls, and tweets attempting to discredit Romney as an acceptable alternate to manage the economy. Although voters dislike negative ads, studies show that voters nevertheless process information from these ads in evaluating candidates. Contrast ads can do more to move voters than straight personal attacks or purely positive ads.[15]

The basic advantages of attack ads have stood the test of time as Pfau and Kenski noted over 25 years ago.[16] The advantages are that attack messages generate more attention, are more likely to be remembered than positive ads, and are effective if the message appears credible and is perceived as not going over the top. Attack messages, however, need an immediate response if they are frequent because a lingering negative message, if not dealt with, could become believable to some voters even if it is false.

Trump's 2016 messages drew heavily on his personal image enhanced by media exposure. His positions were right-wing populism-nativist, protectionist, and semi-isolationist and differed in many ways from traditional conservatism.[17] He declared Washington broken and opposed free trade deals and military interventionist policies that conservatives traditionally support. Domestically, he opposed cuts in Medicare and Social Security benefits. His support was high among working and middle-class white male voters with annual incomes of less than $50,000 and no college degree. He benefitted from free media more than any other candidate—estimated at $2 billion and twice the amount Clinton received.[18]

Clinton, of course, ran on the economy and domestic issues and sought to frame Trump as reactionary on domestic policy. There were many controversies for both candidates during the campaign. Clinton, for example, had to cover a tough political challenge over her practice of using a private email address during her work as Secretary of State. Security claims were raised, and she was initially exonerated in an FBI probe that concluded on July 15, 2016. On October 28, the controversial probe was reopened. It was later cancelled on November 6, 2016, before the election, but the Clinton team felt it had done considerable political damage. In September Clinton made a controversial speech that referred to Trump's supporters as "the basket of deplorables. They're racist, sexist, homophobic, xenophobic, Islamaphobic—you name it." Trump criticized her rhetoric as insulting to his supporters.[19] Clinton later expressed regret for making the statement. On the other side, Trump encountered criticism in October for an audio tape he made in 2005 that was derogatory and referred obscenely to women. He was forced to apologize. There was considerable controversy about the messages used by both candidates in the campaign.[20]

CHANNELS OF COMMUNICATION

The electoral environment is changing with respect to channels of communications voters utilize to get information on presidential campaigns. General news consumption habits of the country are changings rapidly. A September 2012 study by the Pew Research Foundation presented data from 1991 to 2012 to assess news consumption. TV news consumption dropped 13% from 68% in 1991 to 55% in 2012, newspapers declined 27% from 56% to 29%, and radio fell from 54% to 33%. Online was nonexistent in 1991, so the study used 2002 and found an increase in online use from 24% to 39%. Television, newspapers, and radio are increasingly less important to the citizenry with respect to general news consumption.[21]

Analyzing the trends, Pew's Andrew Kohut writes: "The transformation of the nation's news landscape has already taken a heavy toll on print news sources, particularly print newspapers. There are now signs that television news—which so far has held onto its audience through the rise on the internet—also is increasingly vulnerable, as it may be losing hold on the next generation of news consumers."[22]

In response to the changing media environment, campaigns are changing and relying less on the reporting from media and are taking a more proactive role in getting their messages out. Campaigns are using the ground game, more direct mail, targeted radio, email, and general print ads to publicize the candidates and to push the messages. The tone of coverage is what is most critical for the candidates. Use of their own direct mail gives more control over their messages as well as their attacks on their opponents. The campaigns of 2016 continued the patterns set forth in previous elections. Both Clinton and Trump used these channels to their advantage, particularly direct mail. Trump did not use as extensive a ground operation as Clinton.

On the topic of channels, Hillary Clinton's campaign established a comprehensive ground game and focused on infrastructure in the swing states. Her campaign felt it would help in winning both absentee and early voting and "withstand Donald Trump's late surge in key battleground states."[23] Trump, on the other hand, did not try to be as competitive on the ground, but instead had his son-in-law Jared Kushner build a comprehensive digital operation that "dictated every campaign decision: travel, fundraising, advertising, rally locations-even the topics of the speeches."[24] It was well orchestrated and successful. For example, when "momentum in Michigan and Pennsylvania was turning Trump's way, Kushner unleashed tailored TV ads, last-minute rallies and thousands of volunteers to knock on doors and make phone calls."[25] The creative use of digital marketing by Trump in 2016 provides a model for other candidates in future campaigns.

THE AUDIENCE

Explaining the vote requires an analysis of both the regional/state strategies and an overview of how various groups voted. We start first with a brief overview of the regional/state strategies.

Hillary Clinton adopted an aggressive Electoral College strategy that provided her multiple pathways to attain an electoral majority. She started first by focusing on 18 "Blue Wall" states that have voted Democratic in every presidential election since 1992. These included the 11 states from "Maryland to Maine, except for New Hampshire; Michigan, Minnesota, Wisconsin, and Illinois in the upper Midwest; the three West Coast states of California, Oregon, and Washington; and Hawaii." All of these states lean Democratic in presidential voting, with the three most contested states likely to be Pennsylvania, Michigan, and Wisconsin. Some 15 blue-wall states were considered solid, and the other three (Pennsylvania, Michigan, and Wisconsin) were put on a list of seven core states that also included New Mexico, Colorado, Virginia, and New Hampshire. The blue-wall list and the core list constituted 273 electoral votes, an electoral majority. To this list, Clinton also added Florida, North Carolina, and Ohio, providing her with a solid Electoral College base.[26]

Donald Trump was left with the traditional list of Republican-oriented states from various parts of the country, mostly medium sized and small states with exception of Texas. This base constituted about 191 electoral votes and was a good start but was not enough win. At the outset, Trump made it clear that he would go beyond the Republican base and he targeted and would seriously contest Clinton in states like Florida, Ohio, North Carolina, Michigan, Wisconsin, Colorado, Virginia, and New Hampshire. He made numerous appearances in these states with a clear goal to win the electoral vote. Trump definitely had to capture some of Clinton's potential core states in order to win.[27]

In order to win states and the electoral vote, candidates have to do well with voting groups. Most demographic groups do not divide evenly between the two parties but have historic tendencies to favor either the Democratic or Republican ticket.[28] Ruy Teixiera observes that Trump's coalition won the demographic battle in 2016 but could lose the political war down the road due to future demographic changes.[29] The single most important factor in Trump's win, he argues, was the staggering 39% margin among white working-class (noncollege) voters, compared to a smaller 25 % Republican advantage in 2012. Teixiera contends that it pushed "Democratic margins down in most states and allowing Trump to eke out an Electoral College victory, despite losing the popular vote."[30] He claims it led to his narrowest victories in "Florida and three Midwestern/Rust Belt states: Florida by 1.3 percentage points. Pennsylvania's one percentage point, Wisconsin by 0.9 points, and Michigan by 0.2 points."[31] Trump's working-class support ranged from 62% to 66%, "which represented very sharp shifts toward the GOP, particularly in Rust Belt states" like Michigan and Wisconsin.[32] This incredibly high working-class Trump support rate coupled with weaker than expected minority support rates for Clinton was the major demographic story in the 2016 election.

Table 11.3   Demographic comparison of 2012 and 2016 presidential vote

Category	2012 (%)			2016 (%)		
	% of 2012 Vote	Obama	Romney	% of 2016 Vote	Clinton	Trump
Total vote	100	51	48	100	48	46
Urban	32	62	36	34	60	34
Suburban	47	48	50	49	45	49
Rural	21	39	59	17	34	61
Democrats	38	92	7	36	89	8
Independents	29	45	50	31	42	46
Republicans	32	6	93	33	8	88
Liberal	25	86	11	26	84	10
Moderate	41	56	41	39	52	40
Conservative	35	17	82	35	16	81
White	72	39	59	71	37	57
Black	13	93	6	12	89	8
Latino	10	71	27	11	66	28
Men	45	45	52	47	41	52
Women	55	53	44	53	54	41
Protestant	29	37	62	27	36	59
Catholic	25	50	48	23	46	50
Weekly Church	42	39	59	33	41	55
Union Household	18	58	40	18	51	42

Sources: 2012 figures retrieved December 30, 2016, from http://elections.nbcnews.com/ns/politics/2012/all/president/#.WGYpL1MrJaQ. 2016 figures retrieved on December 30, 2016, from http://www.cnn.com/election/results/president.

Table 11.3 outlines a comparison for demographic categories where data are available from both the 2012 and 2016 presidential elections. The data clearly underscore that the partisan preferences for demographic groups held for both elections, but that the Clinton percentages were slightly lower than Obama's across the board. She dropped slightly in the area categories of urban, suburban, and rural. Partisan identification showed a drop in support for the Democratic candidate from 92% to 89%, while the Republican decrease was from 93% to 88%. Independents were pretty even with a 45% to 50% split favoring the Republican in the Obama/Romney contest and a 42% to 46% split for Trump in Clinton/Trump matchup.

Similar small drops appear in all of the categories on ideology (liberal, moderate, and conservative), with Clinton registering in lower percentages than did Obama. The same holds true for race/ethnic, and the percentages work against Clinton. Clinton, for example, won 37% of whites compared to 39% for Obama in 2012. The gender gap was fairly similar with Clinton losing men 52% to 41 % and winning women 54% to 41% in 2016. The same pattern of small decreases for Clinton occur for religious categories of Protestant, Catholic, and weekly church attendance. The Catholic vote stood out, however, because it shifted from 50% to 48% Democratic in 2012 to 50% to 46% Republican in 2016. Finally, union household is one of the key Democratic coalitions, and it registered one of the biggest decreases from 58% to 40% for Obama to only 51% to 42% for Clinton. The bottom line on audience is that Clinton was able to win various Democratic-oriented groups, but her margins were smaller than were Obama's, and this contributed to a close election.

Moving on to gender, scholars and the media have long been concerned about a gender gap.[33] The gender gap, or differences in how men and women vote, exists and emerges during presidential elections. An equally important marital gap is also manifest in recent elections, with Republican candidates like Romney winning married voters 56% to 42%, Bush 57% to 42%, and McCain by a smaller 52% to 47% margin. Kerry carried the unmarried 58% to 40%, but Obama improved the support levels for single voters to 65% to 33% in 2008 and 62% to 35% in 2012.

Gender was a key demographic variable in explaining the vote in 2004 and 2008. Gender has attracted media and scholarly attention since the election of Ronald Reagan in 1980. Beginning in 1980, differences seemed more apparent between men and women on party identification, presidential job approval, issues, and candidate choice. There is a tendency of men overall to be more Republican and women more Democratic. On issues, women are less inclined than men to favor the use force in foreign policy and to express more support for domestic issues like education, health care, the environment, and financial support for the poor. In presidential elections, men have been more supportive of Republican candidates than have women.[34]

A historical overview of gender in presidential elections is presented in Table 11.4. These data demonstrate that the differences between how men and women voted from 1952 to 1976 are minimal. Of interest, however, is that both sexes voted Republican in 1952, 1956, and 1972. Despite media emphasis on Kennedy's youthful image and physical attractiveness, women nevertheless preferred Nixon in 1960 (51% to 49%), while men favored Kennedy (52% to 48%). In 1968 women supported

Table 11.4   Gender and the presidential vote: 1952–2016 (% vote by gender)

Year	Males (%)			Females (%)		
	Democrat	Republican	Other	Democrat	Republican	Other
1952	47	53	0	42	58	0
1956	45	55	0	39	61	0
1960	52	48	0	49	51	0
1964	60	40	0	62	38	0
1968	41	43	16	45	43	12
1972	37	63	0	38	62	0
1976	53	45	1	48	51	0
1980	38	53	7	44	49	6
1984	36	64	0	45	55	0
1988	44	56	0	48	52	0
1992	41	37	22	46	38	16
1996	43	44	10	54	38	7
2000	42	53	3	54	43	2
2004	44	55	0	51	48	0
2008	49	48	3	56	43	1
2012	45	52	3	55	44	1
2016	41	53	5	54	42	3

Sources: Gallup polls from 1952 to 1992 in Stanley and Niemi (1994, pp. 105–108); 1996 and 2000 Voter News Service exit polls reported in Kenski and Kenski (2005); 2004 reported by CNN.com/election/ 2004 and 2008 reported in Kenski and Kenski (2009). 2012 reported in http://elections.nbcnews.com/ ns/politics/2012/all/president/#.WGYpL1MrJaQ. 2016 data retrieved on December 30, 2016, from http://www.cnn.com/election/results/president.

Humphrey (45% to 43%) and men Nixon (43% to 41%). In 1976 females leaned toward Ford (51% to 48%), while men opted for Carter (53% to 45%). Although these differences grew in the latter three elections, the margins of difference were not great.

Larger percentage differences emerged in 1980 and were labeled in mass media as the gender gap. The data in Table 11.4 confirm the existence of a gap, but the more significant point in 1980 is that Reagan was preferred by both sexes, although more by men than women. In 1980 Reagan had a 15% advantage with men and a 5% edge with women, while in 1984 his male margin was a striking 28% and 10% with women. In 1988 Bush led among men by 12% and among women by 4%. There was a gap in these three elections, but it did not threaten the Republican presidential ticket since it was favored by both sexes.

The 1992 race was a three-way race with an Independent Ross Perot pulling 19% of the total vote. In this matchup Bill Clinton won both a plurality of males (41%) and a larger margin with females support at 46%. In 1996, there was a gap, but Clinton surpassed Dole with both men (4%) and women (8%). Clinton's campaign strategy in 1996 sought to capture both sexes, and to win as many white males as possible. This election, however, recorded the largest gender gap in U.S. history as men favored Dole by a slim 1% and women favored Clinton by a striking 16% advantage. In 2000, Bush was able to increase the Republicans' male advantage from 1% to 11%, while Gore experienced a drop in the Democratic female edge from 16% to 11%. The gender gap was alive and well in 2000.

By contrast the Kerry campaign in 2004 was unable to exploit the traditional gender gap effectively, and only 51% of females chose him compared to 48% for Bush, who increased his female support by 5% from 2000. Bush won males 55% to 44% in 2004, increasing his male support by 2% from 2000. John Kerry's pollster Mark Mellman observed that a major constraint on capturing women in 2004 was that Bush campaign was so successful in getting an increased number of women to be concerned with the national security issue.[35]

In 2008, Obama carried males narrowly 49% to 48%, but made major inroads with women with a 56% to 43% advantage. As we previously noted, Romney carried males 52% to 45% and Obama scored higher with females 55% to 44% overall. The norm since 1980 is that women are less Republican than men in the vote, but some candidates are sufficiently strong to carry both groups. This what Obama did in 2008 but not in 2012. A good performance in gender voting is carrying these groups by a margin of 10% or more. Obama was especially strong with females as he registered victory margins of 13% in 2008 and 11% in 2012. Romney did win males but only by a margin of 7%. In 2016, the traditional gender gap emerged. Males voted 53% to 41% Republican and females voted 54% to 42% Democratic. It was a major disappointment for Hillary Clinton, the Democratic nominee. As the first female presidential candidate, she expected to do considerably better with women. The bottom line was that her 54% to 42% edge with women differed little from Obama's 55% to 44% female presidential vote in 2012.

A further consideration is race and ethnicity by gender, as such a data disaggregation captures a more complex gender reality. Table 11.5 contains data that note the overall gender vote for 2016 and 2012 but then disaggregates the data by white men, white women, Latino men, Latino women,

Table 11.5   Presidential vote in 2016 and 2012 by race and gender (%)

Category	% of 2016 Total Vote	2016 (%)		% of 2012 Total Vote	2012 (%)	
		Clinton	Trump		Obama	Romney
Total vote	100	48	47	100	51	48
White men	34	31	62	34	35	62
White women	37	43	52	38	42	56
Latino men	5	62	33	5	65	33
Latino women	6	68	26	6	76	23
Black men	5	80	13	5	87	11
Black women	7	94	4	8	96	3

Sources: 2012 reported at http://elections.nbcnews.com/ns/politics/2012/all/president/#.
WGY1qVMrJaR. 2016 reported at http://www.nbcnews.com/politics/2016-election/president.

black men, and black women. Both white men and white women were Republican in both elections, with white males registering higher levels of support of 62% compared to women at 52% in 2016 compared to 62% male and 56% Republican female support in 2012. Latino women were more Democratic than men in 2016 (68%to 62%) and 2012 (76% to 65%). Black women were more Democratic than men in 2016 (94% to 80%) and 2016 (96% to 87%). The race divisions are clear, and the overall pattern in all three racial categories is that women are less likely to vote Republican than men. Clinton did well, but not as well as Obama in race and gender voting.

CONCLUSIONS

The election of 2016 was significant in that Hillary Clinton was trying to make it three straight presidential wins for the Democrats. History underscores how difficult it is for one party to win three straight presidential elections, as the public historically is oriented to change. The Republican Party achieved this goal with two Reagan and one Bush victories in 1980, 1984, and 1988. The Democrats failed for the third win in 2000 as did the Republicans in 2008. For the last three consecutive partisan presidential election victories, one has to go back to Franklin Roosevelt. There appears to be a third consecutive term political curse on parties, which Clinton could not overcome in 2016.

The 2016 presidential race resulted in an impressive victory for Donald Trump. Hillary Clinton led in the polls throughout September and

October with Trump reducing her margins and finally coming close to parity by the day of the election. As our analysis has indicated, the traditional Democratic regional/state strategy fell short, and six states changed from Democratic in 2012 to Republican in 2016. They were Pennsylvania, Florida, Iowa, Ohio, Michigan, and Wisconsin. Trump was able to eke out close victories, especially in the Rust Belt. The survey data reveal that Clinton was able to win traditional Democratic demographic categories but not by the margins that Obama registered in 2012. Before the election, Ronald Brownstein argued that four demographic groups would decide the election. They were noncollege whites, minorities, females, and millennials.[36] Clinton did poorly with noncollege whites and won the other three groups by margins that were lower than expected.

There was no single reason for Trump's win, but numerous factors were involved. We draw upon an excellent comprehensive list identified by Carl Cannon[37] and utilize factors on his list to explain why Trump won. First, we look at Donald Trump. It turns out that it was an advantage to never have held elective office. He was never really a Republican, having been both a Democrat, and an Independent. He chose to be a Republican in 2016. His pick of Mike Pence as his running mate was an asset that appealed to conservatives. Trump performed well in the polls with the one-fifth of the electorate concerned about Supreme Court appointments. Trump called his effort a "movement, not a campaign." He reimagined the electoral map and stunned people by focusing on Michigan, Wisconsin, and Pennsylvania. Trump was the one candidate who truly recognized the importance of working-class whites. He took a critical position on free trade that blamed the Clintons for NAFTA. Along with Democrat Bernie Sanders, he attacked corporate greed and the closing of plants that moved to Mexico. He inoculated against his wealth and his billions by claiming he was too rich to be bribed. Trump finessed his early negative rhetoric on Mexican immigrants by claiming that he had the courage to speak when others did not. Finally, Trump was an icon in his opposition to political correctness.[38]

Second, we utilize Cannon's list and turn to Hillary Clinton. She went off script and called Trump voters a "basket of deplorables." Clinton like Trump had to address voters who felt that both candidates supported crony capitalism. There was the problem of media reports on all the Clinton cash they made on speeches, and with the Clinton Foundation's solicitation of massive donations from U.S. billionaires, foreign governments, etc. There was a need to defend her record on Benghazi, and many were critical of her secret email system. Clinton had to deal with James Comey, the FBI director who questioned her use of the email server but absolved her of criminality. There was the glass ceiling that she felt limited her from expanding the gender gap and the female vote. There was a passion problem and a difficulty of motivating voters. Obama tried but was not able to help much, as voters seemed less inclined to support without Obama on the ballot. Clinton had to deal with the troublesome issues of Obamacare and the position of the Democratic Party on terrorism.[39]

Third, the Republicans had problems, as Cannon noted, but were helped when Kellyanne Conway and Steve Bannon came on to manage the campaign. Trump lacked a strong get-out-the-vote effort, but was helped by strong turnout efforts of Republican Senate candidates in Florida, Ohio, and Wisconsin. The Libertarian Party candidate who was viewed as a greater threat to the Republicans turned out to be weak.[40]

The final factor, as Carl Cannon put it, was public opinion. An exhaustive 2016 YouGov poll of some 5,000 voters showed a consistent but narrow lead for Hillary Clinton. A large cohort of respondents consistently refused to choose either Clinton or Trump. When pressed in surveys, as many said they would vote for Clinton as would vote for Trump. The reality was that in the end a majority who claimed they disliked both candidates ended up voting for Trump.[41] Hence, Trump ended as the winner in the 2016 presidential election.

NOTES

1. Eric Sondermann, "The Myths and Miscalculations of the 2016 Election," *The Denver Post*, November 12, 2016. Accessed December 6, 2016, from http://www.denverpost.com/2016/11/12/the-myths-and-miscalculations-of-the-2016-election/.
2. Fred Barnes, "Trump Didn't Split the GOP–He Strengthened It," *The Weekly Standard*, November 9, 2016. Accessed December 6, 2016, http://www.weeklystandard.com/trump-didnt-split-the-gop-he-strengthened-it/article/2005302.
3. Karen Tumulty, Philip Rucker, and Anne Gearan, "Donald Trump Wins the Presidency in Stunning Upset Over Clinton," *The Washington Post*, November 9, 2016. Accessed December 23, 2016, https://www.washingtonpost.com/politics/election-day-an-acrimonious-race-reaches-its-end-point/2016/11/08/32b96c72-a557-11e6-ba59-a7d93165c6d4_story.html?utm_term=.7c51bab20fef.

4. Tumulty, Rucker, and Gearan. "Donald Trump Wins the Presidency in Stunning Upset Over Clinton."
5. Chuck Todd and Sheldon Gawiser. *How Barack Obama Won* (New York: Vintage Books, 2009).
6. Wikipedia. "United States Presidential Election, 2016." Accessed December 23, 2016, https://en.wikipedia.org/wiki/United_States_presidential_elec tion,_2016.
7. Jay Cost, "Can Obama Sustain Enthusiasm with African Americans?" *The Weekly Standard*, October 22, 2016. Retrieved December 9, 2016, from http://www.weeklystandard.com/can-obama-sustain-enthusiasm-with-afri can-americans/article/655182.
8. Samuel L. Popkin. *The Candidate: What It Takes to Win—and Hold—the White House* (New York: Oxford University Press, 2012).
9. Henry Kenski and Kate M. Kenski, "Explaining the Vote in a Divided Country," in Robert E. Denton, Jr, ed., *The 2004 Presidential Campaign: A Communication Perspective* (Lanham, Maryland: Rowman and Littlefield Publishers, Inc. 2005), pp. 301–33.
10. Exit poll data from NBC News. Retrieved December 30, 2016, from http://elections.nbcnews.com/ns/politics/2012/all/president/#. WGZBxFMrJaQ.
11. Dan Balz. "8 Questions," *The Washington Post*, September 2, 2012. Retrieved December 23, 2016, from http://www.washingtonpost.com/ wp-srv/special/politics/8-questions-democratic-convention/.
12. Election Polls 2016. Retrieved December 23, 2016, from http://www.cnn. com/election/results/president.
13. Balz, September 2, 2012.
14. Balz, September 2, 2012.
15. Balz, September 2, 2012.
16. Michael Pfau and Henry C. Kenski. *Attack Politics: Strategy and Defense.* (New York: Greenwood Publishing Group Inc., 1990)
17. Wikipedia, "United States Presidential Election, 2016."
18. Wikipedia, "United States Presidential Election, 2016."
19. Wikipedia, "United States Presidential Election, 2016."
20. Wikipedia, "United States Presidential Election, 2016."
21. Chris Cillizza, "The Rapidly Changing Media Landscape and What It Means for Politics—in 1 Chart," *The Washington Post*, October 1, 2012. Retrieved December 23, 2016 from https://www.washingtonpost.com/ news/the-fix/wp/2012/10/01/the-rapidly-changing-media-landscape-and-what-it-means-for-politics-in-1-chart/?utm_term=.04d628932668.
22. Cillizza "The Rapidly Changing Media Landscape and What It Means for Politics—in 1 Chart."

23. Steven Shepard, "Democratic Insiders: Clinton's Ground Game Will Sink Trump," *Politico*. November 4, 2016. Accessed December 6, 2016, http://www.politico.com/story/2016/11/democratic-insiders-hillarys-ground-game-will-sink-trump-230718.

24. Steven Bertoni, "Exclusive Interview: How Jared Kushner Won Trump The White House," *Forbes*, November 22, 2016. Retrieved December 23, 2016, from http://www.forbes.com/sites/stevenbertoni/2016/11/22/exclusive-interview-how-jared-kushner-won-trump-the-white-house/#6534e1842f50.

25. Bertoni, "Exclusive Interview: How Jared Kushner Won Trump The White House."

26. Ronald Brownstein, "Is Donald Trump Outflanking Hillary Clinton?" *The Atlantic*, November 2, 2016. Retrieved December 10, 2016, from http://www.theatlantic.com/politics/archive/2016/11/trump-clinton-electoral-college/506306/.

27. Brownstein, "Is Donald Trump Outflanking Hillary Clinton?"

28. Henry C. Kenski and Lee Sigelman, "Where the Votes Come From: Group Components of the 1988 Senate Vote," *Legislative Studies Quarterly*, 28 (3), (1993), pp. 367–390, and Michael Barone, *Our Country: The Shaping of America From Roosevelt to Reagan* (New York: Free Press, 1990).

29. Ruy Teixeira, "Trump's Coalition Won the Demographic Battle. It'll Still Lose the War," Vox Explain the News, November 15, 2016. Retrieved December 23, 2016, from http://www.vox.com/the-big-idea/2016/11/15/13629814/trump-coalition-white-demographics-working-class.

30. Teixeira, "Trump's Coalition Won the Demographic Battle. It'll Still Lose the War."

31. Teixeira, "Trump's Coalition Won the Demographic Battle. It'll Still Lose the War."

32. Teixeira, "Trump's Coalition Won the Demographic Battle. It'll Still Lose the War."

33. Henry C. Kenski, "The Gender Gap in a Changing Electorate," in Carol Mueller, ed., *The Politics of the Gender Gap: The Social Construction of Political Influence* (Newbury Park; CA Sage Publications, 1988, pp. 36–69, and Kate Kenski and Kathleen Hall Jamieson, "The Gender Gap in Political Knowledge: Are Women Less Knowledgeable Than Men About Politics?" in Kathleen Hall Jamieson, ed., *Everything You Want to Know About Politics… and Why You're Wrong* (New York: Basic Books, 2000), pp. 83–89.

34. Henry C. Kenski and Kate M. Kenski, "Explaining the Vote in the Election of 2008," in Robert E. Denton Jr., ed., *The 2008 Presidential Campaign: A Communication Perspective* (Lanham, Maryland: Rowman and Littlefield Publishers, Inc., 2009), pp. 244–290.

35. Mark Mellman, Comments at the Annenberg Public Policy Center Election debriefing. Philadelphia: University of Pennsylvania, December 3, 2004.
36. Ronald Brownstein, "The Four Groups That Will Decide the Presidential Race," *The Atlantic*, November 7, 2016. Retrieved December 23, 2016, from https://www.theatlantic.com/politics/archive/2016/11/clinton-trump-demographics/506714/.
37. Carl M. Cannon, "How Donald Trump Won," RealClearPolitics.com, November 10, 2016. Retrieved December 23, 2016, from http://www.realclearpolitics.com/articles/2016/11/10/how-donald-trump-won-132321.html.
38. Cannon, "How Donald Trump Won."
39. Cannon, "How Donald Trump Won."
40. Cannon, "How Donald trump Won."
41. Cannon, "How Donald Trump Won."

Henry C. Kenski is a retired professor, currently teaching one course each semester as an adjunct professor at the University of Arizona. His research and teaching interests are in media, public opinion, campaigns, and presidential leadership. He has published two books: *Saving the Hidden Treasure: The Evolution of Ground Water Policy* and a co-authored endeavor with Michael Pfau entitled *Attack Politics: Strategy and Defense*. In addition, he has published numerous articles on different facets of political communication. He believes, however, that his most important contribution to the field of political communication is his daughter Kate Kenski.

Kate M. Kenski is an associate professor of Communication and Government & Public Policy at the University of Arizona where she teaches political communication, public opinion, and research methods. Her book *The Obama Victory: How Media, Money, and Message Shaped the 2008 Election* (co-authored with Bruce W. Hardy and Kathleen Hall Jamieson; 2010, Oxford University Press) has won several awards including the 2011 ICA Outstanding Book Award and the 2012 NCA Diamond Anniversary Book Award. Her current research focuses on political messaging in social media, incivility in online forums, and multimedia teaching strategies to mitigate cognitive biases.

SELECTED BIBLIOGRAPHY

An, Chasu, and Michael Pfau. "The Efficacy of Inoculation in Televised Political Debates." *Journal of Communication* 54, no. 3 (2004): 421–36.

Barone, Michael. *Our Country: The Shaping of America from Roosevelt to Reagan.* New York: Free Press. 1990.

Bennett, W. Lance. "Myth, Ritual, and Political Control." *Journal of Communication* 30, no. 4 (1980): 166–79.

Bormann, Ernest G. "Fantasy and Rhetorical Vision: The Rhetorical Criticism of Social Reality." *Quarterly Journal of Speech* 58, no. 4 (1980): 396–407.

Bramlett, Brittany H., James G. Gimpel, and Frances E. Lee. "The Political Ecology of Opinion in Big-Donor Neighborhoods." *Political Behavior* 33, no. 4 (2010): 565–600.

Burke, Kenneth. *The Philosophy of Literary Form: Studies in Symbolic Action.* New York: Vintage Books. 1957.

Burke, Kenneth. *A Rhetoric of Motives.* Berkeley: University of California Press. 1969.

Cali, Dennis D. "Personae in the 2012 Presidential Election," In *Studies of Communication in the 2012 Presidential Election,* edited by Robert Denton Jr., 41–70. New York: Lexington Book Series on Political Communication. 2014.

Chandler, Alfred D. *The Visible Hand: The Managerial Revolution in American Business.* Cambridge, Massachusetts: Belknap Press. 1977.

Chou, Hsuan-Yi, and Nai-Hwa Lien. "How Do Candidate Poll Ranking and Election Status Affect the Effects of Negative Political Advertising?" *International Journal of Advertising* 29, no. 5 (2010): 815–34.

© The Author(s) 2017
R.E. Denton, Jr. (ed.), *The 2016 US Presidential Campaign,*
Political Campaigning and Communication,
DOI 10.1007/978-3-319-52599-0

Clark Paul, W., and Monica B. Fine. "Expanding Direction-of-Comparison Theory and Its Applications for Political Advertising Practitioners." *Journal of Management and Marketing Research* 10 (2012): http://www.aabri.com/manuscripts/111031.pdf.

Cohen, Marty, David Karol, Hans Noel, and John Zaller. *The Party Decides: Presidential nominations before and after reform.* Chicago: University of Chicago Press. 2009.

Compton, Josh, and Michael Pfau. "Spreading Inoculation: Inoculation, Resistance to Influence, and Word-of-Mouth Communication." *Communication Theory* 19, no. 1 (2009): 9–28.

Cortese, Anthony Joseph Paul. *Opposing Hate Speech.* Westport, Connecticut: Praeger Publishers. 2006.

Cosgrove, Ken. "The Emotional Brand Wins," *U. S. Election Analysis 2016.* http://www.electionanalysis2016.us/us-election-analysis-2016/section-2-campaign/the-emotional-brand-wins/. 2016

Delli Carpini, Michael X. "The New Normal? Campaigns and Elections in the Contemporary Media Environment," *U.S. Election Analysis 2016.* http://www.electionanalysis2016.us/us-election-analysis-2016/section-1-media/the-new-normal-campaigns-elections-in-the-contemporary-media-environment/. 2016

Denton Jr, Robert E, and Ben Voth. *Social Fragmentation and the Decline of American Democracy: The End of the Social Contract.* New York: Springer. 2016.

Denton, Jr., Robert E editor. *The 2008 Presidential Campaign: A Communication Perspective.* Lanham, MD: Rowman & Littlefield. 2009.

Dewberry, David R. 2015. *The American Political Scandal: Free Speech, Public Discourse, and Democracy.* Lanham, MD: Rowman & Littlefield. 2015.

Elovitz, Paul. "A Psychobiographical and Psycho-political Comparison of Clinton and Trump." *Journal of Psychohistory* 44 (2016): 100.

Fisher, Walter R. "Reaffirmation and Subversion of the American Dream." *Quarterly Journal of Speech* 59 (1973): 160.

Fowler, Evelyn Franklin, and Travis N. Ridout. "Negative, Angry, and Ubiquitous: Political Advertising in 2012." *The Forum: A Journal of Applied Research in Contemporary Politics* 10, no. 4 (2012): 51–61.

Friedenberg, Robert V. *Rhetorical Studies of National Political Debates, 1960-1992.* Santa Barbara: Praeger Publishers. 1993.

Gronbeck, Bruce E. "The Rhetoric of Political Corruption: Sociolinguistic, Dialectical, and Ceremonial Processes." *Quarterly Journal of Speech* 64, no. 2 (1978): 155–72.

Hasen, Richard L. *Plutocrats United: Campaign Money, the Supreme Court, and the Distortion of American Elections.* New Haven: Yale University Press. 2016.

Holloway, Rachel L. "The 2012 Presidential –Nominating Conventions and the American Dream: Narrative Unity and Political Division," In *The 2012 Presidential Campaign: A Communication Perspective*, edited by Robert E. Denton Jr., 1–22. Lanham, MD: Rowman & Littlefield. 2014.

Ivanov, Bobi, Michael Pfau, and Kimberly A. Parker. "Can Inoculation Withstand Multiple Attacks? An Examination of the Effectiveness of the Inoculation Strategy Compared to the Supportive and Restoration Strategies." *Communication Research* 36 (2009): 655–76.

Jasperson, Amy C., and David P. Fan. "An Aggregate Examination of the Backlash Effect in Political Advertising: The Case of the 1996 U.S. Senate Race in Minnesota." *Journal of Advertising* 31, no. 1 (2002): 1–12.

Johnston, Anne, and Lynda Lee Kaid. "Image Ads and Issue Ads in U.S. Presidential Advertising: Using Videostyle to Explore Stylistic Differences in Televised Political Ads from 1952 to 2000." *Journal of Communication* 52, no. 2 (2002): 281–300.

Karol, David. "Forcing Their Hands? Campaign Finance Law, Retirement Announcements and the Rise of the Permanent Campaign in U.S. Senate Elections." *Congress & the Presidency* 42, no. 1 (2015): 79–94.

Kenski, Henry C. "The Gender Gap in a Changing Electorate," In *The Politics of the Gender Gap. The Social Construction of Political Influence*, edited by Carol Mueller, Newbury Park: Sage Publications. 1988.

Kenski, Henry C., Brooks Aylor, and Kate Kenski. "Explaining the vote in a divided country," In *The 2004 Presidential Campaign: A Communication Perspective*, edited by Robert E. Denton Jr., Lanham, Maryland: Rowman and Littlefield Publishers, Inc. 2005.

Kenski, Henry C., and Kate M. Kenski. "Explaining the Vote in the Election of 2008," In *The 2008 Presidential Campaign: A Communication Perspective*, edited by Robert E. Denton Jr., Lanham, Maryland: Rowman and Littlefield Publishers, Inc. 2009.

Kenski, Henry C., and Lee Sigelman. "Where the Votes Come from: Group Components of the 1988 Senate Vote." *Legislative Studies Quarterly* 18, no. 3 (1993): 367.

Kenski, Kate, and Kathleen Hall Jamieson. "The gender gap in political knowledge: Are women less knowledgeable than men about politics," In *Everything you think you know about politics... and why you're wrong*, edited by Kathleen Hall Jamieson, 83–89. New York: Basic Books. 2000.

Kintz, Linda. *Between Jesus and the Market: The Emotions that Matter in Right-Wing America*. Durham, North Carolina: Duke University Press. 1997.

Kuypers, Jim. *Partisan Journalism: A History of Media Bias in America*. Lanham, Maryland: Rowman and Littlefield. 2014.

La Raja, Raymond J., and Brian F. Schaffner. "The Effects of Campaign Finance Spending Bans on Electoral Outcomes: Evidence from the States about the

Potential impact of Citizens United v. FEC." *Electoral Studies* 33 (2014): 102–14.

La Raja, Raymond J., and David L. Wiltse. "Don't Blame Donors for Ideological Polarization of Political Parties: Ideological Change and Stability Among Political Contributors, 1972-2008." *American Politics Research* 40, no. 3 (2012): 501–30.

Le Guin, Ursula K. *The Wave in the Mind: Talks and Essays on the Writer, the Reader, and the Imagination.* Boulder, Colorado: Shambhala Publications. 2004.

Lewis, Seth C., and Matt Carlson. "The Dissolution of News: Selective Exposure, Filter Bubbles, and the Boundaries of Journalism," *U.S. Election Analysis 2016*, http://www.electionanalysis2016.us/us-election-analysis-2016/section-6-internet/the-dissolution-of-news-selective-exposure-filter-bubbles-and-the-boundaries-of-journalism/. 2016

Lutgen-Sandvik, Pamela, and Virginia McDermott. "The Constitution of Employee-Abusive Organizations: A Communication Flow Theory." *Communication Theory* 18, no. 2 (2008): 304–33.

McGee, Michael Calvin. "The "ideograph": A Link Between Rhetoric and Ideology." *Quarterly Journal of Speech* 66, no. 1 (1980): 1–16.

McGuire, William J. "The Effectiveness of Supportive and Refutational Defenses in Immunizing and Restoring Beliefs against Persuasion." *Sociometry* 24, no. 2 (1961): 184–97.

McKinney, Mitchell S., and Benjamin R. Warner. "Do Presidential Debates matter? Examining a Decade of Campaign Debate Effects." *Argumentation and Advocacy* 49 (2013): 238–58.

Mutch, Robert E. *Campaign Finance.* Oxford: Oxford University Press. 2016.

Myers, Cayce, and Ruthann Lariscy. "Corporate PR in a Post-Citizens United World." *Journal of Communication Management* 18, no. 2 (2014): 146–57.

Patterson, Thomas E. "Research: Media Coverage of the 2016 Election," (blog) Shorenstein Center, Harvard University. Accessed September 7, 2016. https://shorensteincenter.org/news-coverage-2016-general-election/. 2016.

Pevnick, Ryan. "The Anatomy of Debate about Campaign Finance." *The Journal of Politics* 78, no. 4 (2016): 1184–95.

Pfau, Michael, Henry C. Kenski, Michael Nitz, and John Sorenson. "Efficacy of Inoculation Strategies in Promoting Resistance to Political Attack Messages: Application to Direct mail." *Communications Monographs* 57, no. 1 (1990): 25–43.

Pfau, Michael, and Michael Burgoon. "Inoculation in Political Campaign Communication." *Human Communication Research* 15, no. 1 (1988): 91–111.

Pfau, Michael, and Henry C. Kenski. *Attack Politics: Strategy and Defense.* Westport, Connecticut: Praeger Publishers. 1990.

Popkin, Samuel L. *The Candidate: What It Takes to Win-and Hold-the White House.* Oxford: Oxford University Press. 2012.

Pörhölä, Maili, Sanna Karhunen, and Sini Rainivaara. "Bullying at School and in the Workplace: A Challenge for Communication Research." *Annals of the International Communication Association* 30, no. 1 (2006): 249–301.

Quine, L. "Workplace Bullying in NHS Community Trust: Staff Questionnaire Survey." *British Medical Journal* 318 (1999): 228–32.

Romney, Mitt. *No Apology: The Case for American Greatness.* New York: Macmillan. 2010.

Rowland, Robert C., and John M. Jones. "Recasting the American Dream and American Politics: Barack Obama's Keynote Address to the 2004 Democratic National Convention." *Quarterly Journal of Speech* 93 (2007): 443.

Shea, Daniel M., and Alex Sproveri. "The Rise and Fall of Nasty Politics in America." *PS: Political Science & Politics* 45, no. 03 (2012): 416–21.

Sheckels, Theodore F., Nichola D. Gutgold, and Diana B. Carlin. *Gender and the American Presidency: Nine Presidential Women and the Barriers They Faced.* Lanham, Maryland: Lexington Books. 2012.

Sheeler, Kristina Horn, and Karrin Vasby Anderson. *Woman President: Confronting Postfeminist Political Culture.* College Station: Texas A&M University Press. 2013.

Smith, Craig Allen. *Presidential Campaign Communication.* Cambridge: Polity Press. 2015.

Stromer-Galley, Jennifer. "In the Age of Social Media, Voters Still Need Journalists," *U. S. Election Analysis 2016.* http://www.electionanalysis2016. us/us-election-analysis-2016/section-6-internet/in-the-age-of-social-media-voters-still-need-journalists/. 2016

Stuckey, Mary E. "One Nation (Pretty Darn) Divisible: National Identity in the 2004 Conventions." *Rhetoric and Public Affairs* 8, no. 4 (2005): 639–56.

Tedesco John, C., and Scott W. Dunn. "Political Advertising in the 2012 U.S. Presidential Election," In *The 2012 Presidential Campaign: A Communication Perspective,* edited by Robert E. Denton Jr., Lanham, MD.: Rowman & Littlefield. 2013.

Thompson, J. B. *Political Scandal: Power and Visibility in the Media Age.* Cambridge: Polity Press. 2000.

Todd, Chuck, Sheldon R. Gawiser, Ana Maria. Arumi, and G. Evans. Witt. *How Barack Obama Won: A State-by-State Guide to the Historic 2008 Presidential Election.* New York: Vintage Books. 2009.

Trent, Judith S., Robert V. Friedenberg, and Robert E. Denton Jr. *Political Campaign Communication: Principles & Practices.* Lanham, MD: Rowman & Littlefield. 2016. 122.

Treviño, A. Javier, and Karen M. McCormack. *Service Sociology and Academic Engagement in Social Problems.* New York: Routledge. 2016.

Van Steenburg, Eric. "Areas of Research in Political Advertising: A Review and Research Agenda." *International Journal of Advertising* 34, no. 2 (2015): 195–231.

Whillock, Rita Kirk, and David Slayden. *Hate Speech.* Thousand Oaks, California: Sage Publications. 1995.

Zuckert, Michael P., and Catherine H. Zucker. *Leo Strauss and the Problem of Political Philosophy.* Chicago: The University of Chicago Press. 2014.

INDEX

© The Author(s) 2017
R.E. Denton, Jr. (ed.), *The 2016 US Presidential Campaign*,
Political Campaigning and Communication,
DOI 10.1007/978-3-319-52599-0

318   INDEX

Bernstein, Carl, 185
Biden, Jill, 55, 183
Biden, Joe, 17, 18, 55, 62, 73, 135,
    157, 187
  Democratic national convention,
    speech of, 73
Big Data, 129, 130, 140
Bin Laden, Osama, 17, 57, 231, 237,
    295
Blackburn, Marcia, 42
Blair, Bruce, 105, 106
Bleeker, Andrew, 126
Bloomberg, Michael, 54, 278
Bondi, Pam, 38
Booker, Corey, 49, 50, 72
Boxer, Barbara, 53
Brazile, Donna, 47, 52, 87
Broaddrick, Juanita, 91, 184, 185
Brown, Kimberlin, 36, 196
Brownstein, Ronald, 305, 308, 309
Buckley vs. Valeo, 262, 264, 267, 279
  campaign finance and, 262, 264, 267
Buffett, Warren, 272
Burke, Kenneth, 210, 211
Burns, Alexander, 212
Burns, Mark, 42
Bush, Barbara
Bush, George W.
  debates and, 79, 80, 94
  Republican National Convention
    and, 31
Bush, Jeb
  Common Core and, 159–161
  Donald Trump's attacks on, 139
  low energy and, 160, 161, 217
Buzzfeed
  Hillary Clinton and, 126, 127

C
Campaign finance
  Bernie Sanders and

Buckley vs. Valeo and, 262, 264,
    267
campaign finance laws, xiii,
    260–267, 278, 280–281
Citizens United vs. Federal Election
    Commission (FEC) and, 52,
    94, 265
debates and, 266
Federal Corrupt Practices Act
    (FCPA) and, 261, 262, 279
Federal Election Commission
    (FEC) vs. Massachusetts
    Citizens for Life, 264, 280
Federal Elections Commission
    (FEC) and, 262
First Amendment and, 260, 264
First National Bank of Boston vs.
    Bellotti, 264
527s and, 265
McCain-Feingold and, 265,
    280–281
McConnell vs. Federal Election
    Commission (FEC) and, 265
Right to Rise super-PAC and, 267
Smith-Connally Act, 262
SpeechNow vs. Federal Election
    Commission (FEC) and, 265
Taft-Hartley amendment, 262
Tillman Act and, 261
Campaign fundraising
  Clinton and, xiii, 260, 272
  Trump and, xiii, 260, 272
Campaigns, x, xi, xii, xiii, xiv, 5, 6, 8,
    14, 20, 30, 47, 65, 87, 99–103,
    108, 118, 121, 122, 125, 135,
    138–140, 154, 168, 180, 181,
    187, 194, 195, 205, 206, 208,
    209, 215, 218, 221, 224, 231,
    232, 238, 251, 259–309
Campaign strategies, xiii, 129, 130,
    234, 277, 286, 295, 303
Campbell, Bill, 85

Made in the USA
Middletown, DE
13 June 2019